MW00678868

2013 U.S. POCKET STAMP CATALOGUE

EDITOR .... Charles Snee
EDITOR EMERITUS .... James E. Kloetzel
ASSOCIATE EDITORS .... David Akin, Donna Houseman
ASSISTANT EDITOR/NEW ISSUES .... Martin J. Frankevicz
VALUING ANALYST .... Steven R. Myers
GRAPHIC DESIGNER .... Jennifer Lenhart
IMAGE COORDINATOR .... Stacey Mahan
ADVERTISING .... Angela Nolte
CIRCULATION/PRODUCT PROMOTION MANAGER .... Tim Wagner
VICE PRESIDENT/EDITORIAL & PRODUCTION .... Steve Collins
PRESIDENT .... Bill Fay

2A

CONTENTS

An overview of the
  world's most popular hobby 7A
How to use this book 7A
United States Postage Stamps 5
Semi-Postal Stamps 467
Air Post Stamps 470
Air Post Special Delivery Stamps 483
Special Delivery Stamps 483
Registration Stamp 485
Certified Mail Stamp 485
Postage Due Stamps 486
U.S. Offices in China 490
Official Stamps 491
Newspaper Stamps 502
Parcel Post Stamps 507
Parcel Post Postage Due Stamps 507
Special Handling Stamps 507
Computer Vended Postage 509
Personal Computer Postage 522
Non-Personalizable Postage 535
Carrier's Stamps 537
Hunting Permit (Duck) Stamps 544
Index to advertisers 551

AN OVERVIEW OF THE WORLD'S MOST POPULAR HOBBY

A fascinating hobby, an engrossing avocation and a universal pastime, stamp collecting is pursued by millions. Young and old, and from all walks of life, stamp collectors are involved in the indoor sport known as "the paper chase."

It was more than 160 years ago that Rowland Hill's far-reaching postal reforms became a reality and the world's first adhesive postage stamp, the Penny Black, was placed on sale at post offices in Great Britain. Not long after, a hobby was born that has continued to grow since.

Although there were only four stamps issued in England from 1840-47, the Penny Black, two types of the 2-penny blue and the 1-penny red, there were people who saved them. One story relates that a woman covered a wall in a room of her home with copies of the Penny Black.

As country after country began to issue postage stamps, the fraternity of stamp collectors flourished. Today, collectors number in the millions, while the number of stamp-issuing entities has exceeded 650.

The hobby of stamp collecting may take many forms. There are those people who collect the stamps of a single country. Others collect a single issue, such as the U.S. Transportation coils. Others specialize in but a single stamp, with all its nuances and variations. Some collectors save one type of postage stamp, such as airmails, commemoratives or other types. Another type of collection would consist only of covers (envelopes) bearing a stamp with a postmark from the first day of that stamp's issue.

Most popular, however, is collecting by country, especially one's own country. This catalogue is designed to aid in forming just such a collection. It lists the postage stamps of the United States and is a simplified edition of information found in Volume I of the *Scott Standard Postage Stamp Catalogue*.

Catalogue Information

The number (1616) in the first column of the example below is the stamp's identifying Scott number. Each stamp issued by the United States has a unique Scott number. Each illustration shows the Scott number beneath. In cases where two or more Scott numbers share a common design, the illustration will show the first Scott number that shows that design. Notes in the text will guide the user to find the correct design of subsequent Scott numbers showing the same design. This will be done by information in the header notes for the stamp or set, or by showing the design type by Scott number in parenthesis after its description (e.g., (1590) following the Scott 1616 listing.) Following in the same line are the denomination of the stamp, its color or other description along with the color of the paper (in italic type) if other than white, and the catalogue value both unused and used.

Scott Number	Denomination	Descrip.	Design, Type	Color	Color of the Stamp Paper	Unused Value	Used Value
1616	9c	Capitol	(1590)	slate grn	gray	.25	.25

8A

Catalogue value

Scott Catalogue value is a retail value; what you could expect to pay for a sound stamp in a grade of Very Fine. The value listed is a reference that reflects recent actual dealer selling prices.

Dealer retail price lists, public auction results, published prices in advertising and individual solicitation of retail prices from dealers, collectors and specialty organizations have been used in establishing the values found in this catalogue.

Use this catalogue as a guide in your own buying and selling. The actual price you pay for a stamp may be higher or lower than the catalogue value because of one or more of the following factors: the grade and condition of the actual stamp; the amount of personal service a dealer offers: increased interest in the country or topic represented by the stamp or set; whether an item is a "loss leader," part of a special sale, or is otherwise being sold for a short period of time at a lower price; or if at a public auction you are able to obtain an item inexpensively because of little interest in the item at that time.

The Scott Catalogue values stamps on the basis of the cost of purchasing them individually. You will find packets, mixtures and collections where the unit cost of the material will be substantially less than the total catalogue value of the component stamps.

Values for pre-1890 unused issues are for stamps with approximately half or more of their original gum. Later issues are assumed to have full original gum.

Unused stamps are valued in never hinged condition beginning with Nos. 772, C19, E17, FA1, J88, O127 and RW1. No. 485 also is valued never hinged.

	1847 ISSUES	1857-61 ISSUES	1861-67 ISSUES
Fine-Very Fine ➡			
SCOTT CATALOGUES VALUE STAMPS IN THIS GRADE **Very Fine**			
Extremely Fine ➡			

Grade

A stamp's grade and condition are crucial to its value. Values quoted in this catalogue are for stamps graded at Very Fine, and with no faults. The accompanying illustrations show an example of a Very Fine grade between the grades immediately below and above it: Fine to Very Fine and Extremely Fine.

FINE to VERY FINE stamps may be somewhat off center on one side, or slightly off center on two sides. Imperforate stamps will have two margins at least normal size and the design will not touch the edge. *Early issues may be printed in such a way that the design is naturally very close to the edges.* Used stamps will not have a cancellation that detracts from the design.

VERY FINE stamps may be slightly off center on one side, but the design will be well clear of the edge. The stamp will present a nice, balanced appearance. Imperforate stamps will have three normal-sized margins. *However, early perforated issues may be printed in such a way that the perforations may touch the design on one or more sides.* Used stamps will have light or otherwise neat cancellations. This is the grade used to establish Scott Catalgoue values.

EXTREMELY FINE stamps are close to being perfectly centered. Imperforate stamps will have even margins that are larger than normal. Even the earliest perforated issues will have perforations clear of the design on all sides.

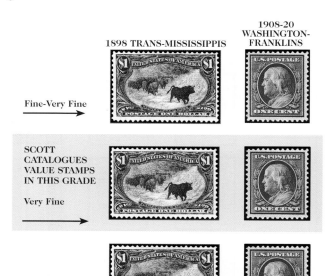

1898 TRANS-MISSISSIPPIS

1908-20 WASHINGTON-FRANKLINS

Fine-Very Fine

SCOTT CATALOGUES VALUE STAMPS IN THIS GRADE

Very Fine

Extremely Fine

Scott Publishing Co. recognizes that there is no formal, enforced grading scheme for postage stamps, and that the final price you pay for a stamp or obtain for a stamp you are selling will be determined by individual agreement at the time of the transaction.

Condition

The definitions given with the illustrations describe *grade*, which is centering and, for used stamps, cancellation. *Condition* refers to the soundness of the stamp; that is, faults, repairs and other factors influencing price.

Copies of a stamp that are of a lesser grade or condition trade at lower prices. Those of exceptional quality often command higher than catalogue prices.

Factors that can increase the value of a stamp include exceptionally wide margins, particularly fresh color, the presence of selvage (sheet margin), and plate or die varieties. Unusual cancels on used stamps (particularly those of the 19th century) can greatly enhance their value as well.

Factors other than faults that decrease the value of a stamp include loss of original gum or regumming, hinge remnants, foreign objects adhering to gum, natural inclusions, straight edges, or notations applied by collectors or dealers.

Faults include a missing piece, tear, clipped perforation, pin or other hole, surface scuff, thin spot, crease, toning, oxidation or other form of color changeling, short or pulled perforation, stains or such man-made changes as reperforations or the chemical removal or lightening of a cancellation.

Forming a collection

Methods of collecting stamps are many and varied. A person may begin by attempting to gather a single specimen of every face-different stamp issued by a country. An extension of that approach is to include the different types of each stamp, such as perforation varieties, watermark varieties, different printings and color changes. The stamps may be collected on cover (envelope) complete with postal markings, thus showing postal rates, types of cancellations and other postal information.

Collections also may be limited to types of stamps. The stamps issued by most countries are divided into such categories as regular postage (made up of definitives and commemoratives), airmail stamps, special delivery stamps, postage due stamps and others. Any of those groups may provide the basis for a good collection.

Definitive stamps are those regular issues used on most mail sent out on a daily basis. They are normally issued in extended sets, sometimes over a period of years. The sets feature a rising series of face values that allows a mailer to meet any current postal rate. Definitive stamps may be printed in huge quantities and are often kept in service by the Postal Service for long periods of time.

Commemorative stamps meet another need. They are primarily issued to celebrate an important event, honor a famous person or promote a special project or cause. Such stamps are issued on a limited basis for a limited time. They are usually more colorful and are often of a larger size than definitives.

Although few airmail stamps are currently issued by the United States, they continue to remain very popular among collectors. Just as with regular issues, airmail stamps are subject to several types of collecting. In addition to amassing the actual stamps, airmail enthusiasts pursue first-flight covers, airport dedication covers and even crash covers.

Not as popular, but still collected as units, are special delivery and postage due stamps. Special delivery stamps ensured speedier delivery of a letter once it reached its destination post office through normal postal means. Postage due stamps were used when a letter or parcel did not carry enough postage to pay for its delivery, subjecting the recipient to a fee to make up the difference. The United States no longer issues postage due stamps.

The resurrection in 1983 of Official Mail stamps-those used only by departments and offices of the federal government-has also brought about a resurgence of interest in them by stamp collectors. Originally issued between 1873 and 1911, Official Mail stamps were obsolete until recently. To be legally used, they must be on cards, envelopes or parcels that bear the return address of a federal office or facility.

"Topical" collecting is becoming more and more popular. Here the paramount attraction to the collector is the subject depicted on the stamp. The topics or themes from which to choose are virtually unlimited, other than by your own imagination. Animals, flowers, music, ships, birds and famous people on stamps make interesting collections. The degree of specializations is limitless, leading to such topics as graduates of a specific college or university, types of aircraft or the work of a specific artist.

There are several ways to obtain topical information, one of which is through the "By Topic" section of the *Scott Stamp Monthly*. "By Topic" is a regular feature of the magazine that divides the stamps of the world into more than 100 topical areas.

The album

To be displayed at their best, stamps should be properly housed. A quality album not only achieves this, but gives protection from dirt, loss and damage. When choosing an album, consider these three points: Is it within your means, does it meet your special interests and is it the best you can afford?

The Scott *Pony Express* and *Minuteman* albums are ideal companions to this Catalogue. Scott also publishes the National Album series for United States stamps, for a more complete collection.

Looseleaf albums are recommended for all collectors beyond the novice level. Not only do looseleaf albums allow for expansion of a collection, but the pages may be removed for mounting stamps as well as for display. A special advantage of a looseleaf album is that in many cases it may be kept current with supplements published annually on matching pages. All Scott albums noted are looseleaf and are supplemented annually.

Mounts and hinges

Mounts and hinges specially manufactured for collectors are used to affix stamps to album pages. Most stamp mounts are pre-gummed, clear plastic containers that hold a stamp safely and may be affixed to an album page with minimum effort. They are available in sizes to fit any stamp, block or even complete envelopes. Mounts are particularly important with unused stamps when there is a desire to not disturb the gum.

Although the mount is important, so is the venerable hinge. Innumerable stamps have been ruined beyond redemption by being glued to an album page. Hinges are inexpensive and effective. Use only peelable hinges. These may be removed from a stamp or album page without leaving an unsightly mark or causing damage to either.

Hinges are perfect for less-expensive stamps, used stamps and stamps that previously have been hinged. The use of stamp hinges is simple. Merely fold back, adhesive side out, about a quarter of the hinge (if it is not pre-folded). Lightly moisten the shorter side and affix it near the top of the back of the stamp. Then, holding the stamp with a pair of tongs, moisten the longer side of the hinge and place it (with stamp attached) in its proper place on the album page.

Stamp tongs

As previously noted, stamp tongs are a simple but important accessory and should always be used when handling a stamp. Fingers can easily damage or soil a stamp. Tongs cost little and will quickly pay for themselves. They come in a variety of styles. Beginners should start with tongs having a blunt or rounded tip. Those with sharp ends may inadvertently cause damage to a stamp. With just a little practice you will find tongs easier to work with than using your fingers...and your stamps will be better for it.

Magnifying glass

A good magnifying glass for scrutinizing stamps in detail is another useful philatelic tool. It allows you to see variations in stamps that may otherwise be invisible to the naked eye. Also, a magnifying glass makes minute parts of a stamp design large enough to see well. Your first glass should be a least 5- to 10-power magnification, with edge-to-edge clarity. Stronger magnifications are available and may also be useful.

Perforation gauge and watermark detector

Although many stamps appear to be alike, they are not. Even though the design may be the same and the color identical, there are at least two other areas where differences occur, and where specialized devices are needed for such identification. These are perforation measurement and watermark detection. A ruler that measures in millimeters is also useful.

The perforation gauge, printed on plastic, cardboard or metal, contains a graded scale that enables you to measure the number of perforation "teeth" in two centimeters. To determine the perforation measurement, place the stamp on the gauge and move the former along the scale until the points on one entry of the scale align perfectly with the teeth of the stamp's perforations. A stamp may have different perforations horizontally and vertically.

Watermarks are a bit more difficult to detect. They are letters or designs impressed into the paper at the time of manufacture. A watermark may occasionally be seen by holding a stamp up to the light, but a watermark detector is often necessary. The simplest of the many types of detectors available consists of a small black tray (glass or hard plastic). The stamp is placed face down in the tray and watermark detection fluid is poured over it. If there is a watermark, or a part of one, it should become visible when the stamp becomes soaked with the fluid.

There are a number of other liquids that over the years have been recommended for use to detect watermarks. The currently available fluids made specifically for that purpose are the safest for the stamp and the collector. We do not recommend anything other than such watermark detection fluids for that use.

Where to get accessories

Your local stamp dealer probably stocks a variety of stamp albums and accessories. Check the Yellow Pages under "Stamps for Collectors." Scott Publishing Co. also has a variety of albums and accessories available for sale. Call 1-800-572-6885 for a Scott Product Guide.

Notes

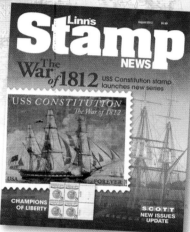
1

Benjamin Franklin
1
3

George Washington
2
4

Reproductions. The letters R.W.H. & E. at the bottom of each stamp are less distinct on the reproductions than on the originals.

5c. On the originals the left side of the white shift frill touches the oval on a level with the top of the "F" of "Five." On the reproductions it touches the oval about on a level with the top of the figure "5."

10c. On the reproductions, line of coat at left points to right tip of "X" and line of coat at right points to center of "S" of CENTS. On the originals, line of coat points to "T" of TEN and between "T" and "S" of CENTS. On the reproductions, the gap between the bottom legs of the left "X" is noticeably wider than the gap on the right "X". On the originals, the gap is of equal width. On the reproductions the eyes have a sleepy look, the line of the mouth is straighter, and in the curl of hair near the left cheek is a strong black dot, while the originals have only a faint one.

Franklin
5

5

ONE CENT.
Type I. Has complete curved lines outside the labels with "U.S. Postage" and "One Cent." The scrolls below the lower label are turned under, forming little balls. The ornaments at top are substantially complete.
Type Ib. Same as I but balls below the bottom label are not so clear. The plume-like scrolls at bottom are not complete.

6

Type Ia. Same as I at bottom but top ornaments and outer line at top are partly cut away.
Type Ic. Same as Ia, but bottom right plume and ball ornament incomplete. Bottom left plume complete or nearly complete.

7

Type II. Same as type I at top, but the little balls of the bottom scrolls and the bottoms of the lower plume ornaments are missing. The side ornaments are substantially complete.

8

Type III. The top and bottom curved lines outside the labels are broken in the middle. The side ornaments are complete.

Type IIIa. Similar to type III with the outer line broken at top or bottom but not both.

9

Type IV. Similar to type II, but with the curved lines outside the labels recut at top or bottom or both.

Prices for types I and III are for stamps showing the marked characteristics plainly. Copies of type I showing the balls indistinctly and of type III with the lines only slightly broken, sell for much lower prices.

Washington
10

Thomas Jefferson
12

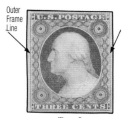

Outer Frame Line

Type I

Outer Frame Line

INNER LINE

Type II

Top, the 1851 3¢ stamp with outer frame lines only on all four sides, type I. Bottom, the 3¢ stamp with outer frame lines and recut inner lines, type II.

12

FIVE CENTS.
Type I. There are projections on all four sides.

13

13

TEN CENTS.

Type I. The "shells" at the lower corners are practically complete. The outer line below the label is very nearly complete. The outer lines are broken above the middle of the top label and the "X" in each upper corner.

14

Type II. The design is complete at the top. The outer line at the bottom is broken in the middle. The shells are partly cut away.

15

Type III. The outer lines are broken above the top label and the "X" numerals. The outer line at the bottom and the shells are partly cut away, as in Type II.

16

Type IV. The outer lines have been recut at top or bottom or both.

Types I, II, III, and IV have complete ornaments at the sides of the stamps and three pearls at each outer edge of the bottom panel.

17

Franklin
24

ONE CENT.

Type V. Similar to type III of 1851-56 but with side ornaments partly cut away.

UNITED STATES

Scott No.	Description	Unused Value	Used Value	/ / / / / /
1847, Imperf.				
1	5c Benjamin Franklin, red brown......	6,750.	450.00	
	Pen cancel..		240.00	
a.	5c dark brown....................................	8,750.	850.00	
b.	5c orange brown.................................	10,000.	950.00	
c.	5c red orange.....................................	25,000.	9,500.	
d.	5c brown orange.................................	—	1,150.	
2	10c George Washington, black.............	35,000.	1,050.	
	Pen cancel..		600.00	
a.	Diagonal half used as 5c on cover		13,000.	
b.	Vert. half used as 5c on cover........		30,000.	
c.	Horiz. half used as 5c on cover		—	
1875, Reproductions, Bluish Paper Without Gum, Imperf.				
3	5c Franklin (1), red brown.................	825.00		
4	10c Washington (2), black	1,000.		
1851-57, Imperf.				
5	1c Franklin, blue, type I.....................	225,000.	75,000.	
5A	1c Franklin (5), blue, type Ib.............	32,500.	10,000.	
6	1c Franklin (5), blue, type Ia	45,000.	11,000.	
b.	Type Ic	7,000.	3,500.	
7	1c Franklin (5), blue, type II..............	1,100.	160.00	
8	1c Franklin (5), blue, type III	25,000.	2,750.	
8A	1c Franklin (5), blue, type IIIa...........	6,000.	900.00	
9	1c Franklin (5), blue, IV	800.00	100.00	
a.	Printed on both sides, reverse inverted		—	
10	3c Washington, orange brown, type I.	4,000.	200.00	
10A	3c Washington, orange brown, type II.	3,250.	160.00	
b.	Printed on both sides.....................		55,000.	
11	3c Washington (10), dull red, type I...	275.00	15.00	
11A	3c Washington (10A), dull red, type II	275.00	15.00	
c.	Vert. half used as 1c on cover.......		5,000.	
d.	Diagonal half used as 1c on cover.		5,000.	
e.	Double impression		30,000.	

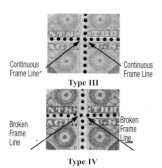

Continuous Frame Line | Continuous Frame Line

Type III

Broken Frame Line | Broken Frame Line

Type IV

THREE CENTS.

Types III & IV. Top, the perforated 1857 3¢ stamp with top and bottom frame lines removed and with continuous side frame lines (type III, No. 26). Bottom, the perforated 3¢ stamp with side frame lines broken between stamps (type IV, No. 26A).

30

30

FIVE CENTS.

Type II. The projections at top and bottom are partly cut away.

35

(Two typical examples).

TEN CENTS.

Type V. The side ornaments are slightly cut away. Usually only one pearl remains at each end of the lower label but some copies show two or three pearls at the right side. At the bottom the outer line is complete and the shells nearly so. The outer lines at top are complete except over the right "X."

TWELVE CENTS.

Plate I. Outer frame lines complete.

Plate III. Outer frame lines noticeably uneven or broken, sometimes partly missing.

37   38

39

63

63

1c. A dash appears under the tip of the ornament at right of the numeral in upper left corner.

64

6

Scott No.	Description	Unused Value	Used Value	/ / / / / /
12	5c Thomas Jefferson, red brown, type I	*30,000.*	700.00	
13	10c Washington, green, type I	*19,000.*	900.00	
14	10c Washington (13), green, type II.....	5,000.	160.00	
15	10c Washington (13), green, type III ...	5,000.	160.00	
16	10c Washington (13), green, type IV ...	*35,000.*	1,650.	
17	12c Washington, black..........................	6,250.	260.00	
a.	Diagonal half used as 6c on cover.		2,750.	
b.	Vert. half used as 6c on cover........		8,500.	
c.	Printed on both sides.....................		40,000.	

1857-61, Perf. 15½

Scott No.	Description	Unused Value	Used Value	/ / / / / /
18	1c Franklin (5), blue, type I................	2,250.	550.00	
19	1c Franklin (5), blue, type Ia	*42,500.*	9,000.	
b.	Type Ic..	*4,250.*	2,500.	
20	1c Franklin (5), blue, type II..............	1,000.	275.00	
21	1c Franklin (5), blue, type III	*17,500.*	2,500.	
22	1c Franklin (5), blue, type IIIa...........	2,600.	500.00	
b.	Horiz. pair, imperf. btwn.		10,000.	
23	1c Franklin (5), blue, type IV	10,000.	900.00	
24	1c Franklin (5), blue, type V..............	150.00	40.00	
b.	Laid paper.......................................		7,500.	
25	3c Washington (10), rose, type I	2,750.	125.00	
25A	3c Washington (10A), rose, type II	7,000.	800.00	
b.	Vert. pair, imperf. horiz.................		10,000.	
26	3c Washington, dull red, type III	65.00	9.00	
b.	Horiz. pair, imperf. vert., type II.................................	*4,000.*	—	
c.	Vert. pair, imperf. horiz., type II..		16,000.	
d.	Horiz. pair, imperf. btwn., type II..		—	
e.	Double impression, type II		2,500.	
26A	3c Washington, dull red, type IV........	600.00	150.00	
f.	As "a," horiz. strip of 3, imperf. vert., on cover		14,500.	
27	5c Jefferson (12), brick red, type I	*80,000.*	1,650.	
28	5c Jefferson (12), red brown, type I ...	*60,000.*	1,200.	
b.	bright red brown...........................	70,000.	2,100.	
28A	5c Jefferson (12), Indian red, type I ...	*175,000.*	3,500.	
29	5c Jefferson (12), brown, type I..........	5,500.	400.00	
30	5c Jefferson, orange brown, type II....	1,250.	*1,400.*	
30A	5c Jefferson (30), brown, type II	2,200.	275.00	
b.	Printed on both sides.....................		45,000.	
31	10c Washington (13), green, type I	*30,000.*	1,350.	
32	10c green, type II..............................	6,250.	200.00	
33	10c green, type III.............................	6,250.	200.00	
34	10c green, type IV.............................	*50,000.*	2,250.	
35	10c green, type V	250.00	65.00	

7

64

3c. Ornaments at corners end in a small ball.

69

67

12c. Ovals and scrolls have been added to the corners.

67

5c. A leaflet appears on the foliated ornaments at each corner.

70

71

68

72

Grill

62B

72

90c. Parallel lines form an angle above the ribbon with "U.S. Postage;" between these lines a row of dashes has been added and a point of color to the apex of the lower pair.

68

10c. A heavy curved line has been cut below the stars and an outer line added to the ornaments above them.

73

77

8

Scott No.	Description	Unused Value	Used Value	/ / / / / /
36	12c black, plate I	1,900.	350.00	
a.	Diagonal half used as 6c on cover (I)		17,500.	
c.	Horiz. pair, imperf. between (I).....		12,500.	
36B	12c black, plate III	775.00	275.00	
37	24c gray lilac	1,500.	400.00	
a.	24c gray	1,500.	400.00	
38	30c orange	2,250.	425.00	
39	90c blue	3,250.	11,000.	

1875, Reprints, Without Gum, Perf. 12

Scott No.	Description	Unused Value	Used Value	/ / / / / /
40	1c bright blue (5).........................	600.00		
41	3c scarlet (10).............................	3,000.		
42	5c orange brown (30)....................	1,200.		
43	10c blue green (13)	2,750.	13,000.	
44	12c greenish black (17)..................	3,000.		
45	24c black violet (37)	3,000.	10,000.	
46	30c yellow orange (38)	3,000.		
47	90c deep blue (39)........................	4,000.		

1861

Scott No.	Description	Unused Value	Used Value	/ / / / / /
62B	10c Washington, dark green (68)	8,000.	1,600.	

1861-62

Scott No.	Description	Unused Value	Used Value	/ / / / / /
63	1c blue	325.00	50.00	
a.	1c ultramarine	2,500.	800.00	
b.	1c dark blue	800.00	800.00	
c.	Laid paper...................................	8,500.	5,000.	
d.	Vert. pair, imperf. horiz...............		—	
e.	Printed on both sides....................	—	50,000.	
64	3c pink	14,000.	850.00	
a.	3c pigeon blood pink	50,000.	5,000.	
b.	3c rose pink	600.00	160.00	
65	3c rose	125.00	3.00	
b.	Laid paper...................................	—	1,250.	
d.	Vert. pair, imperf. horiz...............	15,000.	1,500.	
e.	Printed on both sides....................	40,000.	8,000.	
f.	Double impression		15,000.	
67	5c buff	27,500.	1,000.	
a.	5c brown yellow	30,000.	1,250.	
b.	5c olive yellow	—	4,000.	
68	10c Washington, yellow green.............	1,200.	60.00	
a.	10c dark green..............................	1,450.	80.00	
b.	Vert. pair, imperf. horiz................		3,500.	
69	12c Washington, black	2,000.	110.00	
70	24c Washington, red lilac	3,000.	275.00	
a.	24c brown lilac.............................	3,250.	300.00	
b.	24c steel blue...............................	16,500.	900.00	
c.	24c violet, thin paper	35,000.	2,250.	
d.	24c pale gray violet, thin paper	25,000.	3,000.	

9

Scott No.	Description	Unused Value	Used Value	/ / / / / /
71	30c Franklin, orange	2,600.	180.00	
a.	Printed on both sides		—	
72	90c Washington, blue	3,250.	600.00	
a.	90c pale blue	3,250.	650.00	
b.	90c dark blue	4,000.	1,000.	

1861-66

Scott No.	Description	Unused Value	Used Value	/ / / / / /
73	2c Andrew Jackson, black	375.00	65.00	
a.	Diagonal half used as 1c as part of 3c rate on cover.		1,500.	
b.	Diagonal half used alone as 1c on cover		3,000.	
c.	Horiz. half used as 1c as part of 3c rate on cover		3,500.	
d.	Vert. half used as 1c as part of 3c rate on cover		2,000.	
e.	Vert. half used alone as 1c on cover		4,000.	
f.	Printed on both sides		30,000.	
g.	Laid paper	—	12,500.	
75	5c Jefferson (67), red brown	5,750.	475.00	
76	5c Jefferson (67), brown	1,500.	120.00	
a.	5c dark brown	2,250.	400.00	
b.	Laid paper		—	
77	15c Abraham Lincoln, black	4,500.	200.00	
78	24c Washington (70), lilac	2,750.	350.00	
a.	24c grayish lilac	2,900.	425.00	
b.	24c gray	2,900.	450.00	
c.	24c blackish violet	100,000.	22,500.	
d.	Printed on both sides		50,000.	

1867, Perf. 12, Grill With Points Up
A. Grill Covering The Entire Stamp

Scott No.	Description	Unused Value	Used Value	/ / / / / /
79	3c Washington (64), rose	8,500.	1,500.	
b.	Printed on both sides		—	
80	5c Jefferson (67), brown		260,000.	
a.	5c dark brown		260,000.	
81	30c Franklin (71), orange		210,000.	

B. Grill About 18 x 15mm (22 by 18 points)

Scott No.	Description	Unused Value	Used Value	/ / / / / /
82	3c Washington (64), rose		1,000,000.	

Grill With Points Down
C. Grill About 13 x 16mm (16 to 17 by 18 to 21 points)

Scott No.	Description	Unused Value	Used Value	/ / / / / /
83	3c Washington (64), rose	6,250.	1,200.	

D. Grill About 12 x 14mm (15 by 17 to 18 points)

Scott No.	Description	Unused Value	Used Value	/ / / / / /
84	2c Jackson (73)	16,000.	4,500.	
85	3c Washington (64), rose	6,500.	1,250.	

Z. Grill About 11 x 14mm (13 to 14 by 17 to 18 points)

Scott No.	Description	Unused Value	Used Value	/ / / / / /
85A	1c Franklin (63), blue		3,000,000.	
85B	2c Jackson (73)	17,500.	1,300.	
85C	3c Washington (64), rose	25,000.	3,750.	

Scott No.	Description	Unused Value	Used Value	/ / / / / /
85D	10c Washington (68), green..............		650,000.	
85E	12c Washington (69)...........................	*17,500.*	2,500.	
85F	15c Lincoln (77).................................		*2,000,000.*	

E. Grill About 11 x 13mm (14 by 15 to 17 points)

86	1c Franklin (63), blue........................	3,500.	525.00	
a.	1c dull blue.......................................	3,500.	500.00	
87	2c Jackson (73)	1,750.	200.00	
a.	Half used as 1c on cover, diagonal or vert.		*2,000.*	
88	3c Washington (64), rose	1,000.	27.50	
a.	3c lake red	1,250.	50.00	
89	10c Washington (68), green..............	5,250.	350.00	
90	12c Washington (69)..........................	4,750.	400.00	
91	15c Lincoln (77)	12,500.	700.00	

F. Grill About 9 x 13mm (11 to 12 by 15 to 17 points)

92	1c Franklin (63), blue........................	3,250.	500.00	
a.	1c pale blue	2,275.	450.00	
93	2c Jackson (73)	500.00	60.00	
a.	Vert. half used as 1c as part of 3c rate on cover		*1,250.*	
b.	Diagonal half used as 1c as part of 3c rate on cover...........................		*1,250.*	
c.	Horiz. half used alone as 1c on cover		*2,500.*	
d.	Diagonal half used alone as 1c on cover.......................................		*2,500.*	
94	3c Washington (64), red.....................	375.00	10.00	
a.	3c rose	375.00	10.00	
c.	Vert. pair, imperf. horiz....................	*15,000.*		
d.	Printed on both sides......................	*9,000.*		
95	5c Jefferson (67), brown	3,750.	1,000.	
a.	5c dark brown...................................	4,750.	2,250.	
96	10c Washington (68), yellow green......	3,000.	275.00	
a.	10c dark green..................................	3,500.	350.00	
97	12c Washington (69)..........................	3,250.	275.00	
98	15c Lincoln (77).................................	4,500.	350.00	
99	24c Washington (70), gray lilac...........	9,000.	1,600.	
100	30c Franklin (71), orange	8,500.	1,000.	
101	90c Washington (72), blue...................	14,500.	2,250.	

1875, Reprints, Without Grill, White Crackly Gum, Hard White Paper, Perf. 12

102	1c Franklin (63), blue........................	*900.00*	*1,500.*	
103	2c Jackson (73)	*4,000.*	*15,000.*	
104	3c Washington (64), brown red	*4,500.*	*17,500.*	
105	5c Jefferson (67), brown	*3,000.*	*10,000.*	
106	10c Washington (68), green................	*3,750.*	*125,000.*	
107	12c Washington (69)..........................	*4,550.*	*15,000.*	
108	15c Lincoln (77).................................	*5,250.*	*35,000.*	

112 **113**

114 **115**

116 **117**

118 **120**

121 **122**

118

FIFTEEN CENTS. Type I. Picture unframed.

Type II. Picture framed.
Type III. Same as type I but without fringe of brown shading lines around central vignette.

134

135

136

137

12

Scott No.	Description	Unused Value	Used Value	/ / / / / /
109	24c Washington (70), deep violet.........	6,500.	20,000.	
110	30c Franklin (71), brownish orange	6,750.	25,000.	
111	90c Washington (72), blue....................	7,250.	225,000.	

1869, Perf. 12
G. Grill Measuring 9½ x 9mm

112	1c Franklin, buff...............................	650.00	160.00	
b.	Without grill....................................	35,000.		
113	2c Pony Express, brown......................	550.00	95.00	
b.	Without grill....................................	7,500.		
c.	Half used as 1c on cover, diagonal, vert. or horiz................		6,000.	
d.	Printed on both sides......................		9,000.	
114	3c Locomotive, ultramarine...............	275.00	18.00	
a.	Without grill....................................	10,000.		
b.	Vert. one third used as 1c on cover	18,000.	—	
c.	Vert. two thirds used as 2c on cover		10,000.	
d.	Double impression		11,000.	
e.	Printed on both sides......................		55,000.	
115	6c Washington, ultramarine...............	2,750.	240.00	
b.	Vert. half used as 3c on cover........		50,000.	
116	10c Shield & Eagle, yellow	2,250.	150.00	
117	12c Ship, green	1,900.	150.00	
118	15c Landing of Columbus, brown & blue, Type I......................................	10,000.	800.00	
a.	Without grill....................................	13,000.		
119	15c Landing of Columbus (118), type II	3,500.	250.00	
b.	Center inverted..............................	1,250,000.	22,500.	
c.	Center double, one inverted...........		80,000.	
120	24c Declaration of Independence, grn & vio	9,000.	700.00	
a.	Without grill....................................	15,000.		
b.	Center inverted..............................	750,000.	37,500.	
121	30c Shield, Eagle & Flags, blue & car.	5,750.	450.00	
a.	Without grill....................................	11,000.		
b.	Flags inverted	1,000,000.	110,000.	
122	90c Lincoln, carmine & black.............	12,500.	2,100.	
a.	Without grill....................................	24,000.		

1875, Re-issues, Without Grill, Hard White Paper

123	1c Franklin (112), buff......................	575.00	400.00	
124	2c Pony Express (113).......................	675.00	800.00	
125	3c Locomotive (114), blue................	5,500.	27,500.	
126	6c Washington (115), blue.................	1,800.	3,250.	
127	10c Shield & Eagle (116)	1,800.	2,000.	
128	12c Ship (117)......................................	2,500.	3,250.	
129	15c Landing of Columbus (118), type III	1,500.	1,250.	
a.	Imperf. horiz., single......................	6,250.	7,000.	
130	24c Declaration of Independence (120)	2,300.	1,750.	
131	30c Shield, Eagle & Flags (121)...........	2,750.	3,000.	

13

138

139

140

141

142

143

144

156

1c. In pearl at left of numeral "1" is a small crescent.

157

2c. Under the scroll at the left of "U.S." there is a small diagonal line. This mark seldom shows clearly. The stamp, No. 157, can be distinguished by its color.

158

3c. The under part of the upper tail of the left ribbon is heavily shaded.

159

6c. The first four vertical lines of the shading in the lower part of the left ribbon have been strengthened.

Scott No.	Description	Unused Value	Used Value	/ / / / / /
132	90c Lincoln (122), carmine and black .	4,250.	6,500.	☐☐☐☐☐
1880, Soft Porous Paper				
133	1c Franklin (112), buff, with gum......	325.00	450.00	☐☐☐☐☐
a.	1c brown orange, without gum..........	250.00	350.00	☐☐☐☐☐
1870-71, Perf. 12, With H Grill, about 10x12mm (11 to 13 by 14 to 16 points)				
134	1c Franklin, ultramarine..................	2,250.	210.00	☐☐☐☐☐
b.	Pair, one without grill	—		☐☐☐☐☐
135	2c Jackson, red brown.......................	1,100.	80.00	☐☐☐☐☐
b.	Diagonal half used as 1c on cover.		—	☐☐☐☐☐
c.	Vert. half used as 1c on cover........		—	☐☐☐☐☐
136	3c Washington, green......................	675.00	32.50	☐☐☐☐☐
b.	Printed on both sides.....................	—		☐☐☐☐☐
137	6c Lincoln, carmine	5,250.	575.00	☐☐☐☐☐
b.	Pair, one without grill	—		☐☐☐☐☐
138	7c Edwin M. Stanton, vermilion	4,500.	550.00	☐☐☐☐☐
139	10c Jefferson, brown	7,000.	850.00	☐☐☐☐☐
b.	Pair, one without grill, one with split grill, on cover		—	☐☐☐☐☐
140	12c Henry Clay, dull violet..................	27,500.	3,750.	☐☐☐☐☐
141	15c Daniel Webster, orange..........	8,000.	1,400.	☐☐☐☐☐
142	24c Gen. Winfield Scott, purple...........		7,500.	☐☐☐☐☐
143	30c Alexander Hamilton, black...........	20,000.	4,000.	☐☐☐☐☐
144	90c Commodore O. H. Perry, carmine .	25,000.	2,500.	☐☐☐☐☐
I Grill, about 8½x10mm (10 to 11 by 10 to 13 points)				
134A	1c Franklin (134), ultramarine...........	2,750.	275.00	☐☐☐☐☐
135A	2c Jackson (135), red brown..............	1,750.	225.00	☐☐☐☐☐
136A	3c Washington (136), green..............	1,000.	95.00	☐☐☐☐☐
a.	Pair, one without grill, on cover		—	☐☐☐☐☐
137A	6c Lincoln (137), carmine	7,000.	900.00	☐☐☐☐☐
138A	7c Stanton (138), vermilion...............	6,750.	1,500.	☐☐☐☐☐
139A	10c Jefferson (139), brown		6,000.	☐☐☐☐☐
140A	12c Clay (140), dull violet..................	35,000.		☐☐☐☐☐
141A	15c Webster (141), orange...............	17,500.	7,500.	☐☐☐☐☐
143A	30c Hamilton (143), black...............	75,000.		☐☐☐☐☐
144A	90c Perry (144), carmine	—	15,000.	☐☐☐☐☐
1870-71, Perf. 12, Without Grill				
145	1c Franklin (134), ultramarine...........	750.00	25.00	☐☐☐☐☐
146	2c Jackson (135), red brown..............	350.00	20.00	☐☐☐☐☐
a.	Diagonal half used as 1c on cover.		700.00	☐☐☐☐☐
b.	Vert. half used as 1c on cover........		800.00	☐☐☐☐☐
c.	Horiz. half used as 1c on cover		800.00	☐☐☐☐☐
d.	Double impression	9,000.		☐☐☐☐☐
147	3c Washington (136), green...............	250.00	2.00	☐☐☐☐☐
a.	Printed on both sides.....................		15,000.	☐☐☐☐☐
b.	Double impression		40,000.	☐☐☐☐☐
148	6c Lincoln (137), carmine	1,100.	35.00	☐☐☐☐☐
a.	Vert. half used as 3c on cover........		6,500.	☐☐☐☐☐
b.	Double impression		13,000.	☐☐☐☐☐

160

7c. Two small semi-circles are drawn around the ends of the lines which outline the ball in the lower right hand corner.

161

10c. There is a small semi-circle in the scroll at the right end of the upper label.

162

12c. The balls of the figure "2" are crescent shaped.

163

15c. In the lower part of the triangle in the upper left corner two lines have been heavier forming a "V". This mark can be found on some of the Continental and American (1879) printings, but not all stamps show it.

Secret marks were added to the dies of the 24c, 30c and 90c but new plates were not made from them. The various printings of these stamps can be distinguished only by the shades and paper.

179   **205**

206

1c. The vertical lines in the upper part of the stamp have been so deepened that the background often appears to be solid. Lines of shading have been added to the upper arabesques.

207

3c. The shading at the sides of the central oval appears only about one-half the previous width. A short horizontal dash has been cut about 1 mm below the "TS" of "CENTS."

208

6c. On the original stamps four vertical lines can be counted from the edge of the panel to the outside of the stamp. On the re-engraved stamps there are but three lines in the same place.

209

10c. On the original stamps there are five vertical lines between the left side of the oval and the edge of the shield. There are only four lines on the re-engraved stamps. In the lower part of the latter, also, the horizontal lines of the background have been strengthened.

210   **211**

Scott No.	Description	Unused Value	Used Value	/ / / / / /
149	7c Stanton (138), vermilion...............	1,100.	100.00	
150	10c Jefferson (139), brown...................	2,250.	35.00	
151	12c Clay (140), dull violet...................	2,750.	220.00	
152	15c Webster (141), bright orange.........	3,000.	220.00	
a.	Double impression..........................		6,000.	
153	24c Scott (142), purple.......................	2,000.	230.00	
154	30c Hamilton (143), black...................	7,500.	300.00	
155	90c Perry (144), carmine.....................	5,500.	350.00	

1873, Perf. 12

Scott No.	Description	Unused Value	Used Value	/ / / / / /
156	1c Franklin (134), ultramarine...........	250.00	6.00	
e.	With grill......................................	2,000.		
f.	Imperf., pair..................................	—	1,500.	
157	2c Jackson (135), brown.....................	400.00	25.00	
c.	With grill......................................	1,850.	750.00	
d.	Double impression.........................	—	5,000.	
e.	Vert. half used as 1c on cover........		1,000.	
158	3c Washington (136), green...............	120.00	1.00	
e.	With grill......................................	500.00		
h.	Horiz. pair, imperf. vert.		—	
i.	Horiz. pair, imperf. btwn.		1,300.	
j.	Double impression.........................		10,000.	
k.	Printed on both sides.....................		15,000.	
159	6c Lincoln (137), dull pink...............	425.00	20.00	
a.	Diagonal half used as 3c on cover...		7,250.	
b.	With grill......................................	1,800.		
160	7c Stanton (138), orange vermilion....	1,250.	90.00	
a.	With grill......................................	3,500.		
161	10c Jefferson (139), brown...................	1,250.	25.00	
c.	With grill......................................	3,750.		
d.	Horiz. pair, imperf. btwn.		2,750.	
162	12c Clay (140), blackish violet............	2,500.	140.00	
a.	With grill......................................	5,500.		
163	15c Webster (141), yellow orange........	2,750.	160.00	
a.	With grill......................................	5,750.		
164	24c Scott (142), purple, vertically ribbed paper		357,500.	
165	30c Hamilton (143), gray blk	3,250.	140.00	
c.	With grill......................................	22,500.		
166	90c Perry(144), rose car.....................	2,400.	300.00	

1875, Re-issues, Without Gum, Hard White Paper, Perf. 12

Scott No.	Description	Unused Value	Used Value	/ / / / / /
167	1c Franklin (134), ultramarine...........	20,000.		
168	2c Jackson (135), dark brown.............	8,000.		
169	3c Washington (136), blue green........	25,000.	—	
170	6c Lincoln (137), dull rose	24,000.		
171	7c Stanton (138), reddish vermilion...	5,250.		
172	10c Jefferson (139), pale brown	23,000.		
173	12c Clay (140), dark violet..................	6,500.		

ScottMounts

Protect your stamps from the harmful effects of dust and moisture. Available in clear or black backs.

Pre-Cut Single Mounts

Size	Description	# Mounts	Item	Price
40 x 25	U.S. Stand. Com.-Hor.	40	901	$3.25
25 x 40	U.S. Stand. Com.-Vert.	40	902	3.25
25 x 22	U.S. Reg Issue-Hor.	40	903	3.25
22 x 25	U.S. Reg. Issue-Vert.	40	904	3.25
41 x 31	U.S. Semi-Jumbo-Hor.	40	905	3.25
31 x 41	U.S. Semi-Jumbo-Vert.	40	906	3.25
50 x 31	U.S. Jumbo-Hor.	40	907	3.25
31 x 50	U.S. Jumbo-Vert.	40	908	3.25
25 x 27	U.S. Famous Americans	40	909	3.25
33 x 27	United Nations	40	910	3.25
40 x 27	United Nations	40	911	3.25
67 x 25	PNC, Strips of Three	40	976	5.79
67 x 34	Pacific '97 Triangle	10	984	3.25
111 x 25	PNC, Strips of Five	25	985	5.29
51 x 36	U.S. Hunting Permit/ Express Mail	40	986	5.79
40 x 26	Stand. Commnem Hor. S/A	40	1045	3.25
25 x41	Stand. Commme Vert. S/A	40	1046	3.25
22 x 46	Definitives Vert. S/A	40	1047	3.25

Pre-Cut Plate Block, FDC & Postal Card Mounts

Size	Description	# Mounts	Item	Price
57 x 55	Reg Issue Plate Block	25	912	$5.75
73 x 63	Champions of Liberty	25	913	5.75
106 x 55	Rotary Press Stand. Com.	20	914	5.75
105 x 57	Giori Press Stand. Com.	20	915	5.75
165 x 94	First Day Cover	10	917	5.75
140 x 90	Postal Card Size	10	918	5.75
152 x 107	Large Postal Card Size	8	1048	9.79

Strips 215mm Long

Size	Description	# Mounts	Item	Price
20	U.S. 19th Century/Hor. Coil	22	919	$ 7.50
22	U.S. Early Air Mail	22	920	7.50
24	U.S., Canada, Great Britain	22	921	7.50
25	U.S. Comm. and Regular	22	922	7.50
27	U.S. Famous Americans	22	923	7.50
28	U.S. 19th Century	22	924	7.50
30	U.S. 19th Century	22	925	7.50
31	U.S. Jumbo and Semi-Jumbo	22	926	7.50
33	United Nations	22	927	7.50
36	U.S. Hunting Permit, Canada	15	928	7.50
39	U.S. Early 20th Century	15	929	7.50
41	U.S. Semi-Jumbo	15	930	7.50
	Multiple Assortment: one strip of each size 22-41 (Two 25mm strips)	12	931	7.50
44	U.S. Vertical Coil Pair	15	932	7.50
48	U.S. Farley, Gutter Pair	15	933	7.50
50	U.S. Jumbo	15	934	7.50
52	U.S. Standard Comm. Block	15	935	7.50
55	U.S. Century of Progress	15	936	7.50
57	U.S. Famous Americans Block	15	937	7.50
61	U.S. Blocks, Israel Tab	15	938	7.50

Strips 240mm Long

Size	Description	# Mounts	Item	Price
63	U.S. Jumbo Com.-Hor.Block	10	939	$8.79
66	Israel Tab Block	10	940	8.79
68	U.S. Farley, Gutter Pair & Souvenir Sheets	10	941	8.79
74	U.S. TIPEX Souvenir Sheet	10	942	8.79
80	U.S. Stand. Com.-Vert. Block	10	943	8.79
82	U.S. Blocks of 4	10	944	8.79
84	Israel Tab Block	10	945	8.79
89	U.S. Postal Card Size	10	946	8.79
100	U.N. Margin Inscribed Block	7	947	8.79
120	Souvenir Sheets and Blocks	7	948	8.79

Strips 265mm Long

Size	Description	# Mounts	Item	Price
40	Standard Comm. Vertical	10	949	$8.79
55	U.S. Reg. Plate Block Strip 20	10	950	8.79
59	U.S. Double Issue Strip	10	951	8.79
70	U.S. Jumbo Com. Plate Block	10	952	11.99
91	Great Britain Souvenir Sheet	10	953	11.99
105	U.S. Stand. Plate No. Strip	10	954	11.99
107	Same as above-Wide Margin	10	955	11.99
111	U.S. Gravure-Intaglio Plate No. Strip	10	956	14.29
127	U.S. Jumbo Comm. Plate No. Strip	10	957	16.75
137	Great Britain Coronation	10	958	16.75
158	U.S. Apollo-Soyuz Plate No. Strip	10	959	17.50
231	U.S. Full Post Office Pane Regular and Comm.	5	961	17.50
75	Lance Armstrong, Prehistoric	10	1032	11.99
95	Mini-Sheet Plate Blocks	10	1033	11.99
25	Coil Strips of 11	12	1035	8.79
46	Long S/A Booklet Panes of 15	10	1036	8.79

Souvenir Sheets/Small Panes

Size	Description	# Mounts	Item	Price
111 x 25	PNC, Strips of Five	25	985	$5.79
204 x 153	U.S. Bicent. New Year 2000	4	962	8.79
187 x 144	U.N. Flag Sheet	10	963	14.99
160 x 200	New U.N., Israel Sheet	10	964	14.99
120 x 207	AMERIPEX President Sht.	4	965	5.79
229 x 131	World War II Com. Sheet	5	968	8.25
111 x 91	Columbian Souv. Sheet	6	970	5.75
148 x 196	Apollo Moon Landing	4	972	7.50
129 x 122	*U.S. Definitive Mini-Sheet*	9	989	9.79
189 x 151	Chinese New Year	5	990	9.79
150 x 185	*Dr. Davis/World Cup*	5	991	9.79
198 x 151	Cherokee	5	992	9.79
198 x 187	Postal Museum	4	994	9.79
156 x 187	Sign Lang., Statehood	5	995	9.79
188 x 197	Country-Western	4	996	9.79
151 x 192	Olympic	5	997	9.79
174 x 185	Buffalo Soldiers	5	998	9.79
130 x 198	Silent Screen Stars	5	999	9.79
190 x 199	Leg. West, Civil, Comic	4	1000	9.79
178 x 181	Cranes	5	1001	9.79
183 x 212	Wonders of the Sea	3	1002	9.79
156 x 264	$14 Eagle	4	1003	9.79
159 x 255	$9.95 Moon Landing	4	1004	9.79
159 x 259	Priority/Express Mail	4	1005	9.79
223 x 187	Marilyn Monroe	3	1006	9.79
185 x 181	Challenger Shuttle	5	1007	9.79
152 x 228	Indian Dances/Antique Autos	5	1008	9.79
165 x 150	River Boat/Hanukkah	6	1009	9.79
275 x 200	Large Gutter Blocks	2	1010	9.79
161 x 160	Pacific '97 Sheet	4	1011	9.79
174 x 130	Bugs Bunny	6	1012	9.79
196 x 158	Football Coaches	4	1013	9.79
184 x 184	American Dolls	4	1014	9.79
186 x 230	Classic Movie Monsters	3	1015	9.79
187 x 160	Trans-Mississippi Sheet	4	1016	9.79
192 x 230	Celebrate The Century	3	1017	9.79
156 x 204	Space Discovery	5	1018	9.79
182 x 209	American Ballet	5	1019	9.79
139 x 151	Christmas Wreaths	5	1020	9.79
129 x 126	Justin Morrill, Henry Luce	8	1021	9.79
184 x 165	Bright Eyes	4	1022	9.79
185 x 172	Shuttle Landing	4	1023	9.79
172 x 233	Sonoran Desert	5	1024	9.79
150 x 166	Prostate Cancer	5	1025	9.79
201 x 176	Famous Trains	4	1026	9.79
176 x 124	Canada Historic Vehicles	4	1027	9.79
245 x 114	Canada Provincial Leaders	5	1028	9.79
177 x 133	Canada Year of Family	5	1029	9.79
181 x 213	Arctic Animals	3	1034	9.79
179 x 242	Louise Nevelson	3	1037	9.79
179 x 217	Library of Congress	3	1038	9.79
182 x 332	Youth Team Sports	3	1039	9.79
183 x 216	Lucille Ball Scott #3523	3	1040	9.79
182 x 244	American Photographers	3	1041	9.79
185 x 255	Andy Warhol	3	1042	9.79

Scott No.	Description	Unused Value	Used Value	/ / / / /
174	15c Webster (141), bright orange	*23,000.*		
175	24c Scott (142), dull purple..................	*4,500.*	*22,500.*	
176	30c Hamilton (143), greenish black	*19,000.*		
177	90c Perry (144), violet carmine............	*30,000.*		

Yellowish Wove Paper, Perf. 12

178	2c Jackson (135), vermilion	375.00	15.00	
b.	Half used as 1c on cover...............		*750.00*	
c.	With grill	900.00	2,750.	
179	5c Zachary Taylor, blue.....................	750.00	25.00	
c.	With grill	4,500.		

Re-issues, Without Gum, Hard White Paper, Perf. 12

180	2c Jackson (135), carmine vermilion .	*85,000.*		
181	2c Taylor (179), bright blue	*500,000.*		

1879, Perf. 12, Soft Paper

182	1c Franklin (134), dark ultramarine ...	275.00	6.00	
183	2c Jackson (135), vermilion	110.00	5.00	
a.	Double impression	—	5,500.	
b.	Half used as 1c on cover...............		750.00	
184	3c Washington (136), green...............	95.00	1.00	
b.	Double impression		5,500	
185	5c Taylor (179), blue........................	475.00	17.50	
186	6c Lincoln (137), pink	950.00	30.00	
187	10c Jefferson (139), brown	3,500.	42.50	
188	10c Jefferson (139), brown w/secret mk.	2,000.	32.50	
189	15c Webster (141), red orange.............	250.00	27.50	
190	30c Hamilton (143), full black	950.00	100.00	
191	90c Perry (144), carmine	2,250.	375.00	

1880, Special Printing, Without Gum, Soft Porous Paper, Perf. 12

192	1c Franklin (134), dark ultramarine ..	*72,500.*		
193	2c Jackson (135), black brown	*24,000.*		
194	3c Washington (136), blue green	*125,000.*		
195	6c Lincoln (137), dull rose	*90,000.*		
196	7c Stanton (138), scarlet vermilion ...	*10,000.*		
197	10c Jefferson (139), deep brown	*55,000.*		
198	12c Clay (140), blackish purple...........	*12,500.*		
199	15c Webster (141), orange	*42,500.*		
200	24c Scott (142), dark violet	*11,500.*		
201	30c Hamilton (143), greenish black	*25,000.*		
202	90c Perry (144), dull carmine	*38,000.*		
203	30c Jackson (135), scarlet vermilion ...	*140,000.*		
204	90c Taylor (179), deep blue	*350,000.*		

1882, Perf. 12

205	5c James Garfield, yellow brown	275.00	12.00	

Special Printing, Soft Porous Paper, Without Gum

205C	5c Garfield (205), gray brown	*85,000.*		

212   219   219D   221

222   223   224   225

226   227   228   229

230   231   232

233   234   235

236   237   238

Scott No.	Description	Unused Value	Used Value	/ / / / / /
1881-82, Perf. 12				
206	1c Franklin (134), gray blue	80.00	1.00	
207	3c Washington (136), blue green........	85.00	.80	
c.	Double impression			
208	6c Lincoln (137), rose........................	775.00	110.00	
a.	6c brown red.......................................	575.00	175.00	
209	10c Jefferson (139), brown	175.00	6.00	
b.	10c black brown	3,000.	350.00	
c.	Double impression		—	
1883, Perf. 12				
210	2c Washington, red brown	42.50	.75	
211	4c Jackson, blue green	300.00	27.50	
Special Printing, Soft Porous Paper, Without Gum				
211B	2c Washington (210), pale red brown,			
	with gum	375.00	—	
c.	Horiz. pair, imperf. btwn.	2,000.	—	
211D	4c Jackson (211), dp blue grn,			
	w/o gum	80,000.		
1887, Perf. 12				
212	1c Franklin, ultramarine.....................	100.00	2.50	
213	2c Washington (210), green...............	45.00	.60	
b.	Printed on both sides.....................		—	
214	3c Washington (136), vermilion.........	65.00	60.00	
1888, Perf. 12				
215	4c Jackson (211), carmine	225.00	27.50	
216	5c Garfield (205), indigo	250.00	17.50	
217	30c Hamilton (143), orange brown	375.00	120.00	
218	90c Perry (144), purple........................	1,000.	250.00	
1890-93, Perf. 12				
219	1c Franklin, dull blue	25.00	.75	
219D	2c Washington, lake............................	220.00	5.50	
220	2c Washington (219D), carmine.........	22.50	.70	
a.	Cap on left "2"	140.00	11.00	
c.	Cap on both "2s".............................	625.00	32.50	
221	3c Jackson, purple...............................	75.00	9.00	
222	4c Lincoln, dark brown.......................	100.00	4.75	
223	5c U. S. Grant, chocolate	80.00	4.75	
224	6c Garfield, brown red	75.00	25.00	
225	8c William T. Sherman, lilac	60.00	17.00	
226	10c Webster, green...............................	190.00	4.50	
227	15c Clay, indigo	250.00	27.50	
228	30c Jefferson, black.............................	400.00	40.00	
229	90c Perry, orange	550.00	150.00	
1893, Perf. 12				
230	1c Columbian Exposition, deep blue .	14.00	.40	
231	2c Columbian Exposition, brown violet	14.00	.30	

239 240 241

242 243 244

245 246 247 248

253 254 255 256

257 258 259 260

261 262 263

22

Scott No.	Description	Unused Value	Used Value	/ / / / / /
232	3c Columbian Exposition, green........	37.50	17.50	
233	4c Columbian Exposition, ultra..........	55.00	9.00	
a.	4c Columbian Exposition, blue (error)	*17,500.*	*16,500.*	
234	5c Columbian Exposition, chocolate..	55.00	9.50	
235	6c Columbian Exposition, purple.......	55.00	25.00	
a.	6c Columbian Exposition, red violet..	55.00	25.00	
236	8c Columbian Exposition, magenta ...	52.50	12.00	
237	10c Columbian Exposition, black brown	110.00	9.00	
238	15c Columbian Exposition, dark green	225.00	82.50	
239	30c Columbian Exposition, orange brown	240.00	100.00	
240	50c Columbian Exposition, slate blue..	500.00	200.00	
241	$1 Columbian Exposition, salmon	1,100.	650.00	
242	$2 Columbian Exposition, brown red.	1,150.	650.00	
243	$3 Columbian Exposition, yellow green	1,600.	900.00	
a.	$3 Columbian Exposition, olive green	1,600.	1,000.	
244	$4 Columbian Exposition, crimson lake	2,100.	1,200.	
a.	$4 Columbian Exposition, rose carmine	2,100.	1,200.	
245	$5 Columbian Exposition, black	2,500.	1,350.	
1894, Perf. 12, Unwatermarked				
246	1c Franklin (247), ultramarine...........	30.00	7.00	
247	1c Franklin, blue	65.00	4.00	
248	2c Washington, pink, type I..............	30.50	9.00	
a.	Vert. pair, imperf. horiz.................	*5,500.*		
249	2c Washington (248), carmine lake, type I..	150.00	7.00	
a.	Double impression		—	
250	2c Washington (248), carmine, type I	30.00	3.00	
a.	2c rose, type I................................	37.50	6.00	
b.	2c scarlet, type I............................	27.50	22.50	
d.	Horiz, pair, imperf. btwn.	*2,000.*		
251	2c Washington (248), carmine, type II	375.00	14.00	
a.	2c scarlet, type II..........................	350.00	13.00	
252	2c Washington (248), carmine, type III	125.00	14.00	
a.	2c scarlet, type III	120.00	16.00	
b.	Horiz. pair, imperf. vert.	*5,000.*		
c.	Horiz. pair, imperf. btwn.	*5,500.*		
253	3c Jackson, purple.............................	110.00	13.00	
254	4c Lincoln, dark brown.....................	175.00	10.00	
255	5c Grant, chocolate	110.00	10.00	
c.	Vert. pair, imperf. horiz.................	*4,000.*		
256	6c Garfield, dull brown.....................	160.00	30.00	
a.	Vert. pair, imperf. horiz.................	*2,000.*		
257	8c Sherman, violet brown..................	175.00	22.50	
258	10c Webster, dark green.....................	300.00	19.00	
259	15c Clay, dark blue............................	300.00	70.00	
260	50c Jefferson, orange	525.00	160.00	

Wmk. 190-"USPS" in Single-lined Capitals

Wmk. 191-Double-lined "USPS" in Capitals

Triangle A (Type I)   **Triangle B (Type II)**

TWO CENTS.

Type I. The horizontal lines of the ground work run across the triangle and are of the same thickness within it as without.

Type II. The horizontal lines cross the triangle but are thinner within it than without.

Triangle C (Type III & IV)

Type IV design

Type III. The horizontal lines do not cross the double frame lines of the triangle. The lines within the triangle are thin, as in type II.

Type IV. Same triangle C as type III, but other design differences including, (1) re-cutting and lengthening of hairline, (2) shaded toga button, (3) strengthening of lines on sleeve, (4) additional dots on ear, (5) "T" of "TWO" straight at right, (6) background lines extend into white oval opposite "U" of "UNITED".

ONE DOLLAR

Type I

Type I. The circles enclosing "$1" are broken where they meet the curved line below "One Dollar." The fifteen left vertical rows of impressions from plate 76 are Type I, the balance being Type II.

Type II

Type II. The circles are complete.

TEN CENTS

Type I

Type I. Tips of foliate ornaments do not impinge on white curved line below "TEN CENTS."

Type II

Type II. Tips of ornaments break curved line below "E" of "TEN" and "T" of "CENTS."

24

Scott No.	Description	Unused Value	Used Value	/ / / / / /
261	$1 Perry, black, type I	1,050.	375.00	
261A	$1 Perry (261), type II......................	2,200.	825.00	
262	$2 James Madison, bright blue..........	2,750.	1,250.	
263	$5 John Marshall, dark green	4,500.	2,750.	

1895, Watermark 191, Perf. 12

Scott No.	Description	Unused Value	Used Value	/ / / / / /
264	1c Franklin (247), blue......................	6.00	.60	
265	2c Washington (248), carmine, type I	27.50	3.50	
266	2c Washington (248), carmine, type II	32.50	5.50	
267	2c Washington (248), carmine, type III	5.50	.50	
a.	2c pink, type III............................	20.00	5.00	
b.	2c vermilion, type III...................	50.00	15.00	
c.	2c rose carmine, type III..............	—	—	
268	3c Jackson (253), purple..................	37.50	2.25	
269	4c Lincoln (254), dark brown............	42.50	3.50	
270	5c Grant (255), chocolate	35.00	3.50	
271	6c Garfield (256), dull brown............	120.00	8.50	
a.	Wmkd. USIR...............................	15,000.	12,500.	
272	8c Sherman (257), violet brown.........	70.00	2.75	
a.	Wmkd. USIR...............................	6,000.	1,000.	
273	10c Webster (258), dark green............	95.00	2.25	
274	15c Clay (259), dark blue	225.00	17.50	
275	50c Jefferson (260), orange	275.00	40.00	
a.	50c Jefferson (260), red orange..........	350.00	47.50	
276	$1 Perry (261), black, type I..............	650.00	100.00	
276A	$1 Perry (261), black, type II............	1,350.	210.00	
277	$2 Madison (262), bright blue	1,000.	450.00	
a.	$2 dark blue..................................	1,000.	450.00	
278	$5 Marshall (263), dark green	2,250.	625.00	

1897-1903, Watermark 191, Perf. 12

Scott No.	Description	Unused Value	Used Value	/ / / / / /
279	1c Franklin (247), deep green............	9.00	.50	
279B	2c Washington (248), red, type IV	9.00	.40	
c.	2c rose carmine, type IV....................	300.00	200.00	
d.	2c orange red, type IV........................	11.50	2.00	
f.	2c carmine, type IV	10.00	2.00	
g.	2c pink, type IV	50.00	5.00	
h.	2c vermilion, type IV.........................	11.00	3.00	
i.	2c brown orange, type IV	150.00	50.00	
j.	Booklet pane of 6 horiz. watermark	500.00	1,250.	
k.	Booklet pane of 6 vert. watermark	500.00	1,250.	
l.	As No. 279B, all color missing (FO)	500.00		
280	4c Lincoln (254), rose brown	27.50	3.50	
a.	4c lilac brown....................................	27.50	3.50	
b.	4c orange brown................................	27.50	3.50	
281	5c Grant (255), dark blue...................	32.50	2.25	
282	6c Garfield (256), lake.......................	45.00	6.50	
a.	6c purple lake....................................	70.00	15.00	
282C	10c Webster (258), brown, type I.........	190.00	6.50	

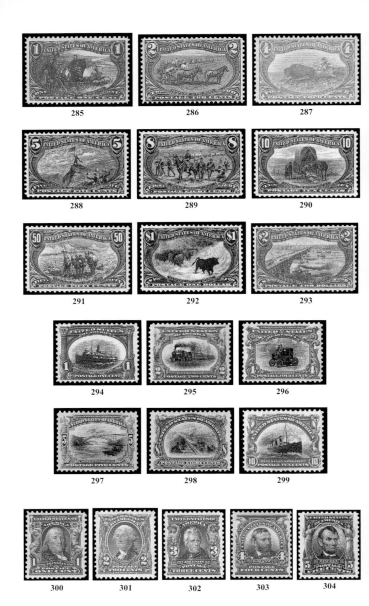

285 286 287

288 289 290

291 292 293

294 295 296

297 298 299

300 301 302 303 304

Scott No.	Description	Unused Value	Used Value	/ / / / / /
283	10c Webster (258), orange brown, type II, horiz. watermark	150.00	5.50	
a.	Type II, vert. watermark	*225.00*	*11.00*	
284	15c Clay (259), olive green	160.00	13.00	
285	1c Trans-Mississippi Expo	25.00	7.00	
286	2c Trans-Mississippi Expo	25.00	2.75	
287	4c Trans-Mississippi Expo	120.00	27.50	
288	5c Trans-Mississippi Expo	100.00	25.00	
289	8c Trans-Mississippi Expo	150.00	50.00	
a.	Vert. pair, imperf. horiz.	*27,500.*		
290	10c Trans-Mississippi Expo	160.00	35.00	
291	50c Trans-Mississippi Expo	650.00	210.00	
292	$1 Trans-Mississippi Expo	1,100.	700.00	
293	$2 Trans-Mississippi Expo	1,900.	1,100.	
1901, Watermark 191, Perf. 12				
294	1c Pan-American Exposition	17.50	3.00	
a.	Center inverted	*12,500.*	*17,500.*	
295	2c Pan-American Exposition	16.50	1.00	
a.	Center inverted	*55,000.*	*60,000.*	
296	4c Pan-American Exposition	75.00	19.00	
a.	Center inverted	*75,000.*		
297	5c Pan-American Exposition	80.00	18.50	
298	8c Pan-American Exposition.	100.00	55.00	
299	10c Pan-American Exposition	130.00	32.50	
1902-03, Watermark 191, Perf. 12				
300	1c Franklin	12.00	.25	
b.	Booklet pane of 6	600.00	*12,500.*	
301	2c Washington	16.00	.50	
c.	Booklet pane of 6	500.00	*4,500.*	
302	3c Jackson	55.00	4.00	
303	4c Grant	60.00	2.50	
304	5c Lincoln	60.00	2.25	
305	6c Garfield	60.00	5.75	
306	8c Martha Washington	40.00	3.50	
307	10c Webster	60.00	3.25	
308	13c Benjamin Harrison	40.00	11.00	
309	15c Clay	200.00	14.00	
310	50c Jefferson	425.00	35.00	
311	$1 David G. Farragut	700.00	90.00	
312	$2 Madison	950.00	225.00	
313	$5 Marshall, dark green	2,500.	750.00	
1906-08, Imperf.				
314	1c Franklin (300)	16.00	18.00	
314A	4c Grant (303), brown	*100,000.*	*50,000.*	
315	5c Lincoln (304), blue	350.00	*1,250.*	
1908, Coil Stamps, Perf. 12 Horizontally				
316	1c Franklin (300)	*115,000.*	—	

305   306   307   308   309

310   311   312   313   319

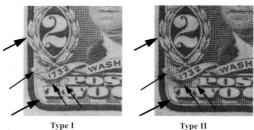

Type I   Type II

The two large arrows in the illustrations highlight the two major differences of the type II
stamps: closing of the thin left border line next to the laurel leaf, and strengthening of the
inner frame line at the lower left corner. The small arrows point out three minor differences
that are not always easily discernible: strengthening of shading lines under the ribbon just
above the "T"of "TWO," a shorter shading line to the left of the "P" in "POSTAGE," and
shortening of a shading line in the left side ribbon.

323   324   325

326   327

Scott No.	Description	Unused Value	Used Value	/ / / / / /
317	5c Lincoln (304)	6,000.	—	☐☐☐☐☐
Perf. 12 Vertically				
318	1c Franklin (300)	5,000.	—	☐☐☐☐☐
1903-1908, Watermark 191, Perf. 12				
319	2c Washington, carmine, type I.........	6.00	.25	☐☐☐☐☐
b.	2c carmine rose, type I.....................	10.00	.40	☐☐☐☐☐
c.	2c scarlet, type I..............................	10.00	.30	☐☐☐☐☐
d.	Vert. pair, imperf. horiz.................	9,000.		☐☐☐☐☐
r.	Vert. pair, rouletted btwn.	2,500.		☐☐☐☐☐
g.	Booklet pane of 6, carmine, type I	125.00	550.00	☐☐☐☐☐
n.	Booklet pane of 6, carmine rose, type I....................................	250.00	650.00	☐☐☐☐☐
p.	Booklet pane of 6, scarlet, type I...	185.00	575.00	☐☐☐☐☐
319F	2c Washington, lake, type II..............	10.00	.30	☐☐☐☐☐
i.	2c carmine, type II............................	75.00	50.00	☐☐☐☐☐
j.	2c carmine rose, type II	70.00	1.75	☐☐☐☐☐
k.	2c scarlet, type II..............................	70.00	2.00	☐☐☐☐☐
h.	Booklet pane of 6, carmine, type II	900.00		☐☐☐☐☐
q.	Booklet pane of 6, lake, type II	300.00	750.00	☐☐☐☐☐
1906-1908, Imperf.				
320	2c Washington (319), carmine, type I	16.00	19.00	☐☐☐☐☐
b.	2c scarlet, type I...............................	18.50	15.00	☐☐☐☐☐
c.	2c carmine rose, type I......................	75.00	42.50	☐☐☐☐☐
320A	2c Washington (319), lake, type II	45.00	50.00	☐☐☐☐☐
d.	2c carmine, type II............................	120.00	250.00	☐☐☐☐☐
1908, Coil Stamps, Perf. 12 Horizontally				
321	2c Washington (319), car., type I, pair	450,000.	250,000.	☐☐☐☐☐
Perf. 12 Vertically				
322	2c Washington (319), car., type II	6,000.	—	☐☐☐☐☐
1904, Watermark 191, Perf. 12				
323	1c Louisiana Purchase	25.00	5.00	☐☐☐☐☐
324	2c Louisiana Purchase	25.00	2.00	☐☐☐☐☐
a.	Vert. pair, imperf. horiz.................	25,000.		☐☐☐☐☐
325	3c Louisiana Purchase	75.00	30.00	☐☐☐☐☐
326	5c Louisiana Purchase	80.00	25.00	☐☐☐☐☐
327	10c Louisiana Purchase	130.00	30.00	☐☐☐☐☐
1907, Watermark 191, Perf. 12				
328	1c Jamestown Exposition	25.00	5.00	☐☐☐☐☐
329	2c Jamestown Exposition	30.00	4.50	☐☐☐☐☐
a.	2c carmine lake	—		☐☐☐☐☐
330	5c Jamestown Exposition	130.00	32.50	☐☐☐☐☐
1908-09, Watermark 191, Perf. 12				
331	1c Franklin, green	6.75	.40	☐☐☐☐☐
a.	Booklet pane of 6...........................	150.00	450.00	☐☐☐☐☐
332	2c Washington, carmine	6.25	.35	☐☐☐☐☐

328 329 330

Franklin
331

Washington
332

Washington
333

Franklin
414

367 370 372

397 398 399

400

TYPE I

THREE CENTS.

Type I. The top line of the toga rope is weak and the rope shading lines are thin. The fifth line from the left is missing.

The line between the lips is thin.

Used on both flat plate and rotary press printings.

Scott No.	Description	Unused Value	Used Value	/ / / / / /
a.	Booklet pane of 6....................	135.00	*400.00*	☐☐☐☐☐
b.	2c lake	*4,250.*		☐☐☐☐☐
333	3c Washington, deep violet, type I.....	30.00	3.00	☐☐☐☐☐
334	4c Washington (333), orange brown ..	37.50	1.50	☐☐☐☐☐
335	5c Washington (333), blue............	50.00	2.50	☐☐☐☐☐
336	6c Washington (333), red orange	65.00	6.50	☐☐☐☐☐
337	8c Washington (333), olive green.......	45.00	3.00	☐☐☐☐☐
338	10c Washington (333), yellow..............	67.50	2.00	☐☐☐☐☐
339	13c Washington (333), blue green........	37.50	19.00	☐☐☐☐☐
340	15c Washington (333), pale ultramarine	65.00	6.50	☐☐☐☐☐
341	50c Washington (333), violet..............	300.00	20.00	☐☐☐☐☐
342	$1 Washington (333), violet brown	500.00	100.00	☐☐☐☐☐
Imperf.				
343	1c Franklin (331)..............................	4.00	5.50	☐☐☐☐☐
344	2c Washington (332)..........................	4.75	3.25	☐☐☐☐☐
345	3c Washington (333), deep violet, type I...................................	9.00	*22.50*	☐☐☐☐☐
346	4c Washington (333), orange brown ..	13.50	*25.00*	☐☐☐☐☐
347	5c Washington (333), blue.................	27.50	37.50	☐☐☐☐☐
1908-10, Coil Stamps, Perf. 12 Horizontally				
348	1c Franklin (331)..............................	35.00	50.00	☐☐☐☐☐
349	2c Washington (332)..........................	90.00	100.00	☐☐☐☐☐
350	4c Washington (333), orange brown ..	140.00	210.00	☐☐☐☐☐
351	5c Washington (333), blue.................	140.00	275.00	☐☐☐☐☐
Coil Stamps, Perf. 12 Vertically				
352	1c Franklin (331)..............................	95.00	190.00	☐☐☐☐☐
353	2c Washington (332)..........................	90.00	220.00	☐☐☐☐☐
354	4c Washington (333), orange brown ..	200.00	275.00	☐☐☐☐☐
355	5c Washington (333), blue.................	210.00	300.00	☐☐☐☐☐
356	10c Washington (333), yellow..............	3,000.	*4,500.*	☐☐☐☐☐
1909, Bluish paper, Perf. 12				
357	1c Franklin (331)..............................	85.00	*100.00*	☐☐☐☐☐
358	2c Washington (332)..........................	80.00	*100.00*	☐☐☐☐☐
359	3c Washington (333), deep violet, type I...................................	1,800.	*5,000.*	☐☐☐☐☐
360	4c Washington (333), orange brown ..	*27,500.*		☐☐☐☐☐
361	5c Washington (333), blue.................	5,750.	*15,000.*	☐☐☐☐☐
362	6c Washington (333), red orange	1,250.	*15,000.*	☐☐☐☐☐
363	8c Washington (333), olive green.......	*30,000.*		☐☐☐☐☐
364	10c Washington (333), yellow..............	1,600.	*7,000.*	☐☐☐☐☐
365	13c Washington (333), blue green........	2,600.	*2,250.*	☐☐☐☐☐
366	15c Washington (333), pale ultra	1,250.	*11,000.*	☐☐☐☐☐
1909, Watermark 191, Perf. 12				
367	2c Lincoln Memorial	5.00	2.00	☐☐☐☐☐
Imperf.				
368	2c Lincoln Memorial (367)	15.00	22.50	☐☐☐☐☐

Scott No.	Description	Unused Value	Used Value	/ / / / / /
Bluish paper				
369	2c Lincoln Memorial (367)	150.00	*250.00*	☐☐☐☐☐
Perf. 12				
370	2c Alaska-Yukon-Pacific Exposition .	7.50	2.25	☐☐☐☐☐
Imperf.				
371	2c Alaska-Yukon-Pacific Exposition (370)	17.50	24.00	☐☐☐☐☐
Perf. 12				
372	2c Hudson-Fulton	10.00	4.75	☐☐☐☐☐
Imperf.				
373	2c Hudson-Fulton (372).....................	20.00	27.50	☐☐☐☐☐
1910-11, Watermark 190, Perf. 12				
374	1c Franklin (331)...............................	6.50	.25	☐☐☐☐☐
a.	Booklet pane of 6..........................	225.00	*300.00*	☐☐☐☐☐
375	2c Washington (332)..........................	6.50	.25	☐☐☐☐☐
a.	Booklet pane of 6..........................	125.00	*200.00*	☐☐☐☐☐
b.	2c lake...	*800.00*		☐☐☐☐☐
c.	As "b," booklet pane of 6	*10,000.*		☐☐☐☐☐
d.	Double impression	*750.00*		☐☐☐☐☐
376	3c Washington (333), deep violet, type I...	20.00	2.00	☐☐☐☐☐
377	4c Washington (333), brown..............	30.00	1.00	☐☐☐☐☐
378	5c Washington (333), blue................	30.00	.75	☐☐☐☐☐
379	6c Washington (333), red orange	35.00	1.00	☐☐☐☐☐
380	8c Washington (333), olive green.......	100.00	15.00	☐☐☐☐☐
381	10c Washington (333), yellow.............	95.00	6.00	☐☐☐☐☐
382	15c Washington (333), pale ultra	240.00	20.00	☐☐☐☐☐
1910, Imperf.				
383	1c Franklin (331)...............................	2.00	2.25	☐☐☐☐☐
384	2c Washington (332)..........................	3.25	2.75	☐☐☐☐☐
1910, Coil Stamps, Perf. 12 Horizontally				
385	1c Franklin (331)...............................	45.00	45.00	☐☐☐☐☐
386	2c Washington (332)..........................	130.00	100.00	☐☐☐☐☐
1910-11, Coil Stamps, Perf. 12 Vertically				
387	1c Franklin (331)...............................	190.00	140.00	☐☐☐☐☐
388	2c Washington (332)..........................	1,300.	2,250.	☐☐☐☐☐
389	3c Washington (333), deep violet, type I	110,000.	10,500.	☐☐☐☐☐
1910, Perf. 8½ Horizontally				
390	1c Franklin (331)...............................	4.50	*14.00*	☐☐☐☐☐
391	2c Washington (332)..........................	42.50	50.00	☐☐☐☐☐
1910-13, Perf. 8½ Vertically				
392	1c Franklin (331)...............................	27.50	55.00	☐☐☐☐☐
393	2c Washington (332)..........................	45.00	45.00	☐☐☐☐☐
394	3c Washington (333), deep violet, type I...	60.00	*67.50*	☐☐☐☐☐

Scott No.	Description	Unused Value	Used Value	/ / / / / /
395	4c Washington (333), brown.............	60.00	70.00	☐☐☐☐☐
396	5c Washington (333), blue.................	60.00	67.50	☐☐☐☐☐
1913, Watermark 190, Perf. 12				
397	1c Panama-Pacific Exposition............	16.50	2.00	☐☐☐☐☐
398	2c Panama-Pacific Exposition............	18.00	1.00	☐☐☐☐☐
a.	2c carmine lake	*1,500.*		☐☐☐☐☐
b.	2c lake	*5,000.*		☐☐☐☐☐
399	5c Panama-Pacific Exposition............	70.00	10.00	☐☐☐☐☐
400	10c Panama-Pacific Expo., orange yellow	120.00	22.50	☐☐☐☐☐
400A	10c Panama-Pacific Expo. (400), orange	180.00	20.00	☐☐☐☐☐
1914-15, Perf. 10				
401	1c Panama-Pacific Expo. (397)..........	25.00	7.00	☐☐☐☐☐
402	2c Panama-Pacific Expo. (398)..........	70.00	2.75	☐☐☐☐☐
403	5c Panama-Pacific Expo. (399)..........	160.00	20.00	☐☐☐☐☐
404	10c Panama-Pacific Expo. (400), orange	725.00	75.00	☐☐☐☐☐
1912-14, Watermark 190, Perf. 12				
405	1c Washington (333), green...............	6.50	.25	☐☐☐☐☐
a.	Vert. pair, imperf. horiz..................	*2,000.*	—	☐☐☐☐☐
b.	Booklet pane of 6..........................	65.00	*75.00*	☐☐☐☐☐
406	2c Washington (333), carmine, type I	6.50	.25	☐☐☐☐☐
a.	Booklet pane of 6..........................	65.00	*90.00*	☐☐☐☐☐
b.	Double impression	*1,250.*		☐☐☐☐☐
c.	2c lake, type I	*2,000.*	*2,750.*	☐☐☐☐☐
407	7c Washington (333), black	70.00	14.00	☐☐☐☐☐
1912, Imperf.				
408	1c Washington (333), green...............	1.00	1.00	☐☐☐☐☐
409	2c Washington (333), carmine, type I	1.20	1.20	☐☐☐☐☐
Coil Stamps, Perf. 8½ Horizontally				
410	1c Washington (333), green...............	6.00	12.50	☐☐☐☐☐
411	2c Washington (333), carmine, type I	10.00	15.00	☐☐☐☐☐
Coil Stamps, Perf. 8½ Vertically				
412	1c Washington (333), green...............	25.00	25.00	☐☐☐☐☐
413	2c Washington (333), carmine, type I	50.00	25.00	☐☐☐☐☐
1912-14, Watermark 190, Perf. 12				
414	8c Franklin, pale olive green	42.50	2.00	☐☐☐☐☐
415	9c Franklin (414), salmon red	52.50	14.00	☐☐☐☐☐
416	10c Franklin (414), orange yellow	40.00	.80	☐☐☐☐☐
a.	10c brown yellow	*1,250.*	—	☐☐☐☐☐
417	12c Franklin (414), claret brown	42.50	5.00	☐☐☐☐☐
418	15c Franklin (414), gray	85.00	4.50	☐☐☐☐☐
419	20c Franklin (414), ultra	190.00	19.00	☐☐☐☐☐
420	30c Franklin (414), orange red	115.00	19.00	☐☐☐☐☐
421	50c Franklin (414), violet	350.00	30.00	☐☐☐☐☐
1912, Watermark 191, Perf. 12				
422	50c Franklin (414), violet	225.00	22.50	☐☐☐☐☐

TYPE I

TWO CENTS.

Type I. There is one shading line in the first curve of the ribbon above the left "2" and one in the second curve of the ribbon above the right "2."

The button of the toga has a faint outline.

The top line of the toga rope, from the button to the front of the throat, is also very faint.

The shading lines at the face terminate in front of the ear with little or no joining, to form a lock of hair.

Used on both flat and rotary press printings.

TYPE II

TWO CENTS.

Type II. Shading lines in ribbons as on type I.

The toga button, rope, and shading lines are heavy.

The shading lines of the face at the lock of hair end in a strong vertical curved line.

Used on rotary press printings only.

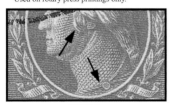

TYPE Ia

TWO CENTS.

Type Ia. Design characteristics similar to type I except that all lines of design are stronger.

The toga button, toga rope and rope shading lines are heavy. The latter characteristics are those of type II, which, however, occur only on impressions from rotary plates.

Used only on flat plates 10208 and 10209.

TYPE III

TWO CENTS.

Type III. Two lines of shading in the curves of the ribbons.

Other characteristics similar to type II.

Used on rotary press printings only.

TYPE II

THREE CENTS.

Type II. The top line of the toga rope is strong and the rope shading lines are heavy and complete.

The line between the lips is heavy.

Used on both flat plate and rotary press printings.

TYPE V

TWO CENTS.

Type V. Top line of toga is complete.

Five vertical shading lines in toga button.

Line of color in left "2" is very thin and usually broken.

Shading dots on the nose and lip are as indicated on the diagram.

Used on offset printings only.

Scott No.	Description	Unused Value	Used Value	//////
423	$1 Franklin (414), violet brown..........	475.00	75.00	☐☐☐☐☐
1914, Watermark 190, Perf. 12 x 10				
423A	1c Washington (333), green...............	*15,000.*	*7,500.*	☐☐☐☐☐
423B	2c Washington (333), rose red, type 1	*175,000.*	*25,000.*	☐☐☐☐☐
423C	5c Washington (333), blue.................		*27,500.*	☐☐☐☐☐
1914, Watermark 190, Perf. 10 x 12				
423D	1c Washington (333), green...............		*15,000.*	☐☐☐☐☐
423E	2c Washington (333), rose red, type 1.		—	☐☐☐☐☐
1914-15, Watermark 190, Perf. 10				
424	1c Washington (333), green...............	2.50	.25	☐☐☐☐☐
c.	Vert. pair, imperf. horiz.................	*3,000.*	*2,500.*	☐☐☐☐☐
d.	Booklet pane of 6.........................	5.25	*7.50*	☐☐☐☐☐
e.	As "d.," imperf............................	*1,750.*		☐☐☐☐☐
f.	Vert. pair, imperf. between and with straight edge at top	*13,000.*		☐☐☐☐☐
425	2c Washington (333), rose red, type I	2.30	.25	☐☐☐☐☐
e.	Booklet pane of 6.........................	17.50	*25.00*	☐☐☐☐☐
426	3c Washington (333), deep violet, type I...	14.00	1.50	☐☐☐☐☐
427	4c Washington (333), brown...............	32.50	1.00	☐☐☐☐☐
428	5c Washington (333), blue.................	32.50	1.00	☐☐☐☐☐
429	6c Washington (333), red orange	45.00	2.00	☐☐☐☐☐
430	7c Washington (333), black	90.00	5.00	☐☐☐☐☐
431	8c Franklin (414), pale olive green	35.00	3.00	☐☐☐☐☐
a.	Double impression	—		☐☐☐☐☐
432	9c Franklin (414), salmon red	45.00	9.00	☐☐☐☐☐
433	10c Franklin (414), orange yellow	45.00	1.00	☐☐☐☐☐
434	11c Franklin (414), dark green............	22.50	8.50	☐☐☐☐☐
435	12c Franklin (414), claret brown	25.00	6.00	☐☐☐☐☐
a.	12c Franklin (414), copper red............	30.00	7.00	☐☐☐☐☐
437	15c Franklin (414), gray	125.00	7.25	☐☐☐☐☐
438	20c Franklin (414), ultramarine............	200.00	6.00	☐☐☐☐☐
439	30c Franklin (414), orange red	220.00	18.00	☐☐☐☐☐
440	50c Franklin (414), violet	475.00	18.00	☐☐☐☐☐
1914, Coil Stamps, Perf. 10 Horizontally				
441	1c Washington (333), green...............	1.00	*1.50*	☐☐☐☐☐
442	2c Washington (333), carmine, type I	10.00	*45.00*	☐☐☐☐☐
Coil Stamps, Perf. 10 Vertically				
443	1c Washington (333), green...............	30.00	45.00	☐☐☐☐☐
444	2c Washington (333), carmine, type I	45.00	35.00	☐☐☐☐☐
a.	2c lake		*1,250.*	☐☐☐☐☐
445	3c Washington (333), violet, type I....	225.00	*250.00*	☐☐☐☐☐
446	4c Washington (333), brown...............	130.00	150.00	☐☐☐☐☐
447	5c Washington (333), blue.................	45.00	115.00	☐☐☐☐☐
1914-16, Coil Stamps, Perf. 10 Horizontally, Rotary Press Printing				
448	1c Washington (333), green...............	7.50	17.50	☐☐☐☐☐

Scott No.	Description	Unused Value	Used Value	`//////`
449	2c Washington (333), red, type I	2,500.	600.00	
450	2c Washington (333), carmine, type III	12.50	22.50	
1914-16, Coil Stamps, Perf. 10 Vertically, Rotary Press Printing				
452	1c Washington (333), green...............	10.00	*17.50*	
453	2c Washington (333), car rose, type I	140.00	17.50	
454	2c Washington (333), red, type II.......	70.00	22.50	
455	2c Washington (333), carmine, type III	8.00	3.50	
456	3c Washington (333), violet, type I....	225.00	170.00	
457	4c Washington (333), brown...............	25.00	30.00	
458	5c Washington (333), blue.................	27.50	30.00	
1914, Coil Stamp, Imperf., Rotary Press Printing				
459	2c Washington (333), carmine, type I	175.00	*1,300.*	
1915, Watermark 191, Perf. 10				
460	$1 Franklin (414), violet black	675.00	140.00	
1915, Watermark 190, Perf. 11				
461	2c Washington (333), pale car red, type I...	140.00	*360.00*	
1916-17, Perf. 10, Unwatermarked				
462	1c Washington (333), green...............	7.00	.35	
a.	Booklet pane of 6...........................	9.50	*12.50*	
463	2c Washington (333), carmine, type I	4.50	.40	
a.	Booklet pane of 6...........................	110.00	*110.00*	
464	3c Washington (333), violet, type I....	70.00	19.00	
465	4c Washington (333), orange brown ..	40.00	2.50	
466	5c Washington (333), blue.................	70.00	2.50	
467	5c Washington (333), car (error in plate of 2c)	475.00	*850.00*	
468	6c Washington (333), red orange	85.00	9.00	
469	7c Washington (333), black...............	120.00	15.00	
470	8c Franklin (414), olive green	55.00	8.00	
471	9c Franklin (414), salmon red	55.00	18.50	
472	10c Franklin (414), orange yellow	100.00	2.50	
473	11c Franklin (414), dark green............	40.00	18.50	
474	12c Franklin (414), claret brown	50.00	7.50	
475	15c Franklin (414), gray	180.00	16.00	
476	20c Franklin (414), light ultramarine ...	225.00	17.50	
476A	30c Franklin (414), orange red	*3,000.*		
477	50c Franklin (414), light violet............	1,000.	85.00	
478	$1 Franklin (414), violet black	700.00	30.00	
479	$2 Madison (312), dark blue.............	225.00	40.00	
480	$5 Marshall (313), light green	180.00	40.00	
Imperf.				
481	1c Washington (333), green...............	.95	.95	
482	2c Washington (333), carmine, type I	1.30	1.30	
482A	2c Washington (333), deep rose, type Ia...	—	*65,000.*	

Scott No.	Description	Unused Value	Used Value	/ / / / / /
483	3c Washington (333), violet, type I....	10.00	10.00	
484	3c Washington (333), violet, type II...	8.00	8.00	
485	5c Washington (333), carmine (error in plate of 2c)		9,000.	

1916-18, Coil Stamps, Perf. 10 Horizontally, Rotary Press Printing

486	1c Washington (333), green................	.85	.85	
487	2c Washington (333), carmine, type II	12.50	14.00	
488	2c Washington (333), carmine, type III	3.00	5.00	
489	3c Washington (333), violet, type I....	4.50	2.25	

1916-22, Coil Stamps, Perf.10 Vertically

490	1c Washington (333), green................	.50	.60	
491	2c Washington (333), carmine, type II	2,500.	800.00	
492	2c Washington (333), carmine, type III	9.00	1.00	
493	3c Washington (333), violet, type I....	14.00	4.50	
494	3c Washington (333), violet, type II...	10.00	2.50	
495	4c Washington (333), orange brown ..	10.00	7.00	
496	5c Washington (333), blue.................	3.25	2.50	
497	10c Franklin (414), orange yellow	17.50	17.50	

Types of 1912-14 Issue
1917-19, Perf. 11

498	1c Washington (333), green................	.35	.25	
a.	Vert. pair, imperf. horiz.................	900.00		
b.	Horiz. pair, imperf. btwn.	700.00		
c.	Vert. pair, imperf. btwn.	700.00	—	
d.	Double impression	250.00	4,000.	
e.	Booklet pane of 6............................	2.50	2.00	
f.	Booklet pane of 30..........................	1,050.	10,000.	
g.	Perf. 10 at top or bottom................	15,000.	45,000.	
499	2c Washington (333), rose, type I	.35	.25	
a.	Vert. pair, imperf. horiz.................	1,000.		
b.	Horiz. pair, imperf. vert.	600.00	225.00	
c.	Vert. pair, imperf. btwn..................	1,000.	300.00	
e.	Booklet pane of 6............................	4.00	2.50	
f.	Booklet pane of 30..........................	25,000.		
g.	Double impression	200.00	—	
h.	2c lake...	500.00	350.00	
500	2c Washington (333), deep rose, type Ia...	250.00	240.00	
501	3c Washington (333), light violet, type I	10.00	.40	
b.	Booklet pane of 6............................	75.00	60.00	
c.	Vert. pair, imperf. horiz.................	3,000.		
d.	Double impression	3,500.	3,500.	
502	3c Washington (333), dark violet, type II	13.00	.75	
b.	Booklet pane of 6............................	60.00	55.00	
c.	Vert. pair, imperf. horiz.................	1,400.	750.00	

TYPE IV

TWO CENTS.
   Type IV. Top line of the toga rope is broken.
Shading lines in toga button are so arranged that the
curving of the first and last form " ID."
   Line of color in left "2" is very thin and usually
broken.
   Used on offset printings only.

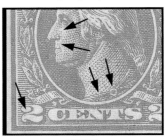

TYPE Va

TWO CENTS.
   Type Va. Characteristics same as type V, except
in shading dots of nose. Third row from bottom has
4 dots instead of 6. Overall height of type Va is
1/3 mm. less than type V.
   Used on offset printings only.

TYPE VI

TWO CENTS.
   Type VI. General characteristics same as
type V, except that line of color in left "2" is
very heavy.
   Used on offset printings only.

TYPE VII

TWO CENTS.
   Type VII. Line of color in left "2" is invari-
ably continuous, clearly defined, and heavier
than in type V or Va, but not as heavy as in
type VI.
   Additional vertical row of dots has been
added to the upper lip.
   Numerous additional dots have been added
to hair on top of head.
   Used on offset printings only.

TYPE III

THREE CENTS.
   Type III. The top line of the toga rope is strong
but the fifth shading line is missing as in type I.
   Center shading line of the toga button consists of
two dashes with a central dot.
   The "P" and "O" of "POSTAGE" are separated
by a line of color.
   The frame line at the bottom of the vignette
is complete.
   Used on offset printings only.

Scott No.	Description	Unused Value	Used Value	/ / / / / /
d.	Double impression	800.00	750.00	
e.	Perf. 10 at top or bottom..............	*15,000.*	*30,000.*	
503	4c Washington (333), brown..............	9.00	.40	
b.	Double impression	—		
504	5c Washington (333), blue.................	8.00	.35	
a.	Horiz. pair, imperf. btwn.	*20,000.*	—	
b.	Double impression	2,000.	*900.00*	
505	5c Washington (333), rose (error in plate of 2c)	300.00	550.00	
506	6c Washington (333), red orange	12.00	.40	
a.	Perf. 10 at top or bottom..............	*30,000.*	*8,000.*	
b.	Double impression	—		
507	7c Washington (333), black	26.00	1.25	
508	8c Franklin (414), olive bister	12.00	.65	
b.	Vert. pair, imperf. btwn.	—		
c.	Perf at 10 at top or bottom...........		*15,000.*	
509	9c Franklin (414), salmon red	12.00	1.75	
a.	Perf. 10 at top or bottom..............	*4,250.*	*12,000.*	
510	10c Franklin (414), orange yellow	16.00	.25	
a.	10c brown yellow	*1,400.*		
511	11c Franklin (414), light green..........	9.00	2.50	
a.	Perf. 10 at top or bottom..............	*5,000.*	*4,500.*	
512	12c Franklin (414), claret brown	8.00	.40	
a.	12c brown carmine........................	9.00	.50	
b.	Perf. 10 at top or bottom..............	*30,000.*	*20,000.*	
513	13c Franklin (414), apple green	10.00	6.00	
514	15c Franklin (414), gray	35.00	1.50	
a.	Perf. 10 at bottom........................		*10,000.*	
515	20c Franklin (414), light ultramarine ...	42.50	.45	
b.	Vert. pair, imperf. btwn.................	5,000.	*3,500.*	
c.	Double impression	*1,250.*		
d.	Perf. at top or bottom	—	*15,000.*	
516	30c Franklin (414), orange red	30.00	1.50	
a.	Perf. at top or bottom	*20,000.*	*7,500.*	
b.	Double impression	—		
517	50c Franklin (414), red violet..............	47.50	.75	
b.	Vert. pair, imperf. btwn. & at bottom		*6,000.*	
c.	Perf. 10 at top or bottom..............		*10,000.*	
518	$1 Franklin (414), violet brown..........	40.00	1.50	
b.	$1 deep brown	*1,900.*	*1,250.*	
1917-19, Watermark 191				
519	2c Washington (332)	400.00	*1,750.*	
1918, Perf. 11, Unwatermarked				
523	$2 Franklin, orange red & black........	525.00	250.00	
524	$5 Franklin (523), deep green & black	170.00	32.50	
1918-20, Perf. 11, Offset Printing				
525	1c Washington (333), gray green	2.50	.90	

TYPE IV

THREE CENTS.

Type IV. Shading lines of toga rope are complete.

Second and fourth shading lines in toga button are broken in the middle and the third line is continuous with a dot in the center.

"P" and "O" of "POSTAGE" are joined.

Frame line at bottom of vignette is broken.

Used on offset printings only.

523

537

548   549   550

551   552   553   554

555   556   557   558

40

Scott No.	Description	Unused Value	Used Value	/ / / / / /
a.	1c dark green...............................	10.00	1.75	
c.	Horiz. pair, imperf. btwn.	*500.00*	*650.00*	
d.	Double impression	40.00	—	
526	2c Washington (333), carmine, type IV	25.00	4.00	
527	2c Washington (333), carmine, type V	18.00	1.25	
a.	Double impression	75.00	—	
b.	Vert. pair, imperf. horiz.................	*850.00*		
c.	Horiz. pair, imperf. vert.	*1,000.*	—	
528	2c Washington (333), carmine, type Va	8.00	.40	
c.	Double impression	55.00		
g.	Vert. pair, imperf. btwn.................	*3,500.*		
528A	2c Washington (333), carmine, type VI	47.50	2.00	
d.	Double impression	180.00	—	
f.	Vert. pair, imperf. horiz.................	—		
h.	Vert. pair, imperf. btwn.................	*1,000.*		
528B	2c Washington (333), carmine, type VII	20.00	.75	
e.	Double impression	77.50	*400.00*	
529	3c Washington (333), violet, type III .	3.50	.50	
a.	Double impression	45.00	—	
b.	Printed on both sides.....................	*2,500.*		
530	3c Washington (333), purple, type IV	2.00	.30	
a.	Double impression	35.00	—	
b.	Printed on both sides.....................	*350.00*		
c.	Triple impression	*1,750.*	—	

Imperf.

Scott No.	Description	Unused Value	Used Value	/ / / / / /
531	1c Washington (333), green...............	10.00	12.00	
532	2c Washington (333), car rose, type IV	32.50	35.00	
533	2c Washington (333), carmine, type V	85.00	100.00	
534	2c Washington (333), carmine, type Va	12.00	11.00	
534A	2c Washington (333), carmine, type VI	35.00	32.50	
534B	2c Washington (333), carmine, type VII	1,750.	1,250.	
535	3c Washington (333), violet, type IV .	8.00	5.00	
a.	Double impression	95.00	—	

Perf. 12½

Scott No.	Description	Unused Value	Used Value	/ / / / / /
536	1c Washington (333), gray green	20.00	*27.50*	
a.	Horiz. pair, imperf. vert.	*1,350.*		

1919, Perf. 11, Flat Plate Printing

Scott No.	Description	Unused Value	Used Value	/ / / / / /
537	3c Victory, violet............................	10.00	3.25	
a.	3c deep red violet..........................	*1,250.*	*2,250.*	
b.	3c light reddish violet	150.00	50.00	
c.	3c red violet.................................	175.00	60.00	

1919, Perf. 11 x 10, Rotary Press Printings,

Size: 19½ to 20mm wide by 22 to 22¼ mm high

Scott No.	Description	Unused Value	Used Value	/ / / / / /
538	1c Washington (333), green...............	10.00	9.00	
a.	Vert. pair, imperf. horiz.................	50.00	*150.00*	
539	2c Washington (333), car rose, type II	2,750.	*5,500.*	

41

Scott No.	Description	Unused Value	Used Value	/ / / / / /
540	2c Washington (333), car rose, type III	12.00	9.50	
a.	Vert. pair, imperf. horiz.................	50.00	*100.00*	
b.	Horiz. pair, imperf. vert.	*1,750.*		
541	3c Washington (333), violet, type II...	40.00	32.50	
1920, Perf. 10 x 11, Size: 19 x 22½-22¾ mm				
542	1c Washington (333), green...............	12.50	1.50	
1921, Perf. 10, Size: 19 x 22½ mm				
543	1c Washington (333), green...............	.70	.40	
a.	Horiz. pair, imperf. btwn.	*2,750.*		
1922, Perf. 11, Size: 19 x 22½ mm				
544	1c Washington (333), green...............	*22,500.*	*3,750.*	
1921, Perf. 11, Size: 19½-20x22mm				
545	1c Washington (333), green...............	170.00	200.00	
546	2c Washington (333), car rose, type III	105.00	*190.00*	
1920, Perf. 11				
547	$2 Franklin (523), carmine & black ...	130.00	40.00	
a.	$2 lake & black	200.00	40.00	
548	1c Pilgrim Tercentenary....................	4.50	2.25	
549	2c Pilgrim Tercentenary....................	5.75	1.60	
550	5c Pilgrim Tercentenary....................	40.00	14.00	
1922-25, Perf. 11				
551	½ c Nathan Hale, olive brown	.25	.25	
552	1c Franklin, deep green	1.40	.25	
a.	Booklet pane of 6...........................	7.50	*4.00*	
553	1½ c Warren G. Harding, yellow brown	2.30	.25	
554	2c Washington, carmine	1.30	.25	
a.	Horiz. pair, imperf. vert.	*275.00*		
b.	Vert. pair, imperf. horiz................	*6,000.*		
c.	Booklet pane of 6...........................	7.00	*3.00*	
d.	Perf. 10 at top or bottom...............	*17,500.*	*10,000.*	
555	3c Lincoln, violet	14.00	1.20	
556	4c Martha Washington, yellow brown	17.50	.50	
a.	Vert. pair, imperf. horiz................	*12,500.*		
b.	Perf. 10 at 10 top or bottom...........	*3,500.*	*25,000.*	
557	5c Theodore Roosevelt, dark blue	17.50	.30	
a.	Imperf., pair...................................	*2,000.*		
b.	Horiz. pair, imperf. vert.	—		
c.	Perf. 10 at top or bottom...............	—	*11,000.*	
558	6c Garfield, red orange	32.50	1.00	
559	7c William McKinley, black...............	7.75	.75	
560	8c Grant, olive green.........................	40.00	1.00	
561	9c Jefferson, rose.............................	12.50	1.25	
562	10c James Monroe, orange..................	15.00	.35	
a.	Vert. pair, imperf. horiz................	*2,250.*		
b.	Imperf., pair...................................	*2,500.*		
c.	Perf. 10 at top or bottom...............	*85,000.*	*25,000.*	

Scott No.	Description	Unused Value	Used Value	/ / / / / /
563	11c Rutherford B. Hayes, light blue.....	1.40	.60	
a.	11c light bluish green..........................	1.40	.60	
d.	Imperf., pair.................................		20,000.	
564	12c Grover Cleveland, brown violet.....	5.25	.35	
a.	Horiz. pair, imperf. vert.	4,500.		
565	14c American Indian, blue..................	4.75	.90	
566	15c Statue of Liberty, gray	17.50	.30	
567	20c Golden Gate, carmine rose	17.50	.30	
a.	Horiz. pair, imperf. vert.	2,750.		
568	25c Niagara Falls, yellow green	15.00	.75	
b.	Vert. pair, imperf. horiz..................	3,250.		
c.	Perf. 10 at one side.......................	5,000.	11,000.	
569	30c American Buffalo, olive brown	25.00	.60	
570	50c Arlington Amphitheater, lilac	35.00	.40	
571	$1 Lincoln Memorial, violet black	37.50	.65	
572	$2 U.S. Capitol, deep blue	70.00	9.00	
573	$5 "America," carmine & blue	110.00	15.00	
a.	$5 carmine lake & dark blue	190.00	30.00	

1923-25, Imperf.

Scott No.	Description	Unused Value	Used Value	
575	1c Franklin (552), green	5.00	5.00	
576	1½ c Harding (553), yellow brown.........	1.25	1.50	
577	2c Washington (554), carmine............	1.30	1.25	
a.	2c carmine lake	—		

Rotary Press Printings, Perf. 11 x 10, Size: 19¾ x 22¼ mm

Scott No.	Description	Unused Value	Used Value	
578	1c Franklin (552), green	85.00	160.00	
579	2c Washington (554), carmine............	80.00	140.00	

Perf. 10

Scott No.	Description	Unused Value	Used Value	
581	1c Franklin (552), green	10.00	.75	
582	1½c Harding (553), brown.....................	6.00	.65	
583	2c Washington (554), carmine............	3.00	.30	
a.	Booklet pane of 6........................	110.00	150.00	
584	3c Lincoln (555), violet	27.50	3.00	
585	4c Martha Washington (556)	18.00	.65	
586	5c Theodore Roosevelt (557), blue	18.00	.40	
a.	Horiz. pair, imperf. vertically.........		8,000.	
587	6c Garfield (558), red orange.............	9.25	.60	
588	7c McKinley (559).............................	12.50	6.25	
589	8c Grant (560)....................................	27.50	4.50	
590	9c Jefferson (561), rose......................	6.00	2.50	
591	10c Monroe (562), orange	45.00	.50	

Perf. 11

Scott No.	Description	Unused Value	Used Value	
594	1c Franklin (552), green	16,000.	10,500.	
595	2c Washington (554), carmine............	275.00	375.00	
596	1c Franklin (552), green		175,000.	

Nos. 578-579, 594-595 were made from coil waste of Nos. 597 and 599 and measure approx. 19³/₄ x 22¹/₄ mm. No 596 was made from rotary press sheet waste and measures approx. 19¹/₄ x 22¹/₂ mm.

559   560   561   562

563   564   565   566

567   568   569   570

571   572   573   610

Type I.

Type II.

Type I.   **Type II.**

Type I–No heavy hair lines at top center of head. Outline of left acanthus scroll generally faint at top and toward base at left side.

Type II–The heavy hair lines at top center of head; two being outstanding in the white area. Outline of left acanthus scroll very strong and clearly defined at top (under left edge of lettered panel) and at lower curve (above and to the left of numeral oval). Type II is found only on Nos. 599A and 634A.

44

614   615   616

617   618

619   620   621

622   623   627

628

629   643

644   645

45

No. 634
Overprinted

Scott 646

MOLLY PITCHER

No. 634 and 637
Overprinted

Scott 647-648

HAWAII
1778 - 1928

649

650

Nos. 632-634,
635-642
Overprinted

Kans.

Scott 658-668

651

Nos. 632-634,
635-642
Overprinted

Nebr.

Scott 669-679

654

657

680

681

682

683

684

685

688

Scott No.	Description	Unused Value	Used Value	/ / / / / /

1923-29, Coil Stamps, Perf. 10 Vertically, Rotary Press Printing

597	1c Franklin (552), green	.30	.25	
598	1½c Harding (553), brown	.90	.25	
599	2c Washington (554), carmine, type I	.35	.25	
b.	2c carmine lake, type I	650.00		
599A	2c Washington (554), carmine, type II	115.00	17.50	
600	3c Lincoln (555), violet	6.25	.25	
601	4c Martha Washington (556)	3.75	.35	
602	5c Theodore Roosevelt (557), dark blue	1.75	.25	
603	10c Monroe (562), orange	3.50	.25	

Perf. 10 Horizontally

604	1c Franklin (552), green	.40	.25	
605	1½c Harding (553), yellow brown	.40	.25	
606	2c Washington (554), carmine	.40	.25	
a.	2c carmine lake, type I	45.00		

1923, Perf. 11, Flat Plate Printing, Size: 19¼ x 22¼ mm

610	2c Harding Memorial, black	.55	.25	
a.	Horiz. pair, imperf. vert.	1,750.		

Imperf.

611	2c Harding Memorial (610)	4.75	4.00	

1923, Perf. 10, Rotary Press Printing, Size: 19¼ x 22½ mm

612	2c Harding Memorial (610)	16.00	1.75	

1923, Perf. 11

613	2c Harding Memorial (610)		45,000.	

1924-26, Perf. 11

614	1c Huguenot-Walloon Tercentenary	2.40	3.25	
615	2c Huguenot-Walloon Tercentenary	4.00	2.25	
616	5c Huguenot-Walloon Tercentenary	16.00	13.00	
617	1c Lexington-Concord	2.00	2.50	
618	2c Lexington-Concord	3.75	4.00	
619	5c Lexington-Concord	15.00	13.00	
620	2c Norse-American	3.25	3.00	
621	5c Norse-American	10.00	10.00	
622	13c Benjamin Harrison, green	11.00	.75	
623	17c Woodrow Wilson, black	11.00	.30	

1926, Perf. 11

627	2c Sesquicentennial Exposition	2.25	.50	
628	5c Ericsson Memorial	5.25	3.25	
629	2c Battle of White Plains	1.75	1.70	
a.	Vert. pair, imperf. btwn.	—		
630	2c Battle of White Plains (629), sht of 25	375.00	475.00	

1926, Imperf., Rotary Press Printings

631	1½c Harding (553), yellow brown	2.00	1.70	

Scott No.	Description	Unused Value	Used Value	/ / / / / /
1926-34, Perf. 1 1x 10½				
632	1c Franklin (552), green	.25	.25	
a.	Booklet pane of 6...........................	5.00	4.00	
b.	Vert. pair, imperf. btwn.	6,000.	—	
c.	Horiz. pair, imperf. btwn.	5,000.		
633	1½c Harding (553), yellow brown........	1.70	.25	
634	2c Washington (554), carmine, type I	.25	.25	
b.	2c carmine lake	190.00	—	
c.	Horiz. pair, imperf. btwn.	7,000.		
d.	Booklet pane of 6...........................	1.50	1.50	
e.	As "d," carmine lake	500.00		
f.	2c lake, on cover		—	
634A	2c Washington (554), carmine, type II	325.00	13.50	
635	3c Lincoln (555), violet	.50	.25	
a.	3c bright violet	.25	.25	
636	4c Martha Washington (556)..............	1.90	.25	
637	5c Theodore Roosevelt (557), dark blue	1.90	.25	
638	6c Garfield (558), red orange............	2.00	.25	
639	7c McKinley (559)...............................	2.00	.25	
a.	Vert. pair, imperf. btwn..................	600.00	250.00	
640	8c Grant (560)....................................	2.00	.25	
641	9c Jefferson (561), orange red............	1.90	.25	
642	10c Monroe (562), orange	3.25	.25	
1927, Perf. 11				
643	2c Vermont Sesquicentennial	1.20	.80	
644	2c Burgoyne Campaign	3.10	2.10	
1928, Perf. 11				
645	2c Valley Forge..................................	1.25	.50	
a.	2c lake	—		
1928, Perf. 11 x 10½, Rotary Press Printing				
646	2c Battle of Monmouth (Molly Pitcher), ovptd. on Washington	1.00	1.00	
a.	"Pitcher" only.................................	675.00		
b.	2c carmine lake		2,500.	
647	2c Hawaii Sesquicentennial, ovptd. on Washington, carmine..................	4.00	4.00	
648	5c Hawaii Sesquicentennial, ovptd. on T. Roosevelt, dark blue	11.00	12.50	
1928, Perf. 11				
649	2c Aeronautics Conference.................	1.10	.80	
650	5c Aeronautics Conference.................	4.50	3.25	
1929, Perf. 11				
651	2c George Rogers Clark......................	.70	.50	
1929, Perf. 11 x 10½, Rotary Press Printing				
653	½c Hale (551), olive brown................	.25	.25	

Scott No.	Description	Unused Value	Used Value	/ / / / / /
1929, Perf. 11				
654	2c Electric Light................................	.60	.65	☐☐☐☐☐
a.	2c lake	—		☐☐☐☐☐
Perf. 11 x 10½, Rotary Press Printing				
655	2c Electric Light (654)........................	.55	.25	☐☐☐☐☐
Coil Stamp (Rotary Press), Perf. 10 Vertically				
656	2c Electric Light (654)........................	11.00	1.75	☐☐☐☐☐
1929, Perf. 11				
657	2c Sullivan Expedition........................	.60	.60	☐☐☐☐☐
a.	2c lake	325.00	300.00	☐☐☐☐☐
1929, Perf. 11 x 10½, Rotary Press Printing, Overprinted				
658	1c Kans. ovpt., on Franklin, green	2.50	2.00	☐☐☐☐☐
a.	Vert. pair, one without ovpt.	*375.00*		☐☐☐☐☐
659	1½c Kans. ovpt., on Harding, brown.....	3.25	2.90	☐☐☐☐☐
a.	Vert. pair, one without ovpt.	*425.00*		☐☐☐☐☐
660	2c Kans. ovpt., on Washington, carmine	4.00	1.00	☐☐☐☐☐
661	3c Kans. ovpt., on Lincoln, violet	17.50	15.00	☐☐☐☐☐
a.	Vert. pair, one without ovpt.	*600.00*		☐☐☐☐☐
662	4c Kans. ovpt., on Martha Washington	17.50	9.00	☐☐☐☐☐
a.	Vert. pair, one without ovpt.	*500.00*		☐☐☐☐☐
663	5c Kans. ovpt., on T. Roosevelt, dp blue	12.50	9.75	☐☐☐☐☐
664	6c Kans. ovpt., on Garfield, red orange	25.00	18.00	☐☐☐☐☐
665	7c Kans. ovpt., on McKinley	25.00	27.50	☐☐☐☐☐
a.	Vert. pair, one without ovpt.	—		☐☐☐☐☐
666	8c Kans. ovpt., on Grant	72.50	65.00	☐☐☐☐☐
667	9c Kans. ovpt., on Jefferson, light rose	14.00	11.50	☐☐☐☐☐
668	10c Kans. ovpt., on Monroe, orange yel	22.50	12.50	☐☐☐☐☐
669	1c Nebr. ovpt., on Franklin, green......	3.25	2.25	☐☐☐☐☐
a.	Vert. pair, one without ovpt.	—		☐☐☐☐☐
670	1½c Nebr. ovpt., on Harding, brown	3.00	2.50	☐☐☐☐☐
671	2c Nebr. ovpt., on Washington, carmine	3.00	1.30	☐☐☐☐☐
672	3c Nebr. ovpt., on Lincoln, violet.......	11.00	12.00	☐☐☐☐☐
a.	Vert. pair, one without ovpt.	*500.00*		☐☐☐☐☐
673	4c Nebr. ovpt., on Martha Washington	17.50	15.00	☐☐☐☐☐
674	5c Nebr. ovpt., on T. Roosevelt, dp blue	15.00	15.00	☐☐☐☐☐
675	6c Nebr. ovpt., on Garfield, red orange	35.00	24.00	☐☐☐☐☐
676	7c Nebr. ovpt., on McKinley	22.50	18.00	☐☐☐☐☐
677	8c Nebr. ovpt., on Grant	30.00	25.00	☐☐☐☐☐
678	9c Nebr. ovpt., on Jefferson, light rose	35.00	27.50	☐☐☐☐☐
a.	Vert. pair, one without ovpt.	*750.00*		☐☐☐☐☐
679	10c Nebr. ovpt., on Monroe, orange yel	90.00	22.50	☐☐☐☐☐

HOW TO USE THIS BOOK

In cases where two or more Scott numbers share a common design, the illustration shows the first Scott number that bears that design. Subsequent Scott numbers showing the same design will have the first Scott number in parentheses following the description to guide the user to the correct design.

689   690   692   693

694   695   696   697

698   699   700   701

702   703   704   705

706   707   708   709

710   711   712   713

Scott No.	Description	Unused Value	Used Value	/ / / / / /
1929, Perf. 11				
680	2c Battle of Fallen Timbers	.70	.70	☐☐☐☐☐
681	2c Ohio River Canalization...............	.60	.60	☐☐☐☐☐
a.	2c lake	—		☐☐☐☐☐
1930, Perf. 11				
682	2c Massachusetts Bay Colony............	.50	.50	☐☐☐☐☐
683	2c Carolina-Charleston......................	1.05	1.05	☐☐☐☐☐
1930, Perf. 11x10½, Rotary Press Printing				
684	1½c Harding, brown..........................	.40	.25	☐☐☐☐☐
685	4c William H. Taft, brown.................	.80	.25	☐☐☐☐☐
Coil Stamps, Perf. 10 Vertically				
686	1½c Harding (684), brown..................	1.75	.25	☐☐☐☐☐
687	4c Taft (685), brown..........................	3.00	.45	☐☐☐☐☐
1930, Perf. 11				
688	2c Battle of Braddock's Field............	.90	.85	☐☐☐☐☐
689	2c Von Steuben.................................	.50	.50	☐☐☐☐☐
a.	Imperf., pair	*2,750.*		☐☐☐☐☐
1931, Perf. 11				
690	2c Pulaski.......................................	.30	.25	☐☐☐☐☐
1931, Perf. 11x10½, Rotary Press Printing				
692	11c Hayes (563)...................................	2.50	.25	☐☐☐☐☐
693	12c Cleveland (564)	5.00	.25	☐☐☐☐☐
694	13c Benjamin Harrison (622), yellow green	2.25	.25	☐☐☐☐☐
695	14c American Indian (565), dark blue.	4.00	.45	☐☐☐☐☐
696	15c Statue of Liberty (566).................	7.75	.25	☐☐☐☐☐
Perf. 10½ x11				
697	17c Wilson (623).................................	4.75	.25	☐☐☐☐☐
698	20c Golden Gate (567)........................	7.75	.25	☐☐☐☐☐
699	25c Niagara Falls (568), blue green.....	8.00	.25	☐☐☐☐☐
700	30c American Buffalo (569), brown....	13.00	.25	☐☐☐☐☐
701	50c Arlington Amphitheater (570).......	30.00	.25	☐☐☐☐☐
1931, Perf. 11, Flat Plate				
702	2c Red Cross.....................................	.25	.25	☐☐☐☐☐
a.	Red cross missing (from a foldover)	*40,000.*		☐☐☐☐☐
703	2c Yorktown, carmine rose & black...	.35	.25	☐☐☐☐☐
a.	2c lake & black	4.50	.75	☐☐☐☐☐
b.	2c dark lake & black	*400.00*		☐☐☐☐☐
c.	Horiz. pair, imperf. vert.................	*5,000.*		☐☐☐☐☐
1932, Perf. 11x10½, Rotary Press Printings				
704	½c Washington Bicentennial, olive brown	.25	.25	☐☐☐☐☐
705	1c Washington Bicentennial, green ...	.25	.25	☐☐☐☐☐
706	1½c Washington Bicentennial, brown..	.45	.25	☐☐☐☐☐
707	2c Washington Bicentennial, car rose	.30	.25	☐☐☐☐☐
708	3c Washington Bicentennial, deep violet	.55	.25	☐☐☐☐☐
709	4c Washington Bicentennial, light brown	.40	.25	☐☐☐☐☐

714 715 716 717
718 719 720 724
725 726 727 728
729 732 733 734
736 737 739
740 741 742

52

Scott No.	Description	Unused Value	Used Value	//////
710	5c Washington Bicentennial, blue......	1.50	.25	
711	6c Washington Bicentennial, red orange	3.00	.25	
712	7c Washington Bicentennial, black....	.50	.25	
713	8c Washington Bicentennial, olive bister	2.75	.50	
714	9c Washington Bicentennial, pale red.....	2.25	.25	
715	10c Washington Bicentennial, orange yel.	10.00	.25	
Perf. 11				
716	2c Olympic Winter Games, carmine rose	.40	.25	
a.	2c lake	—		
Perf. 11x10½, Rotary Press Printing				
717	2c Arbor Day	.25	.25	
Perf. 11x10½				
718	3c Olympic Games.............................	1.50	.25	
719	5c Olympic Games.............................	2.25	.25	
720	3c Washington, deep violet...............	.25	.25	
b.	Booklet pane of 6	35.00	*12.50*	
c.	Vert. pair, imperf. btwn.	*700.00*	*1,350.*	
Coil Stamps, Perf. 10 Vertically, Rotary Press Printing				
721	3c Washington (720)	2.75	.25	
Perf. 10 Horizontally				
722	3c Washington (720)	1.50	.35	
Perf. 10 Vertically				
723	6c Garfield (558), deep orange..........	11.00	.30	
1932-33, Perf. 11				
724	3c William Penn	.45	.25	
a.	Vert. pair, imperf. horiz.	—		
725	3c Daniel Webster.............................	.45	.25	
726	3c Georgia Bicentennial.....................	.45	.25	
1933, Perf. 101/2 x11, Rotary Press Printing				
727	3c Peace of 1783...............................	.25	.25	
728	1c Century of Progress, yellow green	.25	.25	
729	3c Century of Progress, violet...........	.25	.25	
1933, Imperf., Flat Plate Printing				
730	American Phil. Society, Sheet of 25	27.50	27.50	
a.	1c Single stamp, Century of Progress (728)	.75	.50	
731	American Phil. Society, Sheet of 25	25.00	25.00	
a.	3c Single stamp, Century of Progress (729)	.65	.50	
1933, Perforated				
732	3c National Recovery Act	.25	.25	
733	3c Byrd Antarctic	.50	.50	
734	5c Kosciuszko...................................	.55	.25	
a.	Horiz. pair, imperf. vert.................	*2,250.*		
1934, Imperf.				
735	3c National Stamp Exhibition, Sheet of 6	12.00	10.00	
a.	Single stamp, Byrd Antarctic	1.90	1.65	

743

744

745

747

746

748

749

754

755

772

773

774

775

Scott No.	Description	Unused Value	Used Value	/ / / / / /

Perf. 11

736	3c Maryland Tercentenary..................	.25	.25	☐☐☐☐☐
a.	Horiz. pair, imperf. btwn.	7,000.		☐☐☐☐☐
b.	3c lake..	—	—	☐☐☐☐☐

Perf. 11x10½

737	3c Mothers of America......................	.25	.25	☐☐☐☐☐

Perf. 11

738	3c Mothers of America (737)............	.25	.25	☐☐☐☐☐
739	3c Wisconsin Tercentenary................	.25	.25	☐☐☐☐☐
a.	Vert. pair, imperf. horiz.	500.00		☐☐☐☐☐
b.	Horiz. pair, imperf. vert.................	750.00		☐☐☐☐☐
740	1c National Parks - Yosemite...........	.25	.25	☐☐☐☐☐
a.	Vert. pair, imperf. horiz., with gum	1,500.		☐☐☐☐☐
741	2c National Parks - Grand Canyon	.30	.25	☐☐☐☐☐
a.	Vert. pair, imperf. horiz., with gum	850.00		☐☐☐☐☐
b.	Horiz. pair, imperf. vert., with gum	850.00		☐☐☐☐☐
742	3c National Parks - Mt. Rainier.........	.35	.25	☐☐☐☐☐
a.	Vert. pair, imperf. horiz., with gum	850.00		☐☐☐☐☐
743	4c National Parks - Mesa Verde........	.50	.40	☐☐☐☐☐
a.	Vert. pair, imperf. horiz., with gum	1,000.		☐☐☐☐☐
744	5c National Parks - Yellowstone........	.80	.65	☐☐☐☐☐
a.	Horiz. pair, imperf. vert., with gum......................................	1,000.		☐☐☐☐☐
745	6c National Parks - Crater Lake.........	1.20	.85	☐☐☐☐☐
746	7c National Parks - Acadia................	.80	.75	☐☐☐☐☐
a.	Horiz. pair, imperf. vert., with gum......................................	850.00		☐☐☐☐☐
747	8c National Parks - Zion	1.75	1.50	☐☐☐☐☐
748	9c National Parks - Glacier	1.60	.65	☐☐☐☐☐
749	10c National Parks - Great Smoky Mountains.....................................	3.25	1.25	☐☐☐☐☐

Imperf.

750	American Philatelic Society, sheet of 6	30.00	27.50	☐☐☐☐☐
a.	3c Single stamp, National Parks (742)	3.75	3.25	☐☐☐☐☐
751	Trans-Mississippi Phil. Exhib, sheet of 6.....................................	12.50	12.50	☐☐☐☐☐
a.	1c Single stamp, National Parks (740)	2.00	1.60	☐☐☐☐☐

1935, Perf. 10½x11, Rotary Press Printing

752	3c Peace of 1783 Issue (727)............	.25	.25	☐☐☐☐☐

Perf. 11, Flat Plate Printing

753	3c Byrd Antarctic (733)......................	.50	.45	☐☐☐☐☐

No. 753 is similar to No. 733. Positive identification is by blocks or pairs showing guide lines between stamps. These lines between stamps are found only on No. 753.

Scott No.	Description	Unused Value	Used Value	/ / / / / /
Imperf.				
754	3c Mothers of America (737).............	.60	.60	☐☐☐☐☐
755	3c Wisconsin Tercentenary (739).......	.60	.60	☐☐☐☐☐
756	1c National Parks - Yosemite (740) ...	.25	.25	☐☐☐☐☐
757	2c National Parks - Grand Canyon (741)	.25	.25	☐☐☐☐☐
758	3c National Parks - Mt. Rainier (742)	.50	.45	☐☐☐☐☐
759	4c National Parks - Mesa Verde (743)	1.00	.95	☐☐☐☐☐
760	5c National Parks - Yellowstone (744)	1.60	1.40	☐☐☐☐☐
761	6c National Parks - Crater Lake (745)	2.40	2.25	☐☐☐☐☐
762	7c National Parks - Acadia (746).........	1.60	1.40	☐☐☐☐☐
763	8c National Parks - Zion (747)	1.90	1.50	☐☐☐☐☐
764	9c National Parks - Glacier (748)......	2.00	1.75	☐☐☐☐☐
765	10c National Parks - Great Smoky Mountains (749).........................	4.00	3.50	☐☐☐☐☐
766	American Phil. Society, Pane of 25	25.00	25.00	☐☐☐☐☐
a.	1c Single stamp, Century of Progress (728)	.70	.50	
767	American Phil. Society, Pane of 25	23.50	23.50	☐☐☐☐☐
a.	3c Single stamp, Century of Progress (729)	.60	.50	
768	National Stamp Exhibition, Pane of 6	20.00	15.00	☐☐☐☐☐
a.	3c Single stamp, Byrd Antarctic (733)	2.80	2.40	
769	Trans-Mississippi Phil. Exhib, Pane of 6	12.50	11.00	☐☐☐☐☐
a.	1c Single stamp - Yosemite (740)	1.85	1.80	
770	American Phil. Society, Pane of 6	30.00	24.00	☐☐☐☐☐
a.	3c Single stamp, Mt. Rainier - (742).	3.25	3.10	
771	16c Air Post Special Delivery (CE1)...	2.60	2.60	☐☐☐☐☐

Nos. 766-770 were issued in sheets of 9 panes of 25 stamps each. Single items from these sheets are identical with other varieties, 766 and 730, 766a and 730a, 767 and 731, 767a and 731a, 768 and 735, 768a and 735a, 769 and 756, 770 and 758. Positive identification is by blocks or pairs showing wide gutters between stamps. These wide gutters occurs only on Nos. 766-770 and measure, horizontally, 13mm on Nos. 766-767, 16mm on No. 768, and 23mm on Nos. 769-770.

1935, Perf. 11x10½, 11

772	3c Connecticut Tercentenary..............	.30	.25	☐☐☐☐☐
773	3c California Pacific Exposition........	.30	.25	☐☐☐☐☐
774	3c Boulder Dam	.30	.25	☐☐☐☐☐
775	3c Michigan Centenary	.30	.25	☐☐☐☐☐
1936				
776	3c Texas Centennial............................	.30	.25	☐☐☐☐☐
777	3c Rhode Island Tercentenary............	.35	.25	☐☐☐☐☐
778	3rd Intl. Phil. Exhib., Sht. of 4, imperf.	1.75	1.25	☐☐☐☐☐
a.	3c Connecticut Tercentenary (772)....	.40	.30	
b.	3c California Pacific Exposition (773)	.40	.30	
c.	3c Michigan Centennial (775)	.40	.30	
d.	3c Texas Centennial (776).................	.40	.30	
782	3c Arkansas Centennial......................	.30	.25	☐☐☐☐☐
783	3c Oregon Territory	.25	.25	☐☐☐☐☐
784	3c Susan B. Anthony	.25	.25	☐☐☐☐☐

Scott No.	Description	Unused Value	Used Value	/ / / / / /
1936-37				
785	1c Army - Washington & Greene	.25	.25	
786	2c Army - A. Jackson & Scott	.25	.25	
787	3c Army - Sherman, Grant & Sheridan	.35	.25	
788	4c Army - Lee & "Stonewall" Jackson	.55	.25	
789	5c Army - West Point	.65	.25	
790	1c Navy - Jones & Barry	.25	.25	
791	2c Navy - Decatur & MacDonough...	.25	.25	
792	3c Navy - Farragut & Porter	.35	.25	
793	4c Navy - Sampson, Dewey & Schley	.55	.25	
794	5c Navy - Academy Seal & Cadets ...	.65	.25	
1937				
795	3c Ordinance of 1787	.30	.25	
796	5c Virginia Dare	.35	.25	
797	10c Society of Philatelic Americans,			
	blue green, imperf	.60	.40	
798	3c Constitution Sesquicentennial	.35	.25	
799	3c Hawaii	.35	.25	
800	3c Alaska	.35	.25	
801	3c Puerto Rico	.35	.25	
802	3c Virgin Islands...............................	.35	.25	
1938-54, Perf. 11x10½, 11				
803	½c Benjamin Franklin	.25	.25	
804	1c George Washington	.25	.25	
b.	Booklet pane of 6	2.00	.50	
805	1½c Martha Washington	.25	.25	
b.	Horiz. pair, imperf. btwn..............	125.00	20.00	
806	2c John Adams	.25	.25	
b.	Booklet pane of 6	5.50	1.00	
807	3c Thomas Jefferson..........................	.25	.25	
a.	Booklet pane of 6	8.50	*2.00*	
b.	Horiz. pair, imperf. btwn..............	*1,750.*	—	
c.	Imperf., pair	*2,750.*		
808	4c James Madison	.75	.25	
809	4½c White House	.30	.25	
810	5c James Monroe	.35	.25	
811	6c John Quincy Adams	.40	.25	
812	7c Andrew Jackson.............................	.40	.25	
813	8c Martin Van Buren	.40	.25	
814	9c William Henry Harrison...............	.40	.25	
815	10c John Tyler	.40	.25	
816	11c James Knox Polk	.75	.25	
817	12c Zachary Taylor.............................	1.00	.25	
818	13c Millard Fillmore	1.30	.25	
819	14c Franklin Pierce.............................	1.00	.25	
820	15c James Buchanan	.70	.25	
821	16c Abraham Lincoln...........................	3.00	.25	
822	17c Andrew Johnson............................	1.00	.25	

776   777   782

783   784   785

786   787

788   789

790   791

HOW TO USE THIS BOOK

The number in the first column is its Scott number or identifying number. Following that is the denomination of the stamp and its color or description. Finally, the values, unused and used, are shown.

792

793

796

799

794

795

797

798

800

801

802

803

804   805

806

59

807 808 809 810

811 812 813 814

815 816 817 818

819 820 821 822

823 824 825 826

827 828 829 830

60

Scott No.	Description	Unused Value	Used Value	/ / / / / /
823	18c Ulysses S. Grant	2.25	.25	
824	19c Rutherford B. Hayes	1.30	.35	
825	20c James A. Garfield	1.00	.25	
826	21c Chester Arthur	1.30	.25	
827	22c Grover Cleveland	1.20	.40	
828	24c Benjamin Harrison	3.50	.25	
829	25c William McKinley	1.00	.25	
830	30c Theodore Roosevelt, deep ultramarine	4.00	.25	
a.	30c blue	15.00	—	
b.	30c deep blue	240.00	—	
831	50c William Howard Taft	5.00	.25	
832	$1 Woodrow Wilson, purple & black	7.00	.25	
a.	Vert. pair, imperf. horiz.	*1,500.*		
b.	Wmkd. USIR	200.00	65.00	
c.	$1 red violet & black	6.00	.25	
d.	As "c," vert. pair, imperf. horiz.	*1,250.*		
e.	Vert. pair, imperf. btwn.	*2,750.*		
f.	As "c," vert. pair, imperf. btwn.	*8,500.*		
g.	As "c," bright magenta & black	*75.00*	—	
h.	As No. 832, red vio. & black	—		
833	$2 Warren G. Harding	17.50	3.75	
834	$5 Calvin Coolidge, carmine and black	85.00	3.00	
a.	$5 red brown & black	*3,000.*	*7,000.*	

1938

Scott No.	Description	Unused Value	Used Value	/ / / / / /
835	3c Constitution Ratification	.45	.25	
836	3c Swedish-Finnish Tercentenary	.35	.25	
837	3c Northwest Territory Sesquicentennial	.30	.25	
838	3c Iowa Territory Centennial	.40	.25	

1939, Coil Stamps, Perf. 10 Vertically

Scott No.	Description	Unused Value	Used Value	/ / / / / /
839	1c George Washington (804)	.30	.25	
840	1½c Martha Washington (805)	.30	.25	
841	2c John Adams (806)	.40	.25	
842	3c Thomas Jefferson (807)	.50	.25	
843	4c James Madison (808)	7.50	.40	
844	4½c White House (809)	.70	.40	
845	5c James Monroe (810)	5.00	.35	
846	6c John Quincy Adams (811)	1.10	.25	
847	10c John Tyler (815)	11.00	1.00	

Perf. 10 Horizontally

Scott No.	Description	Unused Value	Used Value	/ / / / / /
848	1c George Washington (804)	.85	.25	
849	1½c Martha Washington (805)	1.25	.30	
850	2c John Adams (806)	2.50	.40	
851	3c Thomas Jefferson (807)	2.50	.40	

1939

Scott No.	Description	Unused Value	Used Value	/ / / / / /
852	3c Golden Gate Intl. Exposition	.30	.25	
853	3c New York World's Fair	.30	.25	
854	3c Washington Inauguration	.60	.25	

831   832   833   834

835   836   837

838   852   853

854   855   856

857   858

Scott No.	Description	Unused Value	Used Value	/ / / / / /
855	3c Baseball Centennial	1.75	.25	
856	3c Panama Canal	.40	.25	
857	3c Printing Tercentenary	.25	.25	
858	3c 50th Anniversary of Statehood	.35	.25	
1940				
859	1c Washington Irving	.25	.25	
860	2c James Fenimore Cooper	.25	.25	
861	3c Ralph Waldo Emerson	.25	.25	
862	5c Louise May Alcott	.35	.25	
863	10c Samuel L. Clemens	1.75	1.20	
864	1c Henry Wadsworth Longfellow	.25	.25	
865	2c John Greenleaf Whittier	.25	.25	
866	3c James Russell Lowell	.25	.25	
867	5c Walt Whitman	.50	.25	
868	10c James Whitcomb Riley	1.75	1.25	
869	1c Horace Mann	.25	.25	
870	2c Mark Hopkins	.25	.25	
871	3c Charles W. Eliot	.25	.25	
872	5c Frances E. Willard	.50	.25	
873	10c Booker T. Washington	2.25	1.10	
874	1c John James Audubon	.25	.25	
875	2c Dr. Crawford W. Long	.25	.25	
876	3c Luther Burbank	.25	.25	
877	5c Dr. Walter Reed	.35	.25	
878	10c Jane Addams	1.50	.85	
879	1c Stephen Collins Foster	.25	.25	
880	2c John Philip Sousa	.25	.25	
881	3c Victor Herbert	.25	.25	
882	5c Edward A. MacDowell	.50	.25	
883	10c Ethelbert Nevin	3.75	1.35	
884	1c Gilbert Charles Stuart	.25	.25	
885	2c James A. McNeill Whistler	.25	.25	
886	3c Augustus Saint-Gaudens	.30	.25	
887	5c Daniel Chester French	.50	.25	
888	10c Frederic Remington	1.75	1.25	
889	1c Eli Whitney	.25	.25	
890	2c Samuel F.B. Morse	.30	.25	
891	3c Cyrus Hall McCormick	.30	.25	
892	5c Elias Howe	1.10	.30	
893	10c Alexander Graham Bell	11.00	2.00	
894	3c Pony Express	.50	.25	
895	3c Pan American Union	.30	.25	
896	3c Idaho Statehood	.35	.25	
897	3c Wyoming Statehood	.35	.25	
898	3c Coronado Expedition	.35	.25	
899	1c National Defense	.25	.25	
a.	Vert. pair, imperf. btwn.	*600.00*	—	
b.	Horiz. pair, imperf. btwn.	35.00	—	

859

860

861

862

863

864

865

866

867

868

869

870

871

872

873

874

875

876

877

878

879

880

881

882

883

884

885

886

887

888

889 890 891 892

893 894

895

896 897 898

899 900 901 905 907

902 903 904

Scott No.	Description	Unused Value	Used Value	/ / / / /
900	2c National Defense	.25	.25	
a.	Horiz. pair, imperf. btwn.	37.50	—	
901	3c National Defense	.25	.25	
a.	Horiz. pair, imperf. btwn.	22.50	—	
902	3c Thirteenth Amendment	.50	.25	

1941

903	3c Vermont Statehood	.45	.25	

1942

904	3c Kentucky Statehood	.30	.25	
905	3c Win the War, violet	.25	.25	
b.	3c reddish violet	750.00	500.00	
906	5c Chinese Resistance	1.50	.25	

1943

907	2c Allied Nations	.25	.25	
908	1c Four Freedoms	.25	.25	

1943-44, Nos. 910-921 like No. 909

909	5c Poland	.25	.25	
a.	Double impression of "Poland"	650.00		
b.	Double impression of black flag color and red "Poland"	—		
910	5c Czechoslovakia	.25	.25	
a.	Double impression of "Czecholovakia"	—		
911	5c Norway	.25	.25	
a.	Double impression of "Norway"	—		
912	5c Luxembourg	.25	.25	
a.	Double impression of "Luxembourg"	—		
913	5c Netherlands	.25	.25	
c.	Double impression of black	—		
914	5c Belgium	.25	.25	
a.	Double impression of "Belgium"	—		
915	5c France	.25	.25	
916	5c Greece	.50	.25	
917	5c Yugoslavia	.40	.25	
b.	Double impression of black.	—		
918	5c Albania	.25	.25	
a.	Double impression of "Albania"	—	—	
919	5c Austria	.30	.25	
a.	Double impression of "Austria"	—		
c.	Double impression of black	—		
920	5c Denmark, blue violet, red & black	.30	.25	
b.	5c blue violet, red & gray	.30	.25	
921	5c Korea reverse printing of flag colors (light blue over gray)	.25	.25	
a.	Double impression of "Korea"	—		
c.	Double impression of red	—	—	

906

908

909

922

923

924

925

926

927

928

929

930

931

932

933

934

935

936

937

938

939

940

941

942

943

944

945

946

947

948

949

950

951

952

953

954

955

956

957

958

959

960

961

962

963

964

965

966

967

968

969

970

971

972

Scott No.	Description	Unused Value	Used Value	/ / / / / /
1944				
922	3c Transcontinental Railroad	.25	.25	
923	3c Steamship	.25	.25	
924	3c Telegraph	.25	.25	
925	3c Philippines	.25	.25	
926	3c Motion Pictures	.25	.25	
1945				
927	3c Florida Statehood	.25	.25	
928	5c United Nations Conference	.25	.25	
929	3c Iwo Jima (Marines)	.30	.25	
1945-46				
930	1c Franklin D. Roosevelt	.25	.25	
931	2c Franklin D. Roosevelt	.25	.25	
932	3c Franklin D. Roosevelt	.25	.25	
933	5c Franklin D. Roosevelt	.25	.25	
1945				
934	3c Army	.25	.25	
935	3c Navy	.25	.25	
936	3c Coast Guard	.25	.25	
937	3c Alfred E. Smith	.25	.25	
938	3c Texas Statehood	.25	.25	
1946				
939	3c Merchant Marine	.25	.25	
940	3c Veterans of World War II	.25	.25	
941	3c Tennessee Statehood	.25	.25	
942	3c Iowa Statehood	.25	.25	
943	3c Smithsonian Institution	.25	.25	
944	3c Kearny Expedition	.25	.25	
1947				
945	3c Thomas A. Edison	.25	.25	
946	3c Joseph Pulitzer	.25	.25	
947	3c Postage Stamp Centenary	.25	.25	
948	CIPEX, Sheet of 2, imperf	.55	.45	
a.	5c Franklin (1), blue	.25	.25	
b.	10c Washington (2), brown orange	.25	.25	
949	3c Doctors	.25	.25	
950	3c Utah	.25	.25	
951	3c U.S. Frigate *Constitution*	.25	.25	
952	3c Everglades National Park	.25	.25	
1948				
953	3c George Washington Carver	.25	.25	
954	3c California Gold	.25	.25	
955	3c Mississippi Territory	.25	.25	
956	3c Four Chaplains	.25	.25	
957	3c Wisconsin Statehood	.25	.25	
958	5c Swedish Pioneers	.25	.25	

973

974

975

976

977

978

979

980

981

982

983

986

984

985

987

988

989

Scott No.	Description	Unused Value	Used Value	/ / / / / /
959	3c Progress of Women	.25	.25	
960	3c William Allen White	.25	.25	
961	3c U.S.-Canada Friendship	.25	.25	
962	3c Francis Scott Key	.25	.25	
963	3c Salute to Youth	.25	.25	
964	3c Oregon Territory	.25	.25	
965	3c Harlan F. Stone	.25	.25	
966	3c Palomar Mountain Observatory	.25	.25	
a.	Vert. pair, imperf. btwn.	350.00		
967	3c Clara Barton	.25	.25	
968	3c Poultry Industry	.25	.25	
969	3c Gold Star Mothers	.25	.25	
970	3c Fort Kearny	.25	.25	
971	3c Volunteer Firemen	.25	.25	
972	3c Indian Centennial	.25	.25	
973	3c Rough Riders	.25	.25	
974	3c Juliette Low	.25	.25	
975	3c Will Rogers	.25	.25	
976	3c Fort Bliss	.25	.25	
977	3c Moina Michael	.25	.25	
978	3c Gettysburg Address	.25	.25	
979	3c American Turners	.25	.25	
980	3c Joel Chandler Harris	.25	.25	

1949

Scott No.	Description	Unused Value	Used Value	/ / / / / /
981	3c Minnesota Territory	.25	.25	
982	3c Washington and Lee University	.25	.25	
983	3c Puerto Rico Election	.25	.25	
984	3c Annapolis Tercentenary	.25	.25	
985	3c Grand Army of the Republic	.25	.25	
986	3c Edgar Allan Poe	.25	.25	

1950

Scott No.	Description	Unused Value	Used Value	/ / / / / /
987	3c American Bankers Association	.25	.25	
988	3c Samuel Gompers	.25	.25	
989	3c Statue of Freedom	.25	.25	
990	3c White House	.25	.25	
991	3c Supreme Court	.25	.25	
992	3c U.S. Capitol	.25	.25	
993	3c Railroad Engineers	.25	.25	
994	3c Kansas City, Missouri	.25	.25	
995	3c Boy Scouts	.25	.25	
996	3c Indiana Territory	.25	.25	
997	3c California Statehood	.25	.25	

1951

Scott No.	Description	Unused Value	Used Value	/ / / / / /
998	3c United Confederate Veterans	.25	.25	
999	3c Nevada Centennial	.25	.25	
1000	3c Landing of Cadillac	.25	.25	
1001	3c Colorado Statehood	.25	.25	

990

991

992

993

994

995

996

997

998

999

1000

1001

1002

1003

1004

1005

1006

1007   1008   1009

1010   1011   1012

1013   1014   1015

1016   1017   1018

1019   1020   1021

1022   1023   1024

75

1025

1026

1027

1028

1029

1030

1031

1031A

1032

1033

1034

1035

1036

1037

1038

1039

1040

1041

1042

1043

1044

Scott No.	Description	Unused Value	Used Value	/ / / / / /
1002	3c American Chemical Society..........	.25	.25	
1003	3c Battle of Brooklyn.........................	.25	.25	
1952				
1004	3c Betsy Ross	.25	.25	
1005	3c 4-H Clubs.......................................	.25	.25	
1006	3c B. & O. Railroad............................	.25	.25	
1007	3c American Automobile Association	.25	.25	
1008	3c NATO..	.25	.25	
1009	3c Grand Coulee Dam........................	.25	.25	
1010	3c Lafayette	.25	.25	
1011	3c Mt. Rushmore................................	.35	.25	
1012	3c Engineering....................................	.25	.25	
1013	3c Service Women..............................	.25	.25	
1014	3c Gutenberg Bible............................	.25	.25	
1015	3c Newspaper Boys	.25	.25	
1016	3c Red Cross.......................................	.25	.25	
1953				
1017	3c National Guard	.25	.25	
1018	3c Ohio Statehood..............................	.25	.25	
1019	3c Washington Territory.....................	.25	.25	
1020	3c Louisiana Purchase........................	.25	.25	
1021	5c Opening of Japan...........................	.25	.25	
1022	3c American Bar Association	.25	.25	
1023	3c Sagamore Hill................................	.25	.25	
1024	3c Future Farmers of America	.25	.25	
1025	3c Trucking Industry	.25	.25	
1026	3c General George S. Patton, Jr.	.25	.25	
1027	3c New York City	.25	.25	
1028	3c Gadsden Purchase..........................	.25	.25	
1954				
1029	3c Columbia University	.25	.25	
1954-68, Perf. 11x10½, 10½ x11, 11				
1030	½c Benjamin Franklin........................	.25	.25	
1031	1c George Washington	.25	.25	
1031A	1¼c Palace of the Governors................	.25	.25	
1032	1½c Mount Vernon	.25	.25	
1033	2c Thomas Jefferson...........................	.25	.25	
1034	2½c Bunker Hill Monument	.25	.25	
1035	3c Statue of Liberty, untagged...........	.25	.25	
a.	Booklet pane of 6	4.00	*1.25*	
b.	Tagged...	.35	.25	
c.	Imperf. pair	*1,750.*		
d.	Horiz. pair, imperf. btwn...............	*1,500.*		
g.	As "d," in #1035a with foldover (one pair)			
	or miscut (three pairs).................	*2,000.*		
1036	4c Abraham Lincoln, untagged..........	.25	.25	
a.	Booklet pane of 6	2.75	1.25	
b.	Tagged..	.65	.40	

1044A

1045

1046

1047

1048

1049

1050

1051

1052

1053

1060

1061

1062

1063

1064

1065

1066

1067

Scott No.		Description	Unused Value	Used Value	/ / / / / /
d.		As "a," vert. imperf. horiz.	*10,000.*		
e.		Horiz. pair, imperf btwn.	*3,500.*		
1037	4½c	Hermitage	.25	.25	
1038	5c	James Monroe................................	.25	.25	
1039	6c	Theodore Roosevelt.......................	.25	.25	
b.		Imperf., blk. of 4 (unique).............	*23,000.*		
1040	7c	Woodrow Wilson	.25	.25	
a.	7c	Dark rose carmine	.25	.25	
1041	8c	Statue of Liberty, 22.7 mm high ...	.25	.25	
a.		Double impression of carmine......	*575.00*	—	
1041B	8c	Statue of Liberty(1041), 2.9 mm high	.40	.25	
1042	8c	Statue of Liberty	.25	.25	
1043	9c	Alamo..	.30	.25	
a.	9c	Dark rose lilac...............................	.30	.25	
1044	10c	Independence Hall, untagged........	.30	.25	
b.	10c	Dark rose lake	.25	.25	
d.		Tagged...	2.00	1.00	
1044A	11c	Statue of Liberty, untagged...........	.30	.25	
c.		Tagged...	2.50	1.60	
1045	12c	Benjamin Harrison, untagged	.35	.25	
a.		Tagged...	.35	.25	
1046	15c	John Jay, untagged........................	.60	.25	
a.		Tagged...	1.10	.80	
1047	20c	Monticello.....................................	.50	.25	
a.	20c	Deep bright ultramarine	.50	.25	
1048	25c	Paul Revere	1.10	.75	
1049	30c	Robert E. Lee	1.00	.25	
a.	30c	Intense black	1.20	.75	
1050	40c	John Marshall	1.50	.25	
1051	50c	Susan B. Anthony	1.50	.25	
1052	$1	Patrick Henry................................	4.50	.25	
1053	$5	Alexander Hamilton	55.00	6.75	

1954-73, Perf. 10 Vertically, Horizontally (1¼c, 4½c)

Scott No.		Description	Unused Value	Used Value	/ / / / / /
1054	1c	George Washington (1031)	.25	.25	
b.		Imperf., pair	*2,500.*	—	
1054A	1¼c	Palace of the Governors (1031A)..	.25	.25	
d.		Imperf. pair	—		
1055	2c	Thomas Jefferson (1033), untagged	.35	.25	
a.		Tagged...	.25	.25	
b.		Imperf. pair, untagged (Bureau precanceled)	*375.00*		
c.		As "a," imperf. pair, tagged...........	*550.00*		
1056	2½c	Bunker Hill Monument (1034)	.30	.25	
1057	3c	Statue of Liberty (1035), untagged	.35	.25	
a.		Imperf., pair	*1,750.*	800.00	
b.		Tagged...	1.00	.50	
1058	4c	Abraham Lincoln (1036)..............	.75	.25	
a.		Imperf., pair	75.00	70.00	

1068

1069

1070

1071

1072

1074

1073

1075

1076

1077

1078

1079

1080

1081

80

Scott No.	Description	Unused Value	Used Value	/ / / / / /
1059	4½c Hermitage (1037)	1.50	1.00	
1059A	25c Paul Revere (1048), untagged	.50	.30	
b.	Tagged	.80	.25	
d.	Imperf., pair	30.00		
1954				
1060	3c Nebraska Territory	.25	.25	
1061	3c Kansas Territory	.25	.25	
1062	3c George Eastman	.25	.25	
1063	3c Lewis and Clark Expedition	.25	.25	
1955				
1064	3c Pennsylvania Academy of the Fine Arts	.25	.25	
1065	3c Land Grant Colleges	.25	.25	
1066	8c Rotary International	.25	.25	
1067	3c Armed Forces Reserve	.25	.25	
1068	3c New Hampshire	.25	.25	
1069	3c Soo Locks	.25	.25	
1070	3c Atoms for Peace	.25	.25	
1071	3c Fort Ticonderoga	.25	.25	
1072	3c Andrew W. Mellon	.25	.25	
1956				
1073	3c Benjamin Franklin	.25	.25	
1074	3c Booker T. Washington	.25	.25	
1075	FIPEX, Sheet of 2, imperf	1.70	1.50	
a.	3c Statue of Liberty (1035)	.75	.60	
b.	8c Statue of Liberty (1041)	.85	.75	
1076	3c FIPEX	.25	.25	
1077	3c Wildlife Conservation, Wild Turkey	.25	.25	
1078	3c Wildlife Conserv., Pronghorn Antelope	.25	.25	
1079	3c Wildlife Conservation, King Salmon	.25	.25	
1080	3c Pure Food and Drug Laws	.25	.25	
1081	3c Wheatland	.25	.25	
1082	3c Labor Day	.25	.25	
1083	3c Nassau Hall	.25	.25	
1084	3c Devils Tower	.25	.25	
1085	3c Children	.25	.25	
1957				
1086	3c Alexander Hamilton	.25	.25	
1087	3c Polio	.25	.25	
1088	3c Coast and Geodetic Survey	.25	.25	
1089	3c Architects	.25	.25	
1090	3c Steel Industry	.25	.25	
1091	3c International Naval Review	.25	.25	
1092	3c Oklahoma Statehood	.25	.25	
1093	3c School Teachers	.25	.25	
1094	4c 48-Star Flag	.25	.25	
1095	3c Shipbuilding	.25	.25	
1096	8c Ramon Magsaysay	.25	.25	

1082   1083   1084   1087

1085   1086   1088

1089   1090   1091

1092   1093   1094

1095   1096   1097

82

1098

1099

1100

1109

1104

1105

1106

1107

1108

1110

1112

1113

1115

1114

1116

1117

1119

83

1120

1121

1122

1123

1124

1125

1127

1128

1129

1130

1131

1132

1133

1134

1135

1136

1138

84

Scott No.	Description	Unused Value	Used Value	/ / / / / /
1097	3c Lafayette Bicentenary...................	.25	.25	☐☐☐☐☐
1098	3c Wildlife Conserv., Whooping Cranes	.25	.25	☐☐☐☐☐
1099	3c Religious Freedom........................	.25	.25	☐☐☐☐☐
1958				
1100	3c Gardening and Horticulture	.25	.25	☐☐☐☐☐
1104	3c Brussels Exhibition.......................	.25	.25	☐☐☐☐☐
1105	3c James Monroe...............................	.25	.25	☐☐☐☐☐
1106	3c Minnesota Statehood....................	.25	.25	☐☐☐☐☐
1107	3c Geophysical Year	.25	.25	☐☐☐☐☐
1108	3c Gunston Hall................................	.25	.25	☐☐☐☐☐
1109	3c Mackinac Bridge	.25	.25	☐☐☐☐☐
1110	4c Simon Bolivar, olive bister...........	.25	.25	☐☐☐☐☐
1111	8c Bolivar (1110), carmine,			
	ultra & ocher................................	.25	.25	☐☐☐☐☐
1112	4c Atlantic Cable	.25	.25	☐☐☐☐☐
1958-59				
1113	1c Lincoln..	.25	.25	☐☐☐☐☐
1114	3c Lincoln Bust	.25	.25	☐☐☐☐☐
1115	4c Lincoln-Douglas Debates.............	.25	.25	☐☐☐☐☐
1116	4c Lincoln Statue.............................	.25	.25	☐☐☐☐☐
1958				
1117	4c Lajos Kossuth, green	.25	.25	☐☐☐☐☐
1118	8c Kossuth (1117), carmine,			
	ultra & ocher................................	.25	.25	☐☐☐☐☐
1119	4c Freedom of Press	.25	.25	☐☐☐☐☐
1120	4c Overland Mail..............................	.25	.25	☐☐☐☐☐
1121	4c Noah Webster..............................	.25	.25	☐☐☐☐☐
1122	4c Forest Conservation......................	.25	.25	☐☐☐☐☐
1123	4c Fort Duquesne.............................	.25	.25	☐☐☐☐☐
1959				
1124	4c Oregon Statehood........................	.25	.25	☐☐☐☐☐
1125	4c Jose de San Martin	.25	.25	☐☐☐☐☐
a.	Horiz. pair, imperf. btwn...............	*1,000.*		☐☐☐☐☐
1126	8c San Martin (1125), car.,			
	ultra & ocher	.25	.25	☐☐☐☐☐
1127	4c NATO..	.25	.25	☐☐☐☐☐
1128	4c Arctic Explorations.......................	.25	.25	☐☐☐☐☐
1129	8c World Peace through World Trade	.25	.25	☐☐☐☐☐
1130	4c Silver Centennial	.25	.25	☐☐☐☐☐
1131	4c St. Lawrence Seaway....................	.25	.25	☐☐☐☐☐
1132	4c 49-Star Flag	.25	.25	☐☐☐☐☐
1133	4c Soil Conservation	.25	.25	☐☐☐☐☐
1134	4c Petroleum Industry	.25	.25	☐☐☐☐☐
1135	4c Dental Health..............................	.25	.25	☐☐☐☐☐
1136	4c Ernst Reuter, gray........................	.25	.25	☐☐☐☐☐
1137	8c Reuter (1136), carmine, ultra & ocher	.25	.25	☐☐☐☐☐
a.	Ocher missing (from extraneous			
	paper)...	*3,500.*		☐☐☐☐☐

1139

1140

1141

1142

1143

1144

1145

1146

1147

1149

1150

1152

1151

1154

1153

1155

Scott No.	Description	Unused Value	Used Value	/ / / / / /
b.	Ultramarine missing (from extraneous paper)	4,250.		☐☐☐☐☐
c.	Ocher & ultramarine missing (from extraneous paper)	4,500.		☐☐☐☐☐
d.	All colors missing (from extraneous paper)	2,500.		☐☐☐☐☐
1138	4c Dr. Ephraim McDowell	.25	.25	☐☐☐☐☐
a.	Vert. pair, imperf. btwn.	400.00		☐☐☐☐☐
b.	Vert. pair, imperf. horiz.	275.00		☐☐☐☐☐
1960-61				
1139	4c Credo - Washington	.25	.25	☐☐☐☐☐
1140	4c Credo - Franklin	.25	.25	☐☐☐☐☐
1141	4c Credo - Jefferson	.25	.25	☐☐☐☐☐
1142	4c Credo - Key	.25	.25	☐☐☐☐☐
1143	4c Credo - Lincoln	.25	.25	☐☐☐☐☐
1144	4c Credo - Henry	.25	.25	☐☐☐☐☐
1960				
1145	4c Boy Scout Jubilee	.25	.25	☐☐☐☐☐
1146	4c Olympic Winter Games	.25	.25	☐☐☐☐☐
1147	4c Thomas G. Masaryk, blue	.25	.25	☐☐☐☐☐
a.	Vert. pair, imperf. btwn.	2,750.		☐☐☐☐☐
1148	8c Masaryk (1147), carmine, ultra & ocher	.25	.25	☐☐☐☐☐
a.	Horiz. pair, imperf. btwn.	—		☐☐☐☐☐
1149	4c World Refugee Year	.25	.25	☐☐☐☐☐
1150	4c Water Conservation	.25	.25	☐☐☐☐☐
a.	Brown orange missing (from extraneous paper)	2,250.		☐☐☐☐☐
1151	4c SEATO	.25	.25	☐☐☐☐☐
a.	Vert. pair, imperf. btwn.	140.00		☐☐☐☐☐
1152	4c American Woman	.25	.25	☐☐☐☐☐
1153	4c 50-Star Flag	.25	.25	☐☐☐☐☐
1154	4c Pony Express	.25	.25	☐☐☐☐☐
1155	4c Employ the Handicapped	.25	.25	☐☐☐☐☐
1156	4c World Forestry Congress	.25	.25	☐☐☐☐☐
1157	4c Mexican Independence	.25	.25	☐☐☐☐☐
1158	4c U.S.-Japan Treaty	.25	.25	☐☐☐☐☐
1159	4c Ignacy Jan Paderewski, blue	.25	.25	☐☐☐☐☐
1160	8c Paderewski (1159), car., ultra & ocher	.25	.25	☐☐☐☐☐
1161	4c Robert A. Taft	.25	.25	☐☐☐☐☐
1162	4c Wheels of Freedom	.25	.25	☐☐☐☐☐
1163	4c Boys' Clubs of America	.25	.25	☐☐☐☐☐
1164	4c First Automated Post Office	.25	.25	☐☐☐☐☐
a.	Red missing (from perf. shift)	250.00		☐☐☐☐☐
1165	4c Gustaf Mannerheim, blue	.25	.25	☐☐☐☐☐
1166	8c Mannerheim (1165), car., ultra & ocher	.25	.25	☐☐☐☐☐
1167	4c Camp Fire Girls	.25	.25	☐☐☐☐☐
1168	4c Giuseppe Garibaldi, green	.25	.25	☐☐☐☐☐
1169	8c Garibaldi (1168), carmine, ultra & ocher	.25	.25	☐☐☐☐☐

1156   1157   1158   1159

1161   1162   1163

1164   1165   1167

1168   1170   1171   1172

1173   1174   1176

88

1177

1178

1179

1180

1181

1183

1184

1185

1191

1182

1186

1187

1193

1188

1189

1190

1192

89

1195

1196

1202

1194

1197

1198

1199

1200

1201

1203

1206

1207

1205

1208

1209

1213

1214

1230

1232

1233

Scott No.	Description	Unused Value	Used Value	/ / / / / /
1170	4c Senator Walter F. George.............	.25	.25	☐☐☐☐☐
1171	4c Andrew Carnegie......................	.25	.25	☐☐☐☐☐
1172	4c John Foster Dulles	.25	.25	☐☐☐☐☐
1173	4c Echo I..	.25	.25	☐☐☐☐☐
1961				
1174	4c Mahatma Gandhi, red orange........	.25	.25	☐☐☐☐☐
1175	8c Gandhi (1174), carmine, ultra & ocher	.25	.25	☐☐☐☐☐
1176	4c Range Conservation	.25	.25	☐☐☐☐☐
1177	4c Horace Greeley..............................	.25	.25	☐☐☐☐☐
1961-65				
1178	4c Firing on Fort Sumter....................	.25	.25	☐☐☐☐☐
1179	4c Battle of Shiloh..............................	.25	.25	☐☐☐☐☐
1180	5c Battle of Gettysburg	.25	.25	☐☐☐☐☐
1181	5c Battle of the Wilderness	.25	.25	☐☐☐☐☐
1182	5c Surrender at Appomattox	.35	.25	☐☐☐☐☐
a.	Horiz. pair, imperf. vert................	4,500.		☐☐☐☐☐
1961				
1183	4c Kansas Statehood	.25	.25	☐☐☐☐☐
1184	4c Senator George W. Norris	.25	.25	☐☐☐☐☐
1185	4c Naval Aviation	.25	.25	☐☐☐☐☐
1186	4c Workmen's Compensation............	.25	.25	☐☐☐☐☐
1187	4c Frederic Remington.......................	.25	.25	☐☐☐☐☐
1188	4c Republic of China..........................	.25	.25	☐☐☐☐☐
1189	4c Naismith - Basketball	.25	.25	☐☐☐☐☐
1190	4c Nursing..	.25	.25	☐☐☐☐☐
1962				
1191	4c New Mexico Statehood................	.25	.25	☐☐☐☐☐
1192	4c Arizona Statehood	.25	.25	☐☐☐☐☐
1193	4c Project Mercury.............................	.25	.25	☐☐☐☐☐
1194	4c Malaria Eradication	.25	.25	☐☐☐☐☐
1195	4c Charles Evans Hughes...................	.25	.25	☐☐☐☐☐
1196	4c Seattle World's Fair.......................	.25	.25	☐☐☐☐☐
1197	4c Louisiana Statehood	.25	.25	☐☐☐☐☐
1198	4c Homestead Act...............................	.25	.25	☐☐☐☐☐
1199	4c Girl Scouts	.25	.25	☐☐☐☐☐
1200	4c Senator Brien McMahon..............	.25	.25	☐☐☐☐☐
1201	4c Apprenticeship..............................	.25	.25	☐☐☐☐☐
1202	4c Sam Rayburn	.25	.25	☐☐☐☐☐
1203	4c Dag Hammarskjold, blk, brn and yel	.25	.25	☐☐☐☐☐
1204	4c Hammarskjold (1203), (yel inverted)	.25	.25	☐☐☐☐☐
1205	4c Christmas	.25	.25	☐☐☐☐☐
1206	4c Higher Education...........................	.25	.25	☐☐☐☐☐
1207	4c Winslow Homer.............................	.25	.25	☐☐☐☐☐
a.	Horiz. pair, imperf. btwn. and at right	6,750.		☐☐☐☐☐
1963-66				
1208	5c Flag, untagged	.25	.25	☐☐☐☐☐
a.	Tagged..	.25	.25	☐☐☐☐☐

1234

1235

1238

1236

1237

1239

1240

1241

1242

1245

1243

1244

1246

1247

1248

1249

1250

92

Scott No.	Description	Unused Value	Used Value	/ / / / / /
b.	Horiz. pair, imperf. btwn...............	*1,500.*		

1961-66, Perf. 11 x 10½

Scott No.	Description	Unused Value	Used Value	/ / / / / /
1209	1c Andrew Jackson, untagged............	.25	.25	
a.	Tagged..	.25	.25	
1213	5c George Washington, untagged	.25	.25	
a.	Booklet pane 5 + label	3.00	*2.00*	
b.	Tagged..	.50	.25	
c.	As "a," tagged	2.25	*1.50*	
d.	Horiz. pair, imperf. btwn..............	*1,500.*		
1214	8c General John J. Pershing	.25	.25	

Coil Stamps, Perf. 10 Vertically

Scott No.	Description	Unused Value	Used Value	/ / / / / /
1225	1c Jackson (1209), untagged..............	.40	.25	
a.	Tagged..	.40	.25	
1229	5c Washington (1213), untagged	1.50	.25	
a.	Tagged..	2.50	.25	
b.	Imperf., pair	*325.00*		

1963

Scott No.	Description	Unused Value	Used Value	/ / / / / /
1230	5c Carolina Charter	.25	.25	
1231	5c Food for Peace	.25	.25	
1232	5c West Virginia Statehood	.25	.25	
1233	5c Emancipation Proclamation	.25	.25	
1234	5c Alliance for Progress.....................	.25	.25	
1235	5c Cordell Hull	.25	.25	
1236	5c Eleanor Roosevelt..........................	.25	.25	
1237	5c Science	.25	.25	
1238	5c City Mail Delivery.........................	.25	.25	
1239	5c Red Cross Centenary.....................	.25	.25	
1240	5c Christmas, untagged......................	.25	.25	
a.	Tagged..	.65	.50	
b.	Horiz. pair, imperf. btwn..............	7,750.		
c.	Red missing (from perf. shift).......	—		
1241	5c John James Audubon.....................	.25	.25	

1964

Scott No.	Description	Unused Value	Used Value	/ / / / / /
1242	5c Sam Houston	.25	.25	
1243	5c Charles M. Russell	.25	.25	
1244	5c New York World's Fair..................	.25	.25	
1245	5c John Muir.......................................	.25	.25	
1246	5c John F. Kennedy	.25	.25	
1247	5c New Jersey Tercentenary...............	.25	.25	
1248	5c Nevada Statehood..........................	.25	.25	
1249	5c Register and Vote..........................	.25	.25	
1250	5c William Shakespeare	.25	.25	
1251	5c Doctors Mayo	.25	.25	
1252	5c American Music	.25	.25	
a.	Blue omitted	*800.00*		
b.	Blue missing (from perf. shift)	—		
1253	5c Homemakers..................................	.25	..20	
1254	5c Christmas - Holly, untagged..........	.25	.25	

1251

1252

1253

1254-1257

1258

1259

1260

1262

1263

1264

1261

1265

1266

Scott No.		Description	Unused Value	Used Value	/ / / / / /
a.		Tagged..................................	.65	.50	
b.		Printed on gummed side...............	1,850.		
1255	5c	Christmas - Mistletoe, untagged....	.25	.25	
a.		Tagged..................................	.65	.50	
1256	5c	Christmas - Poinsettia, untagged....	.25	.25	
a.		Tagged..................................	.65	.50	
1257	5c	Christmas - Conifer, untagged......	.25	.25	
a.		Tagged..................................	.65	.50	
b.		Block of 4, #1254-1257	1.00	1.00	
c.		Block of 4, #1254a-1257a.............	3.00	2.25	
1258	5c	Verrazano-Narrows Bridge	.25	.25	
1259	5c	Fine Arts..................................	.25	.25	
1260	5c	Amateur Radio.............................	.25	.25	
1965					
1261	5c	Battle of New Orleans..................	.25	.25	
1262	5c	Physical Fitness - Sokol	.25	.25	
1263	5c	Crusade against Cancer..............	.25	.25	
1264	5c	Winston Churchill........................	.25	.25	
1265	5c	Magna Carta	.25	.25	
1266	5c	International Cooperation Year......	.25	.25	
1267	5c	Salvation Army	.25	.25	
1268	5c	Dante Alighieri	.25	.25	
1269	5c	Herbert Hoover............................	.25	.25	
1270	5c	Robert Fulton...............................	.25	.25	
1271	5c	Florida Settlement	.25	.25	
a.		Yellow omitted............................	250.00		
1272	5c	Traffic Safety..............................	.25	.25	
1273	5c	John Singleton Copley	.25	.25	
1274	11c	Intl. Telecommunication Union.....	.35	.25	
1275	5c	Adlai Stevenson...........................	.25	.25	
1276	5c	Christmas, untagged.....................	.25	.25	
a.		Tagged..................................	.75	.25	
1965-78, Perf. 11 x 10½ , 10½ x11					
1278	1c	Thomas Jefferson, tagged.............	.25	.25	
a.		Booklet pane of 8	1.00	.75	
b.		Booklet pane of 4 + 2 labels	.80	.60	
c.		Untagged (Bureau precanceled)....	6.25	1.25	
1279	1¼c	Albert Gallatin.............................	.25	.25	
1280	2c	Frank Lloyd Wright, tagged..........	.25	.25	
a.		Booklet pane of 5 + label.............	1.25	.80	
b.		Untagged (Bureau precanceled)....	1.35	.40	
c.		Booklet pane of 6	1.00	.75	
1281	3c	Francis Parkman, tagged..............	.25	.25	
a.		Untagged (Bureau precanceled)....	3.00	.75	
1282	4c	Abraham Lincoln, untagged..........	.25	.25	
a.		Tagged..................................	.25	.25	
1283	5c	Washington, untagged	.25	.25	
a.		Tagged..................................	.25	.25	

1267

1268

1269

1271

1270

1272

1273

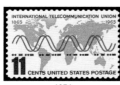
1274

1275

1276

1278

1279

1280

1281

1282

1283

1283B

1284

1285

Redrawn

96

Scott No.		Description	Unused Value	Used Value	/ / / / / /
1283B	5c	Washington, redrawn, tagged........	.25	.25	
d.		Untagged (Bureau precanceled)....	12.50	1.00	
1284	6c	Franklin D. Roosevelt, untagged...	.25	.25	
a.		Tagged.....................................	.25	.25	
b.		Booklet pane of 8	1.50	1.00	
c.		Booklet pane of 5 + label............	1.50	1.00	
d.		Horiz. pair, imperf. between..........	2,400.		
1285	8c	Albert Einstein, untagged..............	.25	.25	
a.		Tagged.....................................	.25	.25	
1286	10c	Andrew Jackson, tagged..............	.25	.25	
b.		Untagged (Bureau precanceled)....	57.50	1.75	
1286A	12c	Henry Ford, tagged......................	.25	.25	
c.		Untagged (Bureau precanceled)....	4.75	1.00	
1287	13c	John F. Kennedy, tagged...............	.30	.25	
a.		Untagged (Bureau precanceled)....	6.00	1.00	
1288	15c	Oliver Wendell Holmes,			
		magenta, tagged........................ .	.30	.25	
a.		Untagged (Bureau precanceled)....	.75	.75	
d.		Type II...	.55	.25	

Type II: The necktie does not touch coat at bottom.

Perf. 10

1288B	15c	Holmes (1288), magenta,			
		(from bklt. pane)........................	.35	.25	
c.		Booklet pane of 8	2.80	*1.75*	
e.		As "c," vert. imperf. btwn.	*1,750.*		

Perf. 11 x 10½, 10½ x 11

1289	20c	George C. Marshall, deep olive,			
		untagged	.40	.25	
a.		Tagged.....................................	.40	.25	
b.	20c	black olive, tagged........................	.50	.25	
1290	25c	Frederick Douglass, rose lake untagged	.55	.25	
a.		Tagged.....................................	.45	.25	
b.	25c	magenta....................................	*25.00*	—	
1291	30c	John Dewey, untagged	.65	.25	
a.		Tagged.....................................	.50	.25	
1292	40c	Thomas Paine, untagged	.80	.25	
a.		Tagged.....................................	.65	.25	
1293	50c	Lucy Stone, untagged	1.00	.25	
a.		Tagged.....................................	.80	.25	
1294	$1	Eugene O'Neill, untagged	2.25	.25	
a.		Tagged.....................................	1.65	.25	
1295	$5	John Bassett Moore, untagged	10.00	2.25	
a.		Tagged.....................................	8.50	2.00	

1966-81, Coil Stamps, Tagged, Perf. 10 Horizontally

1297	3c	Francis Parkman (1281)	.25	.25	
a.		Imperf., pair................................	*22.50*		
b.		Untagged (Bureau precanceled)....	.40	.25	
c.		As "b," imperf. pair	*6.00*	—	

1286

1286A

1287

1288

1289

1290

1291

1292

1293

1294

1295

1305

1306

1307

1308

1309

1310

1312

1313

1311

98

Scott No.	Description	Unused Value	Used Value	/ / / / / /
1298	6c Franklin D. Roosevelt (1284)	.25	.25	
a.	Imperf., pair	1,750.		

Tagged Perf. 10 Vertically

Scott No.	Description	Unused Value	Used Value	/ / / / / /
1299	1c Thomas Jefferson (1278)...............	.25	.25	
a.	Untagged (Bureau precanceled)....	8.00	1.75	
b.	Imperf., pair	22.50	—	
1303	4c Abraham Lincoln (1282)...............	.25	.25	
a.	Untagged (Bureau precanceled)....	8.75	.75	
b.	Imperf., pair	750.00		
1304	5c George Washington (1283)	.25	.25	
a.	Untagged (Bureau precanceled)....	6.50	.65	
b.	Imperf., pair	125.00		
e.	As "a," imperf. pair	275.00		
1304C	5c Washington, redrawn (1283B)	.25	.25	
d.	Imperf., pair	375.00		
1305	6c Franklin D. Roosevelt....................	.25	.25	
a.	Imperf., pair	60.00		
b.	Untagged (Bureau precanceled)....	20.00	1.00	
1305E	15c Oliver Wendell Holmes (1288), type I	.25	.25	
f.	Untagged (Bureau precanceled)....	32.50	—	
g.	Imperf., pair	20.00		
h.	Pair, imperf. btwn.	150.00		
i.	Type II...	1.50	.25	
j.	Imperf., pair, type II	65.00		
1305C	$1 Eugene O'Neill (1294)...................	3.25	.40	
d.	Imperf., pair	1,750.		

1966

Scott No.	Description	Unused Value	Used Value	/ / / / / /
1306	5c Migratory Bird Treaty	.25	.25	
1307	5c Humane Treatment of Animals	.25	.25	
1308	5c Indiana Statehood.........................	.25	.25	
1309	5c American Circus............................	.25	.25	
1310	5c SIPEX	.25	.25	
1311	5c SIPEX Souvenir Sheet, imperf.....	.25	.25	
1312	5c Bill of Rights	.25	.25	
1313	5c Polish Millennium	.25	.25	
1314	5c National Park Service, untagged ..	.25	.25	
a.	Tagged..	.35	.35	
1315	5c Marine Corps Reserve, untagged .	.25	.25	
a.	Tagged..	.40	.25	
b.	missing (from extraneous paper)..	16,000.		
1316	5c Women's Clubs, untagged	.25	.25	
a.	Tagged..	.40	.25	
1317	5c Johnny Appleseed, untagged	.25	.25	
a.	Tagged..	.40	.25	
1318	5c Beautification of America, untagged	.25	.25	
a.	Tagged..	.40	.25	
1319	5c Great River Road, untagged	.25	.25	
a.	Tagged..	.40	.25	
1320	5c Savings Bond, untagged	.25	.25	

1315

1317

1319

1320

1314

1316

1318

1321

1322

1324

1325

1326

1328

1323

1327

1329

1330

Scott No.	Description	Unused Value	Used Value	/ / / / /
a.	Tagged..	.40	.25	☐☐☐☐☐
b.	Red, dark blue & black missing (from extraneous paper).............	4,500.		☐☐☐☐☐
c.	Dark blue (engr.) missing (from extraneous paper).............	5,500.		☐☐☐☐☐
1321	5c Christmas, untagged.....................	.25	.25	☐☐☐☐☐
a.	Tagged..	.40	.25	☐☐☐☐☐
1322	5c Mary Cassatt, untagged...............	.25	.25	☐☐☐☐☐
a.	Tagged..	.40	.25	☐☐☐☐☐

1967

Scott No.	Description	Unused Value	Used Value	/ / / / /
1323	5c National Grange..........................	.25	.25	☐☐☐☐☐
1324	5c Canada Centenary.......................	.25	.25	☐☐☐☐☐
1325	5c Erie Canal	.25	.25	☐☐☐☐☐
1326	5c Search for Peace	.25	.25	☐☐☐☐☐
1327	5c Henry David Thoreau	.25	.25	☐☐☐☐☐
1328	5c Nebraska Statehood.....................	.25	.25	☐☐☐☐☐
1329	5c Voice of America	.25	.25	☐☐☐☐☐
1330	5c Davy Crockett..............................	.25	.25	☐☐☐☐☐
a.	Vert. pair, imperf. btwn.	7,000.		☐☐☐☐☐
b.	Green (engr.) missing (from a foldover)	—		☐☐☐☐☐
c.	Black & green (engr.) missing (from a foldover)...........	—		☐☐☐☐☐
1331	5c Astronaut	.50	.25	☐☐☐☐☐
1332	5c Gemini 4 Capsule	.50	.25	☐☐☐☐☐
b.	Pair, #1331-1332...........................	1.10	1.25	☐☐☐☐☐
1333	5c Urban Planning............................	.25	.25	☐☐☐☐☐
1334	5c Finnish Independence	.25	.25	☐☐☐☐☐
1335	5c Thomas Eakins	.25	.25	☐☐☐☐☐
1336	5c Christmas	.25	.25	☐☐☐☐☐
1337	5c Mississippi Statehood..................	.25	.25	☐☐☐☐☐

1968-71, Perf. 11

Scott No.	Description	Unused Value	Used Value	/ / / / /
1338	6c Flag	.25	.25	☐☐☐☐☐
k.	Vert. pair, imperf. btwn.	325.00	175.00	☐☐☐☐☐
s.	Red missing (from a foldover)	—		☐☐☐☐☐
u.	Vert. pair, imperf horiz.	475.00	—	☐☐☐☐☐
v.	All color omitted	—		☐☐☐☐☐

Coil Stamp, Perf. 10 Vertically

Scott No.	Description	Unused Value	Used Value	/ / / / /
1338A	6c Flag (1338).................................	.25	.25	☐☐☐☐☐
b.	Imperf., pair..................................	400.00		☐☐☐☐☐

Perf. 11x10½

Scott No.	Description	Unused Value	Used Value	/ / / / /
1338D	6c Flag (1338).................................	.25	.25	☐☐☐☐☐
e.	Horiz. pair, imperf. btwn.	125.00		☐☐☐☐☐
1338F	8c Flag (1338), red denomination	.25	.25	☐☐☐☐☐
i.	Vert. pair, imperf...........................	35.00		☐☐☐☐☐
j.	Horiz. pair, imperf. btwn.	45.00		☐☐☐☐☐
p.	Slate green omitted........................	325.00		☐☐☐☐☐

1331-1332

1333

1334

1336

1339

1335

1337

1338

1341

1342

1340

1343

1344

Scott No.	Description	Unused Value	Used Value	/ / / / / /
t.	Horiz. pair, imperf. vertically	—		

Coil Stamp, Perf. 10 Vertically

1338G	8c Flag (1338), red denomination	.30	.25	
h.	Imperf., pair	45.00		

1968

1339	6c Illinois Statehood.........................	.25	.25	
1340	6c HemisFair '68	.25	.25	
a.	White omitted	925.00		
1341	$1 Airlift...	2.00	1.25	
1342	6c Support our Youth	.25	.25	
1343	6c Law and Order..............................	.25	.25	
1344	6c Register and Vote.........................	.25	.25	
1345	6c Fort Moultrie Flag	.40	.25	
1346	6c Fort McHenry Flag	.40	.25	
1347	6c Washington's Cruisers Flag	.30	.25	
1348	6c Bennington Flag	.30	.25	
1349	6c Rhode Island Flag.........................	.30	.25	
1350	6c First Stars and Stripes..................	.30	.25	
1351	6c Bunker Hill Flag	.30	.25	
1352	6c Grand Union Flag.........................	.30	.25	
1353	6c Philadelphia Light Horse Flag......	.30	.25	
1354	6c First Navy Jack	.30	.25	
a.	Strip of 10, #1345-1354	3.25	3.25	
c.	As "a," imperf.............................	4,500.		
1355	6c Walt Disney	.40	.25	
a.	Ocher (Walt Disney, 6c, etc.) omitted	400.00	—	
b.	Vert. pair, imperf. horiz.	575.00		
c.	Imperf., pair................................	425.00		
d.	Black omitted...............................	1,850.		
e.	Horiz. pair, imperf. btwn.	3,500.		
f.	Blue omitted	1,850.		
1356	6c Father Marquette..........................	.25	.25	
1357	6c Daniel Boone	.25	.25	
1358	6c Arkansas River Navigation...........	.25	.25	
1359	6c Leif Erikson	.25	.25	
1360	6c Cherokee Strip	.25	.25	
1361	6c John Trumbull..............................	.25	.25	
b.	missing (from a foldover).............	11,000.	—	
1362	6c Waterfowl Conservation	.25	.25	
a.	Vert. pair, imperf. btwn.	275.00	—	
b.	Red & dark blue omitted	475.00		
c.	Red omitted		1,500.	
1363	6c Christmas, tagged	.25	.25	
a.	Untagged......................................	.25	.25	
b.	Imperf., pair, tagged	175.00		
c.	Light yellow omitted	50.00	—	
d.	Imperf., pair, untagged	250.00		
1364	6c Chief Joseph	.25	.25	

1345

1346

1347

1348

1349

1350

1351

1352

1353

1354

1356

1357

1358

1355

1359

1361

1363

1360

1362

1364

1365-1368

1369

1370

1371

1373

1372

1374

1375

1376-1379

1380

1381

1382

1383

1384

1385

1387-1390

1386

1391

1392

106

Scott No.	Description	Unused Value	Used Value	/ / / / / /
1969				
1365	6c Beautification - Cities	.25	.25	
1366	6c Beautification - Parks	.25	.25	
1367	6c Beautification - Highways..........	.25	.25	
1368	6c Beautification - Streets..............	.25	.25	
a.	Block of 4, #1365-1368..............	1.00	1.25	
1369	6c American Legion	.25	.25	
1370	6c Grandma Moses.........................	.25	.25	
a.	Horiz. pair, imperf. btwn.	165.00	—	
b.	Black and Prussian blue omitted..	575.00		
1371	6c Apollo 8.......................................	.25	.25	
1372	6c W.C. Handy.................................	.25	.25	
1373	6c California Settlement..................	.25	.25	
b.	Red (engr.) missing (from perf. shift).................	400.00		
1374	6c John Wesley Powell	.25	.25	
1375	6c Alabama Statehood.....................	.25	.25	
1376	6c Douglas Fir	.35	.25	
1377	6c Lady's Slipper	.35	.25	
1378	6c Ocotillo	.35	.25	
1379	6c Franklinia...................................	.35	.25	
a.	Block of 4, #1376-1379..............	1.40	1.75	
1380	6c Dartmouth College Case	.25	.25	
1381	6c Professional Baseball..................	.50	.25	
a.	Black (1869-1969, United States, 6c, Professional Baseball) omitted...	800.00		
1382	6c Intercollegiate Football................	.25	.25	
a.	Vert. pair, imperf. horizontally	—		
1383	6c Dwight D. Eisenhower.................	.25	.25	
1384	6c Christmas	.25	.25	
	Precanceled	.60	.25	
b.	Imperf., pair	800.00		
c.	Light green omitted	25.00		
d.	Lt green, red & yellow omitted	700.00	—	
e.	Yellow omitted..............................	2,000.		
g.	Red & yellow omitted	2,750.		
h.	Light green & yellow omitted	—		
i.	Light green & red omitted...........	—		
j.	Vert. pair, top stamp Baltimore precancel, bottom stamp precancel missing (from foldover)..........................	—		
k.	Baltimore precancel printed on gum side	—		
l.	Baltimore precancel, vert. pair, top stamp missing precancel, bottom stamp precancel printed inverted on reverse (from foldover)..........................	—		
m.	Inverted Baltimore precancel........	700.00		
n.	Baltimore precancel printed inverted on reverse (FO)..........................	150.00		

1393

1393D

1394

1396

1397

1398

1399

1400

1405

1406

1407

1408

1409

1410-1413

Scott No.	Description	Unused Value	Used Value	/ / / / / /
p.	Double impression of New Haven precancel....................................	—		
1385	6c Hope for the Crippled..............	.25	.25	
1386	6c William M. Harnett	.25	.25	
a.	Red (engr.) missing (from color misregistration).........................	—		

1970

Scott No.	Description	Unused Value	Used Value	/ / / / / /
1387	6c American Bald Eagle..................	.25	.25	
1388	6c African Elephant Herd..............	.25	.25	
1389	6c Haida Ceremonial Canoe...........	.25	.25	
1390	6c Age of Reptiles.........................	.25	.25	
a.	Block of 4, #1387-1390...............	1.00	1.00	
1391	6c Maine Statehood.......................	.25	.25	
1392	6c Wildlife Conservation...............	.25	.25	

1970-74, Tagged, Perf. 11x10½ , 10½ x11, 11 (#1394)

Scott No.	Description	Unused Value	Used Value	/ / / / / /
1393	6c Dwight D. Eisenhower, untagged .	.25	.25	
a.	Booklet pane of 8	2.00	2.00	
b.	Booklet pane of 5 + label............	1.50	1.50	
c.	Untagged (Bureau precanceled) ...	12.75	3.00	
1393D	7c Benjamin Franklin, tagged	.25	.25	
e.	Untagged (Bureau precanceled) ...	4.25	1.00	
1394	8c Eisenhower................................	.25	.25	
b.	Red missing (from perf. shift)......	*150.00*		
c.	Red missing (from perf. shift)......	*1,000.*		
d.	Red, blue missing (from perf. shift)	—		
e.	Red, blue missing (from foldover)	*1,000.*		
1395	8c Eisenhower (1393), deep claret (from bklt. pane).......................	.25	.25	
a.	Booklet pane of 8	2.00	2.00	
b.	Booklet pane of 6	1.50	1.50	
c.	Booklet pane of 4 + 2 labels	1.65	1.10	
d.	Booklet pane of 7 + label............	1.90	1.90	
e.	Vert. pair, imperf btwn.	*600.00*		
1396	8c Postal Service Emblem................	.25	.25	
1397	14c Fiorello LaGuardia, tagged..........	.25	.25	
a.	Untagged (Bureau precanceled) ...	*140.00*	17.50	
1398	16c Ernie Pyle, tagged.....................	.35	.25	
a.	Untagged (Bureau precanceled) ...	22.50	5.00	
1399	18c Dr. Elizabeth Blackwell...............	.35	.25	
1400	21c Amadeo P. Giannini.....................	.40	.25	

Coil Stamps, Perf. 10 Vertically

Scott No.	Description	Unused Value	Used Value	/ / / / / /
1401	6c Eisenhower (1393), dk bl gray, tagged	.25	.25	
a.	Untagged (Bureau precanceled) ...	19.50	3.00	
b.	Imperf., pair..................................	*1,750.*		
1402	8c Eisenhower (1393), dp claret, tagged	.25	.25	
a.	Imperf., pair.................................	37.50		
b.	Untagged (Bureau precanceled) ...	6.75	.75	

1415-1418

1414

1419

1420

1421-1422

1423

1424

1425

1426

Scott No.	Description	Unused Value	Used Value	/ / / / / /
c.	Pair, imperf. btwn.	6,250.		
1970				
1405	6c Edgar Lee Masters....................	.25	.25	
1406	6c Woman Suffrage	.25	.25	
1407	6c South Carolina.........................	.25	.25	
1408	6c Stone Mountain Memorial...........	.25	.25	
1409	6c Fort Snelling	.25	.25	
1410	6c Save Our Soil...........................	.25	.25	
1411	6c Save Our Cities.........................	.25	.25	
1412	6c Save Our Water.........................	.25	.25	
1413	6c Save Our Air	.25	.25	
a.	Block of 4, #1410-1413...............	1.10	1.25	
1414	6c Christmas - Religious	.25	.25	
a.	Precanceled...................................	.25	.25	
b.	Black omitted................................	450.00		
c.	As "a," blue omitted	1,450.		
1415	6c Christmas - Locomotive	.30	.25	
a.	Precanceled...................................	.75	.25	
b.	Black omitted................................	2,500.		
1416	6c Christmas - Toy Horse	.30	.25	
a.	Precanceled...................................	.75	.25	
b.	Black omitted................................	2,500.		
c.	Imperf., pair (#1416, 1418)		2,500.	
1417	6c Christmas - Tricycle....................	.30	.25	
a.	Precanceled...................................	.75	.25	
b.	Black omitted................................	2,500.		
1418	6c Christmas - Doll Carriage	.30	.25	
a.	Precanceled...................................	.75	.25	
b.	Block of 4, #1415-1418................	1.25	1.40	
c.	As "b," precanceled	3.25	3.50	
d.	Black omitted................................	2,500.		
e.	As "b," black omitted.	10,000.		
1419	6c United Nations............................	.25	.25	
1420	6c Landing of the Pilgrims...............	.25	.25	
a.	Orange & yellow omitted	625.00		
1421	6c Disabled American Veterans.........	.25	.25	
1422	6c Servicemen	.25	.25	
a.	Pair, #1421-1422...........................	.30	.30	
1971				
1423	6c Wool Industry	.25	.25	
b.	Teal blue ("United States") missing (from a color misregistration)	350.00		
1424	6c General Douglas MacArthur	.25	.25	
a.	Red missing (from perf. shift)......	—		
c.	Blue missing (from perf. shift).....	—		
1425	6c Blood Donors.............................	.25	.25	
1426	8c Missouri Statehood......................	.25	.25	
1427	8c Trout	.25	.25	

1427-1430

1431

1432

1433

1434-1435

1436

1437

1438

1439

Scott No.	Description	Unused Value	Used Value	/ / / / / /
a.	red omitted		1,250.	
b.	Green (engr.) omitted.	—		
1428	8c Alligator	.25	.25	
1429	8c Polar Bear	.25	.25	
1430	8c California Condor	.25	.25	
a.	Block of 4, #1427-1430	1.00	1.00	
b.	As "a," lt grn & dk grn omitted from #1427-1428	4,500.		
c.	As "a," red omitted from #1427, 1429-1430	3,500.		
1431	8c Antarctic Treaty	.25	.25	
b.	Both colors missing (from extraneous paper)	500.00		
1432	8c Bicentennial Emblem	.25	.25	
a.	Gray & black missing (from extraneous paper)	500.00		
b.	Gray ("U.S. Postage 8c") missing (from extraneous paper)	750.00		
1433	8c John Sloan	.25	.25	
b.	Red engr. ("John Sloan" and "8") missing (from a color misregistration)	950.00		
1434	8c Lunar Module	.25	.25	
1435	8c Lunar Rover	.30	.25	
b.	Pair, #1434-1435	.50	.50	
d.	As "b," blue & red (litho.) omitted	1,00.		
1436	8c Emily Dickinson	.25	.25	
a.	Black & olive (engr.) omitted	525.00		
b.	Pale rose missing (from extraneous paper)	6,000.		
c.	Red omitted	—		
1437	8c San Juan	.25	.25	
b.	Dark brown (engr.) omitted	—		
1438	8c Prevent Drug Abuse	.25	.25	
1439	8c CARE	.25	.25	
a.	Black omitted	1,750.		
1440	8c Decatur House	.25	.25	
1441	8c Whaler Charles W. Morgan	.25	.25	
1442	8c Cable Car	.25	.25	
1443	8c San Xavier del Bac Mission	.25	.25	
a.	Block of 4, #1440-1443	1.00	1.00	
b.	As "a," black brown omitted	1,250.		
c.	As "a," ocher omitted	3,000.		
1444	8c Christmas - Religious	.25	.25	
a.	Gold omitted	400.00		
1445	8c Christmas - Partridge	.25	.25	
1972				
1446	8c Sidney Lanier	.25	.25	
1447	8c Peace Corps	.25	.25	

1440-1443

1444

1445

1446

1447

1452

1454

1448-1451

1453

1455   1456-1459

1460

1461

1462

1463

1464-1467

1468   1469

1470   1471   1472

1473   1474   1475

1476   1477

1478   1479

116

Scott No.	Description	Unused Value	Used Value	/ / / / / /
1448	2c Cape Hatteras - Ship	.25	.25	
1449	2c Cape Hatteras - Lighthouse	.25	.25	
1450	2c Cape Hatteras - Three Gulls	.25	.25	
1451	2c Cape Hatteras - Dunes	.25	.25	
a.	Block of 4, #1448-1451	.50	.50	
b.	As "a," black (litho.) omitted	1,400.		
1452	6c Wolf Trap Farm	.25	.25	
1453	8c Yellowstone	.25	.25	
1454	15c Mt. McKinley	.30	.25	
b.	Yellow omitted	3,500.		
1455	8c Family Planning	.25	.25	
a.	Yellow omitted	400.00		
c.	Dark brown missing (from foldover)	9,000.		
1456	8c Glass Blower	.25	.25	
1457	8c Silversmith	.25	.25	
1458	8c Wigmaker	.25	.25	
1459	8c Hatter	.25	.25	
a.	Block of 4, #1456-1459	1.00	1.00	
1460	6c Olympics - Bicycling	.25	.25	
1461	8c Olympics - Bobsledding	.25	.25	
1462	15c Olympics - Running	.30	.25	
1463	8c Parent Teacher Association	.25	.25	
1464	8c Fur Seal	.25	.25	
1465	8c Cardinal	.25	.25	
1466	8c Brown Pelican	.25	.25	
1467	8c Bighorn Sheep	.25	.25	
a.	Block of 4, #1464-1467	1.00	1.00	
b.	As "a," brown omitted	3,750.		
c.	As "a," green & blue omitted	3,750.		
d.	As "a," red & brown omitted	4,000.		
1468	8c Mail Order Business	.25	.25	
1469	8c Osteopathic Medicine	.25	.25	
1470	8c Tom Sawyer	.25	.25	
a.	Horiz. pair, imperf. btwn.	7,250.		
b.	Red & black (engr.) omitted	1,250.		
c.	Yellow & tan (litho.) omitted	1,750.		
e.	Red (engr. 8c) missing (from color misregistration)	1,000.		
1471	8c Christmas - Religious	.25	.25	
a.	Pink omitted	120.00		
b.	Black omitted	3,250.		
1472	8c Christmas - Santa Claus	.25	.25	
1473	8c Pharmacy	.25	.25	
a.	Blue & orange omitted	675.00		
b.	Blue omitted	1,750.		
c.	Orange omitted	1,750.		
e.	Vertical pair, imperf. horiz.	2,100.		
1474	8c Stamp Collecting	.25	.25	

1480-1483

1484

1485

1486

1487

1488

1489-1493

1494-1498

1499

1500

1501

1502

1503

1507

1508

1504

1505

1506

1509

1510

1511

1518

1525

1526

1527

1528

1529

Scott No.	Description	Unused Value	Used Value	/ / / / / /
a.	Black (litho.) omitted	*475.00*		
1973				
1475	8c Love	.25	.25	
1476	8c Printer	.25	.25	
1477	8c Posting a Broadside	.25	.25	
1478	8c Postrider.....................................	.25	.25	
a.	Red missing (from a color misregistration)	—		
1479	8c Drummer.....................................	.25	.25	
1480	8c Boston Tea Party - upper left........	.25	.25	
1481	8c Boston Tea Party - upper right......	.25	.25	
1482	8c Boston Tea Party - lower left	.25	.25	
1483	8c Boston Tea Party - lower right	.25	.25	
a.	Block of 4, #1480-1483...............	1.00	1.00	
b.	As "a," black (engr.) omitted........	*1,100.*		
c.	As "a," black (litho.) omitted........	*1,000.*		
1484	8c George Gershwin..........................	.25	.25	
a.	Vert. pair, imperf. horiz.	*175.00*		
1485	8c Robinson Jeffers	.25	.25	
a.	Vert. pair, imperf. horiz.	*200.00*		
1486	8c Henry Ossawa Tanner..................	.25	.25	
1487	8c Willa Cather................................	.25	.25	
a.	Vert. pair, imperf. horiz.	*225.00*		
1488	8c Nicolaus Copernicus....................	.25	.25	
a.	Orange omitted	*650.00*		
b.	Black (engraved) omitted	*875.00*		
1489	8c Stamp Counter	.25	.25	
1490	8c Mail Collection............................	.25	.25	
1491	8c Letters on Conveyor Belt.............	.25	.25	
1492	8c Parcel Post Sorting......................	.25	.25	
1493	8c Mail Canceling	.25	.25	
1494	8c Manual Letter Routing	.25	.25	
1495	8c Electronic Letter Routing	.25	.25	
1496	8c Loading Mail on Truck................	.25	.25	
1497	8c Mailman......................................	.25	.25	
1498	8c Rural Mail Delivery......................	.25	.25	
a.	Strip of 10, #1489-1498	2.50	2.50	
1499	8c Harry S Truman...........................	.25	.25	
1500	6c Spark Coil and Spark Gap...........	.25	.25	
1501	8c Transistors...................................	.25	.25	
a.	Black (inscriptions & U.S. 8c) omitted	*350.00*		
b.	Tan (background) & lilac omitted	*850.00*		
1502	15c Microphone, Tubes and Speaker...	.30	.25	
a.	Black (inscriptions & U.S. 15c) omitted	*1,250.*		
1503	15c Lyndon B. Johnson	.25	.25	
a.	Horiz. pair, imperf. vert.................	*250.00*		
1973-74				
1504	8c Angus Cattle	.25	.25	
a.	Green & red brown omitted..........	*750.00*		

121

1530-1537

1538-1541

Scott No.		Description	Unused Value	Used Value	/ / / / / /
b.		Vert. pair, imperf. between		5,000.	
1505	10c	Chautauqua	.25	.25	
a.		Black (litho.) omitted		1,750.	
1506	10c	Kansas Hard Winter Wheat	.25	.25	
a.		Black & blue (engr.) omitted........	650.00		

1973

1507	8c	Christmas - Religious	.25	.25	
1508	8c	Christmas - Tree	.25	.25	
a.		Vert. pair, imperf. btwn.	225.00		

1973-74, Tagged, Perf. 11x10½

1509	10c	Crossed Flags	.25	.25	
a.		Horiz. pair, imperf. btwn	40.00	—	
b.		Blue omitted	160.00	—	
c.		Vert. pair, imperf.	750.00		
d.		Horiz. pair, imperf. vert.	900.00		
f.		Vert. pair, imperf. btwn.	—		
1510	10c	Jefferson Memorial, tagged	.25	.25	
a.		Untagged (Bureau precanceled) ...	4.00	1.00	
b.		Booklet pane of 5 + label	1.65	1.25	
c.		Booklet pane of 8	2.00	2.00	
d.		Booklet pane of 6	5.25	1.75	
e.		Vert. pair, imperf. horiz.	375.00		
f.		Vert. pair, imperf. btwn., in #1510c with miscut or with folder..........	475.00		
i.		As "b," double booklet pane of 10 + stamps with 2 horiz. pairs imperf. btwn. plus stamp and label imperf. btwn. (from foldover)................	1,500.		
1511	10c	Zip Code	.25	.25	
a.		Yellow omitted.............................	45.00		

Coil Stamps, Perf. 10 Vertically

1518	6.3c	Liberty Bell, tagged.....................	.25	.25	
a.		Untagged (Bureau precanceled) ...	.35	.25	
b.		Imperf., pair	130.00		
c.		As "a," imperf. pair......................	80.00		
1519	10c	Crossed Flags (1509)...................	.25	.25	
a.		Imperf., pair	35.00		
1520	10c	Jefferson Memorial (1510), tagged	.25	.25	
a.		Untagged (Bureau precanceled) ...	5.50	1.25	
b.		Imperf., pair	30.00		

1974

1525	10c	Veterans of Foreign Wars.............	.25	.25	
b.		Blue missing (from perf. shift).....	—		
1526	10c	Robert Frost	.25	.25	
1527	10c	Expo '74 World's Fair...................	.25	.25	
1528	10c	Horse Racing	.25	.25	
a.		Blue (Horse Racing) omitted........	800.00		

1543-1546

1542

1547

1548

1549

1550

1553

1554

1551

1552

1555

124

Scott No.	Description	Unused Value	Used Value	/ / / / / /
b.	Red (U.S. postage 10 cents) omitted	*2,250.*		
1529	10c Skylab	.25	.25	
a.	Vert. pair, imperf. btwn.	—		
c.	Vert. pair, imperf. horiz.	—		
1530	10c Raphael	.25	.25	
1531	10c Hokusai	.25	.25	
1532	10c Peto	.25	.25	
1533	10c Liotard	.25	.25	
1534	10c Terborch	.25	.25	
1535	10c Chardin	.25	.25	
1536	10c Gainsborough	.25	.25	
1537	10c Goya	.25	.25	
a.	Block or strip of 8, #1530-1537	2.00	2.00	
b.	As "a" (block), imperf. vert.	*3,500.*		
1538	10c Petrified Wood	.25	.25	
a.	Light blue & yellow omitted	—		
1539	10c Tourmaline	.25	.25	
a.	Light blue omitted	—		
b.	Black & purple omitted	—		
1540	10c Amethyst	.25	.25	
a.	Light blue & yellow omitted	—		
1541	10c Rhodochrosite	.25	.25	
a.	Block or strip of 4, #1538-1541	1.00	1.00	
b.	As "a," lt blue & yellow omitted	*1,500.*	—	
c.	Light blue omitted	—		
d.	Black & red omitted	—		
1542	10c Kentucky Settlement	.25	.25	
a.	Dull black (litho.) omitted	*575.00*		
b.	Green (engr. & litho.), black (engr. & litho.) & blue missing (from extraneous paper)	*3,000.*		
c.	Green (engr.) missing (from extraneous paper)	*3,750.*		
d.	Green (engr.) & black (litho) missing (from extraneous paper)	—		
f.	Blue (litho.) omitted	—		
1543	10c Carpenter's Hall	.25	.25	
1544	10c "We ask but for peace . . . "	.25	.25	
1545	10c "Deriving their just powers . . . ".	.25	.25	
1546	10c Independence Hall	.25	.25	
a.	Block of 4, #1543-1546	1.00	1.00	
1547	10c Energy Conservation	.25	.25	
a.	Blue & orange omitted	*750.00*		
b.	Orange & green omitted	*500.00*		
c.	Green omitted	*700.00*		
1548	10c Legend of Sleepy Hollow	.25	.25	
1549	10c Retarded Children	.25	.25	
1550	10c Christmas - Angel	.25	.25	

1556

1557

1559

1560

1561

1562

1558

1563

1564

Scott No.	Description	Unused Value	Used Value	/ / / / / /
1551	10c Christmas - Currier & Ives	.25	.25	
a.	Buff omitted	12.50		
1552	10c Christmas - Dove	.25	.25	
1975				
1553	10c Benjamin West	.25	.25	
1554	10c Paul Laurence Dunbar	.25	.25	
a.	Imperf., pair	*1,100.*		
1555	10c D.W. Griffith	.25	.25	
a.	Brown (engr.) omitted	575.00		
1556	10c Pioneer 10	.25	.25	
a.	Red & dark yellow omitted	*1,000.*		
b.	Dark blue (engr.) omitted	675.00		
d.	Dark yellow omitted	—		
1557	10c Mariner 10	.25	.25	
a.	Red omitted	375.00	—	
b.	Ultra & bister omitted	*1,575.*		
d.	Red missing (from perf. shift)	575.00		
1558	10c Collective Bargaining	.25	.25	
1559	8c Sybil Ludington	.25	.25	
a.	Back inscription omitted	175.00		
1560	10c Salem Poor	.25	.25	
a.	Back inscription omitted	175.00		
1561	10c Haym Salomon	.25	.25	
a.	Back inscription omitted	175.00		
1562	18c Peter Francisco	.35	.25	
1563	10c Battle of Lexington & Concord	.25	.25	
a.	Vert. pair, imperf. horiz.	400.00		
1564	10c Battle of Bunker Hill	.25	.25	
1565	10c Continental Army	.25	.25	
1566	10c Continental Navy	.25	.25	
1567	10c Continental Marines	.25	.25	
1568	10c American Militia	.25	.25	
a.	Block of 4, #1565-1568	1.00	1.00	
1569	10c Apollo and Soyuz Linked	.25	.25	
1570	10c Apollo and Soyuz Separated	.25	.25	
a.	Pair, #1569-1570	.50	.50	
c.	As "a," vert. pair, imperf. horiz.	*2,100.*		
d.	As "a," yellow omitted	1,000.		
1571	10c International Women's Year	.25	.25	
1572	10c Stagecoach & Truck	.25	.25	
1573	10c Locomotives	.25	.25	
1574	10c Airplanes	.25	.25	
1575	10c Satellites	.25	.25	
a.	Block of 4, #1572-1575	1.00	1.00	
b.	As "a," red (10c) omitted	—		
1576	10c World Peace Through Law	.25	.25	
b.	Horiz. pair, imperf. vert.	*7,500.*		
c.	All colors omitted	—		

1565-1568

1569-1570

1571

1576

1572-1575

1577-1578

1579   1580

1581   1582   1584   1585

RIGHT OF PEOPLE PEACEABLY TO ASSEMBLE · USA 9c
1591

PEOPLE'S RIGHT TO PETITION FOR REDRESS · USA 10c
1592

FREEDOM OF THE PRESS · USA 11c
1593

FREEDOM OF CONSCIENCE—AN AMERICAN RIGHT · USA 12c
1594

PROCLAIM LIBERTY THROUGHOUT ALL THE LAND · USA 13c
1595

ONE NATION INDIVISIBLE · E PLURIBUS UNUM · USA 13c
1596

THE LAND OF THE FREE · THE HOME OF THE BRAVE · USA 15c
1597

I LIFT MY LAMP BESIDE THE GOLDEN DOOR · USA 16c
1599

MIDNIGHT RIDE—ONE IF BY LAND, TWO IF BY SEA · USA 24c
1603

REMOTE OUTPOST—NEW NATION BUILDING WESTWARD · USA 28c
1604

LONELY BEACON—PROTECTING THOSE UPON THE SEA · USA 29c
1605

AMERICAN SCHOOLS—LAYING FUTURE FOUNDATIONS · USA 30c
1606

AMERICA'S LIGHT SUSTAINED BY LOVE OF LIBERTY · USA 50c
1608

AMERICA'S LIGHT FUELED BY TRUTH AND REASON · 1.00 USA
1610

AMERICA'S LIGHT WILL SHINE OVER ALL THE LAND · 2.00
1611

AMERICA'S LIGHT LEADS FREE GENERATIONS ONWARD · 5.00 USA
1612

LISTEN WITH LOVE TO THE MUSIC OF THE LAND · USA 3.1c AUTH NON-PROFIT ORG.
1613

MARCHING IN STEP TO THE MUSIC OF THE UNION · USA 7.7c BULK RATE
1614

BEAT THE DRUM FOR LIBERTY AND THE SPIRIT OF '76 · USA 7.9c BULK RATE
1615

PEACE UNITES A NATION LIKE HARMONY IN MUSIC · USA 8.4c BULK RATE
1615C

United States 13c
1622

USA 13c
1623

130

Scott No.	Description	Unused Value	Used Value	/ / / / / /
1577	10c Banking...	.25	.25	
1578	10c Commerce..	.25	.25	
a.	Pair, #1577-1578..............................	.50	.50	
b.	As "a," brown & blue (litho.) omitted	2,000.		
c.	As "a," brown, blue & yellow (litho.) omitted.............................	2,500.		
1579	(10c) Christmas - Religious	.25	.25	
a.	Imperf., pair.....................................	90.00		
1580	(10c) Christmas Card, by Louis Prang, perf. 11	.25	.25	
a.	Imperf., pair.....................................	90.00		
c.	Perf. 10.9..	.25	.25	
1580B	(10c) Christmas Card, by Louis Prang, 1878, perf. 10.5 x 11.3 (1580) ..	.65	.25	

1975-81, Perf. 11x10½

Scott No.	Description	Unused Value	Used Value	/ / / / / /
1581	1c Inkwell & Quill, tagged...............	.25	.25	
a.	Untagged (Bureau precanceled) ...	4.50	1.50	
1582	2c Speaker's Stand, red brn, *grnish*, tagged	.25	.25	
a.	Untagged (Bureau precanceled) ...	4.50	1.50	
b.	Cream paper....................................	.25	.25	
1584	3c Ballot Box, tagged.......................	.25	.25	
a.	Untagged (Bureau precanceled) ...	.75	.50	
1585	4c Books, tagged	.25	.25	
a.	Untagged (Bureau precanceled) ...	1.00	.75	
1590	9c Capitol, slate green (from bklt. pane #1623a), perf. 11 x 10½	.45	.25	
1590A	9c Capitol (from bklt. pane #1623Bc), perf. 10 x 9¾ (1590)...	14.00	14.00	
1591	9c Capitol, slate green, *gray*.............	.25	.25	
a.	Untagged (Bureau precanceled) ...	1.75	1.00	
1592	10c Justice, tagged.............................	.25	.25	
a.	Untagged (Bureau precanceled) ...	9.50	5.00	
1593	11c Printing Press..............................	.25	.25	
1594	12c Torch...	.25	.25	
1595	13c Liberty Bell (from bklt. pane)......	.30	.25	
a.	Booklet pane of 6	2.25	1.50	
b.	Booklet pane of 7 + label	2.25	1.50	
c.	Booklet pane of 8	2.25	1.50	
d.	Booklet pane of 5 + label	1.75	1.25	
e.	Vert. pair, imperf. btwn.	1,250.		
g.	Horiz. pair, imperf. btwn., in #1595d with foldover	—		
h.	As "a," miscut and inserted upside-down into bklt. cover, imperf. below bottom stamps and with "tab" at bottom.	—		

Perf. 11

Scott No.	Description	Unused Value	Used Value	/ / / / / /
1596	13c Eagle & Shield.............................	.25	.25	
a.	Imperf., pair....................................	40.00	—	

Scott No.	Description	Unused Value	Used Value	/ / / / / /
b.	Yellow omitted...............................	*115.00*		
1597	15c Flag...	.30	.25	
a.	Vert. pair, imperf............................	*17.50*		
b.	Gray omitted....................................	*350.00*		
c.	Vert. strip of 3, imperf. btwn. & at top or bottom......................	*375.00*		

Perf. 11x10½

1598	15c Flag (1597, from bklt. pane).........	.40	.25	
a.	Booklet pane of 8	4.25	*1.50*	
1599	16c Statue of Liberty............................	.35	.25	
1603	24c Old North Church, Boston	.50	.25	
1604	28c Fort Nisqually, Washington	.55	.25	
1605	29c Sandy Hook Lighthouse, N.J.	.60	.25	
1606	30c School, North Dakota...................	.55	.25	

Perf. 11

1608	50c Iron "Betty" Lamp.......................	.85	.25	
a.	Black omitted................................	*250.00*		
b.	Vert. pair, imperf. horiz.	*1,500.*		
1610	$1 Rush Lamp & Candle Holder.......	2.00	.25	
a.	Brown (engraved) omitted.............	*225.00*		
b.	Tan, orange & yellow omitted......	*250.00*		
c.	Brown (engraved) inverted	*20,000.*		
1611	$2 Kerosene Lamp.............................	3.75	.75	
1612	$5 Railroad Lantern..........................	8.50	1.75	

Coil Stamps, Perf. 10 Vertically, Tagged

1613	3.1c Guitar..	.25	.25	
a.	Untagged (Bureau precanceled) ...	.35	.35	
b.	Imperf., pair..................................	*1,200.*		
1614	7.7c Saxhorns	.25	.25	
a.	Untagged (Bureau precanceled) ...	.40	.30	
b.	As "a," imperf., pair.....................	*1,400.*		
1615	7.9c Drum...	.25	.25	
a.	Untagged (Bureau precanceled) ...	.40	.40	
b.	Imperf., pair..................................	*525.00*		
1615C	8.4c Piano	.25	.25	
d.	Untagged (Bureau precanceled) ...	.50	.40	
e.	As "d," pair, imperf. btwn............	45.00		
f.	As "d," imperf., pair.....................	15.00		
1616	9c Capitol (1590), slate grn, *gray*	.25	.25	
a.	Imperf., pair..................................	*135.00*		
b.	Untagged (Bureau precanceled) ...	1.15	.75	
c.	As "b," imperf., pair	*650.00*		
1617	10c Justice (1592)..............................	.25	.25	
a.	Untagged (Bureau precanceled) ...	42.50	1.35	
b.	Imperf., pair..................................	60.00		
c.	As "a," imperf., pair, dull gum	*3,500.*		
1618	13c Liberty Bell (1595)......................	.25	.25	

Scott No.	Description	Unused Value	Used Value	/ / / / / /
a.	Untagged (Bureau precanceled) ...	5.75	.75	
b.	Imperf., pair................................	22.50		
g.	Vertical pair, imperf. btwn............	—		
h.	As "a," imperf., pair.....................	—		
1618C	15c Flag (1597).................................	.75	.25	
d.	Imperf., pair................................	22.50		
e.	Pair, imperf. btwn.	*125.00*		
f.	Gray omitted................................	*30.00*		
1619	16c Statue of Liberty (1599)..............	.35	.25	
a.	Block tagging...............................	.50	.25	

1975-81, Perf. 11x10¾

Scott No.	Description	Unused Value	Used Value	/ / / / / /
1622	13c Flag, Independence Hall.............	.25	.25	
a.	Horizontal pair, imperf. btwn.	*40.00*		
b.	Vertical pair, imperf.....................	*375.00*		
e.	Horiz. pair, imperf. vert...............	—		
1622C	13c Flag, Independence Hall,			
	perf. 11¼ (1622)..........................	1.00	.25	
d.	Vert. pair, imperf.........................	*120.00*		
1623	13c Flag over Capitol (from bklt. pane)			
	perf. 11x10½..............................	.25	.25	
a.	Bklt. pane of 8, #1590 + 7 #1623...	2.25	*2.00*	
d.	Pair, #1590 & 1623.......................	.70	*1.00*	
1623B	13c Flag over Capitol (from bklt. pane			
	#1623Bc), perf. 10 x 9¾ (1623)..	.80	.80	
c.	Booklet pane, 1 #1590A + 7 #1623B	20.00	—	
e.	Pair, #1590A & #1623B	15.00	15.00	

Coil Stamp, Perf. 10 Vertically

Scott No.	Description	Unused Value	Used Value	/ / / / / /
1625	13c Flag, Independence Hall (1622)...	.35	.25	
a.	Imperf., pair................................	20.00		

1976 , Perf. 11

Scott No.	Description	Unused Value	Used Value	/ / / / / /
1629	13c Drummer Boy............................	.25	.25	
1630	13c Old Drummer	.25	.25	
1631	13c Fifer..	.25	.25	
a.	Strip of 3, #1629-1631	.75	.75	
b.	As "a," imperf..............................	*800.00*		
c.	Imperf., vert. pair, #1631.............	*700.00*		
1632	13c Interphil 76..............................	.25	.25	
a.	Dark blue and red (engr.) missing			
	(from a color misregistration).......	—		
b.	Red (engr.) missing (from a color			
	misregistration)	—		
1633	13c Delaware	.30	.25	
1634	13c Pennsylvania	.30	.25	
1635	13c New Jersey................................	.30	.25	
1636	13c Georgia	.30	.25	
1637	13c Connecticut...............................	.30	.25	
1638	13c Massachusetts............................	.30	.25	

1629-1631

1632

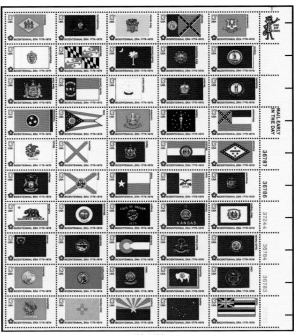

1633-1682

Scott No.	Description	Unused Value	Used Value	/ / / / / /
1639	13c Maryland	.30	.25	
1640	13c South Carolina	.30	.25	
1641	13c New Hampshire	.30	.25	
1642	13c Virginia	.30	.25	
1643	13c New York	.30	.25	
1644	13c North Carolina	.30	.25	
1645	13c Rhode Island	.30	.25	
1646	13c Vermont	.30	.25	
1647	13c Kentucky	.30	.25	
1648	13c Tennessee	.30	.25	
1649	13c Ohio	.30	.25	
1650	13c Louisiana	.30	.25	
1651	13c Indiana	.30	.25	
1652	13c Mississippi	.30	.25	
1653	13c Illinois	.30	.25	
1654	13c Alabama	.30	.25	
1655	13c Maine	.30	.25	
1656	13c Missouri	.30	.25	
1657	13c Arkansas	.30	.25	
1658	13c Michigan	.30	.25	
1659	13c Florida	.30	.25	
1660	13c Texas	.30	.25	
1661	13c Iowa	.30	.25	
1662	13c Wisconsin	.30	.25	
1663	13c California	.30	.25	
1664	13c Minnesota	.30	.25	
1665	13c Oregon	.30	.25	
1666	13c Kansas	.30	.25	
1667	13c West Virginia	.30	.25	
1668	13c Nevada	.30	.25	
1669	13c Nebraska	.30	.25	
1670	13c Colorado	.30	.25	
1671	13c North Dakota	.30	.25	
1672	13c South Dakota	.30	.25	
1673	13c Montana	.30	.25	
1674	13c Washington	.30	.25	
1675	13c Idaho	.30	.25	
1676	13c Wyoming	.30	.25	
1677	13c Utah	.30	.25	
1678	13c Oklahoma	.30	.25	
1679	13c New Mexico	.30	.25	
1680	13c Arizona	.30	.25	
1681	13c Alaska	.30	.25	
1682	13c Hawaii	.30	.25	
a.	Pane of 50	17.50	15.00	
1683	13c Telephone Centennial	.25	.25	
a.	Black and purple missing (from extraneous paper)	*450.00*		

1683

1684

1685

1686

1687

136

Scott No.	Description	Unused Value	Used Value	/ / / / / /
b.	Red missing (from extraneous paper)	—		
c.	All colors missing (from extraneous paper)	—		
1684	13c Commercial Aviation	.25	.25	
1685	13c Chemistry	.25	.25	
1686	Surrender of Cornwallis, Sheet of 5	3.25	2.25	
a.-e.	13c Any single	.45	.40	
f.	USA/13c omitted on b, c & d., imperf.	—	1,750.	
g.	USA/13c omitted on a & e	450.00	—	
h.	Imperf., tagging omitted		2,250.	
i.	USA/13c omitted on b, c & d	450.00		
j.	USA/13c double on b	—		
k.	USA/13c omitted on c & d	750.00		
l.	USA/13c omitted on e	550.00		
m.	USA/13c omitted, imperf., tagging omitted	—		
n.	As "g," imperf., tagging omitted	—		
o.	USA/13c missing on a (from perf. shift)	500.00		
q.	USA/13c omitted on a	—		
r.	Imperf., tagged	—		
s.	USA/13c missing on b & d (from perf. shift)	—		
1687	Declaration of Independence, Sht. of 5	4.25	3.25	
a.-e.	18c Any single	.55	.55	
f.	Design & margin inscriptions omitted	2,750.		
g.	USA/18c omitted on a & c	600.00	—	
h.	USA/18c omitted on b, d & e	400.00		
i.	USA/18c omitted on d	425.00	475.00	
j.	Black omitted in design	1,750.		
k.	USA/18c omitted, imperf., tagging omitted	1,750.		
m.	USA/18c omitted on b & e	500.00		
n.	USA/18c omitted on b & d	1,000.		
p.	Imperf., tagged	1,000.		
q.	USA/18c omitted on c	—		
r.	Yellow omitted	—		
s.	USA/18c missing on a, c and d (from perf. shift)	—		
1688	Washington Crossing the Delaware, Sheet of 5	5.25	4.25	
a.-e.	24c Any single	.70	.70	
f.	USA/24c omitted, imperf.	950.00		
g.	USA/24c omitted on d & e	450.00	450.00	
h.	Design & margin inscriptions omitted	2,500.		
i.	USA/24c omitted on a, b & c	450.00	450.00	
j.	Imperf., tagging omitted	1,450.		
k.	USA/24c of d & e inverted	40,000.		

Washington Crossing the Delaware
From a Painting by Emanuel Leutze / Eastman Johnson

1688

Washington Reviewing His Ragged Army at Valley Forge
From a Painting by William T. Trego

1689

1690

138

Scott No.	Description	Unused Value	Used Value	/ / / / /
l.	As "i," imperf, tagging omitted	3,250.	—	
n.	As No. 1688, perfs inverted..........	450.00		
p.	USA 24c missing on d and e (from color misregistration)......	—		
q.	USA 24c omitted on b and c	—		
1689	Washington Reviewing Army, Sheet of 5....................................	6.25	5.25	
a.-e.	31c multi, any single	.85	.85	
f.	USA/31c omitted	1,450.		
g.	USA/31c omitted on a & c..........	375.00		
h.	USA/31c omitted on b, d & e.......	500.00	—	
i.	USA/31c omitted on e	375.00		
j.	Black omitted in design................	1,450.		
k.	Imperf., tagging omitted................		1,250.	
l.	USA/31c omitted on b & d..........	375.00		
m.	USA/31c omitted on a, c & e.......	750.00		
n.	As "m," imperf., tagging omitted .	—		
p.	As "h," imperf., tagging omitted ..		1,250.	
q.	As "g," imperf., tagging omitted ..	2,500.		
r.	USA/31c omitted on d & e..........	500.00		
t.	USA/31c omitted on d..................	500.00		
v.	As No. 1689, perfs and tagging inverted......................................	10,000.		
w.	USA/31c missing on a, b, c and d (from perf. shift)........................	—		
x.	USA 31c missing on e (from color misregistration)	—		
1690	13c Benjamin Franklin	.25	.25	
a.	Light blue omitted	200.00		
1691	13c Declaration of Independence - Left	.30	.25	
1692	13c Declaration of Independence - Gathered Curtains......................	.30	.25	
1693	13c Declaration of Independence - Table	.30	.25	
1694	13c Declaration of Independence - Right	.30	.25	
a.	Strip of 4, #1691-1694	1.20	1.10	
1695	13c Olympics - Diving	.30	.25	
1696	13c Olympics - Skiing........................	.30	.25	
1697	13c Olympics - Running	.30	.25	
1698	13c Olympics - Skating..................	.30	.25	
a.	Block of 4, #1695-1698..............	1.20	1.20	
b.	As "a," imperf.	550.00		
1699	13c Clara Maass	.25	.25	
a.	Horiz. pair, imperf. vert...............	400.00		
1700	13c Adolph S. Ochs........................	.25	.25	
1701	13c Christmas - Religious	.25	.25	
a.	Imperf., pair..................................	85.00		
1702	13c Christmas - "Winter Pastime"	.25	.25	
a.	Imperf., pair..................................	85.00		

1691-1694

1695-1698

1699

1700

1701

1702

1704

1705

1706-1709

1710

1711

1716

1712-1715

141

1717-1720

1721

1722

1725

1723-1724

1726

1727

1728

1729

1730

1731

142

Scott No.	Description	Unused Value	Used Value	/ / / / / /
1703	13c Christmas - "Winter Pastime" (1702), block tagging	.25	.25	
a.	Imperf., pair	90.00		
b.	Vert. pair, imperf. btwn.	325.00		
d.	Red omitted	650.00		
e.	Yellow omitted	—		
1977				
1704	13c Washington at Princeton	.25	.25	
a.	Horiz. pair, imperf. vert.	500.00		
b.	Black (inscriptions) missing (from perf. shift)	—		
1705	13c Sound Recording	.25	.25	
1706	13c Zia Pot	.25	.25	
1707	13c San Ildefonso Pot	.25	.25	
1708	13c Hopi Pot	.25	.25	
1709	13c Acoma Pot	.25	.25	
a.	Block or strip of 4	1.00	1.00	
b.	As "a," imperf. vert.	2,000.		
1710	13c Lindbergh Flight	.25	.25	
a.	Imperf., pair	825.00		
1711	13c Colorado Statehood	.25	.25	
a.	Horiz. pair, imperf. btwn. and with natural straight edge at right	—		
b.	Horiz. pair, imperf. vert.	750.00		
1712	13c Swallowtail Butterfly	.25	.25	
1713	13c Checkerspot Butterfly	.25	.25	
1714	13c Dogface Butterfly	.25	.25	
1715	13c Orange-tip Butterfly	.25	.25	
a.	Block of 4, #1712-1715	1.00	1.00	
b.	As "a," imperf. horiz.	15,000.		
1716	13c Marquis de Lafayette	.25	.25	
a.	Red missing (from perf. shift)	250.00		
1717	13c Seamstress	.25	.25	
1718	13c Blacksmith	.25	.25	
1719	13c Wheelwright	.25	.25	
1720	13c Leatherworker	.25	.25	
a.	Block of 4, #1717-1720	1.00	1.00	
1721	13c Peace Bridge	.25	.25	
1722	13c Battle of Oriskany	.25	.25	
1723	13c Energy Conservation	.25	.25	
1724	13c Energy Development	.25	.25	
a.	Pair, #1723-1724	.50	.50	
1725	13c Alta California	.25	.25	
1726	13c Articles of Confederation	.25	.25	
b.	Red omitted	600.00		
c.	Red & brown omitted	400.00		
1727	13c Talking Pictures	.25	.25	
1728	13c Surrender at Saratoga	.25	.25	

1732-1733

1734

1735

1745-1748

1737

1738-1742

1749-1752

1744

1753

144

Scott No.	Description	Unused Value	Used Value	/ / / / / /
1729	13c Christmas - Washington Praying ..	.25	.25	
a.	Imperf., pair.................................	65.00		
1730	13c Christmas - Mailbox....................	.25	.25	
a.	Imperf., pair.................................	200.00		
1978				
1731	13c Carl Sandburg............................	.25	.25	
a.	Brown omitted	2,250.		
c.	All colors omitted........................	—		
1732	13c Capt. James Cook - Portrait..........	.25	.25	
1733	13c Capt. James Cook - Ships..............	.25	.25	
a.	Vert. pair, imperf. horiz.	—		
b.	Pair, #1732-1733..........................	.50	.50	
c.	As "a," imperf. btwn.....................	4,250.		
1978-80				
1734	13c Indian Head Penny......................	.25	.25	
a.	Horiz. pair, imperf. vert................	250.00		
1735	(15c) "A" & Eagle, photogravure	.30	.25	
a.	Imperf., pair.................................	85.00		
b.	Vert. pair, imperf. horiz.	600.00		
c.	Perf 11.2.....................................	.35	.25	
Booklet Stamps, Engraved				
1736	(15c) "A" & Eagle (1735)......................	.30	.25	
a.	Booklet pane of 8	2.50	1.50	
c.	Vert. pair, imperf. btwn., in #1736a			
	with foldover	1,000.		
1737	15c Roses......................................	.30	.25	
a.	Booklet pane of 8	2.50	2.00	
b.	Imperf. pair.................................	450.00		
1738	15c Virginia Windmill.......................	.30	.25	
1739	15c Rhode Island Windmill................	.30	.25	
1740	15c Massachusetts Windmill...............	.30	.25	
1741	15c Illinois Windmill.........................	.30	.25	
1742	15c Texas Windmill..........................	.30	.25	
a.	Bklt. pane, 2 each #1738-1742.....	3.50	3.00	
b.	Strip of 5, #1738-1742	1.50	1.40	
Coil Stamp, Perf. 10 Vertically				
1743	(15c) "A" & Eagle (1735)......................	.30	.25	
a.	Imperf., pair.................................	75.00		
1978				
1744	13c Harriet Tubman..........................	.25	.25	
1745	13c Quilts - Orange Flowered Fabric ..	.25	.25	
1746	13c Quilts - Red & White Fabric	.25	.25	
1747	13c Quilts - Orange Striped Fabric	.25	.25	
1748	13c Quilts - Black Plaid Fabric	.25	.25	
a.	Block of 4, #1745-1748...............	1.00	1.00	
1749	13c Ballet.......................................	.25	.25	
1750	13c Dance in Theater........................	.25	.25	
1751	13c Folk Dancing	.25	.25	

1754

1755

1756

1757

1758

1759

1760-1763

Scott No.	Description	Unused Value	Used Value	/ / / / / /
1752	13c Modern Dance	.25	.25	
a.	Block of 4, #1749-1752	1.00	1.00	
1753	13c French Alliance	.25	.25	
a.	Red missing (from a perf. shift)	—		
1754	13c Early Cancer Detection	.25	.25	
1755	13c Jimmie Rodgers	.25	.25	
1756	15c George M. Cohan	.30	.25	
1757	CAPEX, block of 8	2.00	2.00	
a.	13c Cardinal	.25	.25	
b.	13c Mallard	.25	.25	
c.	13c Canada goose	.25	.25	
d.	13c Blue jay	.25	.25	
e.	13c Moose	.25	.25	
f.	13c Chipmunk	.25	.25	
g.	13c Red fox	.25	.25	
h.	13c Raccoon	.25	.25	
i.	Yellow, green, red, brown, blue, and black (litho.) omitted	7,000.		
j.	Strip of 4 (a.-d.), imperf. vert.	5,000.		
k.	Strip of 4 (e.-h.), imperf. vert.	3,000.		
l.	As No. 1757, 'd' and 'h' with black omitted	—		
m.	As No. 1757, 'b' with blue missing (from perf. shift)	—		
1758	15c Photography	.30	.25	
1759	15c Viking Missions to Mars	.30	.25	
1760	15c Great Gray Owl	.30	.25	
1761	15c Saw-whet Owl	.30	.25	
1762	15c Barred Owl	.30	.25	
1763	15c Great Horned Owl	.30	.25	
a.	Block of 4, #1760-1763	1.25	1.25	
1764	15c Giant Sequoia	.30	.25	
1765	15c White Pine	.30	.25	
1766	15c White Oak	.30	.25	
1767	15c Gray Birch	.30	.25	
a.	Block of 4, #1764-1767	1.25	1.25	
b.	As "a," imperf. horiz.	17,500.		
1768	15c Christmas - Religious	.30	.25	
a.	Imperf., pair	80.00		
1769	15c Christmas - Hobby Horse	.30	.25	
a.	Imperf., pair	85.00		
b.	Vert. pair, imperf. horiz.	1,250.		
1979				
1770	15c Robert F. Kennedy	.35	.25	
1771	15c Dr. Martin Luther King, Jr.	.40	.25	
a.	Imperf., pair	1,400.		
1772	15c International Year of the Child	.30	.25	
1773	15c John Steinbeck	.30	.25	
1774	15c Albert Einstein	.35	.25	
1775	15c Toleware - Straight-spouted coffeepot	.30	.25	

1764-1767

1768

1769

1770

1771

1772

1773

1774

1775-1778

148

Scott No.		Description	Unused Value	Used Value	/ / / / / /
1776	15c	Toleware - Tea Caddy	.30	.25	
1777	15c	Toleware - Sugar Bowl	.30	.25	
1778	15c	Toleware - Curved-spouted coffeepot	.30	.25	
a.		Block of 4, #1775-1778	1.25	1.25	
b.		As "a," imperf. horiz.	3,000.		
1779	15c	Architecture - Jefferson	.30	.25	
1780	15c	Architecture - Latrobe	.30	.25	
1781	15c	Architecture - Bulfinch	.30	.25	
1782	15c	Architecture - Strickland	.30	.25	
a.		Block of 4, #1779-1782	1.25	1.25	
1783	5c	Persistent Trillium	.30	.25	
1784	15c	Hawaiian Wild Broadbean	.30	.25	
1785	15c	Contra Costa Wallflower	.30	.25	
1786	15c	Antioch Dunes Evening Primrose	.30	.25	
a.		Block of 4, #1783-1786	1.25	1.25	
b.		As "a," imperf.	275.00		
1787	15c	Seeing Eye Dogs	.30	.25	
a.		Imperf., pair	375.00		
1788	15c	Special Olympics	.30	.25	
1789	15c	John Paul Jones, perf. 11x12	.30	.25	
c.		Vert. pair, imperf. horiz.	150.00		
1789A	15c	John Paul Jones, perf. 11 (1789)	.55	.25	
d.		Vert. pair, imperf horiz.	125.00		
1789B	15c	John Paul Jones, perf. 12 (1789)	3,500.	4,000.	
1979-80					
1790	10c	Olympics - Decathlon	.25	.25	
1791	15c	Olympics - Running	.30	.25	
1792	15c	Olympics - Women's Swimming	.30	.25	
1793	15c	Olympics - Rowing	.30	.25	
1794	15c	Olympics - Equestrian	.30	.25	
a.		Block of 4, #1791-1794	1.25	1.25	
b.		As "a," imperf.	1,400.		
1795	15c	Olympics - Speed Skating, perf. 11¼ x 10½	.35	.25	
1796	15c	Olympics - Downhill Skiing, perf. 11¼ x 10½	.35	.25	
1797	15c	Olympics - Ski Jump, perf. 11¼ x 10½	.35	.25	
1798	15c	Olympics - Ice Hockey, perf. 11¼ x 10½	.35	.25	
b.		Block of 4, #1795-1798	1.50	1.40	
1795A	15c	Olympics - Speed Skating, perf. 11 (1795)	1.10	.60	
1796A	15c	Olympics - Downhill Skiing, perf. 11 (1796)	1.10	.60	
1797A	15c	Olympics - Ski Jump, perf. 11 (1797)	1.10	.60	
1798A	15c	Olympics - Ice Hockey, perf. 11 (1798)	1.10	.60	
c.		Block of 4, #1795A-1798A (1795-1798)	4.50	3.50	

1779-1782

1783-1786

1787   1788   1789

1790

1791-1794

1795-1798

1799

1800

1802

1801

1803

1804

1805

1806

1807

1809

1813

1818

1821

1822

1823

1824

1825

1826

Scott No.	Description	Unused Value	Used Value	/ / / / / /
1979				
1799	15c Christmas - Religious....................	.30	.25	
a.	Imperf., pair.................................	80.00		
b.	Vert. pair, imperf. horiz.................	575.00		
c.	Vert. pair, imperf. btwn.................	1,100.		
1800	15c Christmas - Santa Claus................	.30	.25	
a.	Green & yellow omitted.................	500.00		
b.	Green, yellow & tan omitted	450.00		
1801	15c Will Rogers....................................	.30	.25	
a.	Imperf., pair.................................	175.00		
1802	15c Vietnam Veterans...........................	.30	.25	
1980				
1803	15c W.C. Fields	.30	.25	
a.	Imperf., pair.................................	—		
1804	15c Benjamin Banneker........................	.30	.25	
a.	Horiz. pair, imperf. vert.	400.00		
1805	15c Letters Preserve Memories	.30	.25	
1806	15c P.S. Write Soon, purple & multi	.30	.25	
1807	15c Letters Lift Spirits	.30	.25	
1808	15c P.S. Write Soon (1806), grn & multi	.30	.25	
1809	15c Letters Shape Opinions	.30	.25	
1810	15c P.S. Write Soon (1806), red & multi	.30	.25	
a.	Vert. strip of 6, #1805-1810............	1.85	2.00	
1980-81, Coil Stamps, Perf. 10 Vertically				
1811	1c Inkwell & Quill (1581)	.25	.25	
a.	Imperf., pair.................................	125.00		
1813	3.5c Violins, tagged...............................	.25	.25	
a.	Untagged (Bureau precanceled, lines only).......................................	.25	.25	
b.	Imperf., pair.................................	150.00		
1816	12c Torch (1594), tagged......................	.25	.25	
a.	Untagged (Bureau precanceled)	1.25	1.25	
b.	Imperf., pair.................................	150.00		
c.	As "a," brownish red, *reddish beige*	75.00	—	
1981				
1818	(18c) "B" & Eagle, photogravure............	.35	.25	
Booklet Stamp, Perf. 10, Engraved				
1819	(18c) "B" & Eagle (1818)	.40	.25	
	a. Booklet pane of 8	3.75	2.25	
Coil Stamp, Perf. 10 Vertically				
1820	(18c) "B" & Eagle (1818), engraved	.40	.25	
a.	Imperf., pair.................................	125.00		
1980				
1821	15c Frances Perkins..............................	.30	.25	
1822	15c Dolley Madison..............................	.30	.25	
a.	Red brown missing (from perf. shift)	500.00		

153

1827-1830

1831

1832

1833

1834-1837

Scott No.		Description	Unused Value	Used Value	/ / / / / /
1823	15c	Emily Bissell	.35	.25	
a.		Vert. pair, imperf. horiz.	325.00		
b.		All colors missing (from extraneous paper)	—		
c.		Red missing (from foldover)	—		
1824	15c	Helen Keller, Anne Sullivan	.30	.25	
1825	15c	Veterans Administration	.30	.25	
a.		Horiz. pair, imperf. vert.	400.00		
1826	15c	Bernardo de Galvez	.30	.25	
a.		Red, brown & blue (engr.) omitted.	625.00		
b.		Blue, brown, red (engr.), yellow (litho.) omitted	1,150.		
1827	15c	Brain Coral	.30	.25	
1828	15c	Elkhorn Coral	.30	.25	
1829	15c	Chalice Coral	.30	.25	
1830	15c	Finger Coral	.30	.25	
a.		Block of 4, #1827-1830	1.25	1.10	
b.		As "a," imperf.	450.00		
c.		As "a," vert. imperf. btwn.	2,000.		
d.		As "a," imperf. vert.	3,000.		
1831	15c	Organized Labor	.30	.25	
a.		Imperf., pair	300.00		
1832	15c	Edith Wharton	.30	.25	
1833	15c	Education	.30	.25	
a.		Horiz. pair, imperf. vert.	175.00		
1834	15c	Bella Bella Mask	.35	.25	
1835	15c	Chilkat Tlingit Mask	.35	.25	
1836	15c	Tlingit Mask	.35	.25	
1837	15c	Bella Coola Mask	.35	.25	
a.		Block of 4, #1834-1837	1.50	1.25	
1838	15c	Architecture - Renwick	.30	.25	
a.		Red missing (PS)	—		
1839	15c	Architecture - Richardson	.30	.25	
1840	15c	Architecture - Furness	.30	.25	
1841	15c	Architecture - Davis	.30	.25	
a.		Block of 4, #1838-1841	1.25	1.25	
b.		As "a," red missing on Nos. 1838, 1839 (from perf. shift)	400.00		
1842	15c	Christmas - Religious	.30	.25	
a.		Imperf., pair	50.00		
1843	15c	Christmas - Wreath & Toys	.30	.25	
a.		Imperf., pair	60.00		
b.		Buff omitted	22.50		
c.		Vert. pair, imperf. horiz.	—		
d.		Horiz. pair, imperf. btwn.	3,750.		
1980-85					
1844	1c	Dorothea Dix	.25	.25	
a.		Imperf. pair	375.00		

1838-1841

1842

1843

1844	1845	1846	1847	1848
1849	1850	1851	1852	1853
1854	1855	1856	1857	1858

1859   1860   1861

1862   1863   1864   1865

1866   1867   1868   1869

HOW TO USE THIS BOOK

The number in the first column is its Scott number or identifying number. Following that is the denomination of the stamp and its color or description. Finally, the values, unused and used, are shown.

1874

1875   1876-1879

157

1880-1889

1890   1891   1892

1893   1895

HOW TO USE THIS BOOK

The number in the first column is its Scott number or identifying number. Following that is the denomination of the stamp and its color or description. Finally, the values, unused and used, are shown.

Scott No.		Description	Unused Value	Used Value	/ / / / / /
b.		Vert. pair, imperf. btwn. & with natural straight edge at bottom..................	1,400.		
e.		Vert. pair, imperf. horiz.................	—		
1845	2c	Igor Stravinsky	.25	.25	
1846	3c	Henry Clay	.25	.25	
1847	4c	Carl Schurz.....................................	.25	.25	
1848	5c	Pearl Buck	.30	.25	
1849	6c	Walter Lippmann.............................	.25	.25	
a.		Vert. pair, imperf. btwn. & with natural straight edge at bottom....	1,750.		
1850	7c	Abraham Baldwin	.25	.25	
1851	8c	Henry Knox.....................................	.25	.25	
1852	9c	Sylvanus Thayer	.25	.25	
1853	10c	Richard Russell	.25	.25	
b.		Vert. pair, imperf. btwn. & at bottom	750.00		
c.		Horiz. pair, imperf. btwn...............	1,850.		
d.		Vert. pair imperf. horiz.	—		
1854	11c	Alden Partridge	.40	.25	
1855	13c	Crazy Horse....................................	.40	.25	
1856	14c	Sinclair Lewis................................	.30	.25	
b.		Vert. pair, imperf. horiz...............	110.00		
c.		Horiz. pair, imperf. btwn...............	8.00		
d.		Vert. pair, imperf. btwn..................	1,650.		
e.		All color omitted.	—		
1857	17c	Rachel Carson	.35	.25	
1858	18c	George Mason	.35	.25	
1859	19c	Sequoyah	.45	.25	
1860	20c	Ralph Bunche	.40	.25	
1861	20c	Thomas H. Gallaudet	.50	.25	
1862	20c	Harry S Truman	.40	.25	
1863	22c	John James Audubon	.75	.25	
d.		Vert. pair, imperf. horiz..................	1,750.		
e.		Vert. pair, imperf. btwn..................	—		
f.		Horiz. pair, imperf. btwn...............	1,750.		
1864	30c	Frank C. Laubach............................	.60	.25	
1865	35c	Dr. Charles R. Drew	.75	.25	
1866	37c	Robert Millikan	.80	.25	
1867	39c	Grenville Clark	.90	.25	
a.		Vert. pair, imperf. horiz.	475.00		
b.		Vert. pair, imperf. btwn.	1,650.		
1868	40c	Lillian M. Gilbreth	.90	.25	
1869	50c	Chester W. Nimitz	.95	.25	
1981					
1874	15c	Everett Dirksen...............................	.30	.25	
a.		All color omitted	500.00		
1875	15c	Whitney M. Young	.35	.25	
1876	18c	Rose	.35	.25	
1877	18c	Camellia..	.35	.25	

HOW TO USE THIS BOOK

The number in the first column is its Scott number or identifying number. Following that is the denomination of the stamp and its color or description. Finally, the values, unused and used, are shown.

Scott No.	Description	Unused Value	Used Value	/ / / / / /
1878	18c Dahlia	.35	.25	
1879	18c Lily...	.35	.25	
a.	Block of 4, #1876-1879	1.40	1.25	
1880	18c Bighorn	.70	.25	
1881	18c Puma	.70	.25	
1882	18c Harbor seal	.70	.25	
1883	18c American Buffalo.........................	.70	.25	
1884	18c Brown bear	.70	.25	
1885	18c Polar bear	.70	.25	
1886	18c Elk (wapiti)..................................	.70	.25	
1887	18c Moose	.70	.25	
1888	18c White-tailed deer.........................	.70	.25	
1889	18c Pronghorn	.70	.25	
a.	Bklt. pane of 10, #1880-1889	7.00	6.00	
1890	18c Flag, Grain Field	.35	.25	
a.	Imperf., pair.................................	*80.00*		
b.	Vert. pair, imperf. horiz................	*600.00*		
c.	Vert. pair, imperf. between.............	—		

Coil Stamp, Perf. 10 Vertically

1891	18c Flag, Sea Coast.............................	.35	.25	
a.	Imperf., pair.................................	17.50	—	
b.	Pair, imperf. btwn...........................	*1,850.*		

Booklet Stamps, Perf. 11

1892	6c Stars (from bklt. pane)	.50	.25	
1893	18c Flag, Mountain (from bklt. pane)...	.30	.25	
a.	Booklet pane of 8 (2 #1892, 6 #1893)	3.00	2.50	
b.	As "a," vert. imperf. btwn..............	*70.00*		
c.	Pair, #1892, 1893	.90	1.00	
1894	20c Flag, Supreme Court (1895)...........	.40	.25	
a.	Vert. pair, imperf.........................	30.00		
b.	Vert. pair, imperf. horiz.................	*400.00*		
c.	Dark blue omitted..........................	70.00		
d.	Black omitted	*275.00*		

Coil Stamp, Perf. 10 Vertically

1895	20c Flag, Supreme Court, tagged..........	.40	.25	
b.	Untagged (Bureau precanceled)	.50	.50	
d.	Imperf., pair.................................	8.00	—	
e.	Pair, imperf. btwn...........................	*800.00*		
f.	Black omitted	*45.00*		
g.	Dark blue omitted...........................	*1,350.*		

Booklet Stamps, Perf. 11 x 10½

1896	20c Flag, Supreme Court (1894)..........	.40	.25	
a.	Booklet pane of 6..........................	3.00	*2.25*	
b.	Booklet pane of 10........................	5.25	*3.25*	

1981-84, Coil Stamps, Perf. 10 Vertically

1897	1c Omnibus	.25	.25	

1910　　　　1911

1912-1919

1921-1924

162

Scott No.		Description	Unused Value	Used Value	/ / / / / /
b.		Imperf., pair............................	*375.00*		
1897A	2c	Locomotive................................	.25	.25	
c.		Imperf., pair............................	45.00		
1898	3c	Handcar	.25	.25	
1898A	4c	Stagecoach, tagged.....................	.25	.25	
b.		Untagged (Bureau precanceled).	.25	.25	
c.		As "b," imperf., pair.....................	*450.00*		
d.		No. 1898A, imperf., pair...............	*450.00*	—	
1899	5c	Motorcycle.................................	.25	.25	
a.		Imperf., pair.............................	*2,750.*		
1900	5.2c	Sleigh, tagged............................	.25	.25	
a.		Untagged (Bureau precanceled).	.25	.25	
1901	5.9c	Bicycle, tagged...........................	.25	.25	
a.		Untagged (Bureau precanceled, lines only)..............................	.25	.25	
b.		As "a," imperf., pair.....................	*160.00*		
1902	7.4c	Baby Buggy, tagged.....................	.25	.25	
a.		Untagged (Bureau precanceled).	.25	.25	
1903	9.3c	Mail Wagon, tagged.....................	.30	.25	
a.		Untagged (Bureau precanceled, lines only)..............................	.25	.25	
b.		As "a," imperf., pair.....................	100.00		
1904	10.9c	Hansom Cab, tagged	.30	.25	
a.		Untagged (Bureau precanceled, lines only)..............................	.30	.25	
b.		As "a," imperf., pair.....................	140.00		
1905	11c	Caboose, tagged..........................	.30	.25	
a.		Untagged...................................	.25	.25	
1906	17c	Electric Auto, tagged....................	.35	.25	
a.		Untagged (Bureau precanceled, Presorted First Class)..................	.35	.35	
b.		Imperf., pair.............................	140.00		
c.		As "a," imperf., pair.....................	*550.00*		
1907	18c	Surrey	.35	.25	
a.		Imperf., pair.............................	110.00		
1908	20c	Fire Pumper...............................	.35	.25	
a.		Imperf., pair.............................	90.00		

1983, Booklet Stamp, Perf. 10 Vertically on 1 or 2 Sides

1909		$9.35 Eagle & Moon....................	19.00	15.00	
a.		Booklet pane of 3........................	57.50	—	

1981

1910	18c	American Red Cross	.35	.25	
1911	18c	Savings & Loan............................	.35	.25	
1912	18c	Moon Walk	.40	.25	
1913	18c	Shuttle - Jettison of Boosters..........	.40	.25	
a.		Black ("USA 18c") missing (from perf. shift)................................	—		

1920   1925   1927

1926   1932   1933

1928-1931

1934   1941   1935

Scott No.		Description	Unused Value	Used Value	/ / / / / /
1914	18c	Shuttle - Cargo Doors Open	.40	.25	
1915	18c	Skylab...	.40	.25	
1916	18c	Pioneer 11, Saturn.........................	.40	.25	
1917	18c	Shuttle - Lifting Off......................	.40	.25	
1918	18c	Shuttle - Landing..........................	.40	.25	
1919	18c	Space Telescope.............................	.40	.25	
a.		Block of 8, #1912-1919	3.25	3.00	
b.		As "a," imperf................................	6,000.		
c.		As "a," imperf. vert.	—		
e.		As "a," top 4 stamps part perf., bottom 4 stamps imperf..............	—		
1920	18c	Professional Management..............	.35	.25	
1921	18c	Save Wetland Habitats...................	.35	.25	
1922	18c	Save Grassland Habitats................	.35	.25	
1923	18c	Save Mountain Habitats.................	.35	.25	
1924	18c	Save Woodland Habitats	.35	.25	
a.		Block of 4, #1921-1924	1.50	1.25	
1925	18c	International Year of the Disabled ..	.35	.25	
a.		Vert. pair, imperf. horiz.................	2,500.		
1926	18c	Edna St. Vincent Millay................	.35	.25	
a.		Black (engr., inscriptions) omitted .	275.00	—	
1927	18c	Alcoholism	.45	.25	
a.		Imperf., pair..................................	375.00		
b.		Vert. pair, imperf. horiz.................	2,400.		
1928	18c	Architecture - White......................	.40	.25	
1929	18c	Architecture - Hunt	.40	.25	
1930	18c	Architecture - Maybeck	.40	.25	
1931	18c	Architecture - Sullivan..................	.40	.25	
a.		Block of 4, #1928-1931	1.65	1.65	
1932	18c	Babe Zaharias................................	.40	.25	
1933	18c	Bobby Jones	.60	.25	
1934	18c	Frederic Remington........................	.35	.25	
a.		Vert. pair, imperf. btwn..................	225.00		
b.		Brown omitted...............................	225.00		
1935	18c	James Hoban	.35	.25	
1936	20c	James Hoban (1935)	.35	.25	
1937	18c	Battle of Yorktown.........................	.35	.25	
1938	18c	Battle of Virginia Capes................	.35	.25	
a.		Pair, #1937-1938	.90	.75	
b.		As "a," black (engr., inscriptions) omitted..	350.00		
d.		As "a," black (litho.) omitted..........	—		
1939	(20c)	Christmas - Religious.....................	.40	.25	
a.		Imperf. pair....................................	100.00		
b.		Vert. pair, imperf. horiz.................	1,000.		
1940	(20c)	Christmas - Bear on Sled	.40	.25	
a.		Imperf., pair..................................	200.00		
b.		Vert. pair, imperf. horiz.................	2,750.		

1937-1938

1939

1940

1942-1945

1946

1948

1949

1950

1951

1952

166

Scott No.	Description	Unused Value	Used Value	//////
1941	20c John Hanson	.40	.25	
1942	20c Barrel Cactus	.35	.25	
1943	20c Agave	.35	.25	
1944	20c Beavertail Cactus	.35	.25	
1945	20c Saguaro	.35	.25	
a.	Block of 4, #1942-1945	1.50	1.25	
b.	As "a," deep brown (litho.) omitted	4,250.		
c.	No. 1945 imperf., vert. pair	3,500.		
d.	As "a," dark green & dark blue (engr.) missing (from extraneous paper)	—		
e.	As "a," dark green (engr.) missing on left stamp (from extraneous paper)	—		
1946 (20c)	"C" & Eagle	.40	.25	
b.	All color omitted	450.00		

Coil Stamp, Perf. 10 Vertically

Scott No.	Description	Unused Value	Used Value	//////
1947 (20c)	"C" & Eagle (1946)	.60	.25	
a.	Imperf., pair	950.00		
1948 (20c)	"C" & Eagle (from bklt. pane), perf. 11	.40	.25	
a.	Booklet pane of 10	4.50	3.25	

1982

Scott No.	Description	Unused Value	Used Value	//////
1949	20c Bighorn, (from bklt. pane)	.55	.25	
a.	Booklet pane of 10	5.50	2.50	
b.	As "a," imperf. vert.	95.00		
c.	Type II	1.40	.25	
d.	As "c," booklet pane of 10	14.00	—	
1950	20c Franklin D. Roosevelt	.40	.25	
1951	20c Love, perf. 11¼	.40	.25	
b.	Imperf., pair	225.00		
c.	Blue omitted	200.00		
d.	Yellow omitted	650.00		
e.	Purple omitted	—		
1951A 20c	Love, Perf. 11¼ x 10½ (1951)	.75	.25	
1952	20c George Washington	.40	.25	

Perf 10½ x 11¼

Scott No.	Description	Unused Value	Used Value	//////
1953	20c Alabama	.55	.30	
1954	20c Alaska	.55	.30	
1955	20c Arizona	.55	.30	
1956	20c Arkansas	.55	.30	
1957	20c California	.55	.30	
1958	20c Colorado	.55	.30	
1959	20c Connecticut	.55	.30	
1960	20c Delaware	.55	.30	
1961	20c Florida	.55	.30	
1962	20c Georgia	.55	.30	
1963	20c Hawaii	.55	.30	

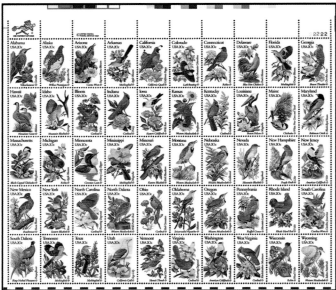

State Birds and Flowers 1953-2002, 1953A-2002A

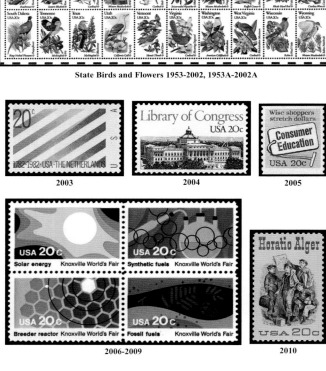

2003

2004

2005

2006-2009

2010

Scott No.	Description	Unused Value	Used Value	/ / / / / /
1964	20c Idaho	.55	.30	
1965	20c Illinois	.55	.30	
1966	20c Indiana	.55	.30	
1967	20c Iowa	.55	.30	
1968	20c Kansas	.55	.30	
1969	20c Kentucky	.55	.30	
1970	20c Louisiana	.55	.30	
1971	20c Maine	.55	.30	
1972	20c Maryland	.55	.30	
1973	20c Massachusetts	.55	.30	
1974	20c Michigan	.55	.30	
1975	20c Minnesota	.55	.30	
1976	20c Mississippi	.55	.30	
1977	20c Missouri	.55	.30	
1978	20c Montana	.55	.30	
1979	20c Nebraska	.55	.30	
1980	20c Nevada	.55	.30	
1981	20c New Hampshire	.55	.30	
b.	Black missing (from extraneous paper)	5,000.		
1982	20c New Jersey	.55	.30	
1983	20c New Mexico	.55	.30	
1984	20c New York	.55	.30	
1985	20c North Carolina	.55	.30	
1986	20c North Dakota	.55	.30	
1987	20c Ohio	.55	.30	
1988	20c Oklahoma	.55	.30	
1989	20c Oregon	.55	.30	
1990	20c Pennsylvania	.55	.30	
1991	20c Rhode Island	.55	.30	
b.	Black missing (from extraneous paper)	5,000.		
1992	20c South Carolina	.55	.30	
1993	20c South Dakota	.55	.30	
1994	20c Tennessee	.55	.30	
1995	20c Texas	.55	.30	
1996	20c Utah	.55	.30	
1997	20c Vermont	.55	.30	
1998	20c Virginia	.55	.30	
1999	20c Washington	.55	.30	
2000	20c West Virginia	.55	.30	
2001	20c Wisconsin	.55	.30	
b.	Black missing (from extraneous paper)	5,000.		
2002	20c Wyoming	.55	.30	
b.	Pane of 50, Nos. 1953-2002	27.50	20.00	
d.	Pane of 50, imperf.	27,500.		
Perf 11¼ x 11				
1953A 20c Alabama		.65	.30	
1954A 20c Alaska		.65	.30	
1955A 20c Arizona		.65	.30	

2011

2014

2012

2013

2015

2016

2017

2018

2019-2022

Scott No.	Description	Unused Value	Used Value	/ / / / /
1956A 20c	Arkansas	.65	.30	
1957A 20c	California	.65	.30	
1958A 20c	Colorado	.65	.30	
1959A 20c	Connecticut	.65	.30	
1960A 20c	Delaware	.65	.30	
1961A 20c	Florida	.65	.30	
1962A 20c	Georgia	.65	.30	
1963A 20c	Hawaii	.65	.30	
1964A 20c	Idaho	.65	.30	
1965A 20c	Illinois	.65	.30	
1966A 20c	Indiana	.65	.30	
1967A 20c	Iowa	.65	.30	
1968A 20c	Kansas	.65	.30	
1969A 20c	Kentucky	.65	.30	
1970A 20c	Louisiana	.65	.30	
1971A 20c	Maine	.65	.30	
1972A 20c	Maryland	.65	.30	
1973A 20c	Massachusetts	.65	.30	
1974A 20c	Michigan	.65	.30	
1975A 20c	Minnesota	.65	.30	
1976A 20c	Mississippi	.65	.30	
1977A 20c	Missouri	.65	.30	
1978A 20c	Montana	.65	.30	
1979A 20c	Nebraska	.65	.30	
1980A 20c	Nevada	.65	.30	
1981A 20c	New Hampshire	.65	.30	
1982A 20c	New Jersey	.65	.30	
1983A 20c	New Mexico	.65	.30	
1984A 20c	New York	.65	.30	
1985A 20c	North Carolina	.65	.30	
1986A 20c	North Dakota	.65	.30	
1987A 20c	Ohio	.65	.30	
1988A 20c	Oklahoma	.65	.30	
1989A 20c	Oregon	.65	.30	
1990A 20c	Pennsylvania	.65	.30	
1991A 20c	Rhode Island	.65	.30	
1992A 20c	South Carolina	.65	.30	
1993A 20c	South Dakota	.65	.30	
1994A 20c	Tennessee	.65	.30	
1995A 20c	Texas	.65	.30	
1996A 20c	Utah	.65	.30	
1997A 20c	Vermont	.65	.30	
1998A 20c	Virginia	.65	.30	
1999A 20c	Washington	.65	.30	
2000A 20c	West Virginia	.65	.30	
2001A 20c	Wisconsin	.65	.30	
2002A 20c	Wyoming	.65	.30	
c.	Pane of 50, Nos. 1953A-2002A	32.50	22.50	

2023

2024

2025

2026

2031

2027-2030

2032-2035

172

Scott No.	Description	Unused Value	Used Value	/ / / / / /
2003	20c U.S. - Netherlands	.40	.25	☐☐☐☐☐
a.	Imperf., pair.....................................	*275.00*		☐☐☐☐☐
2004	20c Library of Congress	.40	.25	☐☐☐☐☐
Coil Stamp, Perf. 10 Vertically				
2005	20c Consumer Education	.55	.25	☐☐☐☐☐
a.	Imperf., pair.....................................	85.00		☐☐☐☐☐
2006	20c Solar Energy	.45	.25	☐☐☐☐☐
2007	20c Synthetic Fuels	.45	.25	☐☐☐☐☐
2008	20c Breeder Reactor..............................	.45	.25	☐☐☐☐☐
2009	20c Fossil Fuels	.45	.25	☐☐☐☐☐
a.	Block of 4, #2006-2009	1.80	1.50	☐☐☐☐☐
2010	20c Horatio Alger..................................	.40	.25	☐☐☐☐☐
b.	Red and black omitted...................	—		☐☐☐☐☐
2011	20c Aging Together	.40	.25	☐☐☐☐☐
2012	20c The Barrymores	.40	.25	☐☐☐☐☐
a.	Black missing (from extraneous paper)	—		☐☐☐☐☐
2013	20c Dr. Mary Walker..............................	.40	.25	☐☐☐☐☐
2014	20c International Peace Garden.............	.50	.25	☐☐☐☐☐
a.	Black & green (engr.) omitted........	*225.00*		☐☐☐☐☐
2015	20c America's Libraries	.40	.25	☐☐☐☐☐
a.	Vert. pair, imperf. horiz..................	*250.00*		☐☐☐☐☐
c.	All colors missing (from extraneous paper)..	*175.00*		☐☐☐☐☐
2016	20c Jackie Robinson	1.10	.25	☐☐☐☐☐
2017	20c Touro Synagogue.............................	.45	.25	☐☐☐☐☐
a.	Imperf., pair.....................................	*2,250.*		☐☐☐☐☐
2018	20c Wolf Trap Farm Park......................	.40	.25	☐☐☐☐☐
2019	20c Architecture - Wright.....................	.45	.25	☐☐☐☐☐
b.	Red omitted	—		☐☐☐☐☐
2020	20c Architecture - Mies van der Rohe..	.45	.25	☐☐☐☐☐
a.	Red omitted	—		☐☐☐☐☐
2021	20c Architecture - Gropius	.45	.25	☐☐☐☐☐
2022	20c Architecture -Saarinen	.45	.25	☐☐☐☐☐
a.	Block of 4, #2019-2022	2.00	1.75	☐☐☐☐☐
2023	20c Francis of Assisi	.40	.25	☐☐☐☐☐
2024	20c Ponce de Leon	.50	.25	☐☐☐☐☐
a.	Imperf., pair.....................................	*425.00*		☐☐☐☐☐
b.	Vert. pair, imperf. between & at top	—		☐☐☐☐☐
2025	13c Christmas - Dog & Cat	.25	.25	☐☐☐☐☐
a.	Imperf., pair.....................................	*350.00*		☐☐☐☐☐
2026	20c Christmas - Religious.....................	.40	.25	☐☐☐☐☐
a.	Imperf., pair.....................................	125.00		☐☐☐☐☐
b.	Horiz. pair, imperf. vert.	—		☐☐☐☐☐
c.	Vert. pair, imperf. horiz..................	—		☐☐☐☐☐
2027	20c Christmas - Sledding......................	.60	.25	☐☐☐☐☐
2028	20c Christmas - Snowman	.60	.25	☐☐☐☐☐
2029	20c Christmas - Skating........................	.60	.25	☐☐☐☐☐
2030	20c Christmas - Tree	.60	.25	☐☐☐☐☐

2036

2037

2039

2038

2040

2041

2042

2043

2044

2045

2046

2047

HOW TO USE THIS BOOK

The number in the first column is its Scott number or identifying number. Following that is the denomination of the stamp and its color or description. Finally, the values, unused and used, are shown.

Scott No.	Description	Unused Value	Used Value	// // //
a.	Block of 4, #2027-2030	2.40	1.50	
b.	As "a," imperf.	*1,750.*		
c.	As "a," imperf. horiz.	*800.00*		
1983				
2031	20c Science & Technology...............	.40	.25	
a.	Black (engr.) omitted	*1,200.*		
2032	20c Intrepid Balloon..........................	.50	.25	
2033	20c Two Large Balloons	.50	.25	
2034	20cLarge Balloon at Right.................	.50	.25	
2035	20c Explorer II Balloon	.50	.25	
a.	Block of 4, #2032-2035	2.00	1.50	
b.	As "a," imperf.	*3,750.*		
c.	As "a," right stamp perf. otherwise imperf.	*3,750.*		
2036	20c U.S. - Sweden	.40	.25	
2037	20c Civilian Conservation Corps...........	.40	.25	
a.	Imperf., pair	*2,750.*		
b.	Vert. pair, imperf. horiz.	—		
2038	20c Joseph Priestley	.40	.25	
2039	20c Voluntarism................................	.40	.25	
a.	Imperf., pair	*300.00*		
2040	20c U.S. - Germany	.40	.25	
2041	20c Brooklyn Bridge..........................	.40	.25	
b.	All color missing (from extraneous paper)...	*75.00*		
2042	20c Tennessee Valley Authority.............	.40	.25	
2043	20c Physical Fitness	.40	.25	
2044	20c Scott Joplin	.50	.25	
a.	Imperf., pair	*400.00*		
2045	20c Medal of Honor...........................	.55	.25	
a.	Red omitted	*200.00*		
2046	20c Babe Ruth	1.40	.25	
2047	20c Nathaniel Hawthorne	.45	.25	
2048	13c Olympics - Discus	.35	.25	
2049	13c Olympics - High Jump	.35	.25	
2050	13c Olympics - Archery......................	.35	.25	
2051	13c Olympics - Boxing	.35	.25	
a.	Block of 4, #2048-2051	1.50	1.25	
2052	20c Treaty of Paris	.40	.25	
2053	20c Civil Service	.40	.25	
2054	20c Metropolitan Opera	.40	.25	
2055	20c Charles Steinmetz........................	.50	.25	
2056	20c Edwin Armstrong	.50	.25	
2057	20c Nikola Tesla	.50	.25	
2058	20c Philo T. Farnsworth.....................	.50	.25	
a.	Block of 4, #2055-2058	2.00	1.50	
b.	As "a," black omitted	*325.00*		
2059	20c Streetcar - New York	.50	.25	

2048-2051

2052

2053

2054

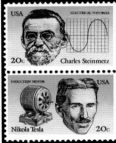

2055-2058

HOW TO USE THIS BOOK

The number in the first column is its Scott number or identifying number. Following that is the denomination of the stamp and its color or description. Finally, the values, unused and used, are shown.

2059-2062

2063

2064

2065

2066

2067-2070

2071

177

2072

2073

2074

2075

2076-2079

2080

2082-2085

2081

2086

2087

2088

2089

178

Scott No.		Description	Unused Value	Used Value	/ / / / / /
2060		20c Streetcar - Alabama.........................	.50	.25	
a.		Horiz. pair, black (engr.) missing on			
		Nos. 2059, 2060 (from extraneous paper)	—		
2061		20c Streetcar - Arkansas........................	.50	.25	
a.		Vert. pair, black (engr.) missing on			
		Nos. 2059, 2061 (from extraneous paper)	—		
2062		20c Streetcar - Louisiana	.50	.25	
a.		Block of 4, #2059-2062	2.00	1.50	
b.		As "a," black (engr.) omitted	300.00		
c.		As "a," black (engr.) omitted			
		on #2059, 2061................................	—		
2063		20c Christmas - Religious......................	.40	.25	
2064		20c Christmas - Santa Claus.................	.40	.25	
a.		Imperf., pair....................................	125.00		
2065		20c Martin Luther	.40	.25	
1984					
2066		20c Alaska Statehood............................	.40	.25	
2067		20c Olympics - Ice Dancing	.55	.25	
2068		20c Olympics - Alpine Skiing	.55	.25	
2069		20c Olympics - Nordic Skiing...............	.55	.25	
2070		20c Olympics - Ice Hockey	.55	.25	
a.		Block of 4, #2067-2070	2.20	1.75	
2071		20c Federal Deposit Insurance Corp.	.40	.25	
2072		20c Love	.40	.25	
a.		Horiz. pair, imperf. vert.	150.00		
2073		20c Carter G. Woodson..........................	.40	.25	
a.		Horiz. pair, imperf. vert.	1,000.		
2074		20c Soil & Water Conservation.............	.40	.25	
2075		20c Credit Union Act	.40	.25	
2076		20c Wild Pink Orchid	.50	.25	
2077		20c Yellow Lady's-slipper Orchid	.50	.25	
2078		20c Spreading Pogonia Orchid	.50	.25	
2079		20c Pacific Calypso Orchid..................	.50	.25	
a.		Block of 4, #2076-2079	2.00	1.50	
2080		20c Hawaii Statehood	.40	.25	
2081		20c National Archives...........................	.40	.25	
2082		20c Olympics - Diving..........................	.55	.25	
2083		20c Olympics - Long Jump	.55	.25	
2084		20c Olympics - Wrestling.....................	.55	.25	
2085		20c Olympics - Kayak	.55	.25	
a.		Block of 4, #2082-2085	2.40	1.90	
b.		As "a," imperf btwn. vertically	9,500.		
2086		20c Louisiana World Exposition............	.50	.25	
2087		20c Health Research	.40	.25	
2088		20c Douglas Fairbanks	.50	.25	
b.		Horiz. pair, imperf. btwn.	—		
2089		20c Jim Thorpe......................................	.50	.25	
2090		20c John McCormack............................	.40	.25	

2091

2092

2090

2093

2094

2095

2096

2097

2098-2101

Scott No.		Description	Unused Value	Used Value	/ / / / / /
2091	20c	St. Lawrence Seaway	.40	.25	
2092	20c	Waterfowl Preservation Act	.50	.25	
a.		Horiz. pair, imperf. vert.	325.00		
2093	20c	Roanoke Voyages	.40	.25	
2094	20c	Herman Melville	.40	.25	
2095	20c	Horace Moses	.45	.25	
2096	20c	Smokey Bear	.40	.25	
a.		Horiz. pair, imperf. btwn.	250.00		
b.		Vert. pair, imperf. btwn.	200.00		
c.		Block of 4, imperf. btwn, vert. & horiz.	4,000.		
d.		Horiz. pair, imperf. vert.	1,000.		
2097	20c	Roberto Clemente	1.40	.25	
a.		Horiz. pair, imperf. vert.	1,800.		
2098	20c	Beagle & Boston Terrier	.50	.25	
2099	20c	Chesapeake Bay Retriever & Cocker Spaniel	.50	.25	
2100	20c	Alaskan Malamute & Collie	.50	.25	
2101	20c	Black & Tan Coonhound & American Foxhound	.50	.25	
a.		Block of 4, #2098-2101	2.00	1.90	
b.		As "a," imperf. horiz.	—		
2102	20c	Crime Prevention	.40	.25	
2103	20c	Hispanic Americans	.40	.25	
a.		Vert. pair, imperf. horiz.	2,000.		
2104	20c	Family Unity	.40	.25	
a.		Horiz. pair, imperf. vert.	425.00		
c.		Vert. pair, imperf. btwn. & at bottom	—		
d.		Horiz. pair, imperf btwn.	—		
2105	20c	Eleanor Roosevelt	.40	.25	
2106	20c	Nation of Readers	.40	.25	
2107	20c	Christmas - Religious	.40	.25	
2108	20c	Christmas - Santa Claus	.40	.25	
a.		Horiz. pair, imperf. vert.	875.00		
2109	20c	Vietnam Veterans' Memorial	.50	.25	
1985					
2110	22c	Jerome Kern	.40	.25	
2111	(22c)	"D" & Eagle	.60	.25	
a.		Vert. pair, imperf.	35.00		
b.		Vert. pair, imperf. horiz.	1,000.		
Coil Stamp, Perf. 10 Vertically					
2112	(22c)	"D" & Eagle (2111)	.60	.25	
a.		Imperf., pair	45.00		
2113	(22c)	"D" & Eagle (from bklt. pane)	.80	.25	
a.		Booklet pane of 10	8.50	3.00	
b.		As "a," horiz. imperf. btwn.	—		
2114	22c	Flag Over Capitol (2115)	.45	.25	

2102

2103

2104

2105

2106

2107

2108

2109

2110

2111

2113

2115

2116

HOW TO USE THIS BOOK

The number in the first column is its Scott number or identifying number. Following that is the denomination of the stamp and its color or description. Finally, the values, unused and used, are shown.

Scott No.	Description	Unused Value	Used Value	/ / / / / /
a.	All color missing (from extraneous paper)..	—		☐☐☐☐☐

Coil Stamp, Perf. 10 Vertically

2115	22c Flag Over Capitol............................	.45	.25	☐☐☐☐☐
c.	Inscribed "T" at bottom	.55	.40	☐☐☐☐☐
f.	Imperf., pair.....................................	10.00		☐☐☐☐☐

Booklet Stamp, Perf. 10 Horizontal on 1 or 2 Sides

2116	22c Flag Over Capitol............................	.50	.25	☐☐☐☐☐
a.	Booklet pane of 5	2.50	1.25	☐☐☐☐☐

Booklet Stamps, Perf. 10

2117	22c Frilled Dogwinkle	.45	.25	☐☐☐☐☐
2118	22c Reticulated Helmet.........................	.45	.25	☐☐☐☐☐
2119	22c New England Neptune	.45	.25	☐☐☐☐☐
2120	22c Calico Scallop	.45	.25	☐☐☐☐☐
2121	22c Lightning Whelk	.45	.25	☐☐☐☐☐
a.	Booklet pane of 10, 2 ea. #2117-2121	4.00	3.00	☐☐☐☐☐
b.	As "a," violet omitted......................	*475.00*		☐☐☐☐☐
c.	As "a," vert. imperf. btwn...............	*450.00*		☐☐☐☐☐
d.	As "a," imperf..............................	—		☐☐☐☐☐
e.	Strip of 5, #2117-2121	2.00	—	☐☐☐☐☐

Booklet Stamp, Perf. 10 Vertically on 1 or 2 Sides

2122	$10.75 Eagle & Half Moon, Type I	19.00	7.50	☐☐☐☐☐
a.	Booklet pane of 3	60.00	—	☐☐☐☐☐
b.	Type II...	21.00	10.00	☐☐☐☐☐
c.	As "b," booklet pane of 3................	65.00	—	☐☐☐☐☐

Type I has a washed out dull appearance. Denomination appears splotchy or grainy. (P#11111) Type II has brighter, more intense colors. Denomination appears smoother (P#22222).

1985-87, Coil Stamps, Perf. 10 Vertically

2123	3.4c School Bus, tagged........................	.25	.25	☐☐☐☐☐
a.	Untagged (Bureau precanceled)	.25	.25	☐☐☐☐☐
2124	4.9c Buckboard, tagged.........................	.25	.25	☐☐☐☐☐
a.	Untagged (Bureau precanceled)	.25	.25	☐☐☐☐☐
2125	5.5c Star Route Truck, tagged	.25	.25	☐☐☐☐☐
a.	Untagged (Bureau precanceled)	.25	.25	☐☐☐☐☐
2126	6c Tricycle, tagged..............................	.25	.25	☐☐☐☐☐
a.	Untagged (Bureau precanceled)	.25	.25	☐☐☐☐☐
b.	Imperf., pair.....................................	200.00		☐☐☐☐☐
2127	7.1c Tractor, tagged...............................	.25	.25	☐☐☐☐☐
a.	Untagged (Bureau precanceled)	.25	.25	☐☐☐☐☐
c.	As "a," black (precancel) omitted...	—		☐☐☐☐☐
2128	8.3c Ambulance, tagged........................	.25	.25	☐☐☐☐☐
a.	Untagged (Bureau precanceled)	.25	.25	☐☐☐☐☐
2129	8.5c Tow Truck, tagged.........................	.25	.25	☐☐☐☐☐
a.	Untagged (Bureau precanceled)	.25	.25	☐☐☐☐☐
2130	10.1c Oil Wagon, tagged..........................	.55	.25	☐☐☐☐☐

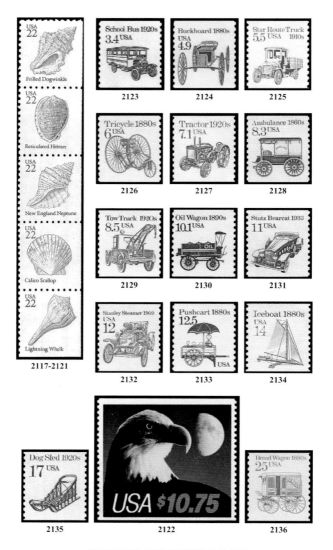

Frilled Dogwinkle
USA 22

Reticulated Helmet
USA 22

New England Neptune
USA 22

Calico Scallop
USA 22

Lightning Whelk
USA 22

2117-2121

School Bus 1920s
3.4 USA
2123

Buckboard 1880s
USA 4.9
2124

Star Route Truck
5.5 USA 1910s
2125

Tricycle 1880s
6 USA
2126

Tractor 1920s
7.1 USA
2127

Ambulance 1860s
8.3 USA
2128

Tow Truck 1920s
8.5 USA
2129

Oil Wagon 1890s
10.1 USA
2130

Stutz Bearcat 1933
11 USA
2131

Stanley Steamer 1909
USA 12
2132

Pushcart 1880s
12.5 USA
2133

Iceboat 1880s
USA 14
2134

Dog Sled 1920s
17 USA
2135

USA $10.75
2122

Bread Wagon 1880s
25 USA
2136

HOW TO USE THIS BOOK

The number in the first column is its Scott number or identifying number. Following that is the denomination of the stamp and its color or description. Finally, the values, unused and used, are shown.

Scott No.		Description	Unused Value	Used Value	/ / / / / /
a.		Untagged (Bureau precanceled)	.25	.25	
b.		As "a," imperf. pair	15.00		
2131	11c	Stutz Bearcat	.25	.25	
2132	12c	Stanley Steamer, Type I, tagged......	.35	.25	
a.		Type I, untagged (Bureau precanceled)	.25	.25	
b.		Type II, untagged (Bureau precanceled)	.40	.30	
		Type II has "Stanley Steamer 1909" 17½ mm. On Type I it is 18 mm.			
2133	12.5c	Pushcart, tagged	.35	.25	
a.		Untagged (Bureau precanceled)	.25	.25	
b.		As "a," imperf., pair	45.00		
2134	14c	Iceboat, Type I	.30	.25	
a.		Imperf. pair....................................	90.00		
b.		Type II	.30	.25	
		Type I design is 17½ mm wide, has overall tagging.			
		Type II is 17¼ mm wide, has block tagging.			
2135	17c	Dog Sled...	.55	.25	
a.		Imperf., pair....................................	*375.00*		
2136	25c	Bread Wagon	.50	.25	
a.		Imperf., pair....................................	12.50		
b.		Pair, imperf. btwn.	*600.00*		
1985					
2137	22c	Mary McLeod Bethune.................	.60	.25	
2138	22c	Broadbill Decoy	1.00	.25	
2139	22c	Mallard Decoy	1.00	.25	
2140	22c	Canvasback Decoy	1.00	.25	
2141	22c	Redhead Decoy	1.00	.25	
a.		Block of 4, #2138-2141	4.00	2.75	
2142	22c	Winter Special Olympics	.50	.25	
a.		Vert. pair, imperf. horiz..................	*400.00*		
2143	22c	Love	.45	.25	
a.		Imperf., pair....................................	*1,250.*		
2144	22c	Rural Electrification Administration	.60	.25	
a.		Vert. pair, imperf. btwn.	—		
2145	22c	AMERIPEX '86..............................	.45	.25	
a.		Red, black & blue omitted	*175.00*		
b.		Red & black omitted.......................	—		
c.		Red omitted....................................	*2,350.*		
d.		Black missing (from perf. shift)	—		
2146	22c	Abigail Adams...............................	.45	.25	
a.		Imperf., pair....................................	*225.00*		
2147	22c	Frederic Auguste Bartholdi............	.45	.25	
Coil Stamps, Perf. 10 Vertically					
2149	18c	George Washington, tagged............	.40	.25	
a.		Untagged (Bureau precanceled)	.35	.35	
b.		Imperf., pair....................................	*825.00*		
c.		As "a," imperf., pair	*625.00*		
2150	21.1c	Envelopes, tagged...........................	.40	.25	

185

2137

2138-2141

2142

2143

2144

2145

2146

2147

2149

2150

2152

2153   2154

2155-2158

2160-2163

2159   2164   2165

Arkansas
Statehood
1836–1986
Old State House
Little Rock
USA 22

2166   2167

2168   2169   2170   2171   2172

2173   2175   2176   2177   2178

2179   2180   2181   2182   2183

2184   2185   2186   2187   2188

2189   2190   2191   2192

Scott No.		Description	Unused Value	Used Value	/ / / / / /
a.		Untagged (Bureau precanceled)	.40	.40	☐☐☐☐☐
1985					
2152	22c	Korean War Veterans......................	.40	.25	☐☐☐☐☐
2153	22c	Social Security Act........................	.40	.25	☐☐☐☐☐
2154	22c	World War I Veterans	.40	.25	☐☐☐☐☐
a.		Red missing (from perf. shift)	*400.00*		☐☐☐☐☐
2155	22c	Quarter Horse...............................	1.25	.25	☐☐☐☐☐
2156	22c	Morgan Horse...............................	1.25	.25	☐☐☐☐☐
2157	22c	Saddlebred Horse	1.25	.25	☐☐☐☐☐
2158	22c	Appaloosa Horse	1.25	.25	☐☐☐☐☐
a.		Block of 4, #2155-2158	6.00	4.00	☐☐☐☐☐
2159	22c	Public Education	.45	.25	☐☐☐☐☐
2160	22c	YMCA Youth Camping..................	.70	.25	☐☐☐☐☐
2161	22c	Boy Scouts....................................	.70	.25	☐☐☐☐☐
2162	22c	Big Brothers/Big Sisters	.70	.25	☐☐☐☐☐
2163	22c	Camp Fire	.70	.25	☐☐☐☐☐
a.		Block of 4, #2160-2163	3.00	2.25	☐☐☐☐☐
2164	22c	Help End Hunger	.45	.25	☐☐☐☐☐
2165	22c	Christmas - Religious.....................	.40	.25	☐☐☐☐☐
a.		Imperf., pair.................................	*65.00*		☐☐☐☐☐
2166	22c	Christmas - Poinsettias..................	.40	.25	☐☐☐☐☐
a.		Imperf., pair.................................	*100.00*		☐☐☐☐☐
1986-93					
2167	22c	Arkansas Statehood.......................	.75	.25	☐☐☐☐☐
a.		Vert. pair, imperf. horiz.................	—		☐☐☐☐☐
2168	1c	Margaret Mitchell..........................	.25	.25	☐☐☐☐☐
b.		1c red brown................................	.30	.30	☐☐☐☐☐
2169	2c	Mary Lyon	.25	.25	☐☐☐☐☐
2170	3c	Dr. Paul Dudley White	.25	.25	☐☐☐☐☐
2171	4c	Father Edward Flanagan	.25	.25	☐☐☐☐☐
a.		4c grayish violet...........................	.25	.25	☐☐☐☐☐
b.		4c deep grayish blue......................	.25	.25	☐☐☐☐☐
d.		All color missing (from extraneous paper)...	—		☐☐☐☐☐
2172	5c	Hugo L. Black	.25	.25	☐☐☐☐☐
b.		5c light olive green........................	.25	.25	☐☐☐☐☐
2173	5c	Luis Munoz Marin, tagged	.25	.25	☐☐☐☐☐
a.		Untagged	.25	.25	☐☐☐☐☐
2175	10c	Red Cloud, lake	.25	.25	☐☐☐☐☐
e.		10c carmine	.50	.25	☐☐☐☐☐
f.		As "c," all color omitted...............	*200.00*		☐☐☐☐☐
2176	14c	Julia Ward Howe	.30	.25	☐☐☐☐☐
2177	15c	Buffalo Bill Cody..........................	.35	.25	☐☐☐☐☐
d.		All color omitted...........................	—		☐☐☐☐☐
2178	17c	Belva Ann Lockwood.....................	.35	.25	☐☐☐☐☐
2179	20c	Dr. Virginia Apgar, red brown	.40	.25	☐☐☐☐☐
a.		20c orange brown..........................	.45	.25	☐☐☐☐☐

2193   2194   2195   2196

2198-2201

2202   2203

2204   2211

2210

2205-2209

Scott No.		Description	Unused Value	Used Value	/ / / / / /
b.		20c bright red brown	1.00	.25	
2180	21c	Chester Carlson	.45	.25	
2181	23c	Mary Cassatt	.45	.25	
2182	25c	Jack London, perf. 11	.50	.25	
a.		Booklet pane of 10	5.00	3.75	
d.		Horiz. pair, imperf btwn	850.00		
e.		As "a," all color omitted on right stamps	—		
f.		As No. 2182 (sheet stamp), vert. pair, bottom stamp all color omitted	—		
2183	28c	Sitting Bull	.65	.35	
2184	29c	Earl Warren	.70	.25	
2185	29c	Thomas Jefferson	.65	.25	
2186	35c	Dennis Chavez	.75	.25	
2187	40c	Claire Chennault, dark blue	.85	.25	
2188	45c	Dr. Harvey Cushing, bright blue	1.00	.25	
a.		45c blue	2.25	.25	
2189	52c	Hubert H. Humphrey	1.10	.25	
2190	56c	John Harvard	1.20	.25	
2191	65c	H.H. 'Hap' Arnold	1.30	.25	
2192	75c	Wendell Willkie	1.60	.25	
2193	$1	Bernard Revel	3.00	.50	
a.		All color omitted	—		
2194	$1	Johns Hopkins, intense deep blue	2.25	.50	
b.		$1 deep blue	2.50	.50	
d.		$1 dark blue	2.50	.50	
e.		$1 blue	2.75	.60	
2195	$2	William Jennings Bryan	4.25	.50	
2196	$5	Bret Harte	9.00	2.50	
Booklet Stamp, Perf. 10 on 2 or 3 Sides					
2197	25c	Jack London (2182)	.55	.25	
a.		Booklet pane of 6	3.30	2.50	
1986					
2198	22c	Handstamped Cover	.45	.25	
2199	22c	Boy, Stamp Collection	.45	.25	
2200	22c	No. 836 Magnified	.45	.25	
2201	22c	No. 2216 on First Day Cover	.45	.25	
a.		Booklet pane of 4, #2198-2201	2.00	1.75	
b.		As "a," black omitted on #2198, 2201	47.50	—	
c.		As "a," blue (litho.) omitted on #2198-2200	2,250.		
d.		As "a," buff (litho.) omitted	—		
2202	22c	Love	.55	.25	
2203	22c	Sojourner Truth	.55	.25	
2204	22c	Republic of Texas	.55	.25	
a.		Horiz. pair, imperf. vert.	900.00		
b.		Dark red omitted	2,250.		

Presidents of
the United States: I

AMERIPEX 86
International
Stamp Show
Chicago, Illinois
May 22–June 1, 1986

2216

Presidents of
the United States: II

AMERIPEX 86
International
Stamp Show
Chicago, Illinois
May 22–June 1, 1986

2217

Presidents of
the United States: III

AMERIPEX 86
International
Stamp Show
Chicago, Illinois
May 22–June 1, 1986

2218

Presidents of
the United States: IV

AMERIPEX 86
International
Stamp Show
Chicago, Illinois
May 22–June 1, 1986

2219

2220-2223

2225   2224   2226

2235-2238

2239

2240-2243

2246

2244

2245

2247

2248

2249

2250

2251

2252

2253

2254

2255

194

Scott No.	Description	Unused Value	Used Value	/ / / / / /
c.	Dark blue omitted............................	*8,000.*		
2205	22c Muskellunge....................................	1.00	.25	
2206	22c Atlantic Cod...................................	1.00	.25	
2207	22c Largemouth Bass............................	1.00	.25	
2208	22c Bluefin Tuna..................................	1.00	.25	
2209	22c Catfish	1.00	.25	
a.	Booklet pane of 5, #2205-2209	6.00	*2.75*	
2210	22c Public Hospitals............................	.45	.25	
a.	Vert. pair, imperf. horiz...................	275.00		
b.	Horiz. pair, imperf. vert.	*1,150.*		
2211	22c Duke Ellington	.45	.25	
a.	Vert. pair, imperf. horiz...................	*750.00*		
2216	Washington-Harrison, sheet of 9	7.50	4.00	
a.-i.	22c Any single.......................................	.75	.40	
j.	Blue omitted...................................	*2,500.*		
k.	Black inscription omitted...............	*2,000.*		
l.	Imperf.	*10,500.*		
m.	As "k," double impression of red ...	—		
n.	Blue omitted on stamps 1-3, 5-6, 8, 9..	—		
2217	Tyler-Grant, sheet of 9	7.50	4.00	
a.-i.	22c Any single.......................................	.75	.40	
j.	Black inscription omitted...............	*2,500.*		
2218	Hayes-Wilson, sheet of 9	7.50	4.00	
a.-i.	22c Any single.......................................	.75	.40	
j.	Brown omitted.................................	—		
k.	Black inscription omitted...............	*2,500.*		
2219	Harding-Johnson, White House, sht. of 9	7.50	—	
a.-i.	22c Any single.......................................	.75	.40	
j.	Blkish blue (engr.) inscription omitted on a.-b., d.-e., g.-h.............	*2,500.*		
l.	Blackish blue (engr.) omitted on all stamps.......................................	—		
2220	22c Elisha Kent Kane	.65	.25	
2221	22c Adolphus W. Greely.......................	.65	.25	
2222	22c Vilhjalmur Stefansson....................	.65	.25	
2223	22c Robert E. Peary & Matthew Henson	.65	.25	
a.	Block of 4, #2220-2223	2.75	2.25	
b.	As "a," black omitted	*6,000.*		
c.	As "a," Nos. 2220, 2221 black (engr.) omitted............................	—		
d.	As "a," Nos. 2222, 2223 black (engr.) omitted............................	—		
2224	22c Statue of Liberty	.40	.25	
a.	Scarlet omitted	—		

1986-87, Coil Stamps, Perf. 10 Vertically

2225	1c Omnibus, tagged	.25	.25	
b.	Untagged	.25	.25	

2256

2257

2258

2259

2260

2261

2262

2263

2264

2265

2266

2268

2267

2269

2271

2270

2272

2273

2274

Scott No.		Description	Unused Value	Used Value	/ / / / / /
c.		Imperf., pair.....................................	*2,000.*		
2226	2c	Locomotive, tagged......................	.25	.25	
a.		Untagged	.25	.25	
2228	4c	Stagecoach (1898A)......................	.25	.25	
b.		Imperf., pair.....................................	175.00		
2231	8.3c	Ambulance (2128), (Bureau precancel)	.65	.25	

On No. 2228 "Stagecoach 1890s" is 17 mm long,
on No. 1898A 19½ mm long. On No. 2231 "Ambulance
1860s" is 18 mm long, on No. 2128 18½ mm long.

1986

2235	22c	Navajo Art - Stripes & Diamonds ..	.80	.25	
2236	22c	Navajo Art - 2 Diamonds Across....	.80	.25	
2237	22c	Navajo Art - 5 Diamonds Across....	.80	.25	
2238	22c	Navajo Art - 4 Diamonds Across....	.80	.25	
a.		Block of 4, #2235-2238	3.25	2.25	
b.		As "a," black (engr.) omitted	*325.00*		
2239	22c	T.S. Eliot.....................................	.55	.25	
2240	22c	Highlander Figure	.50	.25	
2241	22c	Ship Figurehead	.50	.25	
2242	22c	Nautical Figure..............................	.50	.25	
2243	22c	Cigar Store Indian.........................	.50	.25	
a.		Block of 4, #2240-2243	2.00	1.50	
b.		As "a," imperf. vert........................	*1,000.*		
2244	22c	Christmas - Religious.....................	.45	.25	
a.		Imperf., pair.....................................	*600.00*		
2245	22c	Christmas - Village........................	.45	.25	

1987

2246	22c	Michigan Statehood	.55	.25	
2247	22c	Pan-American Games	.45	.25	
a.		Silver omitted	*1,250.*		
2248	22c	Love...	.45	.25	
2249	22c	Jean Baptiste Pointe du Sable	.50	.25	
2250	22c	Enrico Caruso................................	.45	.25	
a.		Black (engr.) omitted	*4,500.*		
2251	22c	Girl Scouts....................................	.45	.25	
a.		All litho. colors omitted	*2,450.*		
b.		Red & black (engr.) omitted	*1,950.*		

1987-88, Coil Stamps, Perf. 10 Vertically

2252	3c	Conestoga Wagon, tagged..............	.25	.25	
a.		Untagged	.25	.25	
b.		Imperf., pair....................................	*1,350.*		
2253	5c	Milk Wagon	.25	.25	
2254	5.3c	Elevator (Bureau precancel in red) ..	.25	.25	
2255	7.6c	Carretta (Bureau precancel in red) .	.25	.25	
2256	8.4c	Wheelchair (Bureau precancel in red)	.25	.25	
a.		Imperf., pair....................................	375.00		
2257	10c	Canal Boat....................................	.40	.25	

Scott No.	Description	Unused Value	Used Value	/ / / / / /
e.	Imperf., pair......................................	*1,750.*		
2258 13c	Patrol Wagon (Bureau precancel in red)	.50	.25	
2259 13.2c	Coal Car (Bureau precancel in red)	.25	.25	
a.	Imperf., pair......................................	80.00		
2260 15c	Tugboat...	.25	.25	
c.	Imperf., pair......................................	*650.00*		
2261 16.7c	Popcorn Wagon (Bureau precancel in blk)	.30	.30	
a.	Imperf., pair......................................	*150.00*		
2262 17.5c	Racing Car, tagged..........................	.65	.25	
a.	Untagged...	.50	.30	
b.	Imperf., pair......................................	*1,600.*		
2263 20c	Cable Car..	.35	.25	
a.	Imperf., pair......................................	50.00		
2264 20.5c	Fire Engine (Bureau precancel in black)	.50	.40	
2265 21c	Railroad Mail Car			
	(Bureau precancel in red)	.40	.40	
a.	Imperf., pair......................................	42.50		
2266 24.1c	Tandem Bicycle (Bureau precancel			
	in red)	.60	.45	

1987, Booklet Stamps

Scott No.	Description	Unused Value	Used Value	/ / / / / /
2267 22c	Congratulations	.65	.25	
2268 22c	Get Well..	.80	.25	
2269 22c	Thank You..	.80	.25	
2270 22c	Love You, Dad..................................	.80	.25	
2271 22c	Best Wishes	.80	.25	
2272 22c	Happy Birthday	.65	.25	
2273 22c	Love You, Mother.............................	1.40	.25	
2274 22c	Keep in Touch...................................	.80	.25	
a.	Booklet pane of 10 (#2268-2271,			
	2273-2274, 2 each #2267, 2272)..	10.00	*5.00*	

1987

Scott No.	Description	Unused Value	Used Value	/ / / / / /
2275 22c	United Way..	.45	.25	
2276 22c	Flag & Fireworks..............................	.45	.25	
a.	Booklet pane of 20..........................	9.00	—	
b.	As "a", vert. pair, imperf. btwn.	*1,500.*	—	
c.	As "a", miscut and inserted upside			
	down into booklet cover, imperf.			
	btwn. stamps and right selvage.....	—		
d.	Yellow omitted.................................	—		
2277 (25c)	"E" & Earth, perf 11	.50	.25	
2278 25c	Flag & Clouds, perf 11	.50	.25	

Coil Stamps, Perf. 10 Vertically

Scott No.	Description	Unused Value	Used Value	/ / / / / /
2279 (25c)	"E" & Earth (2277).........................	.50	.25	
a.	Imperf., pair......................................	60.00	—	
2280 25c	Flag Over Yosemite, Green Trees ...	.50	.25	
c.	Imperf., pair......................................	10.00		
e.	Black trees..	*700.00*	—	
f.	Pair, imperf. btwn.............................	*450.00*		

Scott No.		Description	Unused Value	Used Value	/ / / / / /
2281	25c	Honeybee	.50	.25	
a.		Imperf., pair	45.00		
b.		Black (engr.) omitted	50.00		
c.		Black (litho.) omitted	450.00		
d.		Pair, imperf. between	700.00		
e.		Yellow (litho.) omitted	1,000.		
Booklet Stamps					
2282	(25c)	"E" & Earth (2277), perf. 10	.50	.25	
a.		Booklet pane of 10	6.50	3.50	
2283	25c	Pheasant, multicolored	.50	.25	
a.		Booklet pane of 10	6.00	3.50	
b.	25c	multi, red removed from sky	5.00	.25	
c.		As "b," booklet pane of 10	40.00	—	
d.		As "a," horiz. imperf. btwn.	—		
2284	25c	Grosbeak	.50	.25	
2285	25c	Owl	.50	.25	
b.		Bklt. pane of 10, 5 each #2284-2285	5.00	3.50	
d.		Pair, #2284-2285	1.10	.25	
2285A	25c	Flag & Clouds (2278), perf. 10	.50	.25	
c.		Booklet pane of 6	3.00	2.00	
1987					
2286	22c	Barn swallow	1.00	.50	
2287	22c	Monarch butterfly	1.00	.50	
2288	22c	Bighorn sheep	1.00	.50	
2289	22c	Broad-tailed hummingbird	1.00	.50	
2290	22c	Cottontail	1.00	.50	
2291	22c	Osprey	1.00	.50	
2292	22c	Mountain lion	1.00	.50	
2293	22c	Luna moth	1.00	.50	
2294	22c	Mule deer	1.00	.50	
2295	22c	Gray squirrel	1.00	.50	
2296	22c	Armadillo	1.00	.50	
2297	22c	Eastern chipmunk	1.00	.50	
2298	22c	Moose	1.00	.50	
2299	22c	Black bear	1.00	.50	
2300	22c	Tiger swallowtail	1.00	.50	
2301	22c	Bobwhite	1.00	.50	
2302	22c	Ringtail	1.00	.50	
2303	22c	Red-winged blackbird	1.00	.50	
2304	22c	American lobster	1.00	.50	
2305	22c	Black-tailed jack rabbit	1.00	.50	
2306	22c	Scarlet tanager	1.00	.50	
2307	22c	Woodchuck	1.00	.50	
2308	22c	Roseate spoonbill	1.00	.50	
2309	22c	Bald eagle	1.00	.50	
2310	22c	Alaskan brown bear	1.00	.50	
2311	22c	Iiwi	1.00	.50	

2275

2276   2277   2278   2280

2281   2283   2284   2285

2286-2335

200

Scott No.	Description	Unused Value	Used Value	/ / / / /
2312	22c Badger	1.00	.50	
2313	22c Pronghorn	1.00	.50	
2314	22c River otter	1.00	.50	
2315	22c Ladybug	1.00	.50	
2316	22c Beaver	1.00	.50	
2317	22c White-tailed deer	1.00	.50	
2318	22c Blue jay	1.00	.50	
2319	22c Pika	1.00	.50	
2320	22c American Buffalo	1.00	.50	
2321	22c Snowy egret	1.00	.50	
2322	22c Gray wolf	1.00	.50	
2323	22c Mountain goat	1.00	.50	
2324	22c Deer mouse	1.00	.50	
2325	22c Black-tailed prairie dog	1.00	.50	
2326	22c Box turtle	1.00	.50	
2327	22c Wolverine	1.00	.50	
2328	22c American elk	1.00	.50	
2329	22c California sea lion	1.00	.50	
2330	22c Mockingbird	1.00	.50	
2331	22c Raccoon	1.00	.50	
2332	22c Bobcat	1.00	.50	
2333	22c Black-footed ferret	1.00	.50	
2334	22c Canada goose	1.00	.50	
2335	22c Red fox	1.00	.50	
a.	Pane of 50, #2286-2335	50.00	35.00	
	2286b-2335b, any single, red omitted	2,500.		

1987-90

2336	22c Delaware Ratification	.60	.25	
2337	22c Pennsylvania Ratification	.60	.25	
2338	22c New Jersey Ratification	.60	.25	
a.	Black (engr.) omitted	5,000.		
2339	22c Georgia Ratification	.60	.25	
2340	22c Connecticut Ratification	.60	.25	
2341	22c Massachusetts Ratification	.60	.25	
2342	22c Maryland Ratification	.60	.25	
2343	25c South Carolina Ratification	.60	.25	
a.	Strip of 3, vert. imperf. btwn.	12,500.		
b.	Red missing (from perf. shift)	—		
2344	25c New Hampshire Ratification	.60	.25	
2345	25c Virginia Ratification	.60	.25	
2346	25c New York Ratification	.60	.25	
2347	25c North Carolina Ratification	.60	.25	
2348	25c Rhode Island Ratification	.60	.25	

1987

2349	22c U.S.-Morocco Diplomatic Relations	.50	.25	
a.	Black (engr.) omitted	250.00		
2350	22c William Faulkner	.55	.25	

Dec 7,1787 USA Delaware 22	Dec 12,1787 Pennsylvania 22	Dec 18,1787 USA New Jersey 22
2336	2337	2338

22 USA January 2, 1788 Georgia	22 USA January 9, 1788 Connecticut	22 USA Feb 6,1788 Massachusetts
2339	2340	2341

April 28,1788 USA Maryland 22	25 USA May 23, 1788 South Carolina	25 USA June 21,1788 New Hampshire
2342	2343	2344

June 25, 1788 USA Virginia 25	July 26, 1788 USA New York 25	25 USA November 21,1789 North Carolina	25 USA May 29, 1790 Rhode Island
2345	2346	2347	2348

2349

2351-2354

2355-2359

2350

2360

2367

2368

2361

2369

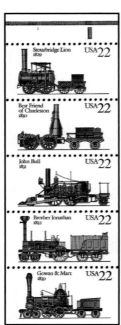

2362-2366

2370

2371

2376

2372-2375

204

Scott No.	Description	Unused Value	Used Value	/ / / / / /
2351	22c Lacemaking - Upper Left..............	.45	.25	
2352	22c Lacemaking - Upper Right.............	.45	.25	
2353	22c Lacemaking - Lower Left..............	.45	.25	
2354	22c Lacemaking - Lower Right	.45	.25	
a.	Block of 4, #2351-2354	1.90	1.90	
b.	As "a," white omitted	*400.00*		
c.	Single stamp, white omitted............	100.00		
2355	22c "The Bicentennial . . ."	.90	.25	
a.	Grayish green (background) omitted	—		
2356	22c "We the People . . ."	.90	.25	
a.	Grayish green (background) omitted	—		
2357	22c "Establish Justice, . . ."	.90	.25	
a.	Grayish green (background) omitted	—		
2358	22c "And Secure . . ."	.90	.25	
a.	Grayish green (background) omitted	—		
2359	22c "Do Ordain . . ."	.90	.25	
a.	Bklt. pane of 5, #2355-2359	4.50	*2.25*	
b.	Grayish green (background) omitted	—		
2360	22c Signing of the Constitution	.55	.25	
2361	22c Certified Public Accounting...........	1.00	.25	
a.	Black (engr.) omitted......................	*675.00*		
2362	22c Stourbridge Lion.............................	.55	.25	
2363	22c Best Friend of Charleston...............	.55	.25	
2364	22c John Bull..	.55	.25	
2365	22c Brother Jonathan............................	.55	.25	
a.	Red omitted....................................	*1,100.*	225.00	
2366	22c Gowan and Marx	.55	.25	
a.	Booklet pane of 5, #2362-2366	2.75	*2.50*	
b.	As "a," black omitted on #2366......	—		
c.	As No. 2366, blue omitted		—	
2367	22c Christmas - Religious.....................	.45	.25	
2368	22c Christmas - Ornaments...................	.45	.25	
1988				
2369	22c Olympics - Skiing..........................	.50	.25	
2370	22c Australia Bicentennial	.45	.25	
2371	22c James Weldon Johnson...................	.50	.25	
2372	22c Siamese, Exotic Shorthair Cats.......	.70	.25	
2373	22c Abyssinian, Himalayan Cats	.70	.25	
2374	22c Maine Coon, Burmese Cats	.70	.25	
2375	22c American Shorthair, Persian Cats ...	.70	.25	
a.	Block of 4, #2372-2375	2.80	1.90	
2376	22c Knute Rockne	.50	.25	
2377	25c Francis Ouimet	.60	.25	
2378	25c Rose	.50	.25	
a.	Imperf., pair	*2,000.*		
2379	45c Roses	.85	.25	
2380	25c Olympics - Gymnastics Rings	.50	.25	
2381	25c 1928 Locomobile............................	.80	.25	

2377

2378

2379

2380

2381-2385

2390-2393

HOW TO USE THIS BOOK

The number in the first column is its Scott number or identifying number. Following that is the denomination of the stamp and its color or description. Finally, the values, unused and used, are shown.

2386-2389

2394

2395

2396

2397

2398

2399

2400

2401

2402

2403

2404

2405-2409

2410

2411

2412

2413

2414

2415

Scott No.	Description	Unused Value	Used Value	/ / / / / /
2382	25c 1929 Pierce-Arrow	.80	.25	
2383	25c 1931 Cord	.80	.25	
2384	25c 1932 Packard	.80	.25	
2385	25c 1935 Duesenberg	.80	.25	
a.	Booklet pane of 5, #2381-2385	5.00	3.50	
2386	25c Nathaniel Palmer	.65	.25	
2387	25c Lt. Charles Wilkes	.65	.25	
2388	25c Richard E. Byrd	.65	.25	
2389	25c Lincoln Ellsworth	.65	.25	
a.	Block of 4, #2386-2389	2.75	2.00	
b.	Black omitted	*1,250.*		
c.	As "a," imperf. horiz.	*1,950.*		
2390	25c Deer	.75	.25	
2391	25c Horse	.75	.25	
2392	25c Camel	.75	.25	
2393	25c Goat	.75	.25	
a.	Block of 4, #2390-2393	3.00	2.00	
b.	As "a," red omitted	—		
2394	$8.75 Eagle and Moon	13.50	8.00	
2395	25c Happy Birthday	.50	.25	
2396	25c Best Wishes	.50	.25	
a.	Bklt. pane, 3 #2395 + 3 #2396 with gutter btwn.	3.50	3.25	
2397	25c Thinking of You	.50	.25	
2398	25c Love You	.50	.25	
a.	Bklt. pane of 6, 3 #2397 + 3 #2398 with gutter btwn.	3.50	3.25	
b.	As "a," imperf. horiz.	—		
c.	As "a," imperf.	—		
2399	25c Christmas - Religious	.50	.25	
a.	Gold omitted	25.00		
2400	25c Christmas - Sleigh	.50	.25	
1989				
2401	25c Montana Statehood	.55	.25	
2402	25c A. Philip Randolph	.50	.25	
2403	25c North Dakota Statehood	.50	.25	
2404	25c Washington Statehood	.50	.25	
2405	25c Experiment	.50	.25	
2406	25c Phoenix	.50	.25	
2407	25c New Orleans	.50	.25	
2408	25c Washington	.50	.25	
2409	25c Walk in the Water	.50	.25	
a.	Booklet pane of 5, #2405-2409	2.50	1.75	
2410	25c World Stamp Expo '89	.50	.25	
2411	25c Arturo Toscanini	.50	.25	
1989-90				
2412	25c House of Representatives	.50	.25	

2416

2417

2418

2419

2420

2421

2422-2425

2426

HOW TO USE THIS BOOK

The number in the first column is its Scott number or identifying number. Following that is the denomination of the stamp and its color or description. Finally, the values, unused and used, are shown.

Scott No.	Description	Unused Value	Used Value	/ / / / / /
2413	25c Senate	.50	.25	
2414	25c Executive Branch	.50	.25	
2415	25c Supreme Court	.50	.25	
1989				
2416	25c South Dakota Statehood	.60	.25	
2417	25c Lou Gehrig	.60	.25	
2418	25c Ernest Hemingway	.50	.25	
a.	Vert. pair, imperf. horiz.	1,500.		
2419	$2.40 Moon Landing	4.75	2.00	
a.	Black (engr.) omitted	2,000.		
b.	Imperf., pair	575.00		
c.	Black (litho.) omitted	2,250.		
2420	25c Letter Carriers	.50	.25	
2421	25c Bill of Rights	.50	.25	
a.	Black (engr.) omitted	250.00		
2422	25c Tyrannosaurus Rex	.70	.25	
a.	Black (engr.) omitted	80.00	—	
2423	25c Pteranodon	.70	.25	
a.	Black (engr.) omitted	80.00	—	
2424	25c Stegosaurus	.70	.25	
a.	Black (engr.) omitted	80.00	—	
2425	25c Brontosaurus	.70	.25	
a.	Black (engr.) omitted	80.00	—	
b.	Block of 4, #2422-2425	2.80	2.00	
c.	As "b," black (engr.) omitted	400.00		
2426	25c Columbian Artifacts	.60	.25	
2427	25c Christmas - Religious	.50	.25	
a.	Booklet pane of 10	5.00	3.50	
b.	Red (litho.) omitted	575.00		
2428	25c Christmas - Sleigh, perf. 11	.50	.25	
a.	Vert. pair, imperf. horiz.	750.00		
Booklet Stamps, Perf. 11½ on 2 or 3 Sides				
2429	25c Christmas - Sleigh (2428)	.50	.25	
a.	Booklet pane of 10	5.00	3.50	
c.	As "a," horiz. imperf. btwn.	3,250.		
d.	As "a," Red omitted	3,250.		
e.	Imperf. pair	—		
Die cut, Self-adhesive				
2431	25c Eagle and Shield	.50	.25	
a.	Booklet pane of 18	11.00		
b.	Vert. pair, no die cutting btwn.	500.00		
c.	Pair, no die cutting	275.00		
1989				
2433	World Stamp Expo '89, sheet of 4	14.00	14.00	
a.	90c like No. 122	3.50	3.00	
b.	90c like No. 132TC (blue frame, brown center)	3.50	3.00	

2427

2433

2428

2431

2439

2434-2437

2442

2440

2443

2444

Scott No.	Description	Unused Value	Used Value	/ / / / / /
c.	90c like No. 132TC (green frame, blue center)	3.50	3.00	
d.	90c like No. 132TC (scarlet frame, blue center)	3.50	3.00	
2434	25c Stagecoach	.50	.25	
2435	25c Paddlewheel Steamer	.50	.25	
2436	25c Biplane	.50	.25	
2437	25c Automobile	.50	.25	
a.	Block of 4, #2434-2437	2.00	1.75	
b.	As "a," dark blue (engr.) omitted	300.00		
2438	UPU Congress, sheet of 4, imperf.	5.25	3.75	
a.	25c Stagecoach (2434)	1.30	.80	
b.	25c Paddlewheel Steamer (2435)	1.30	.80	
c.	25c Biplane (2436)	1.30	.80	
d.	25c Automobile (2437)	1.30	.80	
e.	Dark blue & gray (engr.) omitted	5,000.		

1990

Scott No.	Description	Unused Value	Used Value	/ / / / / /
2439	25c Idaho Statehood	.55	.25	
2440	25c Love, perf. 12½ x 13	.50	.25	
a.	Imperf., pair	675.00		

Booklet Stamp, Perf. 11½ on 2 or 3 Sides

Scott No.	Description	Unused Value	Used Value	/ / / / / /
2441	25c Love (2440)	.50	.25	
a.	Booklet pane of 10	5.00	3.50	
b.	As "a," bright pink omitted	85.00		
c.	As "b," single stamp	950.00		
2442	25c Ida B. Wells	.75	.25	
2443	15c Beach Umbrella	.30	.25	
a.	Booklet pane of 10	3.00	2.50	
b.	As "a," blue omitted	125.00		
c.	As 2443, blue omitted	1,250.		
2444	25c Wyoming Statehood	.80	.25	
a.	Black (engr.) omitted	1,000.	—	
2445	25c The Wizard of Oz	1.50	.25	
2446	25c Gone With the Wind	1.50	.25	
2447	25c Beau Geste	1.50	.25	
2448	25c Stagecoach	1.50	.25	
a.	Block of 4, #2445-2448	6.00	3.50	
2449	25c Marianne Moore	.60	.25	
a.	All colors missing (from extraneous paper)	—		

1990-95, Coil Stamps, Perf. 10 Vertically

Scott No.	Description	Unused Value	Used Value	/ / / / / /
2451	4c Steam Carriage, tagged	.25	.25	
a.	Imperf., pair	525.00		
b.	Untagged	.25	.25	
2452	5c Circus Wagon, engr., tagged	.25	.25	
a.	Untagged	.25	.25	
c.	Imperf., pair	425.00		

2445-2448   2449

2451   2452   2453

2457   2464   2468

2470-2474

Scott No.	Description	Unused Value	Used Value	//////
2452B	5c Circus Wagon (2452), photo.	.25	.25	
2452D	5c Circus Wagon with cent sign (2452).	.25	.25	
e.	Imperf., pair......................................	135.00		
2453	5c Canoe, brown, engr.			
	(Bureau precancel in gray)...........	.25	.25	
a.	Imperf., pair......................................	300.00		
b.	Gray omitted....................................		—	
2454	5c Canoe (2453), red, photo.			
	(Bureau precancel in gray)...........	.30	.25	
2457	10c Tractor Trailer, engr.			
	(Bureau precancel in gray)........... .	.35	.25	
a.	Imperf., pair......................................	125.00		
b.	All color omitted	—		
2458	10c Tractor Trailer (2457), photo.			
	(Bureau precancel in black).	.45	.25	
2463	20c Cog Railway (2451)....................	.40	.25	
a.	Imperf., pair......................................	75.00		
2464	23c Lunch Wagon..............................	.45	.25	
b.	Imperf., pair......................................	110.00		
2466	32c Ferryboat (2451)..........................	.80	.25	
a.	Imperf., pair......................................	475.00		
b.	Bright blue	3.00	2.25	
2468	$1 Seaplane.......................................	2.25	.50	
a.	Imperf., pair......................................	2,500.	1,350.	

1990, Booklet Stamps

2470	25c Admiralty Head Lighthouse............	1.90	.25	
2471	25c Cape Hatteras Lighthouse	1.90	.25	
2472	25c West Quoddy Head Lighthouse	1.90	.25	
2473	25c American Shoals Lighthouse	1.90	.25	
2474	25c Sandy Hook Lighthouse..................	1.90	.25	
a.	Bklt. pane of 5, #2470-2474	9.50	2.00	
b.	As "a," white (USA 25) omitted	100.00	—	

Die cut, Self-adhesive

2475	25c Flag	.55	.25	
a.	Pane of 12	6.60		

1990-95

2476	1c American Kestrel............................	.25	.25	
a.	Quadruple impression of black inscriptions & denom.	850.00		
b.	Quintuple impression of black inscriptions & denom.	1,500.		
2477	1c American Kestrel with cent sign	.25	.25	
2478	3c Eastern Bluebird, no cent sign	.25	.25	
a.	Vert. pair, imperf. horiz.	—		
b.	Double impression of all colors except yellow................................	200.00		
2479	19c Fawn..	.35	.25	

2475

2482

2476

2477

2478

2479

2480

2481

2483

2484

2486

2487

2488

2489

2490

2491

2496-2500

Scott No.	Description	Unused Value	Used Value	/ / / / / /
b.	Red omitted.....................................	*725.00*		
c.	Imperf., pair...................................	*1,000.*		
2480	30c Cardinal..	.60	.25	
2481	45c Pumpkinseed Sunfish.......................	.90	.25	
a.	Black (engr.) omitted......................	*375.00*	—	
2482	$2 Bobcat..	3.50	1.25	
a.	Black (engr.) omitted......................	*225.00*		

1991-95, Booklet Stamps

2483	20c Blue Jay	.50	.25	
a.	Booklet pane of 10	5.25	2.50	
b.	As "a," imperf.................................	—		
2484	29c Wood Duck, black denomination....	.60	.25	
a.	Booklet pane of 10	6.00	3.75	
b.	Vert. pair, imperf. btwn.	*190.00*		
c.	As "b," bklt. pane of 10	*1,000.*		
f.	Vert. pair imperf. btwn. and with natural straight edge at top or bottom	*170.00*		
2485	29c Wood Duck (2484), red denomination	.60	.25	
a.	Booklet pane of 10	6.00	4.00	
b.	Vert. pair, imperf. btwn.	*3,000.*		
c.	Imperf., pair.	*2,000.*		
2486	29c African Violets...............................	.60	.25	
a.	Booklet pane of 10	6.00	4.00	
2487	32c Peach	.65	.25	
2488	32c Pear	.65	.25	
a.	Booklet pane, 5 each #2487-2488 ..	6.50	4.25	
b.	Pair, #2487-2488.............................	1.30	.30	

1993-95, Booklet Stamps, Die cut, Self-adhesive

2489	29c Red Squirrel....................................	.65	.25	
a.	Booklet pane of 18	12.00		
b.	As "a," die cutting omitted.............	—		
2490	29c Rose, red, green & black.................	.65	.25	
a.	Booklet pane of 18	12.00		
2491	29c Pine Cone.......................................	.60	.25	
a.	Booklet pane of 18	11.00		
b.	Horiz. pair, no die cutting between.	*200.00*	*150.00*	

Serpentine Die Cut

2492	32c Rose (2490), pink, green & black...	.65	.25	
a.	Bklt. pane of 20 + label..................	13.00		
b.	Bklt. pane of 15 + label..................	9.75		
c.	Horiz. pair, no die cutting btwn.	—		
d.	As "a," 2 stamps and parts of 7 others printed on backing liner	—		
e.	Booklet pane of 14	20.00		
f.	Booklet pane of 16	20.00		
h.	Vertical pair, no die cutting btwn....	—		

2501-2505

2506-2507

2508-2511

2512   **2513**

2514   **2515**   **2517**

2521   **2522**

Scott No.	Description	Unused Value	Used Value	/ / / / / /
i.	As "a," 6 pairs plus stamp and label die cutting omitted vert. btwn. (due to miscutting)	—		
j.	As "f," with 2 pairs die cutting omitted horiz., in full bklt. #BK178D	—		
2493	32c Peach (2487)	.65	.25	
2494	32c Pear (2488)	.65	.25	
a.	Bklt. pane, 10 each #2493-2494 + label	13.00		
b.	Pair, #2493-2494	1.30		
c.	As "b," die cutting omitted			

1995, Coil Stamps, Serpentine Die Cut Vert.

Scott No.	Description	Unused Value	Used Value	/ / / / / /
2495	32c Peach (2487)	2.00	.25	
2495A	32c Pear (2488)	2.00	.25	

1990

Scott No.	Description	Unused Value	Used Value	/ / / / / /
2496	25c Jesse Owens	.60	.25	
2497	25c Ray Ewry	.60	.25	
2498	25c Hazel Wightman	.60	.25	
2499	25c Eddie Eagan	.60	.25	
2500	25c Helene Madison	.60	.25	
a.	Strip of 5, #2496-2500	3.25	2.50	
b.	As "a," blue omitted	—		
2501	25c Assiniboine	1.60	.25	
2502	25c Cheyenne	1.60	.25	
2503	25c Comanche	1.60	.25	
a.	Black (engr.) omitted	—		
2504	25c Flathead	1.60	.25	
a.	Black (engr.) omitted	—		
2505	25c Shoshone	1.60	.25	
a.	Bklt. pane, 2 each #2501-2505	16.00	7.50	
b.	As "a," black (engr.) omitted	3,500.		
c.	Strip of 5, #2501-2505	8.00	2.50	
d.	As "a," horiz. imperf. btwn.	2,400.		
2506	25c Micronesia	.50	.25	
2507	25c Marshall Islands	.50	.25	
a.	Pair, #2506-2507	1.00	.75	
b.	As "a," black (engr.) omitted	2,750.		
2508	25c Killer Whale	.55	.25	
2509	25c Northern Sea Lion	.55	.25	
2510	25c Sea Otter	.55	.25	
2511	25c Common Dolphin	.55	.25	
a.	Block of 4, #2508-2511	2.25	1.90	
b.	As "a," black (engr.) omitted	350.00		
2512	25c Grand Canyon	.55	.25	
2513	25c Dwight D. Eisenhower	.90	.25	
a.	Imperf., pair	2,250.		
2514	25c Christmas - Religious	.50	.25	
a.	Booklet pane of 10	5.00	3.25	

2523

2524

2528

2529

2530

2531

2531A

2532

2533

2534

2535

2537

2538

2544

2544A

Scott No.	Description	Unused Value	Used Value	/ / / / / /
2515	25c Christmas - Tree, perf. 11...............	.50	.25	☐☐☐☐☐
a.	Vert. pair, imperf. horiz.	625.00.		☐☐☐☐☐
b.	All colors missing (from extraneous paper)..	—		☐☐☐☐☐

Booklet Stamp, Perf. 11½ x11 on 2 or 3 Sides

2516	25c Christmas - Tree (2515)	.50	.25	☐☐☐☐☐
a.	Booklet pane of 10	5.00	3.25	☐☐☐☐☐

1991

2517	(29c) "F" & Flower, perf. 13, yellow, black, red & yellow green......................	.60	.25	☐☐☐☐☐
a.	Imperf., pair	1,000.		☐☐☐☐☐
b.	Horiz. pair, imperf. vert..................	950.00		☐☐☐☐☐

Coil Stamp, Perf. 10 Vertically

2518	(29c) "F" & Flower (2517), yellow, black, dull red & dark yellow green........	.60	.25	☐☐☐☐☐
a.	Imperf., pair	27.50		☐☐☐☐☐

Booklet Stamps, Perf. 11 on 2 or 3 Sides

2519	(29c) "F" & Flower (2517), yellow, black, dull red & dk green, bullseye perfs.	.60	.25	☐☐☐☐☐
a.	Booklet pane of 10	6.50	4.50	☐☐☐☐☐
b.	As "a," imperf. horiz.	—		☐☐☐☐☐
2520	(29c) "F" & Flower (2517), pale yellow, black, red & brt green	1.75	.25	☐☐☐☐☐
a.	Booklet pane of 10	18.00	4.50	☐☐☐☐☐
b.	As "a," imperf. horiz.	—		☐☐☐☐☐
c.	Horiz. pair, imperf. btwn................	500.00		☐☐☐☐☐
d.	Imperf. vert., pair............................	—		☐☐☐☐☐

1991

2521	(4c) Text..	.25	.25	☐☐☐☐☐
a.	Vert. pair, imperf. horiz.	95.00		☐☐☐☐☐
b.	Imperf., pair	60.00		☐☐☐☐☐

Die cut, Self-adhesive

2522	(29c) "F" & Flag	.60	.25	☐☐☐☐☐
a.	Pane of 12	7.25		☐☐☐☐☐

Coil Stamps, Perf. 10 Vertically

2523	29c Flag over Mt. Rushmore, blue, red & claret, engraved...................	.65	.25	☐☐☐☐☐
b.	Imperf., pair	20.00		☐☐☐☐☐
c.	Blue, red & brown............................	5.00	—	☐☐☐☐☐
2523A	29c Flag over Mt. Rushmore (2523), blue, red & brown, photogravure...........	.75	.25	☐☐☐☐☐

1991-92, Perf. 11

2524	29c Flower, dull yellow, black, red & yellow green	.60	.25	☐☐☐☐☐

2539

2540

2541

2542

2543

2550

2545-2549

HOW TO USE THIS BOOK

The number in the first column is its Scott number or identifying number.
Following that is the denomination of the stamp and its color or description.
Finally, the values, unused and used, are shown.

Scott No.	Description	Unused Value	Used Value	/ / / / / /

Perf. 13 x 12½

2524A 29c Flower, dull yellow, black, red & yellow green (2524) .... 1.00 .25 ☐☐☐☐☐

Coil Stamps, Rouletted 10 Vertically

2525 29c Flower (2524), pale yellow, black, red & yellow green........................ .60 .25 ☐☐☐☐☐

Perf. 10 Vertically

2526 29c Flower (2524), pale yellow, black, red & yellow green .... .80 .25 ☐☐☐☐☐

Booklet Stamp, Perf. 11 on 2 or 3 sides

2527 29c Flower (2524), pale yellow, black, red & bright green........................ .60 .25 ☐☐☐☐☐
a.   Booklet pane of 10 .... 6.00 3.50 ☐☐☐☐☐
b.   Horiz. pair, imperf. btwn.............. — ☐☐☐☐☐
c.   Horiz. pair, imperf. vert. .... *100.00* ☐☐☐☐☐
d.   As "a," imperf. horiz. .... *750.00* ☐☐☐☐☐
e.   As "a," imperf. vert. .... *500.00* ☐☐☐☐☐

1991

2528 29c Flag & Olympic Rings .... .60 .25 ☐☐☐☐☐
a.   Booklet pane of 10 .... 6.00 3.50 ☐☐☐☐☐
b.   As "a," imperf. horiz. .... *3,250.* ☐☐☐☐☐
c.   Vert. pair, imperf. btwn., perfed at top and bottom............................. *250.00* ☐☐☐☐☐
d.   Vert. strip of 3, top or bottom pair imperf. btwn .... — ☐☐☐☐☐
e.   Vert. pair, imperf. horiz.. .... *700.00* ☐☐☐☐☐
f.   As "d" two pairs in #2528a with foldover.. — ☐☐☐☐☐

1991-94, Coil Stamps, Perf. 9.8 Vertically

2529 19c Fishing Boat..................................... .40 .25 ☐☐☐☐☐
a.   Type II (finer dot pattern), tagged... .40 .25 ☐☐☐☐☐
b.   As "a," untagged .... 1.00 .40 ☐☐☐☐☐
2529C 19c Fishing Boat (2529), one loop of rope .50 .25 ☐☐☐☐☐

Booklet Stamp, Perf. 10 on 2 or 3 Sides

2530 19c Balloon....................................... .40 .25 ☐☐☐☐☐
a.   Booklet pane of 10 .... 4.00 2.75 ☐☐☐☐☐

1991

2531 29c Flags on Parade............................... .60 .25 ☐☐☐☐☐

Die cut, Self-adhesive

2531A 29c Liberty Torch .... .60 .25 ☐☐☐☐☐
b.   Pane of 18 .... 11.00 ☐☐☐☐☐
c.   Pair, imperf. .... *1,400.* ☐☐☐☐☐

1991

2532 50c Switzerland .... 1.00 .25 ☐☐☐☐☐

2551

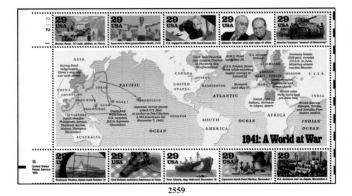

2559

2558

2560

2567

2561

Scott No.	Description	Unused Value	Used Value	/ / / / / /
a.	Vert. pair, imperf. horiz.	*2,250.*		
2533	29c Vermont Statehood	.90	.25	
2534	29c Savings Bonds	.60	.25	

Perf. 12½ x13

2535	29c Love..	.60	.25	
b.	Imperf., pair.....................................	*1,650.*		

Perf. 11

2535A	29c Love (2535)	.85	.25	

Booklet Stamp, Perf. 11 on 2 or 3 Sides

2536	29c Love (2535)....................................	.60	.25	
a.	Booklet pane of 10	6.00	3.50	
2537	52c Love..	.90	.25	
2538	29c William Saroyan	.60	.25	
a.	All colors missing (from extraneous paper)	—		
b.	All colors except black missing (from extraneous paper)..............	—		
2539	$1 Eagle & Olympic Rings	2.00	.50	
a.	Black omitted....................................	—		

1991-95

2540	$2.90 Eagle	6.00	1.50	
a.	Vert. pair, imperf. horiz.	*1,000.*		
b.	Black (engr.) omitted.......................	—		
2541	$9.95 Eagle	20.00	6.00	
a.	Imperf., pair	—		
2542	$14 Eagle	25.00	15.00	
a.	Red (engr. inscriptions) omitted......	—		
2543	$2.90 Futuristic Space Shuttle..................	6.00	1.75	
2544	$3 Space Shuttle *Challenger,* dated "1995"	5.75	1.75	
b.	Dated "1996"....................................	5.75	1.75	
c.	Horiz. pair, imperf. btwn.	—		
d.	Imperf, pair......................................	*1,250.*		
2544A	$10.75 Space Shuttle *Endeavour*	20.00	9.00	

1991

2545	29c Royal Wulff..................................	2.00	.25	
a.	Black omitted....................................	—		
b.	Horiz. pair, imperf. btwn., in #2549b with foldover	*2,400.*		
2546	29c Jock Scott....................................	2.00	.25	
a.	Black omitted....................................	—		
2547	29c Apte Tarpon Fly...........................	2.00	.25	
a.	Black omitted....................................	—		
2548	29c Lefty's Deceiver...........................	2.00	.25	
2549	29c Muddler Minnow..........................	2.00	.25	
a.	Booklet pane of 5, #2545-2549	10.00	3.50	
2550	29c Cole Porter..................................	.60	.25	
a.	Vert. pair, imperf. horiz.	*500.00*		

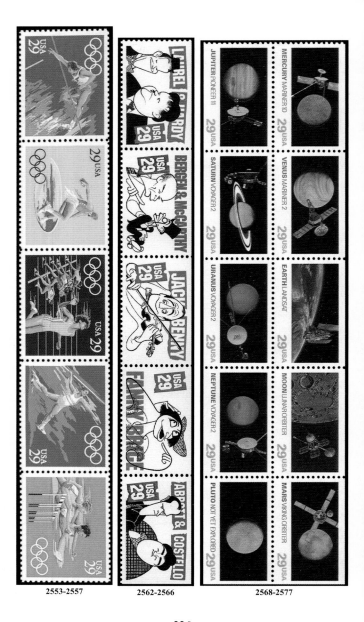

2553-2557   2562-2566   2568-2577

226

Scott No.	Description	Unused Value	Used Value	/ / / / / /
2551	29c Desert Shield & Desert Storm........	.60	.25	
a.	Vert. pair, imperf. horiz.	1,250.		
2552	29c Desert Shield & Desert Storm (2551)			
	20½mm wide (from bklt. pane)..	.60	.25	
a.	Booklet pane of 5	3.00	2.25	
2553	29c Olympics - Pole Vault....................	.60	.25	
2554	29c Olympics - Discus...........................	.60	.25	
2555	29c Olympics - Women's Sprints...........	.60	.25	
2556	29c Olympics - Javelin...........................	.60	.25	
2557	29c Olympics - Women's Hurdles..........	.60	.25	
a.	Strip of #2553-2557	3.00	2.25	
2558	29c Numismatics....................................	.60	.25	
2559	World War II, block of 10...............	7.50	5.00	
a.-j.	29c Any single....................................	.75	.45	
k.	Black (engr.) omitted......................	12,500.		
2560	29c Basketball..	.60	.25	
2561	29c District of Columbia.......................	.60	.25	
a.	Black (engr.) omitted......................	100.00		
2562	29c Laurel and Hardy............................	1.00	.25	
2563	29c Bergen and McCarthy	1.00	.25	
2564	29c Jack Benny.....................................	1.00	.25	
2565	29c Fanny Brice.....................................	1.00	.25	
2566	29c Abbott and Costello.........................	1.00	.25	
a.	Strip of 5, #2562-2566	5.00	2.50	
b.	Booklet pane of 10, 2 ea. #2562-2566	10.00	5.00	
c.	As "b," scarlet & bright violet			
	(engr.) omitted................................	450.00		
d.	As "b," purple (litho.) omitted on			
	Nos. 2562, 2564-2565..................	—		
2567	29c Jan E. Matzeliger............................	.60	.25	
a.	Horiz. pair, imperf. vert..................	650.00		
b.	Vert. pair, imperf. horiz.	650.00		
c.	Imperf. pair.....................................	400.00		
2568	29c Mercury...	1.10	.25	
2569	29c Venus...	1.10	.25	
2570	29c Earth..	1.10	.25	
2571	29c Moon..	1.10	.25	
2572	29c Mars	1.10	.25	
2573	29c Jupiter..	1.10	.25	
2574	29c Saturn..	1.10	.25	
2575	29c Uranus...	1.10	.25	
2576	29c Neptune...	1.10	.25	
2577	29c Pluto..	1.10	.25	
a.	Booklet pane of 10, #2568-2577	10.00	4.50	
2578	(29c) Christmas - Religious.....................	.60	.25	
a.	Booklet pane of 10	6.00	3.25	
b.	As "a," single, red & black			
	(engr.) omitted................................	3,250.		
2579	(29c) Christmas - Santa in Chimney, perf 11	.60	.25	

227

2578

2579

2582

2583

2584

2585

2587

2592

2590

2593

2595

HOW TO USE THIS BOOK

The number in the first column is its Scott number or identifying number. Following that is the denomination of the stamp and its color or description. Finally, the values, unused and used, are shown.

Scott No.	Description	Unused Value	Used Value	/ / / / / /
a.	Horiz. pair, imperf. vert....................	*225.00*		
b.	Vert. pair, imperf. horiz.	*375.00*		

Booklet Stamps, Size: 25 x 18½ mm, Perf. 11 on 2 or 3 sides

Scott No.	Description	Unused Value	Used Value	/ / / / / /
2580	(29c) Christmas - Santa in Chimney (2579), Type I..	2.25	.25	
2581	(29c) Christmas - Santa in Chimney (2579), Type II.	2.75	.25	
a.	Pair, #2580, 2581.......................	5.00	.55	
b.	Bklt. pane, 2 each #2580, 2581......	11.00	1.25	
	The extreme left brick in the top row of chimney is missing on Type II, No. 2581.			
2582	(29c) Christmas - Santa Checking List	.60	.25	
a.	Booklet pane of 4	2.40	1.25	
2583	(29c) Christmas - Santa with Presents......	.60	.25	
a.	Booklet pane of 4	2.40	1.25	
2584	(29c) Christmas - Santa at Fireplace	.60	.25	
a.	Booklet pane of 4	2.40	1.25	
2585	(29c) Christmas - Santa and Sleigh..........	.60	.25	
a.	Booklet pane of 4	2.40	1.25	

1995, Perf. 11.2

2587	32c James K. Polk	.65	.25	

1994, Perf. 11.5

2590	$1 Surrender of Gen. John Burgoyne ..	1.90	.50	
2592	$5 Washington and Jackson	8.00	2.50	

1992-93, Booklet Stamps
Perf. 10 on 2 or 3 sides

2593	29c Flag, black denomination	.60	.25	
a.	Booklet pane of 10	6.00	4.25	

Perf. 11 x 10 on 2 or 3 sides

2593B	29c Flag, black denomination (2593) ...	1.70	.50	
c.	Booklet pane of 10	20.00	7.50	

Perf. 11 x 10 on 2 or 3 Sides

2594	29c Flag (2593), red denomination........	.65	.25	
a.	Booklet pane of 10	6.50	4.25	
b.	Imperf., pair	900.00		

1992-94, Die cut, Self-adhesive

2595	29c Eagle & Shield, brown denomination	.60	.25	
a.	Booklet pane of 17 + label..............	13.00		
b.	Pair, no die cutting........................	*135.00*		
c.	Brown (engr.) omitted	*350.00*		
d.	As "a," die cutting omitted..............	*1,150.*		
2596	29c Eagle & Shield (2595), green denom.	.60	.25	
a.	Booklet pane of 17 + label..............	12.00		
2597	29c Eagle & Shield (2595), red denom.	.60	.25	
a.	Booklet pane of 17 + label..............	10.50		

2598   2599

2602   2603   2605

2606   2609   2618

2616   2617

2619   2611-2615

Scott No.	Description	Unused Value	Used Value	/ / / / / /
2598	29c Eagle	.60	.25	
a.	Booklet pane of 18	11.00		
b.	Coil with P#111	—	5.00	
c.	Die-cutting omitted, pair	1,000.		
2599	29c Statue of Liberty.............................	.60	.25	
a.	Booklet pane of 18	11.00		
b.	Coil with P#D1111..........................	—	5.00	

1991-93, Coil Stamps, Perf. 10 Vertically

2602	(10c) Eagle & Shield (Bureau precancel, Bulk Rate, in blue)	.30	.25	
a.	Imperf. pair	—		
2603	(10c) Eagle & Shield, orange yellow & multi (Bureau precancel, Bulk Rate, in red)	.30	.25	
a.	Imperf., pair	20.00		
2604	(10c) Eagle & Shield (2603), gold & multi (Bureau precancel, Bulk Rate, in red)	.30	.25	
2605	23c Flag (Bureau precancel in blue)......	.45	.40	
a.	Imperf., pair	—		
2606	23c Reflected Flag (Bureau precanceled)	.45	.40	
2607	23c Reflected Flag (2606), multi (Bureau precanceled)	.45	.40	
c.	Imperf., pair	70.00		
2608	23c Reflected Flag (2606), violet blue, red & black (Bureau precanceled)	.80	.40	
	On No. 2607 "First Class" is 9mm long.			
	On No. 2608 "First Class" is 8½mm long.			
2609	29c Flag over White House...................	.60	.25	
a.	Imperf. pair	15.00		
b.	Pair, imperf. btwn.	90.00		
c.	29c Indigo blue and red...................	22.50	—	

1992

2611	29c Olympics - Ice Hockey....................	.60	.25	
2612	29c Olympics - Figure Skating	.60	.25	
2613	29c Olympics - Speed Skating...............	.60	.25	
2614	29c Olympics - Skiing...........................	.60	.25	
2615	29c Olympics - Bobsledding.................	.60	.25	
a.	Strip of 5, #2611-2615	3.00	2.50	
2616	29c World Columbian Stamp Expo	.60	.25	
2617	29c W.E.B. DuBois...............................	.60	.25	
2618	29c Love..	.60	.25	
a.	Horiz. pair, imperf. vert...................	300.00		
b.	As "a," green omitted on right stamp	2,500.		
2619	29c Olympic Baseball	.65	.25	
2620	29c Seeking Queen Isabella's Support...	.65	.25	
2621	29c Crossing the Atlantic	.65	.25	
2622	29c Approaching Land...........................	.65	.25	
2623	29c Coming Ashore...............................	.65	.25	

2620-2623

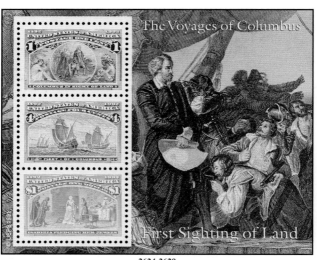

2624-2629

2630

Scott No.	Description	Unused Value	Used Value	/ / / / / /
a.	Block of 4, #2620-2623	2.60	2.00	
2624	First Sighting of Land, sheet of 3....	2.25	1.50	
a.	1c deep blue (like No. 230)............	.25	.25	
b.	4c ultramarine (like No. 233).............	.25	.25	
c.	$1 salmon (like No. 241)......................	1.75	1.00	
2625	Claiming a New World (2624), sht. of 3	7.50	5.00	
a.	2c brown violet (like No. 231)............	.25	.25	
b.	3c green (like No. 232)	.25	.25	
c.	$4 crimson lake (like No. 244)	7.00	4.00	
2626	Seeking Royal Support (2624), sheet of 3	1.75	1.25	
a.	5c chocolate (like No. 234)..................	.25	.25	
b.	30c orange brown (like No. 239)..........	.60	.30	
c.	50c slate blue (like No. 240)................	.90	.50	
2627	Royal Favor Restored (2624), sheet of 3	6.00	3.75	
a.	6c purple (like No. 235)......................	.25	.25	
b.	8c magenta (like No. 236)..................	.25	.25	
c.	$3 yellow green (like No. 243)	5.50	3.00	
2628	Reporting Discoveries (2624) Sht. of 3	4.25	3.00	
a.	10c black brown (like No. 237)	.25	.25	
b.	15c dark green (like No. 238)................	.30	.25	
c.	$2 brown red (like No. 242)................	3.50	2.00	
2629	$5 Christopher Columbus (2624), sheet of 1 (like No. 245)	8.75	6.00	
a.	$5 black, single stamp	8.50	5.00	
2630	29c New York Stock Exchange..............	.60	.25	
a.	Black missing (from extraneous paper)	—		
b.	Black missing (from a color misregistration)............................	—		
c.	Center inverted....................	*22,500.*		
d.	Se-tenant pair, #2630b & #2360c..	*25,000.*		
2631	29c Cosmonaut..	.60	.25	
2632	29c Astronaut..	.60	.25	
2633	29c Apollo Modules................................	.60	.25	
2634	29c Soyuz..	.60	.25	
a.	Block of 4, #2631-2634	2.40	2.00	
b.	As "a," yellow omitted	—		
2635	29c Alaska Highway................................	.60	.25	
a.	Black (engr.) omitted......................	650.00		
2636	29c Kentucky Statehood........................	.60	.25	
a.	Dark blue missing (from extraneous paper)...	—		
b.	Dark blue and red missing (from extraneous paper)	—		
c.	All colors missing (from extraneous paper)...	—		

2631-2634

2635

2636

2637-2641

234

2642-2646

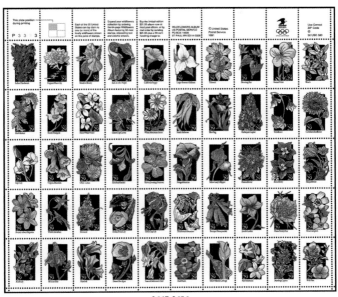

2647-2696

HOW TO USE THIS BOOK

The number in the first column is its Scott number or identifying number. Following that is the denomination of the stamp and its color or description. Finally, the values, unused and used, are shown.

2697

2698

2699

2700-2703

HOW TO USE THIS BOOK

The number in the first column is its Scott number or identifying number. Following that is the denomination of the stamp and its color or description. Finally, the values, unused and used, are shown.

Scott No.	Description	Unused Value	Used Value	/ / / / / /
2637	29c Olympics - Soccer	.60	.25	
2638	29c Olympics - Gymnastics	.60	.25	
2639	29c Olympics - Volleyball	.60	.25	
2640	29c Olympics - Boxing	.60	.25	
2641	29c Olympics - Swimming	.60	.25	
a.	Strip of 5, #2637-2641	3.00	2.50	
2642	29c Ruby-Throated Hummingbird	.60	.25	
2643	29c Broad-billed Hummingbird	.60	.25	
2644	29c Costa's Hummingbird	.60	.25	
2645	29c Rufous Hummingbird	.60	.25	
2646	29c Calliope Hummingbird	.60	.25	
a.	Booklet pane of 5, #2642-2646	3.00	2.50	
2647	29c Indian Paintbrush	.80	.60	
2648	29c Fragrant Water Lily	.80	.60	
2649	29c Meadow Beauty	.80	.60	
2650	29c Jack-in-the-Pulpit	.80	.60	
2651	29c California Poppy	.80	.60	
2652	29c Large-flowered Trillium	.80	.60	
2653	29c Tickseed	.80	.60	
2654	29c Shooting Star	.80	.60	
2655	29c Stream Violet	.80	.60	
2656	29c Bluets	.80	.60	
2657	29c Herb Robert	.80	.60	
2658	29c Marsh Marigold	.80	.60	
2659	29c Sweet White Violet	.80	.60	
2660	29c Claret Cup Cactus	.80	.60	
2661	29c White Mountain Avens	.80	.60	
2662	29c Sessile Bellwort	.80	.60	
2663	29c Blue Flag	.80	.60	
2664	29c Harlequin Lupine	.80	.60	
2665	29c Twinflower	.80	.60	
2666	29c Common Sunflower	.80	.60	
2667	29c Sego Lily	.80	.60	
2668	29c Virginia Bluebells	.80	.60	
2669	29c Ohia Lehua	.80	.60	
2670	29c Rosebud Orchid	.80	.60	
2671	29c Showy Evening Primrose	.80	.60	
2672	29c Fringed Gentian	.80	.60	
2673	29c Yellow Lady's Slipper	.80	.60	
2674	29c Passionflower	.80	.60	
2675	29c Bunchberry	.80	.60	
2676	29c Pasqueflower	.80	.60	
2677	29c Round-lobed Hepatica	.80	.60	
2678	29c Wild Columbine	.80	.60	
2679	29c Fireweed	.80	.60	
2680	29c Indian Pond Lily	.80	.60	
2681	29c Turk's Cap Lily	.80	.60	
2682	29c Dutchman's Breeches	.80	.60	
2683	29c Trumpet Honeysuckle	.80	.60	

2704

2705-2709

2710

2720

2711-2714

2722

2723

2724-2730

Scott No.	Description	Unused Value	Used Value	/ / / / / /
2684	29c Jacobs Ladder	.80	.60	
2685	29c Plains Prickly Pear	.80	.60	
2686	29c Moss Campion	.80	.60	
2687	29c Bearberry	.80	.60	
2688	29c Mexican Hat	.80	.60	
2689	29c Harebell	.80	.60	
2690	29c Desert Five Spot	.80	.60	
2691	29c Smooth Solomon's Seal	.80	.60	
2692	29c Red Maids	.80	.60	
2693	29c Yellow Skunk Cabbage	.80	.60	
2694	29c Rue Anemone	.80	.60	
2695	29c Standing Cypress	.80	.60	
2696	29c Wild Flax	.80	.60	
a.	Pane of 50, #2647-2696	40.00	—	
2697	World War II, block of 10	7.50	5.00	
a.-j.	29c Any single	.75	.30	
k.	Red (litho.) omitted	5,000.		
2698	29c Dorothy Parker	.60	.25	
2699	29c Theodore von Karman	.60	.25	
2700	29c Azurite	.60	.25	
2701	29c Copper	.60	.25	
2702	29c Variscite	.60	.25	
2703	29c Wulfenite	.60	.25	
a.	Block or strip of 4, #2700-2703	2.40	2.00	
b.	As "a," silver (litho.) omitted	7,750.		
c.	As "a," red (litho.) omitted	—		
2704	29c Juan Rodriguez Cabrillo	.60	.25	
a.	Black (engr.) omitted	3,250.		
2705	29c Giraffe	.65	.25	
2706	29c Giant Panda	.65	.25	
2707	29c Flamingo	.65	.25	
2708	29c King Penguins	.65	.25	
2709	29c White Bengal Tiger	.65	.25	
a.	Booklet pane of 5, #2705-2709	3.25	2.25	
b.	As "a," imperforate	2,250.		
2710	29c Christmas - Religious	.60	.25	
a.	Booklet pane of 10	6.00	3.50	
2711	29c Christmas - Horse	.75	.25	
2712	29c Christmas - Locomotive	.75	.25	
2713	29c Christmas - Fire Pumper	.75	.25	
2714	29c Christmas - Boat	.75	.25	
a.	Block of 4, #2711-2714	3.00	1.10	

Booklet Stamps, Perf. 11 on 2 or 3 sides

Scott No.	Description	Unused Value	Used Value	/ / / / / /
2715	29c Christmas - Horse (2711)	.85	.25	
2716	29c Christmas - Locomotive (2712)	.85	.25	
2717	29c Christmas - Fire Pumper (2713)	.85	.25	
2718	29c Christmas - Boat (2714)	.85	.25	
a.	Booklet pane of 4, #2715-2718	3.50	1.25	

2741-2745

2746

2749

2755

2747

2748

2754

2750-2753

Scott No.	Description	Unused Value	Used Value	/ / / / / /
b.	As "a," imperf. horiz.	—		
Die cut, Self-adhesive				
2719	29c Christmas - Locomotive (2712)......	.65	.25	
a.	Booklet pane of 18	12.00		
1992				
2720	29c Year of the Rooster..........................	.60	.25	
1993 Issues				
2721	29c Elvis Presley, "Elvis" only (2724) ..	.60	.25	
a.	Imperf, pair.	—		
2722	29c Oklahoma!, no frameline	.60	.25	
Perf. 10				
2723	29c Hank Williams, 27½mm inscription	.75	.25	
Perf. 11.2 x 11.5				
2723A	29c Hank Williams, 27½mm inscription (2723).........................	20.00	10.00	
Perf. 10				
2724	29c Elvis Presley, with "Presley," no frameline	.70	.25	
2725	29c Bill Haley	.70	.25	
2726	29c Clyde McPhatter	.70	.25	
2727	29c Ritchie Valens	.70	.25	
2728	29c Otis Redding	.70	.25	
2729	29c Buddy Holly	.70	.25	
2730	29c Dinah Washington	.70	.25	
a.	Vert. strip of 7, #2724-2730............	5.50	3.00	
Booklet stamps, Perf. 11 Horiz., with Framelines				
2731	29c Presley (2724)	.60	.25	
2732	29c Haley (2725)..................................	.60	.25	
2733	29c McPhatter (2726)............................	.60	.25	
2734	29c Valens (2727).................................	.60	.25	
2735	29c Redding (2728)...............................	.60	.25	
2736	29c Holly (2729)..................................	.60	.25	
2737	29c Washington (2730)	.60	.25	
a.	Booklet pane, 2 #2731, 1 each #2732-2737.....................................	5.00	2.25	
b.	Booklet pane, #2731, 2735-2737 + tab	2.40	1.50	
2741	29c Ringed Planet.................................	.60	.25	
2742	29c Craft without Wings	.60	.25	
2743	29c Astronauts.....................................	.60	.25	
2744	29c Craft with Long Wings...................	.60	.25	
2745	29c Craft with Short Wings	.60	.25	
a.	Booklet pane of 5, #2741-2745	3.00	2.25	
2746	29c Percy Lavon Julian	.60	.25	
2747	29c Oregon Trail...................................	.60	.25	
b.	Blue omitted	—		
2748	29c World University Games.................	.60	.25	

2756-2759

2760-2764

2765

242

2766

2772-2774

2767-2770

2779-2782

2783-2784

HOW TO USE THIS BOOK

The number in the first column is its Scott number or identifying number. Following that is the denomination of the stamp and its color or description. Finally, the values, unused and used, are shown.

2785-2788

2789

2791-2794

2804

2805

2806

244

Scott No.	Description	Unused Value	Used Value	/ / / / /
2749	29c Grace Kelly	.60	.25	
2750	29c Clown	.60	.25	
2751	29c Ringmaster	.60	.25	
2752	29c Trapeze Artist	.60	.25	
2753	29c Elephant	.60	.25	
a.	Block of 4, #2750-2753	2.40	1.75	
2754	29c Cherokee Strip Land Run	.60	.25	
2755	29c Dean Acheson	.60	.25	
2756	29c Steeplechase	.60	.25	
2757	29c Thoroughbred Racing	.60	.25	
2758	29c Harness Racing	.60	.25	
2759	29c Polo	.60	.25	
a.	Block of 4, #2756-2759	2.40	2.00	
b.	As "a," black (engr.) omitted	700.00		
2760	29c Hyacinth	.75	.25	
2761	29c Daffodil	.75	.25	
2762	29c Tulip	.75	.25	
2763	29c Iris	.75	.25	
2764	29c Lilac	.75	.25	
a.	Booklet pane of 5, #2760-2764	3.75	2.25	
b.	As "a," black (engr.) omitted	150.00		
c.	As "a," imperf.	1,000.		
2765	World War II, block of 10	7.50	5.00	
a.-j.	29c Any single	.75	.40	
2766	29c Joe Louis	.60	.25	
2767	29c Show Boat	.60	.25	
2768	29c Porgy & Bess	.60	.25	
2769	29c Oklahoma! with frameline	.60	.25	
2770	29c My Fair Lady	.60	.25	
a.	Booklet pane of 4, #2767-2770	2.75	2.25	
2771	29c Hank Williams (2723), 27mm inscription	.75	.25	
2772	29c Patsy Cline	.75	.25	
2773	29c Carter Family	.75	.25	
2774	29c Bob Wills	.75	.25	
a.	Block or horiz. strip of 4, #2771-2774	3.00	1.75	
Booklet stamps, Perf. 11 Horiz., with Frameline				
2775	29c Hank Williams (2723), 22mm inscript.	.60	.25	
2776	29c Carter Family	.60	.25	
2777	29c Patsy Cline	.60	.25	
2778	29c Bob Wills	.60	.25	
a.	Booklet pane of 4, #2775-2778	2.50	2.00	
2779	29c Benjamin Franklin	.60	.25	
2780	29c Civil War Soldier	.60	.25	
2781	29c Charles Lindbergh	.60	.25	
2782	29c Stamps	.60	.25	
a.	Block or strip of 4, #2779-2782	2.40	2.00	
b.	As "a," black and maroon omitted	—		

2807-2811

2812   2813   2814

2815   2817

2816   2818

HOW TO USE THIS BOOK

The number in the first column is its Scott number or identifying number. Following that is the denomination of the stamp and its color or description. Finally, the values, unused and used, are shown.

Scott No.	Description	Unused Value	Used Value	/ / / / / /
c.	As "a," imperf.	3,250.		
2783	29c Recognizing Deafness	.60	.25	
2784	29c American Sign Language	.60	.25	
a.	Pair, #2783-2784	1.20	.75	
2785	29c Rebecca of Sunnybrook Farm	.60	.25	
2786	29c Little House on the Prairie	.60	.25	
2787	29c Adventures of Huckleberry Finn	.60	.25	
2788	29c Little Women	.60	.25	
a.	Block or horiz. strip of 4, #2785-2788	2.40	2.00	
2789	29c Christmas - Religious	.60	.25	

Booklet Stamp, Perf. 11½ x 11 on 2 or 3 Sides, 18 x 25mm

Scott No.	Description	Unused Value	Used Value	/ / / / / /
2790	29c Christmas - Religious (2789)	.60	.25	
a.	Booklet pane of 4	2.40	1.75	
b.	Pair, imperf.	—		
c.	As "a," imperf.	—		

Perf. 11½

Scott No.	Description	Unused Value	Used Value	/ / / / / /
2791	29c Christmas - Jack-in-the-Box	.60	.25	
2792	29c Christmas - Reindeer	.60	.25	
2793	29c Christmas - Snowman	.60	.25	
2794	29c Christmas - Toy Soldier	.60	.25	
a.	Block or strip of 4, #2791-2794	2.40	2.00	

Booklet Stamps, Perf. 11 x 10 on 2 or 3 Sides

Scott No.	Description	Unused Value	Used Value	/ / / / / /
2795	29c Christmas - Toy Soldier (2794)	.85	.25	
2796	29c Christmas - Snowman (2793)	.85	.25	
2797	29c Christmas - Reindeer (2792)	.85	.25	
2798	29c Christmas - Jack-in-the-Box (2791)	.85	.25	
a.	Booklet pane, 3 each #2795-2796, 2 each #2797-2798	8.50	4.00	
b.	Booklet pane, 3 each #2797-2798, 2 each #2795-2796	8.50	4.00	
c.	Block of 4, #2795-2798.	3.40	1.75	

Die cut, Self-adhesive, 19½ x 26½mm

Scott No.	Description	Unused Value	Used Value	/ / / / / /
2799	29c Christmas - Snowman (2793)	.65	.25	
2800	29c Christmas - Toy Soldier (2794)	.65	.25	
2801	29c Christmas - Jack-in-the-Box (2791)	.65	.25	
2802	29c Christmas - Reindeer (2792)	.65	.25	
a.	Booklet pane, 3 each #2799-2802	8.00		
b.	Block of 4, #2799-2802	2.60		

Die cut, Self-adhesive, 17 x 20 mm

Scott No.	Description	Unused Value	Used Value	/ / / / / /
2803	29c Christmas - Snowman (2793)	.60	.25	
a.	Booklet pane of 18	11.00		

Perf. 11

Scott No.	Description	Unused Value	Used Value	/ / / / / /
2804	29c Mariana Islands	.60	.25	

Perf. 11.2

Scott No.	Description	Unused Value	Used Value	/ / / / / /
2805	29c Columbus' Landing in Puerto Rico	.60	.25	

2819-2828

2829-2833

2834   2835   2836

248

Scott No.	Description	Unused Value	Used Value	/ / / / / /
2806	29c AIDS Awareness	.60	.25	
a.	Perf. 11 vert. on 1 or 2 sides	.70	.25	
b.	As "a," booklet pane of 5	3.50	2.00	

1994 Issues

2807	29c Olympics - Slalom	.60	.25	
2808	29c Olympics - Luge	.60	.25	
2809	29c Olympics - Ice Dancing	.60	.25	
2810	29c Olympics - Cross-Country Skiing...	.60	.25	
2811	29c Olympics - Ice Hockey	.60	.25	
a.	Strip of 5, #2807-2811	3.00	2.50	
2812	29c Edward R. Murrow	.60	.25	

Die cut, Self-adhesive

2813	29c Love	.60	.25	
a.	Pane of 18	11.00		
b.	Coil with plate #B1	—	3.75	

Booklet stamp, Perf. 10.9 x 11.1

2814	29c Love, photogravure	.60	.25	
a.	Booklet pane of 10	6.00	3.50	
b.	Imperf., pair	—		
d.	As "a," imperf.	—		

Perf. 11.1

2814C	29c Love (2814), litho. & engr.	.70	.25	
2815	52c Love	1.00	.25	
2816	29c Dr. Allison Davis	.60	.25	
2817	29c Year of the Dog	.80	.25	
2818	29c Buffalo Soldier	.60	.25	
a.	Double impression of red brown (engr. inscriptions)	—		
2819	29c Rudolph Valentino	1.10	.30	
2820	29c Clara Bow	1.10	.30	
2821	29c Charlie Chaplin	1.10	.30	
2822	29c Lon Chaney	1.10	.30	
2823	29c John Gilbert	1.10	.30	
2824	29c Zasu Pitts	1.10	.30	
2825	29c Harold Lloyd	1.10	.30	
2826	29c Keystone Cops	1.10	.30	
2827	29c Theda Bara	1.10	.30	
2828	29c Buster Keaton	1.10	.30	
a.	Block of 10, #2819-2828	11.00	5.00	
b.	As "a," black (litho.) omitted	—		
c.	As "a," red, black & bright violet (litho.) omitted	—		
2829	29c Lily	.65	.25	
2830	29c Zinnia	.65	.25	
2831	29c Gladiola	.65	.25	
2832	29c Marigold	.65	.25	
2833	29c Rose	.65	.25	

2837

2839

2838a

2840

2841a

2843-2847

HOW TO USE THIS BOOK

The number in the first column is its Scott number or identifying number. Following that is the denomination of the stamp and its color or description. Finally, the values, unused and used, are shown.

Scott No.	Description	Unused Value	Used Value	/ / / / / /
a.	Booklet pane of 5, #2829-2833	3.00	2.25	
b.	As "a," imperf.	*800.00*		
c.	As "a," black (engr.) omitted...........	*150.00*		
2834	29c World Cup Soccer............................	.60	.25	
2835	40c World Cup Soccer	.80	.25	
2836	50c World Cup Soccer............................	1.00	.25	
2837	World Cup Soccer, Sheet of 3, #a.-c. (like #2834-2836).........................	4.50	3.00	
2838	World War II, block of 10 (2765) ...	17.00	10.00	
a.-j.	29c Any single	1.70	.50	
2839	29c Norman Rockwell............................	.60	.25	
2840	Norman Rockwell, sheet of 4	4.50	2.75	
a.	50c Freedom from Want.......................	1.10	.65	
b.	50c Freedom from Fear........................	1.10	.65	
c.	50c Freedom of Speech........................	1.10	.65	
d.	50c Freedom of Worship......................	1.10	.65	
2841	Moon Landing, sheet of 12..............	10.50	—	
a.	29c Single stamp	.85	.60	
2842	$9.95 Moon Landing	20.00	16.00	
2843	29c Hudson's General............................	.70	.25	
2844	29c McQueen's Jupiter..........................	.70	.25	
2845	29c Eddy's No. 242	.70	.25	
2846	29c Ely's No. 10	.70	.25	
2847	29c Buchanan's No. 999........................	.70	.25	
a.	Booklet pane of 5, #2843-2847	3.50	2.00	
b.	As "a," imperf.	*2,500.*		
2848	29c George Meany	.60	.25	
2849	29c Al Jolson.......................................	.85	.25	
2850	29c Bing Crosby...................................	.85	.25	
2851	29c Ethel Waters...................................	.85	.25	
2852	29c Nat "King" Cole	.85	.25	
2853	29c Ethel Merman	.85	.25	
a.	Vert. strip of 5, #2849-2853	4.25	2.00	
b.	Pane of 20, imperf.	*4,600.*		
2854	29c Bessie Smith	1.50	.25	
2855	29c Muddy Waters................................	1.50	.25	
2856	29c Billie Holiday.................................	1.50	.25	
2857	29c Robert Johnson	1.50	.25	
2858	29c Jimmy Rushing	1.50	.25	
2859	29c "Ma" Rainey	1.50	.25	
2860	29c Mildred Bailey	1.50	.25	
2861	29c Howlin' Wolf.................................	1.50	.25	
a.	Block of 8, #2854-2861 +2 additional stamps	15.00	4.50	
2862	29c James Thurber...............................	.75	.25	
2863	29c Motorboat......................................	.75	.25	
2864	29c Ship	.75	.25	
2865	29c Ship's Wheel	.75	.25	

2854-2861

2849-2853

2842

2848   2862

2863-2866

2867   2868

2869

2871

2872

2873

2874

2875

2876

2877

2879

2881

2888

2893

2897

2902

2905

2907

2908

2911

2919

2933

2934

2938

2940

2941

2942

2943

2948

2950

HOW TO USE THIS BOOK

The number in the first column is its Scott number or identifying number. Following that is the denomination of the stamp and its color or description. Finally, the values, unused and used, are shown.

Scott No.	Description	Unused Value	Used Value	/ / / / / /
2866	29c Coral	.75	.25	
a.	Block of 4, #2963-2966	3.00	1.50	
b.	As "a," imperf	600.00		
2867	29c Black-necked Crane	.70	.25	
2868	29c Whooping Crane	.70	.25	
a.	Pair, #2867-2868	1.40	.75	
b.	Black and magenta (engr.) omitted	1,650.		
c.	As "a," double impression of engr. black (Birds' names and "USA") & magenta ("29")	5,000.		
d.	As "a," double impression of engr. black ("USA") & magenta ("29")	—		
2869	Legends of the West, pane of 20	15.00	10.00	
a.-t.	29c Any single	.75	.50	
u.	As No. 2869, a.-e. imperf, f.-j. part perf	—		
2870	29c Legends of the West (2869), pane of 20	240.00	—	

Nos. 2869 and 2870 have different Bill Pickett stamps.
Framelines on No. 2870 are thinner than on No. 2869.

Scott No.	Description	Unused Value	Used Value	/ / / / / /
2871	29c Christmas - Religious, perf. 11¼	.60	.25	
2871A	29c Christmas-Religious, perf. 9¾ x 11 (2871)	.60	.25	
b.	Booklet Pane of 10	6.25	3.50	
c.	Imperf. pair	475.00		
2872	29c Christmas - Stocking	.60	.25	
a.	Booklet pane of 20	12.50	6.00	
b.	Imperf., pair	—		
c.	As "a," imperf horiz.	—		
d.	Quadruple impression of black, triple impression of blue, double impression of red and yellow, green normal	—		
e.	Vert. pair, imperf. btwn.	—		
f.	As "a," imperf	—		
2873	29c Christmas - Santa Claus	.70	.25	
a.	Booklet pane of 12	8.50		
b.	Coil with plate #V1111	—	6.00	
2874	29c Christmas - Cardinal	.60	.25	
a.	Booklet pane of 18	11.00		
2875	$2 Bureau of Engraving & Printing, Sheet of 4, perf. 11	16.00	13.50	
a.	Single stamp (like No. 262)	4.00	2.00	
2876	29c Year of the Boar	.70	.25	
2877	(3c) Dove, tan, brt bl & red, thin inscript.	.25	.25	
a.	Imperf., pair	135.00		
b.	Double impression of red	190.00		
2878	(3c) Dove (2877), tan, dk blue & red, heavy inscriptions	.25	.25	
2879	(20c) Flag, black "G," yellow & multi	.40	.25	

Scott No.	Description	Unused Value	Used Value	/ / / / / /
a.	Imperf pair......................................	—		
2880 (20c)	Flag (2879), red "G," yellow & multi	.75	.25	
2881 (32c)	Flag, black "G" & multi, perf			
	11.2 x 11.1	1.25	.25	
a.	Booklet pane of 10.........................	12.50	5.00	
2882 (32c)	Flag (2881), red "G" & multi..........	.60	.25	

Distance on No. 2882 from bottom of red G to top of flag immediately above is 13¾mm, on No. 2885 13½mm.

Booklet stamps

2883 (32c)	Flag (2881), black "G" & multi,			
	perf.10 x 9.9..............................	.65	.25	
a.	Booklet pane of 10.........................	6.50	3.75	
2884 (32c)	Flag (2881), blue "G" & multi	.65	.25	
a.	Booklet pane of 10.........................	6.50	3.75	
b.	As "a," imperf.	*1,700.*		
2885 (32c)	Flag (2881), red "G" & multi..........	.90	.25	
a.	Booklet pane of 10.........................	9.00	4.50	
b.	Pair, imperf. vert.	*750.00*		
c.	Pair, imperf. btwn.	—		
d.	Horiz. pair, imperf. btwn., in #2885a			
	with foldover...............................	—		

Self-adhesive, Die Cut

2886 (32c)	Flag (2881), gray, blue, light blue,			
	red & black	.75	.25	
a.	Booklet pane of 18.........................	14.00		
b.	Coil with plate #V1111	—	10.00	
2887 (32c)	Flag (2881), black, blue & red	.75	.25	
a.	Booklet pane of 18.........................	13.50		

No. 2886 has a small number of blue shading dots in white stripes immediately below the blue field. No. 2887 has noticeable blue shading.

1994-95, Coil Stamps, Perf. 9.8 Vert.

2888 (25c)	Flag, blue & multi..........................	.90	.50	
2889 (32c)	Flag (2881), black "G" & multi	1.50	.25	
a.	Imperf., pair...................................	*275.00*		
2890 (32c)	Flag (2881), blue "G" & multi	.65	.25	
2891 (32c)	Flag (2881), red "G" & multi.........	.85	.25	

Rouletted 9.8 Vert.

2892 (32c)	Flag (2881), red "G" & multi.........	.75	.25	

Perf. 9.8 Vert.

2893 (5c)	Flag, green & multi (Bureau precancel)	.50	.25	

1995

2897	32c Flag over Porch	.65	.25	
a.	Imperf., vert. pair	60.00		

Coil Stamps

2902 (5c)	Butte, perf......................................	.25	.25	
a.	Imperf., pair...................................	600.00		
2902B (5c)	Butte (2902), Serpentine Die Cut Vert.	.35	.25	
2903 (5c)	Mountain, perf, purple & multi......	.25	.25	

Scott No.	Description	Unused Value	Used Value	/ / / / / /
2904 (5c)	Mountain (2903), perf, blue & multi	.25	.25	
c.	Imperf., pair	400.00		
2904A (5c)	Mountain (2903), Serpentine Die Cut Vert., 11.2 Vert., purple & multi...	.25	.25	
2904B (5c)	Mountain (2903), Serpentine Die cut 9.8 vert.	.25	.25	
2905 (10c)	Auto, perf., small "1995" date	.25	.25	
a.	Medium "1995" date	.25	.25	
b.	Large "1995" date	.25	.25	
c.	As "a," brown omitted, P#S33 single		400.00	
2906 (10c)	Auto (2905), Serpentine Die Cut Vert.	.50	.25	
2907 (10c)	Eagle and Shield (2603), Serpentine Die Cut Vert., gold & multi	.75	.25	
2908 (15c)	Auto Tail Fin, perf, dk org yel & multi	.30	.30	
2909 (15c)	Auto Tail Fin (2908), perf., buff & multi	.30	.30	
2910 (15c)	Auto Tail Fin (2908), Serpentine Die Cut Vert., buff & multi	.30	.30	

No. 2908 has dark bold colors and heavy shading lines, and heavily shaded chrome.
No. 2909 has shinier chrome, more subdued colors and finer details.

Scott No.	Description	Unused Value	Used Value	/ / / / / /
2911 (25c)	Juke Box, dark red, dark yellow green & multi, perf.	.50	.50	
a.	Imperf., pair	425.00		
2912 (25c)	Juke Box (2911), brt org red, brt yel grn & multi, perf.	.50	.50	
2912A (25c)	Juke Box (2911), brt org red, brt yel grn & multi, Serpentine Die Cut 11½ Vert.	.50	.50	

No. 2911 has dark saturated colors, dark blue lines in music selection board.
No. 2912 has bright colors, less shading and light blue lines in music selection board.

Scott No.	Description	Unused Value	Used Value	/ / / / / /
2912B (25c)	Juke Box (2911) perf. 9.8 Vert.	.75	.50	
2913	32c Flag (2897), blue, tan, brown, red & lt blue, perf. 9.8 vert.	.65	.25	
a.	Imperf., pair	30.00		
2914	32c Flag (2897), blue, yellow brown, red & gray, perf. 9.8 vert.	.80	.25	

No. 2913 has light blue shading in flag, No. 2914 has pale gray shading.

Self-Adhesive, Serpentine Die Cut Vert.

Scott No.	Description	Unused Value	Used Value	/ / / / / /
2915	32c Flag (2897), cut 8.7 vert.	1.25	.30	
2915A	32c Flag (2897), cut 9.8 vert., 10 or 11 "peaks" on each side	.65	.25	
h.	Imperf., pair	32.50		
i.	Tan omitted		2,000.	
j.	Double die cutting	30.00		
2915B	32c Flag (2897), cut 11½ vert.	1.00	.90	
2915C	32c Flag (2897), cut 10.9 vert.	2.50	.40	
2915D	32c Flag (2897), cut 9.8 vert., 9 and/or 10 "peaks" on each side	2.00	.90	

Booklet Stamps, Perf. 10.8 x 9.8 on 2 or 3 sides

Scott No.	Description	Unused Value	Used Value	/ / / / / /
2916	32c Flag (2897), blue, tan, brn, red & lt blue	.65	.25	

Scott No.	Description	Unused Value	Used Value	/ / / / / /
a.	Booklet pane of 10.........................	6.50	3.25	
b.	As "a," imperf.	—		

Self-Adhesive

2919	32c Flag over Field, Die Cut.................	.65	.25	
a.	Booklet pane of 18..........................	12.00		
b.	Vert. pair, no die cutting btwn.	—		
2920	32c Flag (2897), large date, Serpentine Die Cut 8.7...	.65	.25	
a.	Booklet pane of 20 + label	13.00		
b.	Small date......................................	6.00	.35	
c.	As "b," booklet pane of 20 + label.	100.00		
f.	As No. 2920, pane of 15 + label	*10.00*		
h.	As No. 2920, booklet pane of 15 ..	*47.50*		
i.	As No. 2920, imperf pair...............	—		
j.	Dark blue omitted (from #2920a) ..	*1,750.*		
k.	Vert. pair, die cutting missing btwn. (from perf. shift) (from No. 2920a)	—		
2920D	32c Flag, Large date, Serpentine die cut 11.3 (2897)...........................	.80	.25	
e.	Booklet pane of 10..........................	8.00		
2921	32c Flag (2897), dk blue, tan, brn, red & lt bl, Serpentine Die Cut 9.8 on 2 or 3 sides	.90	.25	
a.	Booklet pane of 10, dated red "1996"	9.00		
b.	As #2921, dated red "1997"..........	.75	.25	
c.	As "a," dated red "1997"...............	7.50		
d.	Booklet pane of 5 + label, dated red "1997".......................................	8.00		
e.	As "a," die cutting omitted.	*200.00*		

1995-96 Great Americans

2933	32c Milton S. Hershey	.65	.25	
2934	32c Cal Farley	.65	.25	
2935	32c Henry R. Luce...............................	.65	.35	
2936	32c Lila and Dewitt Wallace, blue	.65	.35	
a.	32c Light blue.................................	.65	.35	
2938	46c Ruth Benedict	.90	.30	
2940	55c Dr. Alice Hamilton	1.10	.25	
a.	Imperf., pair...................................	—		
2941	55c Justin S. Morrill, Self-adhesive	1.10	.25	
2942	77c Mary Breckinridge, Self-adhesive..	1.50	.40	
2943	78c Alice Paul, bright violet.................	1.60	.25	
a.	78c Dull violet	1.60	.25	
b.	78c Pale violet................................	1.75	.30	

Perf. 11.2

2948	(32c) Love..	.65	.25	

Self-Adhesive

2949	(32c) Love (2948).....................................	.65	.25	
a.	Booklet pane of 20 + label	13.00		
b.	Red (engr.) omitted.........................	*275.00*		

Scott No.		Description	Unused Value	Used Value	/ / / / / /
c.		As "a," red (engr.) omitted..............	*5,500.*		
d.		Red (engr.) missing (from a color misregistration)..............................	—		
2950		32c Florida Statehood...........................	.65	.25	
2951		32c Earth in Tub...................................	.65	.25	
2952		32c Solar Energy..................................	.65	.25	
2953		32c Tree Planting..................................	.65	.25	
2954		32c Beach Clean-up	.65	.25	
a.		Block of 4, #2951-2954..................	2.60	1.75	
2955		32c Richard M. Nixon	.65	.25	
a.		Red (engr.) missing (from a color misregistration).............................	*950.00*		
2956		32c Bessie Coleman.............................	.85	.25	
2957		32c Love...	.65	.25	
2958		55c Love...	1.10	.25	
Booklet stamps					
2959		32c Love (2957), Perf 9.8 x 10.8..........	.65	.25	
a.		Booklet pane of 10..........................	6.50	3.25	
b.		Imperf., pair..................................	*100.00*		
c.		As "a," imperf	*500.00*		
Self-Adhesive					
2960		55c Love...	1.10	.25	
a.		Booklet pane of 20 + label	22.50		
1995					
2961		32c Volleyball......................................	.65	.25	
2962		32c Softball..	.65	.25	
2963		32c Bowling..	.65	.25	
2964		32c Tennis..	.65	.25	
2965		32c Golf...	.65	.25	
a.		Vert. strip of 5, #2961-2965	3.25	2.00	
b.		As "a," imperf.	*2,250.*		
c.		As "a," yellow omitted	*2,000.*		
d.		As "a," yellow, blue & mag. omitted	*2,000.*		
2966		32c Prisoners of War & Missing in Action	.65	.25	
2967		32c Legends of Hollywood – Marilyn Monroe..............................	.80	.25	
a.		Imperf., pair	*400.00*		
2968		32c Texas Statehood	.75	.25	
2969		32c Split Rock Lighthouse	1.25	.30	
2970		32c St. Joseph Lighthouse	1.25	.30	
2971		32c Spectacle Reef Lighthouse	1.25	.30	
2972		32c Marblehead Lighthouse	1.25	.30	
2973		32c Thirty Mile Point Lighthouse	1.25	.30	
a.		Booklet pane of 5, #2969-2973......	6.25	*3.00*	
b.		As "a," 2 vert. pairs imperf. horiz. of #2972 and 2973, in pane of 7+ stamps in cplt. bklt. #BK230 (due to foldover)	—		
2974		32c United Nations	.65	.25	
2975		Civil War, pane of 20	32.50	17.50	

2951-2954

2955

2976-2979

2980

2956

2967

HOW TO USE THIS BOOK

The number in the first column is its Scott number or identifying number.
Following that is the denomination of the stamp and its color or description.
Finally, the values, unused and used, are shown.

2975

2981

32 USA JAZZ COMPOSER AND SAXOPHONIST COLEMAN HAWKINS

32 USA JAZZ COMPOSER AND TRUMPETER LOUIS ARMSTRONG

32 USA JAZZ COMPOSER AND PIANIST JAMES P. JOHNSON

32 USA JAZZ COMPOSER AND PIANIST JELLY ROLL MORTON

32 USA JAZZ COMPOSER AND SAXOPHONIST CHARLIE PARKER

32 USA JAZZ COMPOSER AND PIANIST EUBIE BLAKE

32 USA JAZZ COMPOSER AND BASSIST CHARLES MINGUS

32 USA JAZZ COMPOSER AND PIANIST THELONIOUS MONK

32 USA JAZZ COMPOSER AND SAXOPHONIST JOHN COLTRANE

32 USA JAZZ COMPOSER AND PIANIST ERROLL GARNER

2983-2992

Eddie Rickenbacker Aviation Pioneer USA 60

2998

Republic of Palau MARINE LIFE USA 32

2999

UNITED STATES NAVAL ACADEMY USA 32 150TH ANNIVERSARY 1845-1995

3001

TENNESSEE WILLIAMS 32 USA

3002

© United States Postal Service 1994

32 USA Aster

32 USA Chrysanthemum

32 USA Dahlia

32 USA Hydrangea

32 USA Rudbeckia

2993-2997

262

Scott No.	Description	Unused Value	Used Value	/ / / / /
a.-t.	32c Any single	1.50	.60	☐☐☐☐☐
u.	As No. 2975, a-e imperf. f-j.			
	part perf., others perf.	—		☐☐☐☐☐
v.	As No. 2975, k-t. imperf. f-j.			
	part perf., others perf.	1,750.		☐☐☐☐☐
w.	As No. 2975, imperf.	1,500.		☐☐☐☐☐
x.	Block of 9 (f-h, k-m, p-r) k-l & p-q			
	imperf. vert....................................	—		☐☐☐☐☐
y.	As No. 2975, a-b perf., c, f-h part perf.,			
	others imperf.	—		☐☐☐☐☐
z.	As No. 2975, o. & t. imperf., j., n. & s.			
	part perf., others perf.	—		☐☐☐☐☐
2976	32c Carousel Horses, upper left	.65	.25	☐☐☐☐☐
2977	32c Carousel Horses, upper right..........	.65	.25	☐☐☐☐☐
2978	32c Carousel Horses, lower left............	.65	.25	☐☐☐☐☐
2979	32c Carousel Horses, lower right	.65	.25	☐☐☐☐☐
a.	Block of 4, #2976-2979..................	2.60	2.00	☐☐☐☐☐
2980	32c Woman Suffrage	.65	.25	☐☐☐☐☐
a.	Black (engr.) omitted......................	375.00		☐☐☐☐☐
b.	Imperf., pair....................................	1,250.		☐☐☐☐☐
c.	Vert. pair, imperf. btwn. and at bottom	750.00		☐☐☐☐☐
2981	World War II, block of 10..............	15.00	7.50	☐☐☐☐☐
a.-j.	32c Any single	1.50	.50	☐☐☐☐☐
2982	32c Louis Armstrong, white denomination			
	(2984)...	.90	.25	☐☐☐☐☐
2983	32c Coleman Hawkins...........................	2.25	.25	☐☐☐☐☐
2984	32c Louis Armstrong, black denom......	2.25	.25	☐☐☐☐☐
2985	32c James P. Johnson............................	2.25	.25	☐☐☐☐☐
2986	32c Jelly Roll Morton...........................	2.25	.25	☐☐☐☐☐
2987	32c Charlie Parker	2.25	.25	☐☐☐☐☐
2988	32c Eubie Blake	2.25	.25	☐☐☐☐☐
2989	32c Charles Mingus	2.25	.25	☐☐☐☐☐
2990	32c Thelonious Monk............................	2.25	.25	☐☐☐☐☐
2991	32c John Coltrane	2.25	.25	☐☐☐☐☐
2992	32c Erroll Garner	2.25	.25	☐☐☐☐☐
a.	Vertical block of 10, #2983-2992...	23.00	7.50	☐☐☐☐☐
b.	Pane of 20, dark blue omitted.........	—		☐☐☐☐☐
c.	Imperf., pair of Nos. 2991-2992.....	—		☐☐☐☐☐
2993	32c Aster	.65	.25	☐☐☐☐☐
2994	32c Chrysanthemum	.65	.25	☐☐☐☐☐
2995	32c Dahlia	.65	.25	☐☐☐☐☐
2996	32c Hydrangea	.65	.25	☐☐☐☐☐
2997	32c Rudbeckia......................................	.65	.25	☐☐☐☐☐
a.	Booklet pane of 5, #2993-2997......	3.25	2.25	☐☐☐☐☐
b.	As "a," imperf.	2,750.		☐☐☐☐☐
2998	60c Eddie Rickenbacker, small "1995" date	1.40	.50	☐☐☐☐☐
a.	60c Large "1995" date............................	2.00	.50	☐☐☐☐☐
2999	32c Republic of Palau............................	.65	.25	☐☐☐☐☐
3000	Comic Strips, pane of 20...............	13.00	10.00	☐☐☐☐☐

3000

3003

3025-3029

264

Scott No.		Description	Unused Value	Used Value	/ / / / / /
a.-t.	32c	Any single	.65	.50	
u.		As No. 3000 a.-h. imperf., i.-l. part perf	—		
v.		As No. 3000 m.-t. imperf., i.-l. part perf	2,750.		
w.		As No. 3000 a.-l. imperf., m.-t. imperf. vertically....................................	—		
x.		As No. 3000, imperf	—		
3001	32c	Naval Academy	.65	.25	
3002	32c	Tennessee Williams........................	.65	.25	
3003	32c	Christmas - Religious, perf. 11.2 ...	.65	.25	
c.		Blk (engr., denomination) omitted	200.00		
3003A	32c	Christmas -Religious, Perf. 9.8 x 10.9 from bklt pane (3003)	.65	.25	
b.		Booklet pane of 10	6.50	4.00	
3004	32c	Christmas - Santa, Chimney...........	.70	.25	
3005	32c	Christmas - Child, Jumping Jack....	.70	.25	
3006	32c	Christmas - Child, Tree	.70	.25	
3007	32c	Christmas - Santa, Sled.................	.70	.25	
a.		Block or strip of 4	2.80	1.25	
b.		Booklet pane of 10, 3 ea. #3004-3005, 2 ea. #3006-3007	8.00	4.00	
c.		Booklet pane of 10, 2 ea. #3004-3005, 3 ea. #3006-3007	8.00	4.00	
d.		As "a," imperf.	475.00		
e.		As "b," miscut and inserted upside down into booklet cover, with full bottom selvage.	—		
Booklet stamps, self-adhesive, Serpentine Die Cut					
3008	32c	Christmas - Santa, Sled (3007).......	.95	.25	
3009	32c	Christmas - Child, Jumping Jack (3005)	.95	.25	
3010	32c	Christmas - Santa, Chimney (3004)	.95	.25	
3011	32c	Christmas - Child, Tree (3006).......	.95	.25	
a.		Booklet pane of 20, 5 ea. #3008-3011 + label...	19.00	—	
3012	32c	Christmas - Angel	.65	.25	
a.		Booklet pane of 20 + label	13.00	—	
b.		Vert. pair, no die cutting btwn.	—		
c.		Booklet pane of 15 + label, 1996...	13.00		
d.		Booklet pane of 15........................	30.00		
3013	32c	Christmas - Children Sledding	.65	.25	
a.		Booklet pane of 18........................	12.00		
Coil stamps, Serpentine Die Cut Vert.					
3014	32c	Christmas - Santa, Sled (3007).......	3.00	.30	
3015	32c	Christmas - Child, Jumping Jack (3005)	3.00	.30	
3016	32c	Christmas - Santa, Chimney (3004)	3.00	.30	
3017	32c	Christmas - Child, Tree (3006).......	3.00	.30	
a.		Strip of 4, #3014-3017....................	12.00		
3018	32c	Christmas - Angel (3012)	1.10	.30	
3019	32c	1893 Duryea..................................	.90	.25	
3020	32c	1894 Haynes..................................	.90	.25	

3004-3007

3012

3013

3024

3030

3036

3019-3023

3032

3033

3051

3052

3059

3058

3060

266

Scott No.		Description	Unused Value	Used Value	/ / / / / /
3021	32c	1898 Columbia	.90	.25	
3022	32c	1899 Winton	.90	.25	
3023	32c	1901 White	.90	.25	
a.		Vert. or horiz. strip of 5, #3019-3023	4.50	2.00	

1996 Issues

3024	32c	Utah Statehood	.75	.25	
3025	32c	Crocus	.75	.25	
3026	32c	Winter Aconite	.75	.25	
3027	32c	Pansy	.75	.25	
3028	32c	Snowdrop	.75	.25	
3029	32c	Anemone	.75	.25	
a.		Booklet pane of 5, #3025-3029	3.75	2.50	
b.		As "a," imperf.	—		

Serpentine Die Cut 11.3, Self-adhesive

3030	32c	Love	.65	.25	
a.		Booklet pane of 20 + label	13.00		
b.		Booklet pane of 15 + label	10.00		
c.		Red (engr. "LOVE") omitted	*175.00*		
d.		Red (engr. "LOVE") missing (from a color misregistration)	—		
e.		Double impression of red (engr. "LOVE")	—		
f.		Die cutting omitted, pair	*275.00*		
g.		As "a," stamp 1-5 double impression of red (engr. "LOVE")	—		
h.		As "a," red (engr. "LOVE") omitted	—		
i.		As "a," die cutting omitted	—		

Serpentine Die Cut

3031	1c	American Kestrel, self-adhesive (2477)	.25	.25	
c.		Die cutting omitted, pair	—		
3031A		American Kestrel, blue inscription and year	.25	.25	
b.		Die cutting omitted, pair	—		

1996-98

3032	2c	Red-headed Woodpecker	.25	.25	
3033	3c	Eastern Bluebird with cent sign	.25	.25	
3036	$1	Red Fox, self-adhesive, serp. die cut 11½ x 11¼	3.75	.50	
a.		Serpentine die cut 11¾ x 11	4.00	.50	

Coil Stamp, Perf. 9¾ Vert.

3044	1c	American Kestrel (2477) with cent sign, small date	.25	.25	
a.		Large date,	.25	.25	
3045	2c	Red-headed Woodpecker, Coil	.25	.25	

Serpentine Die Cut 10½ x 10¾, Booklet Stamp, Self-Adhesive

3048	20c	Blue Jay (2483)	.40	.25	
a.		Booklet pane of 10	4.00		
b.		Booklet pane of 4	35.00		
c.		Booklet pane of 6	50.00		

3061-3064

3065

3066

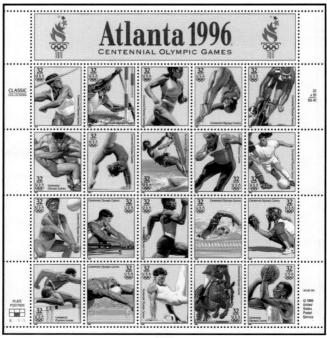

3068

Scott No.	Description	Unused Value	Used Value	/ / / / / /
3049	32c Yellow Rose, serp. die cut 11¼ x 11¾ (2490)	.65	.25	
a.	Booklet pane of 20 + label	13.00		
b.	Booklet pane of 4	2.60		
c.	Booklet pane of 5 + label	3.50		
d.	Booklet pane of 6	6.00		
3050	20c Ring-necked Pheasant, serp. die cut 11¼	.65	.25	
a.	Booklet pane of 10	6.50		
b.	Serp. die cut 11	3.25	.25	
c.	As "b," booklet pane of 10, all stamps upright	35.00		
3051	20c Ring-Necked Pheasant, serp. die cut 10½ x 11, self-adhesive bklt. stamps (3050)	.75	.25	
3051A	20c Ring-Necked Pheasant, serp. die cut 10.6 x 10.4	7.00	.50	
b.	Booklet pane of 5, 4 #3051, 1 #3051A turned sideways at top.	10.00		
c.	Booklet pane of 5, 4 #3051, 1 #3051A turned sideways at bottom	10.00		

Booklet Stamp, Serpentine Die Cut 11½ x 11¼

Scott No.	Description	Unused Value	Used Value	/ / / / / /
3052	33c Coral Pink Rose, serp. die cut 11½ x 11¼	.90	.25	
a.	Booklet pane of 4	3.60		
b.	Booklet pane of 5 + label	4.50		
c.	Booklet pane of 6	5.50		
d.	Booklet pane of 20 + label	17.50		
j.	Die cutting omitted, pair	—		
k.	As "d," die cutting omitted	—		

Serpentine Die Cut 10¾ x 10½ on 2 or 3 sides, Booklet Stamp

Scott No.	Description	Unused Value	Used Value	/ / / / / /
3052E	33c Coral Pink Rose (3052)	.80	.25	
f.	Booklet pane of 20	16.00		
g.	Black ("33 USA," etc.) omitted	375.00		
h.	As "f," all 12 stamps on one side with black ("33 USA," etc.) omitted	—		
i.	Horiz. pair, die cutting omitted btwn.	—		
j.	As "f," vert. die cutting missing between (due to perf. shift)	—		

Coil Stamp, Serpentine Die Cut 11½ Vert.

Scott No.	Description	Unused Value	Used Value	/ / / / / /
3053	20c Blue Jay (2483)	.50	.25	
3054	32c Yellow Rose, serp. die cut 9¾ vert.	.65	.25	
a.	Die cutting omitted, pair	*85.00*		
b.	Black, yellow & green omitted	—		
c.	As "b," die cutting omitted, pair	—		
d.	Black omitted	—		
e.	As "d," die cutting omitted, pair	—		
f.	All colors omitted, die cutting omitted	—		
g.	Pair, die cutting omitted, containing one stamp each of "c" and "e"	—		

269

3067   3069   3070

3072-3076

3077-3080

3081   3082   3087   3088

270

Scott No.	Description	Unused Value	Used Value	/ / / / / /
3055	20c Ring-Necked Pheasant, serp. die cut 9¾ vert. (3051)	.40	.25	
a.	Die cutting omitted, pair	150.00		
1996				
3058	32c Ernest E. Just	.65	.25	
3059	32c Smithsonian Institution	.65	.25	
3060	32c Chinese New Year - Year of the Rat.	.90	.25	
a.	Imperf., pair	725.00		
3061	32c Eadweard Muybridge	.65	.25	
3062	32c Ottmar Mergenthaler	.65	.25	
3063	32c Frederic E. Ives	.65	.25	
3064	32c William Dickson	.65	.25	
a.	Block or strip of 4, #3061-3064	2.60	2.00	
3065	32c Fulbright Scholarship	.75	.25	
3066	50c Jacqueline Cochran	1.00	.40	
a.	Black (engr.) omitted	55.00		
3067	32c Marathon	.65	.25	
3068	Olympic Games, pane of 20	14.00	10.00	
a.-t.	Any single	.70	.50	
u.	As No. 3068, imperf.	1,000.		
v.	As No. 3068, back inscriptions omitted on a., f., k. & p., incorrect back inscriptions on others	—		
w.	As No. 3068, e. imperf., d., i.-j. part perf., all others perf.	—		
3069	32c Georgia O'Keeffe	.85	.25	
a.	Imperf., pair	125.00		
3070	32c Tennessee Statehood, perf.	.65	.25	
3071	32c Tennessee Statehood (3070), serpentine die cut	.75	.30	
a.	Booklet pane of 20	15.00		
b.	Horiz. pair, no die cutting btwn.	—	—	
c.	Die cutting omitted, pair	—		
d.	Horiz. pair, die cutting omitted vert.	—	—	
3072	32c Fancy Dance	1.20	.25	
3073	32c Butterfly Dance	1.20	.25	
3074	32c Traditional Dance	1.20	.25	
3075	32c Raven Dance	1.20	.25	
3076	32c Hoop Dance	1.20	.25	
a.	Strip of 5, #3072-3076	6.00	2.50	
3077	32c Eohippus	.65	.25	
3078	32c Woolly Mammoth	.65	.25	
3079	32c Mastodon	.65	.25	
3080	32c Saber-tooth Cat	.65	.25	
a.	Block or Strip of 5, #3077-3080	2.60	2.00	
3081	32c Breast Cancer Awareness	.65	.25	
3082	32c Legends of Hollywood – James Dean	.65	.25	
a.	Imperf., pair	150.00		

3083-3086

3090

3095

3096-3099

272

Scott No.	Description	Unused Value	Used Value	/ / / / / /
b.	As "a," red (USA 32c) missing (from a color misregistration) and tan (James Dean) omitted............	—		
c.	As "a," tan (James Dean) omitted ..	—		
d.	As "a," top stamp red missing (from a color misregistration) and tan (James Dean) omitted, bottom stamp tan omitted	—		
e.	As No. 3082, pane of 20, right two columns perf., left three columns imperf..	1,750.		
3083	32c Mighty Casey.....................................	.65	.25	
3084	32c Paul Bunyan.....................................	.65	.25	
3085	32c John Henry......................................	.65	.25	
3086	32c Pecos Bill..	.65	.25	
a.	Block or Strip of 5, #3083-3086	2.60	2.00	
3087	32c Centennial Olympic Games...........	.75	.25	
3088	32c Iowa Statehood, perf.	.80	.25	
3089	32c Iowa Statehood, self-adhesive (3088)	.70	.30	
a.	Booklet pane of 20........................	14.00		
3090	32c Rural Free Delivery, Centenary......	.65	.25	
3091	32c Riverboats - "Robert E. Lee"	.65	.25	
3092	32c Riverboats - "Sylvan Dell"	.65	.25	
3093	32c Riverboats - "Far West"	.65	.25	
3094	32c Riverboats - "Rebecca Everingham"	.65	.25	
3095	32c Riverboats - "Bailey Gatzert".........	.65	.25	
a.	Vertical strip of 5, #3091-3095.......	3.25		
b.	Strip of 5, #3091-3095, with special die cutting	65.00	50.00	
3096	32c Count Basie.....................................	.75	.25	
3097	32c Tommy and Jimmy Dorsey.............	.75	.25	
3098	32c Glenn Miller	.75	.25	
3099	32c Benny Goodman	.75	.25	
a.	Block or Strip of 4, #3096-3099	3.00	2.00	
3100	32c Harold Arlen....................................	.75	.25	
3101	32c Johnny Mercer	.75	.25	
3102	32c Dorothy Fields.................................	.75	.25	
3103	32c Hoagy Carmichael	.75	.25	
a.	Block or Strip of 4, #3100-3103	3.00	2.00	
3104	23c F. Scott Fitzgerald	.55	.25	
3105	Endangered Species, Pane of 15	12.00	8.00	
a.-o.	32c Any single	.80	.50	
3106	32c Computer Technology.....................	.65	.25	
3107	32c Christmas - Madonna and Child	.65	.25	
3108	32c Christmas - Family at Fireplace.....	.65	.25	
3109	32c Christmas - Decorating Tree...........	.65	.25	
3110	32c Christmas - Dreaming of Santa Claus	.65	.25	
3111	32c Christmas - Holiday Shopping	.65	.25	
a.	Block or Strip of 4, #3108-3111	2.60	1.75	

3100-3103

3104

3106

3105

3107

3108-3111

3117

3118

3119

3120

3121

3123

3124

3125

3126

3127

3130-3131

3134

3137

3139a

3143-3146

3140a

3141

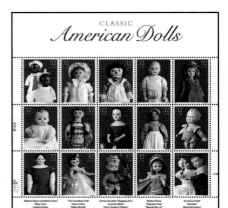

3152

3151

Scott No.		Description	Unused Value	Used Value	/ / / / / /

Serpentine Die Cut 10, Self-Adhesive Booklet Stamps

3112	32c	Christmas - Madonna and Child (3107)	.75	.25	
a.		Booklet pane of 20 + label	15.00		
b.		Die cutting omitted, pair	60.00		
c.		As "a," die cutting omitted	—		
3113	32c	Christmas - Family at Fireplace (3108)	.75	.25	
3114	32c	Christmas - Decorating Tree (3109)	.75	.25	
3115	32c	Christmas - Dreaming of Santa Claus (3110)	.75	.25	
3116	32c	Christmas - Holiday Shopping (3111)	.75	.25	
a.		Booklet pane of 20, 5 ea. #3113-3116	15.00		
b.		Strip of 4, #3113-3116, die cutting omitted	*550.00*		
c.		Block of 6, die cutting omitted	*775.00*		
d.		As "a," die cutting omitted	*2,100.*		

Self-Adhesive, Die Cut

3117	32c	Christmas - Skaters	.65	.25	
a.		Booklet pane of 18	12.00		
3118	32c	Hanukkah	.65	.25	

Perf. 11x11.1

3119		Cycling, Souvenir Sheet of 2	2.75	2.00	
a.	50c	Orange and multi	1.30	1.00	
b.	50c	Blue green and multi	1.30	1.00	

1997 Issues

3120	32c	Year of the Ox	.80	.25	
3121	32c	Brig. Gen. Benjamin O. Davis, Sr., self-adhesive	.70	.25	
3122	32c	Statue of Liberty, self-adhesive (2599)	.70	.25	
a.		Booklet pane of 20 + label	14.00		
b.		Booklet pane of 4	2.80		
c.		Booklet pane of 5 + label	3.75		
d.		Booklet pane of 6	4.25		
h.		As "a," die cutting omitted	—		
3122E	32c	Statue of Liberty, self-adhesive booklet stamp	1.50	.25	
f.		Booklet pane of 20 + label	40.00		
g.		Booklet pane of 6	9.00		
3123	32c	Love - Swans, self-adhesive, booklet stamp	.65	.25	
a.		Booklet pane of 20 + label	13.00		
b.		Die cutting omitted, pair	*135.00*		
c.		As "a," die cutting omitted	*1,350.*		
d.		As "a," black omitted	—		
3124	55c	Love - Swans, self-adhesive, booklet stamp	1.10	.25	
a.		Booklet pane of 20 + label	22.00		
3125	32c	Helping Children Learn, self-adhesive	.65	.25	
3126	32c	Merian Prints (citron), self-adhesive, booklet stamp	.65	.25	

3153

3154-57

3158-3165

3168-3172

3166

3167

3173

Scott No.		Description	Unused Value	Used Value	/ / / / / /
3127	32c	Merian Prints (pineapple), self-adhesive, booklet stamp	.65	.25	
a.		Booklet pane, 10 ea. #3126-3127 + label..	13.00		
b.		Pair, #3126-3127.............................	1.30		
c.		Vert. pair, die cutting omitted btwn..	475.00		
3128	32c	Merian Botanical Prints, self-adhesive booklet stamp 18½ x 24mm (3126)	1.00	.25	
a.		Perf. 11.2 broken on right..............	2.50	.25	
b.		Booklet pane, 2 ea. #3128-3129 + 3128a	6.50		
3129	32c	Merian Botanical Prints, self-adhesive booklet stamp 18½ x 24mm (3127)....................	1.00	.25	
a.		Perf. 11.2 broken on right..............	4.50	.35	
b.		Booklet pane, 2 ea. #3128-3129 + 3129a	8.50		
c.		Pair, #3128-3129.............................	2.00		
3130	32c	Sailing Ship - Pacific '97	.65	.30	
3131	32c	Stagecoach - Pacific '97.................	.65	.30	
a.		Pair, #3130-3131.............................	1.30	.75	
3132	32c	Juke Box, Imperf Coil (2911)	1.00	.50	
3133	32c	Flag Over Porch, Linerless Coil, serpentine die cut 9.9 vert. (2897)	1.75	.25	
3134	32c	Thornton Wilder - Literary Arts.....	.65	.25	
3135	32c	Raoul Wallenberg............................	.65	.25	
3136		Dinosaurs.......................................	10.00	8.00	
a.-o.	32c	Any single	.65	.50	
p.		As No. 3136, bottom seven stamps imperf................................	3,750.		
q.		As No. 3136, top 8 stamps imperf .	3,750.		
r.		As No. 3136, all colors and tagging missing (from extraneous paper)..	—		
3137		Bugs Bunny, self-adhesive pane of 10, die cutting does not extend through backing	6.75		
a.	32c	Single stamp....................................	.65	.25	
b.		Pane of 9 #3137a	6.00		
c.		Pane of 1 #3137a	.65		
3138		Bugs Bunny, self-adhesive pane of 10, die cut through backing, right stamp with no die cutting.............	160.00		
a.	32c	Single stamp....................................	3.50		
b.		Pane of 9 #3138a	32.50		
c.		Pane of 1, no die cutting.................	120.00		
3139	$6	Benjamin Franklin - Pacific '97, pane of 12	12.00	9.00	
a.	50c	Single stamp....................................	1.00	.50	
3140	$7.20	Washington - Pacific '97, pane of 12	14.50	11.00	

3174

3175

3176

3177

3179

3180

3178

3181

3182

3183

3184

HOW TO USE THIS BOOK

The number in the first column is its Scott number or identifying number. Following that is the denomination of the stamp and its color or description. Finally, the values, unused and used, are shown.

Scott No.	Description	Unused Value	Used Value	//////
a.	60c Single stamp...........................	1.20	.60	
3141	32c Marshall Plan, 50th Anniversary....	.65	.25	
3142	Classic American Aircraft, pane of 20	13.00	10.00	
a.-t.	32c Any single	.65	.50	
1997 Perf. 11.2				
3143	32c Bear Bryant.................................	.65	.25	
3144	32c Pop Warner.................................	.65	.25	
3145	32c Vince Lombardi	.65	.25	
3146	32c George Halas...............................	.65	.25	
a.	Block or strip of 4, #3143-3146.....	2.60	1.50	
With Red Bar Above Coach's Name, Perf. 11				
3147	32c Vince Lombardi	.65	.45	
3148	32c Bear Bryant.................................	.65	.45	
3149	32c Pop Warner.................................	.65	.45	
3150	32c George Halas...............................	.65	.45	
1997, July 28 Perf. 10.9x11.1				
3151	American Dolls, pane of 15...........	13.50	—	
a.-o.	32c Any single	.90	.60	
1997, July 31 Perf. 11.1				
3152	32c Legends of Hollywood – Humphrey Bogart (1899-1957)....	.85	.25	
1997, Aug. 21 Perf. 11.1				
3153	32c *The Stars And Stripes Forever!*.......	.65	.25	
1997 Perf. 11				
3154	32c Lily Pons	.75	.25	
3155	32c Richard Tucker.............................	.75	.25	
3156	32c Lawrence Tibbett..........................	.75	.25	
3157	32c Rosa Ponselle	.75	.25	
a.	Block or strip of 4, #3154-3157.....	3.00	2.00	
3158	32c Leopold Stokowski	1.10	.25	
3159	32c Arthur Fiedler..............................	1.10	.25	
3160	32c George Szell.................................	1.10	.25	
3161	32c Eugene Ormandy	1.10	.25	
3162	32c Samuel Barber..............................	1.10	.25	
3163	32c Ferde Grofe	1.10	.25	
3164	32c Charles Ives.................................	1.10	.25	
3165	32c Louis Moreau Gottschalk	1.10	.25	
a.	Block of 8, #3158-3165.................	9.00	4.00	
1997, Sept. 15 Perf. 11.2				
3166	32c Padre Felix Varela (1788-1853)......	.65	.25	
1997, Sept. 18 Perf. 11.2 x 11.1				
3167	32c Department Of The Air Force, 50th Anniv.	.65	.25	
1997, Sept. 30 Perf. 10.2				
3168	32c Lon Chaney as The Phantom of the Opera	.75	.25	
3169	32c Bela Lugosi as Dracula...................	.75	.25	
3170	32c Boris Karloff as Frankenstein's Monster	.75	.25	
3171	32c Boris Karloff as The Mummy	.75	.25	

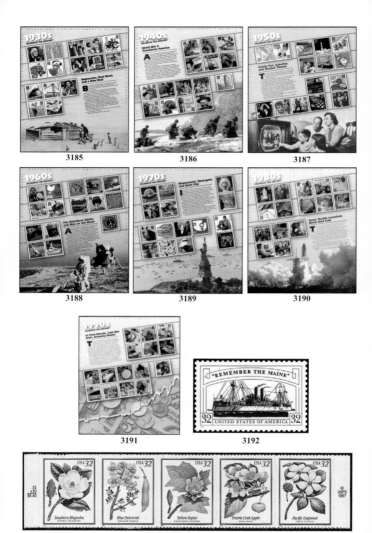

3185

3186

3187

3188

3189

3190

3191

3192

3193-3197

HOW TO USE THIS BOOK

The number in the first column is its Scott number or identifying number. Following that is the denomination of the stamp and its color or description. Finally, the values, unused and used, are shown.

Scott No.	Description	Unused Value	Used Value	/ / / / /
3172	32c Lon Chaney, Jr. as The Wolf Man ..	.75	.25	☐☐☐☐☐
a.	Strip of 5, #3168-3172....................	3.75	2.25	☐☐☐☐☐
1997, Oct. 14 Serpentine Die Cut 11.4, Self-Adhesive				
3173	32c First Supersonic Flight, 50th Anniv.	.65	.25	☐☐☐☐☐
1997, Oct. 18 Perf. 11.1				
3174	32c Women In Military Service............	.65	.25	☐☐☐☐☐
1996, Oct. 22 Serpentine Die Cut 11, Self-Adhesive				
3175	32c Kwanzaa..	.65	.25	☐☐☐☐☐
1997 Serpentine Die Cut 9.9 Booklet Stamps, Self-Adhesive				
3176	32c Madonna and Child, by Sano di Pietro, self-adhesive booklet stamp	.65	.25	☐☐☐☐☐
a.	Booklet pane of 20 + label	13.00		☐☐☐☐☐
Serpentine Die Cut 11.2 x 11.8 on 2, 3 or 4 Sides				
3177	32c Holly..	.65	.25	☐☐☐☐☐
a.	Booklet pane of 20 + label	13.00		☐☐☐☐☐
b.	Booklet pane of 4............................	2.60		☐☐☐☐☐
c.	Booklet pane of 5 + label	3.25		☐☐☐☐☐
d.	Booklet pane of 6............................	3.90		☐☐☐☐☐
Souvenir Sheet 1997, Dec. 10 Perf. 11 x 11.1				
3178	$3 Mars Pathfinder	6.00	4.00	☐☐☐☐☐
a.	$3 Single stamp.................................	5.50	3.00	☐☐☐☐☐
1998 Issues				
3179	32c Year of the Tiger............................	.80	.25	☐☐☐☐☐
3180	32c Alpine Skiing	.75	.25	☐☐☐☐☐
Self-Adhesive				
3181	32c Madam C.J. Walker (1867-1919), Entrepreneur....................................	.70	.25	☐☐☐☐☐
1998-2000, Lithographed, Engraved (#3182m, 3183f, 3184m, 3185b, 3186k, 3187a, 3188c, 3189h), Perf. 11½				
3182	Celebrate The Century, 1900s, pane of 15	10.00	8.50	☐☐☐☐☐
a.-o.	32c any single	.80	.65	☐☐☐☐☐
p.	Engraved red (No. 3182m, Gibson girl) omitted, in pane of 15..........	3,000.		☐☐☐☐☐
3183	Celebrate The Century, 1910s, pane of 15	10.00	8.50	☐☐☐☐☐
a.-o.	32c any single	.80	.65	☐☐☐☐☐
p.	Nos. 3183g, 3183l-3183o imperf. in pane of 15................................	7,000.		☐☐☐☐☐
3184	Celebrate The Century, 1920s, pane of 15	12.50	8.50	☐☐☐☐☐
a.-o.	32c any single	.80	.65	☐☐☐☐☐
3185	32c Celebrate The Century, 1930s, pane of 15	12.50	8.50	☐☐☐☐☐
a.-o.	32c any single	.80	.65	☐☐☐☐☐
3186	Celebrate The Century, 1940s, pane of 15	13.00	8.50	☐☐☐☐☐
a.-o.	33c any single	.85	.65	☐☐☐☐☐

3198-3202

3203

3204

3206

3207

3208

3209

3211

3212-3215

3216-3219

284

Scott No.	Description	Unused Value	Used Value	/ / / / / /
3187	Celebrate The Century, 1950s, pane of 15	13.00	8.50	☐☐☐☐☐
a.-o.	33c any single	.85	.65	☐☐☐☐☐
3188	Celebrate The Century, 1960s,			
	pane of 15	13.00	8.50	☐☐☐☐☐
a.-o.	33c any single	.85	.65	☐☐☐☐☐
3189	Celebrate The Century, 1970s,			
	pane of 15	13.00	8.50	☐☐☐☐☐
a.-o.	33c any single	.85	.65	☐☐☐☐☐
3190	Celebrate The Century, 1980s,			
	pane of 15	13.00	8.50	☐☐☐☐☐
a.-o.	33c any single	.85	.65	☐☐☐☐☐
3191	Celebrate The Century, 1990s,			
	pane of 15	13.00	8.50	☐☐☐☐☐
a.-o.	33c any single	.85	.65	☐☐☐☐☐

1998, Feb. 15 Perf. 11.2 x 11

3192	32c *Remember The Maine*	.70	.25	☐☐☐☐☐

1998, Mar. 19 Die Cut Perf 11.3, Self-Adhesive

3193	32c Southern Magnolia	.65	.25	☐☐☐☐☐
3194	32c Blue Paloverde	.65	.25	☐☐☐☐☐
3195	32c Yellow Poplar	.65	.25	☐☐☐☐☐
3196	32c Prairie Crab Apple	.65	.25	☐☐☐☐☐
3197	32c Pacific Dogwood	.65	.25	☐☐☐☐☐
a.	Strip of 5, #3193-3197	3.25		☐☐☐☐☐
b.	As "a," die cutting omitted	—		☐☐☐☐☐

1998, Mar. 25 Perf. 10.2 Alexander Calder

3198	32c Black Cascade, 13 Verticals, 1959	.65	.25	☐☐☐☐☐
3199	32c Untitled, 1965	.65	.25	☐☐☐☐☐
3200	32c Rearing Stallion, 1928	.65	.25	☐☐☐☐☐
3201	32c Portrait of a Young Man, c. 1945	.65	.25	☐☐☐☐☐
3202	32c Un Effet du Japonais, 1945	.65	.25	☐☐☐☐☐
a.	Strip of 5, #3198-3202	3.25	2.25	☐☐☐☐☐

1998, Apr. 16 Serpentine Die Cut 11.7 x 10.9, Self-Adhesive

3203	32c Cinco De Mayo	.65	.25	☐☐☐☐☐

1998, Apr. 27 Serpentine Die Cut 11.1, Self-Adhesive

3204	Sylvester & Tweety, pane of 10	6.75		☐☐☐☐☐
a.	32c any single	.65	.25	☐☐☐☐☐
b.	Pane of 9 #3204a	6.00		☐☐☐☐☐
c.	Pane of 1 #3204a	.65		☐☐☐☐☐
3205	Pane of 10, right stamp with no			
	die cutting	15.00		☐☐☐☐☐
a.	32c single	1.00		☐☐☐☐☐
b.	Pane of 9 #3205a	9.00		☐☐☐☐☐
c.	Pane of 1, no die cutting	4.00		☐☐☐☐☐

1998, May 29 Serpentine Die Cut 10.8 x 10.9, Self-Adhesive

3206	32c Wisconsin Statehood	.65	.30	☐☐☐☐☐

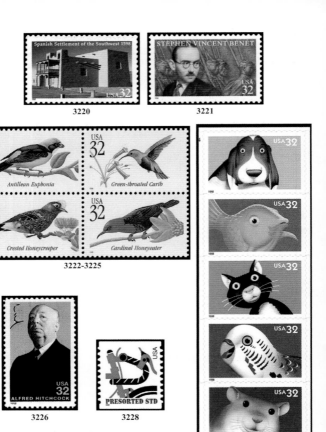

3220

3221

3222-3225

3226

3228

3230-3234

3235

HOW TO USE THIS BOOK

The number in the first column is its Scott number or identifying number.
Following that is the denomination of the stamp and its color or description.
Finally, the values, unused and used, are shown.

Scott No.	Description	Unused Value	Used Value	/ / / / / /

1998, June 5 Perf. 10 Vert., Coil Stamps

3207	(5c) Wetlands......................................	.25	.25	
3207A	(5c) Wetlands, small dates, self-adhesive Coil	.25	.25	
b.	Large date...................................	.30	.25	
3208	(25c) Diner...	.50	.50	
3208A	(25c) Diner, self-adhesive Coil	.50	.50	

1998, June 18 Perf. 12 x 12.4

3209	1898 Trans-Mississippi Stamps, Cent., pane of 9	9.50	7.00	
a.	1c green & black.............................	.25	.25	
b.	2c red brown & black	.25	.25	
c.	4c orange & black	.25	.25	
d.	5c blue & black...............................	.25	.25	
e.	8c dark lilac & black.......................	.25	.25	
f.	10c purple & black	.25	.25	
g.	50c green & black............................	1.25	.60	
h.	$1 red & black................................	2.50	1.25	
i.	$2 red brown & black	4.25	2.50	
3210	$1 Pane of 9, #3209h	22.50	—	

1998, June 26 Perf. 11.2

3211	32c Berlin Airlift, 50th Anniv.	.65	.25	

1998, June 26 Perf. 10.1 x 10.2

3212	32c Huddie "Leadbelly" Ledbetter (1888-1949)	.90	.25	
3213	32c Woody Guthrie (1912-67)	.90	.25	
3214	32c Sonny Terry (1911-86)...................	.90	.25	
3215	32c Josh White (1908-69)	.90	.25	
a.	Block or strip of 4, #3212-3215	3.60	2.00	

1998, July 15 Perf. 10.1 x 10.3

3216	32c Mahalia Jackson (1911-72)	1.00	.25	
3217	32c Roberta Martin (1917-69)	1.00	.25	
3218	32c Clara Ward (1924-73)	1.00	.25	
3219	32c Sister Rosetta Tharpe (1921-73).....	1.00	.25	
a.	Block or strip of 4, #3216-3219	4.00	2.00	

1998, June 26 Perf. 11.2

3220	32c La Mision de San Miguel de San Gabriel, Espanola, NM.....	.65	.25	

1998, July 22 Perf. 11.2

3221	32c Stephen Vincent Benet (1898-43) ..	.65	.25	

1998, July 29 Perf. 11.2

3222	32c Antillean Euphonia	.65	.25	
3223	32c Green-throated Carib	.65	.25	
3224	32c Crested Honeycreeper....................	.65	.25	
3225	32c Cardinal Honeyeater	.65	.25	
a.	Block of 4, #3222-3225.................	2.60	2.00	

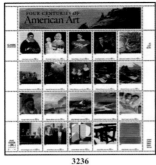

3236

3237

3238-3242

3243

3244

3245

3246

3247

3248

3257

3259

3260

288

Scott No.	Description	Unused Value	Used Value	/ / / / / /
1998, Aug. 3 Perf. 11.1				
3226	32c Legends of Hollywood – Alfred Hitchcock (1899-1980).....	.75	.25	☐☐☐☐☐
1998, Aug. 5 Serpentine Die Cut 11.7, Self-Adhesive				
3227	32c Organ & Tissue Donation...............	.65	.25	☐☐☐☐☐
3228	(10c) Modern Bicycle, self-adhesive Coil, small "1998" year date	.25	.25	☐☐☐☐☐
a.	Large date....................................	.25	.25	☐☐☐☐☐
3229	(10c) Modern Bicycle coil (3228), perf. 9.9 vert...............................	.25	.25	☐☐☐☐☐
3230	32c Bright Eyes - Dog, self-adhesive....	.75	.25	☐☐☐☐☐
3231	32c Bright Eyes - Fish, self-adhesive....	.75	.25	☐☐☐☐☐
3232	32c Bright Eyes - Cat, self-adhesive	.75	.25	☐☐☐☐☐
3233	32c Bright Eyes - Parakeet, self-adhesive	.75	.25	☐☐☐☐☐
3234	32c Bright eyes - Hamster, self-adhesive	.75	.25	☐☐☐☐☐
a.	Strip of 5, #3230-3234....................	3.75		
3235	32c Klondike Gold Rush Centennial	.65	.25	☐☐☐☐☐
3236	32c American Art, pane of 20..............	18.00	17.50	☐☐☐☐☐
a.-t.	any single	.90	.85	☐☐☐☐☐
3237	32c American Ballet	.65	.25	☐☐☐☐☐
3238	32c Space Discovery - Space City	.65	.25	☐☐☐☐☐
3239	32c Space Discovery - Space ship landing	.65	.25	☐☐☐☐☐
3240	32c Space Discovery - Person in space suit	.65	.25	☐☐☐☐☐
3241	32c Space Discovery - Space ship taking off	.65	.25	☐☐☐☐☐
3242	32c Space Discovery - Large domed structure	.65	.25	☐☐☐☐☐
a.	Strip of 5, #3238-3242....................	3.25	2.25	
3243	32c Giving and Sharing, self-adhesive..	.65	.25	☐☐☐☐☐
3244	32c Christmas - Madonna and Child, self-adhesive booklet stamp	.65	.25	☐☐☐☐☐
a.	Booklet pane of 20 + label	13.00		☐☐☐☐☐
b.	Die cutting omitted, pair................	—		☐☐☐☐☐
Size: 22x25mm				
3245	32c Wreath - Evergreen, self-adhesive booklet stamp..............................	5.00	.25	☐☐☐☐☐
3246	32c Wreath - Victorian, self-adhesive booklet stamp..............................	5.00	.25	☐☐☐☐☐
3247	32c Wreath - Chili Pepper, self-adhesive booklet stamp..............................	5.00	.25	☐☐☐☐☐
3248	32c Wreath - Tropical, self-adhesive booklet stamp..............................	5.00	.25	☐☐☐☐☐
a.	Booklet pane of 4, #3245-3248......	20.00		☐☐☐☐☐
b.	Booklet pane of 5, #3245-3246, 3248, 2 #3247 + label	27.50		☐☐☐☐☐
c.	Booklet pane of 6, #3247-3248, 2 each #3245-3246	35.00		☐☐☐☐☐
d.	As "a," die cutting omitted	—		☐☐☐☐☐
e.	As "b," die cutting omitted.............	—		☐☐☐☐☐
f.	As "c," die cutting omitted	—		☐☐☐☐☐

3261

3262

3272

3273

3274

3275

3276

3277

3283

3286

3270

3287

3288-3292

290

Scott No.	Description	Unused Value	Used Value	//////
Size: 23x30mm				
3249	32c Wreath (Large) - Evergreen, self-adhesive, serp. die cut 11.4 x 11.5	1.75	.25	
a.	Serp. die cut 11.7 x 11.6.................	3.00	.25	
3250	32c Wreath (Large) - Victorian, self-adhesive, serp. die cut 11.4 x 11.5	1.75	.25	
a.	Serp. die cut 11.7 x 11.6.................	3.00	.25	
3251	32c Wreath (Large) - Chili Pepper, self-adhesive, serp. die cut 11.4 x 11.5	1.75	.25	
a.	Serp. die cut 11.7 x 11.7.................	3.00	.25	
3252	32c Wreath (Large) - Tropical, self-adhesive, serp. die cut 11.4 x 11.5	1.75	.25	
a.	Serp. die cut 11.7 x 11.6.................	2.50	.25	
b.	Block or strip of 4, #3249-3252.....	7.00		
c.	Booklet pane, 5 each #3249-3252..	40.00		
d.	Block or strip of 4, #3249a-3252a .	10.00		
e.	Booklet pane, 5 each #3249a-3252a	50.00		
f.	Block or strip of 4, red ("Greetings 32 USA" and "1998") omitted on #3249, 3252	*675.00*		
g.	Block or strip of 4, #3249-3252, red ("Greetings 32 USA" and "1998") omitted on #3250, #3251	—		
h.	As "b," die cutting omitted............	—		
i.	As "c," die cutting omitted............	—		
3257	(1c) Weather Vane, white "USA"...........	.25	.25	
a.	Black omitted...................................	125.00		
3258	(1c) Weather Vane, pale blue "USA".....	.25	.25	
3259	22c Uncle Sam, self-adhesive, Die Cut 10.8	.45	.25	
a.	Die cut 10, 8 x 10½	2.50	.25	
b.	Vert. pair, #3259 & 3259a	3.50		
3260	(33c) Uncle Sam's Hat..............................	.65	.25	
3261	$3.20 Space Shuttle Landing, self-adhesive Priority Mail Rate...	6.00	1.50	
3262	$11.75 Piggyback Space Shuttle, self-adhesive Express Mail Rate ..	22.50	10.00	
3263	22c Uncle Sam, self-adhesive Coil	.45	.25	
a.	Die cutting omitted, pair	—		
3264	(33c) Uncle Sam's Hat (3260), coil	.65	.25	
a.	Imperf., pair......................................	—		
3265	(33c) Uncle Sam's Hat (3260), self-adhesive coil, square corners......................	.80	.25	
a.	Die cutting omitted, pair.................	70.00	—	
b.	Red, omitted	*575.00*		
c.	Black omitted...................................	—		
d.	Black omitted, die cutting omitted, pair	*575.00*		
e.	Red omitted, die cutting omitted, pair	*500.00*		
3266	(33c) Uncle Sam's Hat (3260), self-adhesive coil, rounded corners...................	1.75	.25	

3294

3295

3296

3297

3293

3306

3308

3314

3315

3310-3313

3316

Scott No.	Description	Unused Value	Used Value	/ / / / / /
3267 (33c)	Uncle Sam's Hat (3260), self-adhesive booklet stamp, serp die cut 9.9	.75	.25	
a.	Booklet pane of 10..........................	7.50		
3268 (33c)	Uncle Sam's Hat (3260), self-adhesive booklet stamp, serp. die cut 11¼ .	.75	.25	
a.	Booklet pane of 10..........................	7.50		
b.	Serpentine die cut 11	.75	.25	
c.	As "b," booklet pane of 20 + label.	15.00		
3269 (33c)	Uncle Sam's Hat (3260), self-adhesive booklet stamp, serp. die cut 8	.65	.25	
a.	Booklet pane of 18..........................	12.00		
3270 (10c)	Eagle & Shield, coil stamp	.25	.25	
a.	Large Date,...................................	.45	.25	
3271 (10c)	Eagle & Shield (3270), self-adhesive coil, Small Date................................	.25	.25	
a.	Large Date	1.00	.25	
1999 Issues				
3272	33c Chinese New Year - Year of the Rabbit	.80	.25	
3273	33c Malcolm X - Black Heritage, self-adhesive..................................	.85	.25	
3274	33c Love, self-adhesive booklet stamp .	.65	.25	
a.	Booklet pane of 20..........................	13.00		
b.	Die cutting omitted, pair.................	125.00		
c.	As "a," die cutting omitted	1,250.		
3275	55c Love, self-adhesive..........................	1.10	.25	
3276	33c Hospice Care, self-adhesive	.65	.25	
3277	33c Flag and City....................................	.70	.25	
3278	33c Flag and City, self-adhesive, serp. die cut 11 (3277)	.65	.25	
a.	Booklet pane of 4............................	2.60		
b.	Booklet pane of 5 + label	3.25		
c.	Booklet pane of 6............................	3.90		
d.	Booklet pane of 10..........................	14.00		
e.	Booklet pane of 20 + label.............	17.00		
h.	As "e," die cutting omitted.	—		
i.	Serpentine die cut 11¼...................	3.00	.25	
j.	As "i," booklet pane of 10.............	30.00		
3278F	33c Flag and City (3277), self-adhesive, serp. die cut 11½ x 11¾...............	1.40	.25	
g.	Booklet pane of 20 + label.............	28.00		
3279	33c Flag and City, self-adhesive booklet stamp, red date	.85	.25	
a.	Booklet pane of 10..........................	8.50		
3280	33c Flag and City, Coil, small date	.65	.25	
a.	Large date	1.25	.25	
b.	Imperf, pair.....................................	—	150.00	
3281	33c Flag and City, self-adhesive coil, square corners, large date	.65	.25	
a.	Die cutting omitted, pair.................	30.00		

3317-3320

3321-3324

3329

3330

3331

3325-3328

Scott No.	Description	Unused Value	Used Value	/ / / / / /
b.	Lt. blue and yellow omitted............	*300.00*		
c.	Small date....................................	.65	.25	
e.	As "c," die cutting omitted, pair.....	—		
3282	33c Flag and City, self-adhesive coil, rounded corners	.65	.25	
3283	33c Flag and Chalkboard, self-adhesive booklet stamp..............................	.65	.25	
a.	Booklet pane of 18..........................	12.00		
3286	33c Irish Immigration.............................	.65	.25	
3287	33c Alfred Lunt and Lynn Fontanne, Actors	.65	.25	
3288	33c Arctic Hare......................................	.85	.25	
3289	33c Arctic Fox.......................................	.85	.25	
3290	33c Snowy Owl......................................	.85	.25	
3291	33c Polar Bear.......................................	.85	.25	
3292	33c Gray Wolf.......................................	.85	.25	
a.	Strip of 5, #3288-3292....................	4.25	—	
3293	33c Sonoran Desert, self-adhesive pane of 10	8.00		
a.-j.	any single	.80	.50	
3294	33c Blueberries, self-adhesive booklet stamp, dated "1999"........	.85	.25	
a.	Dated "2000"...................................	1.25	.25	
3295	33c Raspberries, self-adhesive booklet stamp, dated "1999"........	.85	.25	
a.	Dated "2000"...................................	1.25	.25	
3296	33c Strawberries, self-adhesive booklet stamp, dated "1999"........	.85	.25	
a.	Dated "2000"...................................	1.25	.25	
3297	33c Blackberries, self-adhesive booklet stamp, dated "1999"........	.85	.25	
a.	Dated 2000......................................	1.25	.25	
b.	Booklet pane, 5 each #3294-3297 + label..	17.50		
c.	Block of 4, #3294-3297..................	3.50		
d.	Booklet pane, 5 #3297e + label......	25.00		
e.	Block of 4, #3294a-3297a..............	5.00		
3298	33c Blueberries (3294), self-adhesive booklet stamp..............................	1.00	.25	
3299	33c Raspberries (3295), self-adhesive booklet stamp..............................	1.00	.25	
3300	33c Strawberries (3296), self-adhesive booklet stamp..............................	1.00	.25	
3301	33c Blackberries (3297), self-adhesive booklet stamp..............................	1.00	.25	
a.	Booklet pane of 4, #3298-3301, ...	4.00		
b.	Booklet pane of 5, #3298, 3299, 3301, 2 #3300 + label..................	5.00		
c.	Booklet pane of 6, #3300, 3301, 2 #3298, 3299	6.00		
d.	Block of 4, #3298-3301..................	4.00		

3333-3337

3332

3338

3339-3344

HOW TO USE THIS BOOK

The number in the first column is its Scott number or identifying number. Following that is the denomination of the stamp and its color or description. Finally, the values, unused and used, are shown.

Scott No.	Description	Unused Value	Used Value	/ / / / /
3302	33c Blueberries (3294), self-adhesive coil	1.40	.25	
3303	33c Raspberries (3295), self-adhesive coil	1.40	.25	
3304	33c Strawberries (3296), self-adhesive coil	1.40	.25	
3305	33c Blackberries (3297), self-adhesive coil	1.40	.25	
a.	Strip of 4, # 3302-3305..................	5.75		
3306	Daffy Duck, self-adhesive pane of 10	6.75		
a.	33c any single	.65	.25	
b.	Pane of 9 #3306a	6.00		
c.	Pane of 1 #3306a	.65		
3307	Daffy Duck, self-adhesive pane of 10, right stamp with no die cutting	15.00		
a.	33c single	1.25		
b.	Pane of 9 #3307a	12.00		
c.	Pane of 1, no die cutting.................	2.75		
d.	As "a," vert. pair, imperf. between .	*3,500.*		
3308	33c Ayn Rand - Literary Arts................	.65	.25	
3309	33c Cinco de Mayo, self-adhesive.........	.70	.25	
3310	33c Tropical Flowers - Bird of Paradise, self-adhesive booklet stamp	.65	.25	
3311	33c Tropical Flowers - Royal Poinciana, self-adhesive booklet stamp	.65	.25	
3312	33c Tropical Flowers - Gloriosa Lily, self-adhesive booklet stamp	.65	.25	
3313	33c Tropical Flowers - Chinese Hibiscus, self-adhesive booklet stamp	.65	.25	
a.	Block of 4, #3310-3313..................	2.60		
b.	Booklet pane of 20, 5 each #3310-3313	13.00		
3314	33c John & William Bartram, self-adhesive	.65	.25	
3315	33c Prostate Cancer Awareness, self-adhesive	.65	.25	
3316	33c California Gold Rush 150th Anniversary	.65	.25	
3317	33c Aquarium Fish, self-adhesive	.65	.25	
3318	33c Aquarium Fish, self-adhesive	.65	.25	
3319	33c Aquarium Fish, self-adhesive	.65	.25	
3320	33c Aquarium Fish, self-adhesive	.65	.25	
b.	Strip of 4, #3317-3320....................	2.60		
3321	33c Extreme Sports - Skateboarding, self-adhesive....................................	.75	.25	
3322	33c Extreme Sports - BMX Biking, self-adhesive....................................	.75	.25	
3323	33c Extreme Sports - Snowboarding, self-adhesive....................................	.75	.25	
3324	33c Extreme Sports - Inline Skating, self-adhesive....................................	.75	.25	
a.	Block or strip of 4, #3321-3324	3.00		
3325	33c American Glass - Free-Blown Glass	1.90	.25	
3326	33c American Glass - Mold-Blown Glass	1.90	.25	
3327	33c American Glass - Pressed Glass.....	1.90	.25	
3328	33c American Glass - Art Glass............	1.90	.25	
a.	Strip or block of 4, #3325-3328	7.75	3.00	

3345-3350

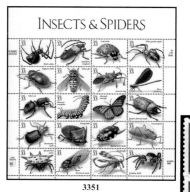

3351

3355

3356-3359

Scott No.	Description	Unused Value	Used Value	/ / / / /
3329	33c James Cagney - Legends of Hollywood	.80	.25	
3330	55c Gen. William "Billy" Mitchell	1.10	.30	
3331	33c Honoring Those Who Served, self-adhesive..................................	.65	.25	

1999, Lithographed, Perf. 11

3332	45c Universal Postal Union	1.00	.45	
3333	33c Famous Trains, Daylight	.75	.25	
3334	33c Famous Trains, Congressional	.75	.25	
3335	33c Famous Trains, 20th Century Limited	.75	.25	
3336	33c Famous Trains, Hiawatha	.75	.25	
3337	33c Famous Trains, Super Chief..........	.75	.25	
a.	Strip of 5, #3333-3337	3.75	—	
3338	33c Frederick Law Olmsted, Landscape Architect...................	.70	.25	
3339	33c Max Steiner	1.40	.25	
3340	33c Dimitri Tiomkin...........................	1.40	.25	
3341	33c Bernard Herrmann	1.40	.25	
3342	33c Franz Waxman...............................	1.40	.25	
3343	33c Alfred Newman	1.40	.25	
3344	33c Erich Wolfgang Korngold	1.40	.25	
a.	Block of 6, #3339-3344	8.50	4.50	
3345	33c Ira & George Gershwin	1.25	.25	
3346	33c Alan Jay Lerner & Frederick Loewe	1.25	.25	
3347	33c Lorenz Hart	1.25	.25	
3348	33c Richard Rodgers & Oscar Hammerstein II................	1.25	.25	
3349	33c Meredith Willson.........................	1.25	.25	
3350	33c Frank Loesser	1.25	.25	
a.	Block of 6, #3345-3350	7.50	4.50	
3351	Insects & Spiders, Pane of 20	14.00	10.00	
a.-t.	33c any single..	.70	.50	

Serpentine Die Cut 11, Self-Adhesive

3352	33c Hanukkah......................................	.65	.25	

Coil Stamp Perf 9¾, Vertically

3353	22c Uncle Sam (3259).........................	.45	.25	

Perf. 11¼

3354	33c NATO, 50th Anniv.	.65	.25	

Serpentine Die Cut 11¼ on 2 or 3 sides, Self-Adhesive Booklet Stamp

3355	33c Madonna and Child, by Bartolomeo Vivarini	1.00	.25	
a.	Booklet pane of 20	20.00		

Serpentine Die Cut 11¼

3356	33c Deer, gold & red............................	1.75	.25	
3357	33c Deer, gold & blue	1.75	.25	
3358	33c Deer, gold & purple	1.75	.25	
3359	33c Deer, gold & green........................	1.75	.25	
a.	Block or strip of 4, #3356-3359....	7.00		

3369

3370

3371

3375a

3378

3379-3383

3384-3388

3389

3390

3391

3393-3396

3397

3398

301

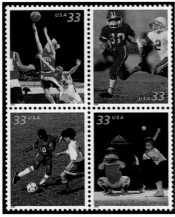

3399-3402

THE STARS AND STRIPES

3403

3404-3407

Legends of Baseball

3408

PROBING THE VASTNESS OF SPACE

3409

Scott No.	Description	Unused Value	Used Value	//////
Booklet Stamps				
Serpentine Die Cut 11¼ on 2, 3 or 4 sides				
3360	33c Deer, gold & red (3356)...............	1.40	.25	☐☐☐☐☐
3361	33c Deer, gold & blue (3357).............	1.40	.25	☐☐☐☐☐
3362	33c Deer, gold & purple (3358)..........	1.40	.25	☐☐☐☐☐
3363	33c Deer, gold & green (3359)...........	1.40	.25	☐☐☐☐☐
a.	Booklet pane of 20, 5 each			
	#3360-3363	28.00		☐☐☐☐☐
b.	Block of 4, #3360-3363.................	5.60		☐☐☐☐☐
c.	As "b," die cutting omitted............	—		☐☐☐☐☐
d.	As "a," die cutting omitted............	—		☐☐☐☐☐
Size: 21x19mm				
Serpentine Die Cut 11½ x11¼ on 2 or 3 sides				
3364	33c Deer, gold & red (3356)...............	2.00	.25	☐☐☐☐☐
3365	33c Deer, gold & blue (3357).............	2.00	.25	☐☐☐☐☐
3366	33c Deer, gold & purple (3358)..........	2.00	.25	☐☐☐☐☐
3367	33c Deer, gold & green (3359)...........	2.00	.25	☐☐☐☐☐
a.	Booklet pane of 4, #3364-3367	8.00		☐☐☐☐☐
b.	Booklet pane of 5, #3364, 3366,			
	3367, 2 #3365 + label	10.00		☐☐☐☐☐
c.	Booklet pane of 6, #3365, 3367,			
	2 each #3364 & 3366.................	12.00		☐☐☐☐☐
d.	Block of 4, #3364-3367.................	8.00		☐☐☐☐☐
Photogravure, Serpentine Die Cut 11, Self-Adhesive				
3368	33c Kwanzaa (3175)	.65	.25	☐☐☐☐☐
Serpentine Die Cut 11¼, Self-Adhesive				
3369	33c Year 2000, Baby New Year...........	.65	.25	☐☐☐☐☐
2000 Issues				
3370	33c Chinese New Year –			
	Year of the Dragon	.80	.25	☐☐☐☐☐
3371	33c Patricia Roberts Harris,			
	self-adhesive..............................	.65	.25	☐☐☐☐☐
Perf. 11				
3372	33c Submarines, Los Angeles Class			
	with microprinted "USPS"			
	at base of sail	.75	.25	☐☐☐☐☐
Booklet Stamps				
3373	22c Submarines, S Class	1.25	.75	☐☐☐☐☐
3374	33c Submarines, Los Angeles Class,			
	no microprinting	1.75	1.00	☐☐☐☐☐
3375	55c Submarines, Ohio Class	2.75	1.25	☐☐☐☐☐
3376	60c Submarines, USS Holland	3.00	1.50	☐☐☐☐☐
3377	$3.20 Submarines, Gato Class	16.00	5.00	☐☐☐☐☐
a.	Booklet pane of 5, #3373-3377	22.50	—	☐☐☐☐☐

3410

3411

3412

3413

3414-3417

HOW TO USE THIS BOOK

The number in the first column is its Scott number or identifying number. Following that is the denomination of the stamp and its color or description. Finally, the values, unused and used, are shown.

Scott No.	Description	Unused Value	Used Value	/ / / / / /
Serpentine Die Cut 11¼ x 11½, 11½ (horiz. stamps), Self-Adhesive				
3378	Pacific Coast Rain Forest, pane of 10	10.00		
a.-j.	33c any single	1.00	.50	
Perf. 11 x 11¼				
3379	33c Louise Nevelson, Sculptor, Silent Music I	.65	.25	
3380	33c Louise Nevelson, Sculptor, Royal Tide I	.65	.25	
3381	33c Louise Nevelson, Sculptor, Black Chord	.65	.25	
3382	33c Louise Nevelson, Sculptor, Nightsphere-Light	.65	.25	
3383	33c Louise Nevelson, Sculptor, Dawn's Wedding Chapel I	.65	.25	
a.	Strip of 5, #3379-3383	3.25	—	
Perf. 11				
3384	33c Hubble Images, Eagle Nebula	.65	.25	
3385	33c Hubble Images, Ring Nebula	.65	.25	
3386	33c Hubble Images, Lagoon Nebula	.65	.25	
3387	33c Hubble Images, Egg Nebula	.65	.25	
3388	33c Hubble Images, Galaxy NGC 1316	.65	.25	
a.	Strip of 5, #3384-3388	3.25	2.00	
b.	As "a," imperf	1,250.		
3389	33c Samoan Double Canoe	.85	.25	
3390	33c Library Of Congress,	.65	.25	
Serpentine Die Cut 11, Self-Adhesive				
3391	Road Runner & Wile E. Coyote, pane of 10	10.00		
a.	33c single	.85	.25	
b.	Pane of 9 #3391a	8.00		
c.	Pane of 1 #3391a	1.50		
d.	All die cutting omitted, pane of 10	2,400.		
3392	Road Runner & Wile E. Coyote, right stamp with no die cutting	40.00		
a.	33c single	2.75		
b.	Pane of 9 #3392a	30.00		
c.	Pane of 1, no die cutting.	5.00		
Perf. 11				
3393	33c Maj. Gen. John L. Hines	.65	.25	
3394	33c Gen. Omar N. Bradley	.65	.25	
3395	33c Sgt. Alvin C. York	.65	.25	
3396	33c Second Lt. Audie L. Murphy	.65	.25	
a.	Block or strip of 4, #3393-3396	2.60	1.50	
3397	33c Summer Sports – Runners	.65	.25	
Serpentine Die Cut 11½, Self-Adhesive				
3398	33c Adoption	.75	.25	
a.	Die cutting omitted, pair	—		
Perf. 11				
3399	33c Youth Team Sports, Basketball	.70	.25	

3420

3422

3426

3427

3427A

3428

3430

3431

3432A

3432B

3433

3434

3435

3438

3443

3444

3445

3446

3447

3448

3451

3457

Scott No.	Description	Unused Value	Used Value	/ / / / / /
3400	33c Youth Team Sports, Football........	.70	.25	
3401	33c Youth Team Sports, Soccer..........	.70	.25	
3402	33c Youth Team Sports, Baseball........	.70	.25	
a.	Block or strip of 4, #3399-3402...	2.80	1.75	

Perf. 10½ x 11

3403	The Stars And Stripes, pane of 20	15.00	11.00	
a.-t.	33c any single	.75	.50	

Photogravure, Serpentine Die Cut 8½ Horiz.,
Self-Adhesive Coil Stamps

3404	33c Blueberries	3.50	.25	
3405	33c Strawberries...............................	3.50	.25	
3406	33c Blackberries	3.50	.25	
3407	33c Raspberries.................................	3.50	.25	
a.	Strip of 4, #3404-3407	15.00		

Serpentine Die Cut 11¼, Self-Adhesive

3408	Legends Of Baseball, pane of 20.	14.00		
a.-t.	33c any single	.70	.50	

Souvenir Sheets

3409	Probing the Vastness of Space, sheet of 6.....................................	15.00	7.00	
a.-f.	60c any single	2.25	1.00	
3410	Exploring the Solar System, sheet of 5 + label......................	17.50	10.00	
a.-e.	$1 any single	3.00	1.75	
f.	As No. 3410, imperf.....................	*3,250.*		
g.	As No. 3410, with hologram from No. 3411b applied	—		

Untagged, Photogravure with Hologram Affixed

3411	Escaping the Gravity of Earth, sheet of 2.....................................	22.50	10.00	
a.-b.	$3.20 any single........	10.00	4.00	
c.	Hologram omitted on right stamp.			
3412	$11.75 Space Achievement and Exploration	40.00	17.50	
a.	$11.75 single.................................	35.00	15.00	
b.	Hologram omitted..........................	—		
3413	$11.75 Landing on the Moon...................	40.00	17.50	
a.	$11.75 single.................................	35.00	15.00	
b.	Double hologram	*4,250.*		

Stampin' The Future – Children's Stamp Design Contest Winners,
Serpentine Die Cut 11¼, Self-Adhesive

3414	33c By Zachary Canter, Space Figures	.65	.25	
3415	33c By Sarah Lipsey, Heart.................	.65	.25	
3416	33c By Morgan Hill, "Mommy, Are We There Yet"	.65	.25	
3417	33c By Ashley Young, Space Dog.......	.65	.25	

Scott No.	Description	Unused Value	Used Value	//////
a.	Horiz. strip of 4, #3414-3417	2.60		

2000-2009 Distinguished Americans Issue

Scott No.	Description	Unused Value	Used Value	//////
3420	10c Joseph W. Stilwell........................	.25	.25	
a.	Imperf., pair..................................	*350.00*		
3422	23c Wilma Rudolph, self-adhesive......	.45	.25	
a.	Imperf., pair..................................	—		
3426	33c Claude Pepper.............................	.65	.25	
3427	58c Margaret Chase Smith, self-adhesive	1.25	.25	
b.	Black (engr.) omitted....................	*500.00*		
3427A	59c James A. Michener, self-adhesive	1.25	.25	
3428	63c Dr. Jonas Salk, self-adhesive........	1.25	.25	
a.	Black (litho.) omitted...................	—		
3430	75c Harriet Beecher Stowe, self-adhesive	1.50	.25	
3431	76c Sen Hattie Caraway, self-adhesive, die cut 11	1.50	.25	
3432	76c Hattie Caraway, die cut 11½ x 11 (3431).............................	3.50	2.00	
3432A	76c Edward Trudeau, self-adhesive.....	1.50	.25	
3432B	78c Mary Lasker, self-adhesive	1.60	.25	
3433	83c Edna Ferber, self-adhesive............	1.60	.30	
3434	83c Edna Ferber, With Curving Shoulder, self-adhesive...............................	1.60	.30	
3435	87c Dr. Albert Sabin, self-adhesive	1.75	.30	
3436	23c Wilma Rudolph, self-adhesive, booklet stamp, litho (3422)........	.45	.25	
a.	Booklet pane of 4.........................	1.80		
b.	Booklet pane of 6.........................	2.70		
c.	Booklet pane of 10.......................	4.50		
d.	As "c," die cutting omitted	—		

2000 Commemoratives

Scott No.	Description	Unused Value	Used Value	//////
3438	33c California Statehood, 150th Anniv.	.75	.25	
3439	33c Deep Sea Creatures – Fanfin Anglerfish	.75	.25	
3440	33c Deep Sea Creatures – Sea Cucumber	.75	.25	
3441	33c Deep Sea Creatures – Fangtooth ..	.75	.25	
3442	33c Deep Sea Creatures – Amphipod..	.75	.25	
3443	33c Deep Sea Creatures – Medusa......	.75	.25	
a.	Vert. strip of 5, #3439-3443	3.75	2.00	
3444	33c Literary Arts – Thomas Wolfe, Novelist	.65	.25	
3445	33c White House, 200th Anniv............	1.00	.25	
3446	33c Legends of Hollywood – Edward G. Robinson	1.75	.25	
3447	(10c) New York Public Library Lion self-adhesive, coil stamp, "2000" year date......................................	.25	.25	
a.	"2003" year date	.25	.25	
3448	(34c) Flag Over Farm, litho., perf 11¼..	1.00	.25	
3449	(34c) Flag Over Farm, litho. self-adhesive	.70	1.00	

Scott No.	Description	Unused Value	Used Value	/ / / / / /
3450	(34c) Flag Over Farm, photo., self-adhesive booklet stamp	.85	.25	
a.	Booklet pane of 18	16.00		
b.	Die cutting omitted, pair	—		
3451	(34c) Statue of Liberty, self-adhesive booklet stamp	.70	.25	
a.	Statue of Liberty, booklet pane of 20	14.00		
b.	Statue of Liberty, booklet pane of 4	3.00		
c.	Statue of Liberty, booklet pane of 6	5.75		
d.	As "a," die cutting omitted	—		
3452	(34c) Statue of Liberty, coil stamp	.70	.25	
3453	(34c) Statue of Liberty self-adhesive coil	.70	.25	
a.	Die cutting omitted, pair	*350.00*		
3454	(34c) Flower, self-adhesive booklet stamp (purple background)	1.05	.25	
3455	(34c) Flower, self-adhesive booklet stamp (tan background)	1.05	.25	
3456	(34c) Flower, self-adhesive booklet stamp (green background)	1.05	.25	
3457	(34c) Flower, self-adhesive booklet stamp (red background)	1.05	.25	
a.	Block of 4, #3454-3457	4.25		
b.	Booklet pane of 4, #3454-3457	4.25		
c.	Booklet pane of 6, #3456, 3457, 2 each #3454-3455	6.50		
d.	Booklet pane of 6, #3454, 3455, 2 each #3456-3457	6.50		
e.	Booklet pane of 20, 5 each #3454-3457 + label	21.00		
3458	(34c) Flower (purple bckgrnd), die cut 11½ x 11¾	3.25	.25	
3459	(34c) Flower (tan bckgrnd), die cut 11½ x 11¾	3.25	.25	
3460	(34c) Flower (green bckgrnd), die cut 11½ x 11¾	3.25	.25	
3461	(34c) Flower (red bckgrnd), die cut 11½ x 11¾	3.25	.25	
a.	Block of 4, #3458-3461	13.00		
b.	Booklet pane of 20, 2 each #3461a, 3 each #3457a	40.00		
c.	Booklet pane of 20, 2 each #3457a, 3 each #3461a	50.00		
3462	(34c) Flower (green bckgrnd), coil stamp	4.00	.25	
3463	(34c) Flower (red bckgrnd), coil stamp	4.00	.25	
3464	(34c) Flower (tan bckgrnd), coil stamp	4.00	.25	
3465	(34c) Flower (purple bckgrnd), coil stamp	4.00	.25	
a.	Strip of 4, #3462-3465	16.00		

3467

3468A

3471A

3472

3473

3491

3495

3496

3499

3500

3501

Scott No.	Description	Unused Value	Used Value	/ / / / / /
2001 Issues				
3466	34c Statue of Liberty, self-adhesive coil (rounded corners).......................	.70	.25	☐☐☐☐☐
3467	21c American Buffalo, perf. 11¼ x 11......................	.50	.25	☐☐☐☐☐
3468	21c American Buffalo (3467), self-adhesive sheet stamp...........	.50	.25	☐☐☐☐☐
3468A	23c George Washington, self-adhesive, serpentine die cut 11¼ x11¾....	.50	.25	☐☐☐☐☐
3469	34c Flag Over Farm, perf 11¼ sheet stamp	.75	.25	
3470	34c Flag Over Farm, self-adhesive sheet stamp...........	1.00	.25	☐☐☐☐☐
3471	55c Eagle, self-adhesive, serpentine die cut 10¾...................	1.10	.25	☐☐☐☐☐
3471A	57c Eagle, self-adhesive	1.10	.25	☐☐☐☐☐
3472	$3.50 Capitol Dome...............................	7.00	2.00	☐☐☐☐☐
a.	Die cutting omitted, pair	—		☐☐☐☐☐
3473	$12.25 Washington Monument.................	22.50	10.00	☐☐☐☐☐
3475	21c American Buffalo (3467), self-adhesive coil stamp...............	.50	.25	☐☐☐☐☐
3475A	23c George Washington (3468A), self-adhesive, coil stamp, serpentine die cut 8½ Vert........	.75	.25	☐☐☐☐☐
3476	34c Statue of Liberty, perforated coil stamp......................	.70	.25	☐☐☐☐☐
3477	34c Statue of Liberty, self-adhesive coil stamp (right angle corners).........	.80	.25	☐☐☐☐☐
a.	Die cutting omitted, pair	75.00		☐☐☐☐☐
3478	34c Flower, self-adhesive coil stamp, die cut 8½ vert.	.70	.25	☐☐☐☐☐
3479	34c Flower , self-adhesive coil stamp, die cut 8½ vert.	.70	.25	☐☐☐☐☐
3480	34c Flowers, self-adhesive coil stamp, die cut 8½ vert.	.70	.25	☐☐☐☐☐
3481	34c Flowers, self-adhesive coil stamp, die cut 8½ vert.	.70	.25	☐☐☐☐☐
a.	Strip of 4, #3478-3481,.................	2.80		☐☐☐☐☐
3482	20c George Washington (3468A), self-adhesive bklt stamp, die cut 11¼	.55	.25	☐☐☐☐☐
a.	Booklet pane of 10.......................	5.50		☐☐☐☐☐
b.	Booklet pane of 4.........................	2.20		☐☐☐☐☐
c.	Booklet pane of 6.........................	3.30		☐☐☐☐☐
3483	20c George Washington (3468A), self-adhesive bklt stamp, die cut 10½ x 11¼	5.00	1.25	☐☐☐☐☐
a.	Booklet pane of 4, 2 #3482 at L, 2 #3483 at R...............................	14.00		☐☐☐☐☐

Scott No.	Description	Unused Value	Used Value	/ / / / /
b.	Booklet pane of 6, 3 #3482 at L, 3 #3483 at R..............................	20.00		☐☐☐☐☐
c.	Booklet pane of 10, 5 #3482 at L, 5 #3483 at R..............................	28.00		☐☐☐☐☐
d.	Booklet pane of 4, 2 #3483 at L, 2 #3482 at R..............................	14.00		☐☐☐☐☐
e.	Booklet pane of 6, 3 #3483 at L, 3 #3482 at R..............................	20.00		☐☐☐☐☐
f.	Booklet pane of 10, 5 #3483 at L, 5 #3482 at R..............................	28.00		☐☐☐☐☐
g.	Pair, #3482 at L, #3483 at R.........	5.75		☐☐☐☐☐
h.	Pair, #3483 at R, #3482 at L.........	5.75		☐☐☐☐☐
3484	21c American Buffalo (3467), self-adhesive, booklet stamp, serpentine die cut 11¼ on 3 Sides	.60	.25	☐☐☐☐☐
b.	Booklet pane of 4.........................	2.40		☐☐☐☐☐
c.	Booklet pane of 6.........................	3.60		☐☐☐☐☐
d.	Booklet pane of 10.......................	6.00		☐☐☐☐☐
3484A	21c American Buffalo (3467), self-adhesive, booklet stamp serpentine die cut 10½ x 11¼	5.00	1.50	☐☐☐☐☐
e.	Booklet pane of 4, 2 #3484 at L, 2 #3484A at R............................	14.00		☐☐☐☐☐
f.	Booklet pane of 6, 3 #3484 at L, 3 #3484A at R, ...	20.00		☐☐☐☐☐
g.	Booklet pane of 10, 5 #3484 at L, 5 #3484A at R............................	28.00		☐☐☐☐☐
h.	Booklet pane of 4, 2 #3484A at L, 2 #3484 at R..............................	14.00		☐☐☐☐☐
i.	Booklet pane of 6, 3 #3484A at L, 3 #3484 at R..............................	20.00		☐☐☐☐☐
j.	Booklet pane of 10, 5 #3484A at L, 5 #3484 at R..............................	28.00		☐☐☐☐☐
k.	Pair, #3484 at L, #3484A at R......	5.75		☐☐☐☐☐
l.	Pair, #3484A at L, #3484 at R......	5.75		☐☐☐☐☐
3485	34c Statue of Liberty, self-adhesive booklet stamp...............................	.70	.25	☐☐☐☐☐
a.	Booklet pane of 10	7.00		☐☐☐☐☐
b.	Booklet pane of 20.......................	14.00		☐☐☐☐☐
c.	Booklet pane of 4.........................	3.00		☐☐☐☐☐
d.	Booklet pane of 6.........................	4.50		☐☐☐☐☐
e.	Die cutting omitted, pair (from No. 3485b)	—		☐☐☐☐☐
f.	As "e," booklet pane of 20............	—		☐☐☐☐☐
3487	34c Flower, self-adhesive booklet stamp, die cut 10¼ x 10¾	.85	.25	☐☐☐☐☐
3488	34c Flower, self-adhesive booklet stamp, die cut 10¼ x 10¾	.85	.25	☐☐☐☐☐

Scott No.	Description	Unused Value	Used Value	/ / / / / /
3489	34c Flower, self-adhesive booklet stamp, die cut 10¼ x 10¾	.85	.25	☐☐☐☐☐
3490	34c Flower, self-adhesive booklet stamp, die cut 10¼ x 10¾	.85	.25	☐☐☐☐☐
a.	Block of 4, #3487-3490	3.50		☐☐☐☐☐
b.	Booklet pane of 4, #3487-3490	3.50		☐☐☐☐☐
c.	Booklet pane of 6, #3489-3490, 2 each #3487-3488	5.00		☐☐☐☐☐
d.	Booklet pane of 6, #3487-3488, 2 each #3489-3490.....................	5.00		☐☐☐☐☐
e.	Booklet pane of 20, 5 each #3490a + label...........................	17.50		☐☐☐☐☐
3491	34c Apple, self-adhesive booklet stamp, serpentine die cut 11¼	.70	.25	☐☐☐☐☐
3492	34c Orange, self-adhesive booklet stamp	.70	.25	☐☐☐☐☐
a.	Pair, #3491-3492	1.40		☐☐☐☐☐
b.	Booklet pane, 10 each #3491-3492	14.00		☐☐☐☐☐
c.	As "a," black ("34 USA") omitted	—		☐☐☐☐☐
d.	As "a," die cutting omitted...........	—		☐☐☐☐☐
e.	As "b," die cutting omitted.	—		☐☐☐☐☐
f.	As "b," right four stamps yellow omitted...........................	3,500.		☐☐☐☐☐
3493	34c Apple, self-adhesive booklet stamp, serpentine die cut 11½ x 10¾....	1.25	.25	☐☐☐☐☐
3494	34c Orange, self-adhesive booklet stamp	1.25	.25	☐☐☐☐☐
a.	Pair, #3493-3494	2.50		☐☐☐☐☐
b.	Booklet pane, 2 each #3493-3494	5.00		☐☐☐☐☐
c.	Booklet pane, 3 each #3493-3494, #3493 at UL..........	7.50		☐☐☐☐☐
d.	Booklet pane, 3 each #3493-3494, #3494 at UL..........	7.50		☐☐☐☐☐
3495	34c Flag Over Farm, self-adhesive, booklet stamp (3469), serpentine die cut 8 on 2, 3 or 4 sides..........	1.25	.25	☐☐☐☐☐
a.	Booklet pane of 18	22.50		☐☐☐☐☐

2001 Commemoratives

Scott No.	Description	Unused Value	Used Value	/ / / / / /
3496	(34c) Love – Rose, Apr. 20, 1763 Love letter by John Adams...........................	.90	.25	☐☐☐☐☐
a.	Booklet pane of 20.......................	18.00		☐☐☐☐☐
b.	Vert. pair, die cutting omitted btwn.	—		☐☐☐☐☐
3497	34c Love – Rose and Apr 20, 1763 Love Letter by John Adams, self-adhesive..............................	.90	.25	☐☐☐☐☐
a.	Booklet pane of 20.......................	18.00		☐☐☐☐☐
b.	Vertical pair, die cutting omitted btwn.	—		☐☐☐☐☐

313

3502

3503

3504

3505

3506

3507

3508

3509

314

Scott No.		Description	Unused Value	Used Value	/ / / / / /
3498	34c	Love – Rose and Apr 20, 1763 Love Letter by John Adams, 18 x 21mm	1.00	.25	☐☐☐☐☐☐
a.		Booklet pane of 4........................	4.00		☐☐☐☐☐☐
b.		Booklet pane of 6........................	6.00		☐☐☐☐☐☐
3499	55c	Rose, Aug. 11 1763 Love Letter by Abigail Adams, self-adhesive	1.10	.25	☐☐☐☐☐☐
3500	34c	Chinese New Year – Year of the Snake	.75	.25	☐☐☐☐☐☐
3501	34c	Black Heritage, Roy Wilkins (1901-81), Civil Rights Leader	.70	.25	☐☐☐☐☐☐
3502		American Illustrators, pane of 20 .	17.50		☐☐☐☐☐☐
3502a-t		American Illustrators, any single ..	.85	.60	☐☐☐☐☐☐
3503	34c	Diabetes Awareness......................	.65	.25	☐☐☐☐☐☐
3504	34c	Nobel Prize, Centenary	.70	.25	☐☐☐☐☐☐
a.		Imperf., pair................................	—		☐☐☐☐☐☐
3505		Pan-American Expo Invert Stamps, Cent., pane	10.00	7.00	☐☐☐☐☐☐
a.	1c	Pan-American Expo Invert Stamps, Cent. – Reproduction of Scott 294a	.75	.25	☐☐☐☐☐☐
b.	2c	Pan-American Expo Invert Stamps, Cent. – Reproduction of Scott 295a	.75	.25	☐☐☐☐☐☐
c.	4c	Pan-American Expo Invert Stamps, Cent. – Reproduction of Scott 296a	.75	.25	☐☐☐☐☐☐
d.	80c	Pan-American Expo Invert Stamps, Cent. – Commemorative (cinderella) stamp depicting a buffalo	1.90	.35	☐☐☐☐☐☐
3506		Great Plains Prairie, pane of 10	10.00		☐☐☐☐☐☐
3506a-j	34c	Great Plains Prairie, any single.....	1.00	.50	☐☐☐☐☐☐
3507	34c	Peanuts Comic Strip......................	.80	.25	☐☐☐☐☐☐
3508	34c	Honoring Veterans, self-adhesive..	.75	.25	☐☐☐☐☐☐
3509	34c	Frida Kahlo (1907-54), Painter, Self-Portrait.................................	.70	.25	☐☐☐☐☐☐
3510	34c	Legendary Playing Fields, Ebbets Field, self-adhesive......................	.90	.60	☐☐☐☐☐☐
3511	34c	Legendary Playing Fields, Tiger Stadium, self-adhesive	.90	.60	☐☐☐☐☐☐
3512	34c	Legendary Playing Fields, Crosley Field, self-adhesive......................	.90	.60	☐☐☐☐☐☐
3513	34c	Legendary Playing Fields, Yankee Stadium, self-adhesive....	.90	.60	☐☐☐☐☐☐
3514	34c	Legendary Playing Fields, Polo Grounds, self-adhesive...............	.90	.60	☐☐☐☐☐☐
3515	34c	Legendary Playing Fields, Forbes Field, self-adhesive......................	.90	.60	☐☐☐☐☐☐
3516	34c	Legendary Playing Fields, Fenway Park, self-adhesive	.90	.60	☐☐☐☐☐☐
3517	34c	Legendary Playing Fields, Comiskey Park, self-adhesive	.90	.60	☐☐☐☐☐☐

3511

3520

3521

3522

3523

3524

3528

3532

3533

3534-3535

HOW TO USE THIS BOOK

The number in the first column is its Scott number or identifying number. Following that is the denomination of the stamp and its color or description. Finally, the values, unused and used, are shown.

Scott No.		Description	Unused Value	Used Value	/ / / / /
3518	34c	Legendary Playing Fields, Shibe Park, self-adhesive..............................	.90	.60	☐☐☐☐☐
3519	34c	Legendary Playing fields, Wrigley Field, self-sdhesive...............................	.90	.60	☐☐☐☐☐
a.		Legendary Playing fields, Block of 10, #3510-3519	9.00		☐☐☐☐☐
3520	(10c)	Atlas Statue, New York City, self-adhesive coil stamp.............	.25	.25	
3521	34c	Leonard Bernstein (1918-90), Conductor	.65	.25	☐☐☐☐☐
3522	(15c)	Woody Wagon, self-adhesive coil stamp	.30	.25	☐☐☐☐☐
3523	34c	Legends of Hollywood – Lucille Ball (1911-89), self-adhesive..............	1.00	.25	☐☐☐☐☐
a.		Die cutting omitted, pair	*925.00*		☐☐☐☐☐
3524	34c	American Treasures Series, Amish Quilts – Diamond in the Square, c. 1920, self-adhesive.................	.70	.25	☐☐☐☐☐
3525	34c	American Treasures Series, Amish Quilts – Lone Star, c. 1920, self-adhesive	.70	.25	☐☐☐☐☐
3526	34c	American Treasures Series, Amish Quilts – Sunshine and Shadow, c. 1910, self-adhesive..............................	.70	.25	☐☐☐☐☐
3527	34c	American Treasures Series, Amish Quilts – Double Ninepatch Variation, self-adhesive..............................	.70	.25	☐☐☐☐☐
a.		Block or strip of 4, #3524-3527....	2.80		☐☐☐☐☐
3528	34c	Carnivorous Plants – Venus Flytrap, self-adhesive..............................	.70	.25	☐☐☐☐☐
3529	34c	Carnivorous Plants – Yellow Trumpet, self-adhesive..............................	.70	.25	☐☐☐☐☐
3530	34c	Carnivorous Plants – Cobra Lily, self-adhesive..............................	.70	.25	☐☐☐☐☐
3531	34c	Carnivorous Plants – English Sundew, self-adhesive..............................	.70	.25	☐☐☐☐☐
a.		Block or strip of 4, #3528-3531....	2.80		☐☐☐☐☐
3532	34c	Eid – 'Eid Mubarak', self adhesive	.70	.25	
3533	34c	Enrico Fermi, Physicist, self-adhesive	.70	.25	☐☐☐☐☐
3534		That's All Folks! Porky Pig at Mailbox, Pane of 10, self-adhesive...........	7.00		☐☐☐☐☐
a.	34c	Single	.70	.25	☐☐☐☐☐
b.		Pane of 9, #3534a........................	6.25		☐☐☐☐☐
c.		Pane of 1, #3534a........................	.70		☐☐☐☐☐
3535		That's All Folks! Porky Pig at Mailbox, Pane of 10, self-adhesive, right stamp with no die cutting...	60.00		☐☐☐☐☐
a.	34c	Single	*3.00*		☐☐☐☐☐
b.		Pane of 9, #3535a........................	*27.50*		☐☐☐☐☐
c.		Pane of 1, no die cutting	*30.00*		☐☐☐☐☐

3536   3537   3538   3539

3540   3541   3542   3543

3544   3545   3546

3547   3548   3549

3551

318

Scott No.		Description	Unused Value	Used Value	/ / / / / /
3536	34c	Virgin and Child, by Lorenzo Costa, self-adhesive, booklet stamp, serpentine die cut 11½ on 2, 3, or 4 Sides ..	.75	.25	☐☐☐☐☐
a.		Booklet pane of 20......................	15.00		☐☐☐☐☐
3537	34c	Santa Claus, large date, self-adhesive serpentine die cut 10¾ x 11........	.70	.25	☐☐☐☐☐
a.		Small date (from booklet pane), self-adhesive, serp. die cut 10¾ x 11	.90	.25	☐☐☐☐☐
b.		Large date (from booklet pane)	2.00	.25	☐☐☐☐☐
3538	34c	Santa Claus, large date, self-adhesive, serpentine die cut 10¾ x 11	.70	.25	☐☐☐☐☐
a.		Small date (from booklet pane), self-adhesive, serp. die cut 10¾ x 11	.90	.25	☐☐☐☐☐
b.		Large date, (from booklet pane) ..	2.00	.25	☐☐☐☐☐
3539	34c	Santa Claus, large date, self-adhesive, serpentine die cut 10¾ x 11	.70	.25	☐☐☐☐☐
a.		Small date (from booklet pane), self-adhesive, serp. die cut 10¾ x 11	.90	.25	☐☐☐☐☐
b.		Large date (from booklet pane) ...	2.00	.25	☐☐☐☐☐
3540	34c	Santa Claus, large date, self-adhesive, serpentine die cut 10¾ x 11	.70	.25	☐☐☐☐☐
a.		Small date (from booklet pane), self-adhesive, serp. die cut 10¾ x 11	.90	.25	☐☐☐☐☐
b.		Santa Claus, Block of 4, #3537-3540	2.80		☐☐☐☐☐
c.		Santa Claus, Block of 4, small date, #3537a-3540a.............................	3.60		☐☐☐☐☐
d.		Santa Claus, Booklet pane, 5 #3540c + label	18.00		☐☐☐☐☐
e.		Large date (from booklet pane) ...	2.00	.25	☐☐☐☐☐
f.		Block of 4, large date, #3537b-3539b, 3540e (from booklet pane)	8.00		☐☐☐☐☐
g.		Booklet pane of 20, 5 #3540f + label	40.00		☐☐☐☐☐
3541	34c	Santa Claus, Green and Red denominations, self-adhesive, serpentine die cut 11...................	1.10	.25	☐☐☐☐☐
3542	34c	Santa Claus, Green and Red denominations, Self-Adhesive, serpentine die cut 11...................	1.10	.25	☐☐☐☐☐
3543	34c	Santa Claus, Green and Red denominations, self-adhesive, serpentine die cut 11	1.10	.25	☐☐☐☐☐
3544	34c	Santa Claus, Green and Red denominations, self-adhesive, serpentine die cut 11..................	1.10	.25	☐☐☐☐☐
a.		Block of 4, #3541-3544	4.40		☐☐☐☐☐
b.		Booklet pane of 4, #3541-3544	4.40		☐☐☐☐☐
c.		Booklet pane of 6, #3543-3544, 2 #3541-3542	6.60		☐☐☐☐☐

3552

3553

3554

3555

3556

3557

3558

3559

3560

HOW TO USE THIS BOOK

The number in the first column is its Scott number or identifying number. Following that is the denomination of the stamp and its color or description. Finally, the values, unused and used, are shown.

Scott No.		Description	Unused Value	Used Value	/ / / / / /
d.		Booklet pane of 6, #3541-3542, 2 #3543-3544	6.60		☐☐☐☐☐
3545	34c	James Madison (1751-1836), Montpelier, self-adhesive............	.70	.25	☐☐☐☐☐
3546	34c	Thanksgiving Cornicopia, self-adhesive	.70	.25	☐☐☐☐☐
3547	34c	Hanukkah Type of 1996 (3118), self-adhesive............................	.70	.25	☐☐☐☐☐
3548	34c	Kwanzaa Type of 1997 (3175), self-adhesive............................	.70	.25	☐☐☐☐☐
3549	34c	United We Stand, self-adhesive, booklet stamp, serpentine die cut 11¼ on 2, 3, or 4 sides	.75	.25	☐☐☐☐☐
a.		Booklet pane of 20........................	15.00		☐☐☐☐☐
3549B	34c	United We Stand (3549), self-adhesive, booklet stamp, serpentine die cut 10½ x 10¾ on 2 or 3 Sides	1.00	.25	☐☐☐☐☐
c.		Booklet pane of 4..........................	4.00		☐☐☐☐☐
d.		Booklet pane of 6..........................	6.00		☐☐☐☐☐
e.		Booklet pane of 20........................	20.00		☐☐☐☐☐
3550	34c	United We Stand (3549), self-adhesive, coil stamp, square corners,......... serpentine die cut 9¾ Vert.	1.25	.25	☐☐☐☐☐
3550A	34c	United We Stand (3549), self-adhesive, coil stamp, round corners, spaced, serpentine die cut 9¾ Vert.	1.25	.25	☐☐☐☐☐
3551	57c	Love Letters (3496), self-adhesive, serpentine die cut 11¼................	1.10	.25	☐☐☐☐☐
2002 Issues					
3552	34c	Winter Olympics – Ski Jumping, self-adhesive	.70	.25	☐☐☐☐☐
3553	34c	Winter Olympics – Snowboarding, self-adhesive	.70	.25	☐☐☐☐☐
3554	34c	Winter Olympics – Ice Hockey, self-adhesive	.70	.25	☐☐☐☐☐
3555	34c	Winter Olympics – Figure Skating, self-adhesive	.70	.25	☐☐☐☐☐
a.		Block or strip of 4, #3552-3555....	2.80		☐☐☐☐☐
b.		Die cutting inverted, pane of 20....	—		☐☐☐☐☐
c.		Die cutting omitted, block of 4	*825.00*		☐☐☐☐☐
3556	34c	Child and Adult, self-adhesive......	.70	.25	☐☐☐☐☐
3557	34c	Langston Hughes, Writer, self-adhesive	.70	.25	☐☐☐☐☐
a.		Die cutting omitted, pair	*850.00*		☐☐☐☐☐
3558	34c	Happy Birthday, self-adhesive	.75	.25	☐☐☐☐☐
3559	34c	Year of the Horse, self-adhesive ...	.75	.25	☐☐☐☐☐
a.		Horiz. pair, vert. die cutting omitted	—		☐☐☐☐☐
3560	34c	Military Academy Coat of Arms, self-adhesive	.75	.45	☐☐☐☐☐
3561	34c	Greetings from Alabama, self-adhesive	.70	.45	☐☐☐☐☐
3562	34c	Greetings from Alaska, self-adhesive	.70	.45	☐☐☐☐☐

3561

3562

3563

3564

3565

3566

3567

3568

3569

3570

3571

3572

3573

3574

3575

3576

3577

3578

3579

3580

3581

3582

3583

3584

3585

3586

3587

3588

3589

3590

Scott No.	Description	Unused Value	Used Value	/ / / / /
3563	34c Greetings from Arizona, self-adhesive	.70	.45	
3564	34c Greetings from Arkansas, self-adhesive	.70	.45	
3565	34c Greetings from California, self-adhesive	.70	.45	
3566	34c Greetings from Colorado, self-adhesive	.70	.45	
3567	34c Greetings from Connecticut, self-adhesive	.70	.45	
3568	34c Greetings from Delaware, self-adhesive	.70	.45	
3569	34c Greetings from Florida, self-adhesive	.70	.45	
3570	34c Greetings from Georgia, self-adhesive	.70	.45	
3571	34c Greetings from Hawaii, self-adhesive	.70	.45	
3572	34c Greetings from Idaho, self-adhesive	.70	.45	
3573	34c Greetings from Illinois, self-adhesive	.70	.45	
3574	34c Greetings from Indiana, self-adhesive	.70	.45	
3575	34c Greetings from Iowa, self-adhesive	.70	.45	
3576	34c Greetings from Kansas, self-adhesive	.70	.45	
3577	34c Greetings from Kentucky, self-adhesive	.70	.45	
3578	34c Greetings from Louisiana, self-adhesive	.70	.45	
3579	34c Greetings from Maine, self-adhesive	.70	.45	
3580	34c Greetings from Maryland, self-adhesive	.70	.45	
3581	34c Greetings from Massachusetts, self-adhesive	.70	.45	
3582	34c Greetings from Michigan, self-adhesive	.70	.45	
3583	34c Greetings from Minnesota, self-adhesive	.70	.45	
3584	34c Greetings from Mississippi, self-adhesive	.70	.45	
3585	34c Greetings from Missouri, self-adhesive	.70	.45	
3586	34c Greetings from Montana, self-adhesive	.70	.45	
3587	34c Greetings from Nebraska, self-adhesive	.70	.45	
3588	34c Greetings from Greetings from Nevada, self-adhesive	.70	.45	
3589	34c Greetings from New Hampshire, self-adhesive	.70	.45	
3590	34c Greetings from New Jersey, self-adhesive	.70	.45	
3591	34c Greetings from New Mexico, self-adhesive	.70	.45	
3592	34c Greetings from New York, self-adhesive	.70	.45	
3593	34c Greetings from North Carolina, self-adhesive	.70	.45	
3594	34c Greetings from North Dakota, self-adhesive	.70	.45	
3595	34c Greetings from Ohio, self-adhesive	.70	.45	
3596	34c Greetings from Oklahoma, self-adhesive	.70	.45	
3597	34c Greetings from Oregon, self-adhesive	.70	.45	
3598	34c Greetings from Pennsylvania, self-adhesive	.70	.45	
3599	34c Greetings from Rhode Island, self-adhesive	.70	.45	
3600	34c Greetings from South Carolina, self-adhesive	.70	.45	

3591

3592

3593

3594

3595

3596

3597

3598

3599

3600

3601

3602

3603

3604

3605

3606

3607

3608

3609

3610

3611

3612

3613-3614

3620

3626

3627

3628

3629

3629F

HOW TO USE THIS BOOK

The number in the first column is its Scott number or identifying number. Following that is the denomination of the stamp and its color or description. Finally, the values, unused and used, are shown.

Scott No.		Description	Unused Value	Used Value	/ / / / / /
3601	34c	Greetings from South Dakota, self-adhesive..............................	.70	.45	☐☐☐☐☐
3602	34c	Greetings from Tennessee, self-adhesive	.70	.45	☐☐☐☐☐
3603	34c	Greetings from Texas, self-adhesive	.70	.45	☐☐☐☐☐
3604	34c	Greetings from Utah, self-adhesive	.70	.45	☐☐☐☐☐
3605	34c	Greetings from Vermont, self-adhesive	.70	.45	☐☐☐☐☐
3606	34c	Greetings from Virginia, self-adhesive	.70	.45	☐☐☐☐☐
3607	34c	Greetings from Washington, self-adhesive..............................	.70	.45	☐☐☐☐☐
3608	34c	Greetings from West Virginia, self-adhesive..............................	.70	.45	☐☐☐☐☐
3609	34c	Greetings from Wisconsin, self-adhesive	.70	.45	☐☐☐☐☐
3610	34c	Greetings from Wyoming, self-adhesive	.70	.45	☐☐☐☐☐
a.		Greetings From America, pane of 50, #3561-3610................................	35.00		☐☐☐☐☐
3611		Longleaf Pine Forest, pane of 10, self-adhesive	19.00		☐☐☐☐☐
a.	34c	Bachman's sparrow, ...	1.90	.50	☐☐☐☐☐
b.	34c	Northern bobwhite, yellow pitcher plants......................................	1.90	.50	☐☐☐☐☐
c.	34c	Fox squirrel, red-bellied woodpecker	1.90	.50	☐☐☐☐☐
d.	34c	Brown-headed nuthatch	1.90	.50	☐☐☐☐☐
e.	34c	Broadhead skink, yellow pitcher plants, pipeworts	1.90	.50	☐☐☐☐☐
f.	34c	Eastern towhee, yellow pitcher plants, Savannah meadow beauties, toothache grass...........................	1.90	.50	☐☐☐☐☐
g.	34c	Gray fox, gopher tortoise	1.90	.50	☐☐☐☐☐
h.	34c	Blind click beetle, sweetbay, pine woods treefrog............................	1.90	.50	☐☐☐☐☐
i.	34c	Rosebud orchid, pipeworts, southern toad, yellow pitcher plants	1.90	.50	☐☐☐☐☐
j.	34c	Grass-pink orchid, yellow-sided skimmer, pipeworts, yellow pitcher plants .	1.90	.50	☐☐☐☐☐
k.		As No. 3611, die cutting omitted..	*2,500.*		☐☐☐☐☐
3612	5c	Toleware Coffeepot, coil stamp, perf. 10 vert...............................	.25	.25	☐☐☐☐☐
a.		Imperf., pair....................................	—		☐☐☐☐☐
3613	3c	Star, self-adhesive, serpentine die cut 11	.25	.25	☐☐☐☐☐
a.		Die cutting omitted, pair	—		☐☐☐☐☐
3614	3c	Star (3613), self-adhesive, serpentine die cut 10, year at lower right....	.25	.25	☐☐☐☐☐
3615	3c	Star, year at lower left	.25	.25	☐☐☐☐☐
3616	23c	Washington (3468A), perf. 11¼...	.50	.25	☐☐☐☐☐
3617	23c	Washington (3468A), self-adhesive, coil stamp, serpentine die cut 11¼	.45	.25	☐☐☐☐☐
a.		Die cutting omitted, pair	—		☐☐☐☐☐

Scott No.	Description	Unused Value	Used Value	/ / / / / /
3618	23c Washington (3468A), booklet stamp, self-adhesive, serp. die cut 11¼	.50	.25	
a.	Booklet pane of 4........................	2.00		
b.	Booklet pane of 6........................	3.00		
c.	Booklet pane of 10......................	5.00		
3619	23c Washington (3468A), booklet stamp, self-adhesive, serpentine die cut 10½ x11¼	4.50	1.75	
a.	Booklet pane of 4, 2 #3619 at L, 2 #3618 at R.............................	10.00		
b.	Booklet pane of 6, 3 #3619 at L, 3 #3618 at R.............................	15.00		
c.	Booklet pane of 4, 2 #3618 at L, 2 #3619 at R.............................	10.00		
d.	Booklet pane of 6, 3 #3618 at L, 3 #3619 at R.............................	15.00		
e.	Booklet pane of 10, 5 #3619 at L, 5 #3618 at R.............................	27.50		
f.	Booklet pane of 10, 5 #3618 at L, 5 #3619 at R.............................	27.50		
g.	Pair, #3619 at L, #3618 at R	5.00		
h.	Pair, #3618 at L, #3619 at R	5.00		
i.	Nos. 3619c and 3619d, in bklt of 10 (#BK289A), imperf. vert. btwn. on both panes	—		
3620 (37c)	Flag perf.11¼ x 11	.85	.25	
3621 (37c)	Flag (3620), self-adhesive, serpentine die cut 11¼ x 11......................	1.00	.25	
3622 (37c)	Flag (3620), coil stamp, self-adhesive, serpentine die cut 10 vert............	.75	.25	
a.	Die cutting omitted, pair	—		
3623 (37c)	Flag (3620), booklet stamps, self-adhesive, serpentine die cut 11¼	.75	.25	
a.	Booklet pane of 20	15.00		
3624 (37c)	Flag (3620), booklet stamp, self-adhesive, serpentine die cut 10½ x10¾	.75	.25	
a.	Booklet pane of 4........................	3.00		
b.	Booklet pane of 6........................	4.50		
c.	Booklet pane of 20	15.00		
3625 (37c)	Flag (3620), booklet stamp, self-adhesive, serp. die cut 8.......	.75	.25	
a.	Booklet pane of 18......................	13.50		
3626 (37c)	Toy Mail Wagon, self-adhesive, booklet stamp.............................	.75	.25	
3627 (37c)	Toy Locomotive, self-adhesive, booklet stamp.............................	.75	.25	
3628 (37c)	Toy Taxicab, self-adhesive, booklet stamp.............................	.75	.25	

Scott No.		Description	Unused Value	Used Value	/ / / / / /
3629	(37c)	Toy Fire Pumper, self-adhesive, booklet stamp	1.00	.25	☐☐☐☐☐☐
a.		Block of 4, #3626-3629	3.00		
b.		Booklet pane of 4, #3626-3629	3.00		
c.		Booklet pane of 6, #3627, 3629, 2 each #3626, 3628	4.50		☐☐☐☐☐☐
d.		Booklet pane of 6, #3626, 3628, 2 each #3627, 3629	4.50		☐☐☐☐☐
e.		Booklet pane of 20, 5 each			
3629F	37c	Flag, perf 11¼	.90	.25	☐☐☐☐☐☐
g.		Imperf., pair	*250.00*		☐☐☐☐☐
3630	37c	Flag (3629F), self-adhesive, serpentine die cut 11¼ x 11	.90	.25	☐☐☐☐☐☐
3631	37c	Flag (3629F), coil stamp, perf. 10 vert.	.75	.25	☐☐☐☐☐
3632	37c	Flag (3629F), self-adhesive, coil stamp, serp. die cut 9¾ vert.	.75	.25	☐☐☐☐☐
b.		Die cutting omitted, pair	55.00	55.00	
3632A	37c	Flag (3629F) self-adhesive, serp. die cut 10¼ vert.	.75	.25	☐☐☐☐☐☐
f.		Die cutting omitted, pair	—		☐☐☐☐☐
3632C	37c	Flag (3629F), self-adhesive, coil stamp, serp. die cut 11¾ vert.	1.00	.25	☐☐☐☐☐
3633	37c	Flag (3629F), self-adhesive, coil stamp, serpentine die cut 8½ vert., dated "2002," rounded corners	.75	.25	☐☐☐☐☐
3633A	37c	Flag (3629F), self-adhesive, coil stamp, serp. die cut 8½ vert., square corners	2.25	.25	☐☐☐☐☐
3633B	37c	Flag (3629F), self-adhesive, coil stamp, serp. die cut 9½ vert.	4.50	.25	☐☐☐☐☐
3634	37c	Flag (3629F), self-adhesive, booklet stamp, serp. die cut 11.1, dated "2002"	.75	.25	☐☐☐☐☐
a.		Booklet pane of 10	7.50		☐☐☐☐☐
b.		Dated "2003"	.75	.25	☐☐☐☐☐
c.		Booklet pane, 4 #3634b	3.00		☐☐☐☐☐
d.		Booklet pane, 6 #3635b	4.50		☐☐☐☐☐
e.		As No. 3634, die cut 11.3	.85	.25	☐☐☐☐☐
f.		As "e," booklet pane of 10	8.50		☐☐☐☐☐
3635	37c	Flag (3629F), self-adhesive, booklet stamp, serp. die cut 11¼	.75	.25	☐☐☐☐☐
a.		Booklet pane of 20	15.00		☐☐☐☐☐
b.		Black omitted	*3,000.*		☐☐☐☐☐
3636	37c	Flag (3629F), self-adhesive, booklet stamp, serp. die cut 10½ x 10¾.	.75	.25	☐☐☐☐☐
a.		Booklet pane of 4	3.00		☐☐☐☐☐
b.		Booklet pane of 6	4.50		☐☐☐☐☐
c.		Booklet pane of 20	15.00		☐☐☐☐☐
f.		As "c," 11 stamps and part of 12th stamp on reverse printed on backing liner, the 8 stamps on front side imperf.	—		☐☐☐☐☐

3638

3639

3640

3641

3646

3647

3648

3649

Scott No.		Description	Unused Value	Used Value	/ / / / /
3636D	37c	Flag (3629F), self-adhesive, booklet stamp, serp. die cut 11¼ x11 on 2 or 3 sides	1.25	.25	
e.		Booklet pane of 20	22.50		
3637	37c	Flag (3629F), self-adhesive, booklet stamp, serpentine die cut 8.........	.75	.25	
a.		Booklet pane of 18......................	13.50		
3638	37c	Toy Locomotive, coil	.85	.25	
3639	37c	Toy Mail Wagon, coil...................	.85	.25	
3640	37c	Toy Fire Pumper, coil...................	.85	.25	
3641	37c	Toy Taxicab, coil	.85	.25	
a.		Strip of 4, #3638-3641	3.40		
3642	37c	Mail Wagon (3639), booklet stamp, serp. die cut 11, dated "2002"	.75	.25	
a.		Serp. die cut 11 x 11¼, dated "2003"	.75	.25	
3643	37c	Locomotive (3638), booklet stamp, serp. die cut 11, dated "2002"	.75	.25	
a.		Serp. die cut 11 x 11¼, dated "2003"	.75	.25	
3644	37c	Taxicab (3641), booklet stamp, serp. die cut 11, dated "2002"	.75	.25	
a.		Serp. die cut 11 x 11¼, dated "2003"	.75	.25	
3645	37c	Fire Pumper (3640), booklet stamp, serp. die cut 11, dated "2002"	.75	.25	
a.		Block of 4, #3642-3645	3.00		
b.		Booklet pane of 4, #3642-3645	3.00		
c.		Booklet pane of 6, #3643, 3645, 2 each #3642, 3644....................	4.50		
d.		Booklet pane of 6, #3642, 3644, 2 each #3643, 3645....................	4.50		
e.		Booklet pane of 20, 5 each #3642-3645	15.00		
f.		Serp. die cut 11 x 11¼, dated "2003"	.75	.25	
g.		Block of 4, #3642a, 3643a, 3644a, 3645f..	3.00		
h.		Booklet pane of 20, 5 #3645g	15.00		
3646	60c	Coverlet eagle, self-adhesive.........	1.25	.25	
3647	$3.85	Jefferson Memorial, self-adhesive, serp. die cut 11¼	7.50	2.00	
3647A	$3.85	Jefferson Memorial (3647), self-adhesive, serp. die cut 11 x 10¾.....	8.50	2.00	
3648	$13.65	Capitol Dome	27.50	10.00	
3649		Masters of American Photography, pane of 20, self-adhesive	15.00		
a.	37c	Portrait of Daniel Webster, by Albert Sands..........................	.75	.50	
b.	37c	Gen. Ulysses S. Grant and Officers, by Timothy H. Olsullivan.............	.75	.50	
c.	37c	Cape Horn, Columbia River, by Carleton E. Watkins	.75	.50	
d.	37c	Blessed Art Thou Among Women, by Gertrude Kasebier.......................	.75	.50	

3650

3651

3652

3653

3654

3655

3656

3657

3658

3659

3660

Scott No.	Description	Unused Value	Used Value	/ / / / / /
e.	37c Looking for Lost Luggage, Ellis Island, by Lewis W. Hine	.75	.50	☐☐☐☐☐
f.	37c The Octopus, by Alvin Langdon Colburn	.75	.50	☐☐☐☐☐
g.	37c Lotus, Mount Kisco, New York, by Edward Steichen	.75	.50	☐☐☐☐☐
h.	37c Hands and Thimble, by Alfred Stieglitz	.75	.50	☐☐☐☐☐
i.	37c Rayograph, by Man Ray	.75	.50	☐☐☐☐☐
j.	37c Two Shells, by Edward Weston	.75	.50	☐☐☐☐☐
k.	37c My Corsage, by James VanDerZee	.75	.50	☐☐☐☐☐
l.	37c Ditched, Stalled, and Stranded, San Joaquin Valley, California, by Dorothea Lange	.75	.50	☐☐☐☐☐
m.	37c Washroom and Dining Area of Floyd Burroughs' Home, Hale County, Alabama, by Walker Evans	.75	.50	☐☐☐☐☐
n.	37c Frontline Soldier with Canteen, Saipan, by W. Eugene Smith	.75	.50	☐☐☐☐☐
o.	37c Steeple, by Paul Strand	.75	.50	☐☐☐☐☐
p.	37c Sand Dunes, Sunrise, by Ansel Adams	.75	.50	☐☐☐☐☐
q.	37c Age and Its Symbols, by Imogen Cunningham	.75	.50	☐☐☐☐☐
r.	37c New York Cityscape, by Andre Kertesz	.75	.50	☐☐☐☐☐
s.	37c Photograph of pedestrians, by Garry Winogrand	.75	.50	☐☐☐☐☐
t.	37c Bristol, Vermont, by Minor White	.75	.50	☐☐☐☐☐
u.	As No. 3649, die cutting omitted	—		☐☐☐☐☐
3650	37c Scarlet and Louisiana Tanagers, self-adhesive	1.00	.25	☐☐☐☐☐
3651	37c Harry Houdini (1874-1926), Magician, self-adhesive	.75	.25	☐☐☐☐☐
3652	37c Andy Warhol (1928-87), Artist – Self-Portrait, self-adhesive	.75	.25	☐☐☐☐☐
3653	37c Teddy Bears, Centennial – Bruin Bear, c. 1907	1.00	.25	☐☐☐☐☐
3654	37c Teddy Bears, Centennial – Stick Bear, 1920s	1.00	.25	☐☐☐☐☐
3655	37c Teddy Bears, Centennial – Bund Bear, c. 1948	1.00	.25	☐☐☐☐☐
3656	37c Teddy Bears, Centennial – Ideal Bear, c. 1905	1.00	.25	☐☐☐☐☐
a.	Block or vert. strip of 4, #3653-3656	4.00		☐☐☐☐☐
3657	37c Love, self-adhesive, booklet stamp	.75	.25	☐☐☐☐☐
a.	Booklet pane of 20	15.00		☐☐☐☐☐
b.	As "a," silver ("Love 37 USA") missing on top 5 stamps (from color misregistration)	750.00		☐☐☐☐☐

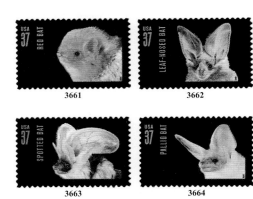

3661

3662

3663

3664

3665

3666

3667

3668

3669

3670

3671

3675

336

Scott No.	Description	Unused Value	Used Value	/ / / / / /
3658	60c Love, self-adhesive......................	1.25	.25	☐☐☐☐☐
3659	37c Ogden Nash (1902-1987), Poet, self-adhesive	.75	.25	☐☐☐☐☐
3660	37c Duke Kahanamoku, 1890-1968, 'Father of Surfing' and Olympic Swimmer, self-adhesive............	.75	.25	☐☐☐☐☐
3661	37c American Bats – Red Bat, self-adhesive	.75	.25	☐☐☐☐☐
3662	37c American Bats – Leaf-nosed Bat, self-adhesive	.75	.25	☐☐☐☐☐
3663	37c American Bats – Pallid Bat, self-adhesive	.75	.25	☐☐☐☐☐
3664	37c American Bat – Spotted Bat, self-adhesive	.75	.25	☐☐☐☐☐
a.	Block or horiz. strip of 4, #3661-3664	3.00		☐☐☐☐☐
3665	37c Women In Journalism – Nellie Bly (1864-1922), self-adhesive..	1.00	.25	☐☐☐☐☐
3666	37c Women In Journalism – Ida M. Tarbell (1857-1944), self-adhesive	1.00	.25	☐☐☐☐☐
3667	37c Women In Journalism – Ethel L. Payne (1911-91), self-adhesive..	1.00	.25	☐☐☐☐☐
3668	37c Women In Journalism – Marguerite Higgins (1920-66), self-adhesive	1.00	.25	☐☐☐☐☐
a.	Block or horiz. strip of 4, #3665-3668	4.00		☐☐☐☐☐
3669	37c Irving Berlin, 1888-1989, Composer, self-adhesive............	.75	.25	☐☐☐☐☐
3670	37c Neuter and Spay – Kitten, self-adhesive	1.00	.25	☐☐☐☐☐
3671	37c Neuter and Spay – Puppy, self-adhesive	1.00	.25	☐☐☐☐☐
a.	Horiz. or vert. pair, #3670-3671 ..	2.00		☐☐☐☐☐
3672	37c Hanukkah Type of 1996 (3118), self-adhesive	.75	.25	☐☐☐☐☐
3673	37c Kwanzaa Type of 1997 (3175) self-adhesive	.75	.25	☐☐☐☐☐
3674	37c Eid Type of 2001 (3532) self-adhesive	.75	.25	☐☐☐☐☐
3675	37c Christmas – Madonna and Child, by Jan Gossaert, self-adhesive, booklet stamp, 19x27mm design size	.75	.25	☐☐☐☐☐
a.	Booklet pane of 20........................	15.00		
3676	37c Snowman with Red and Green Plaid Scarf, self-adhesive...........	.90	.25	☐☐☐☐☐
3677	37c Snowman with Blue Plaid Scarf, self-adhesive	.90	.25	☐☐☐☐☐
3678	37c Snowman with Pipe, self-adhesive	.90	.25	☐☐☐☐☐
3679	37c Snowman with Top Hat, self-adhesive	.90	.25	☐☐☐☐☐
a.	Block or vert. strip of 4, #3676-3679	3.75		☐☐☐☐☐
3680	37c Snowman with Blue Plaid Scarf, self-adhesive, coil stamp............	2.75	.25	☐☐☐☐☐

3676

3677

3678

3679

3680

3681

3682

3683

3692

3693

3694

3746

3747

3748

3750

338

Scott No.	Description	Unused Value	Used Value	/ / / / / /
3681	37c Snowman with Pipe, self-adhesive, coil stamp..................	2.75	.25	☐☐☐☐☐
3682	37c Snowman with Top Hat, self-adhesive, coil stamp............	2.75	.25	☐☐☐☐☐
3683	37c Snowman with Red and Green Plaid Scarf, self-adhesive, coil stamp	2.75	.25	☐☐☐☐☐
a.	Strip of 4, #3680-3683.................	11.00		☐☐☐☐☐
3684	37c Snowman with Red and Green Plaid Scarf, self-adhesive, booklet stamp, serp. die cut 10¾ x 11..............	1.25	.25	☐☐☐☐☐
3685	37c Snowman with Blue Plaid Scarf, self-adhesive, booklet stamp, serp. die cut 10¾ x 11..............	1.25	.25	☐☐☐☐☐
3686	37c Snowman with Pipe, self-adhesive, booklet stamp, serp. die cut 10¾ x 11....................................	1.25	.25	☐☐☐☐☐
3687	37c Snowman with Top Hat, self-adhesive, booklet stamp, serp. die cut 10¾ x 11..............	1.25	.25	☐☐☐☐☐
a.	Block of 4, #3684-3687..............	5.00		☐☐☐☐☐
b.	Booklet pane, 5 #3687a + label...	25.00		☐☐☐☐☐
3688	37c Snowman with Blue Plaid Scarf, self-adhesive, booklet stamp, serp. die cut 11..........................	1.25	.25	☐☐☐☐☐
3689	37c Snowman with Blue Plaid Scarf, self-adhesive, booklet stamp, serp. die cut 11..........................	1.25	.25	☐☐☐☐☐
3690	37c Snowman with Pipe, self-adhesive, booklet stamp, serp. die cut 11..	1.25	.25	☐☐☐☐☐
3691	37c Snowman with Top Hat, self-adhesive, booklet stamp, serp. die cut 11..........................	1.25	.25	☐☐☐☐☐
a.	Block of 4, #3688-3691..............	5.00		☐☐☐☐☐
b.	Booklet pane of 4, #3688-3691 ...	5.00		☐☐☐☐☐
c.	Booklet pane of 6, #3690-3691, 2 each #3688-3689.....................	7.50		☐☐☐☐☐
d.	Booklet pane of 6, #3688-3689, 2 each #3690-3691.....................	7.50		☐☐☐☐☐
3692	37c Legends of Hollywood – Cary Grant (1904-86), self-adhesive	1.25	.25	☐☐☐☐☐
3693	5c Sea Coast, self-adhesive, coil stamp, serpentine die cut 8½ vert.	.25	.25	☐☐☐☐☐
3694	Hawaiian Missionary Stamps – Pane of 4......................................	5.00	2.50	☐☐☐☐☐
a.	37c 2c stamp of 1851, Hawaii Scott 1	1.25	.50	☐☐☐☐☐
b.	37c 5c stamp of 1851, Hawaii Scott 2	1.25	.50	☐☐☐☐☐
c.	37c 13c stamp of 1851, Hawaii Scott 3	1.25	.50	☐☐☐☐☐
d.	37c 13c stamp of 1852, Hawaii Scott 4	1.25	.50	☐☐☐☐☐

Scott No.	Description	Unused Value	Used Value	/ / / / /
3695	37c Happy Birthday Type of 2002 (3558), self-adhesive..................	.75	.25	☐☐☐☐☐
3696	37c Greetings From Alabama type (3561), self-adhesive..................	.75	.60	☐☐☐☐☐
3697	37c Greetings From Alaska type (3562), self-adhesive..................	.75	.60	☐☐☐☐☐
3698	37c Greetings From Arizona type (3563), self-adhesive..................	.75	.60	☐☐☐☐☐
3699	37c Greetings From Arkansas type (3564), self-adhesive..................	.75	.60	☐☐☐☐☐
3700	37c Greetings From California type (3565), self-adhesive..................	.75	.60	☐☐☐☐☐
3701	37c Greetings From Colorado type (3566), self-adhesive..................	.75	.60	☐☐☐☐☐
3702	37c Greetings From Connecticut type (3567), self-adhesive..................	.75	.60	☐☐☐☐☐
3703	37c Greetings From Delaware type (3568), self-adhesive..................	.75	.60	☐☐☐☐☐
3704	37c Greetings From Florida type (3569), self-adhesive..................	.75	.60	☐☐☐☐☐
3705	37c Greetings From Georgia type (3570), self-adhesive..................	.75	.60	☐☐☐☐☐
3706	37c Greetings From Hawaii type (3571), self-adhesive..................	.75	.60	☐☐☐☐☐
3707	37c Greetings From Idaho type (3572), self-adhesive..................	.75	.60	☐☐☐☐☐
3708	37c Greetings From Illinois type (3573), self-adhesive..................	.75	.60	☐☐☐☐☐
3709	37c Greetings From Indiana type (3574), self-adhesive..................	.75	.60	☐☐☐☐☐
3710	37c Greetings From Iowa type (3575), self-adhesive..................	.75	.60	☐☐☐☐☐
3711	37c Greetings From Kansas type (3576), self-adhesive..................	.75	.60	☐☐☐☐☐
3712	37c Greetings From Kentucky type (3577), self-adhesive..................	.75	.60	☐☐☐☐☐
3713	37c Greetings From Louisiana type (3578), self-adhesive..................	.75	.60	☐☐☐☐☐
3714	37c Greetings From Maine type (3579), self-adhesive..................	.75	.60	☐☐☐☐☐
3715	37c Greetings From Maryland type (3580), self-adhesive..................	.75	.60	☐☐☐☐☐
3716	37c Greetings From Massachusetts type (3581), self-adhesive..................	.75	.60	☐☐☐☐☐
3717	37c Greetings From Michigan type (3582), self-adhesive..................	.75	.60	☐☐☐☐☐
3718	37c Greetings From Minnesota type (3583), self-adhesive..................	.75	.60	☐☐☐☐☐

Scott No.	Description	Unused Value	Used Value	/ / / / / /
3719	37c Greetings From Mississippi type (3584), self-adhesive................	.75	.60	□□□□□
3720	37c Greetings From Missouri type (3585), self-adhesive................	.75	.60	□□□□□
3721	37c Greetings From Montana type (3586), self-adhesive................	.75	.60	□□□□□
3722	37c Greetings From Nebraska type (3587), self-adhesive................	.75	.60	□□□□□
3723	37c Greetings From Nevada type (3588), self-adhesive................	.75	.60	□□□□□
3724	37c Greetings From New Hampshire type (3589), self-adhesive..........	.75	.60	□□□□□
3725	37c Greetings From New Jersey type (3590), self-adhesive................	.75	.60	□□□□□
3726	37c Greetings From New Mexico type (3591), self-adhesive................	.75	.60	□□□□□
3727	37c Greetings From New York type (3592), self-adhesive................	.75	.60	□□□□□
3728	37c Greetings From North Carolina type (3593), self-adhesive................	.75	.60	□□□□□
3729	37c Greetings From North Dakota type (3594), self-adhesive................	.75	.60	□□□□□
3730	37c Greetings From Ohio type (3595), self-adhesive	.75	.60	□□□□□
3731	37c Greetings From Oklahoma type (3596), self-adhesive................	.75	.60	□□□□□
3732	37c Greetings From Oregon type (3597), self-adhesive................	.75	.60	□□□□□
3733	37c Greetings From Pennsylvania type (3598), self-adhesive................	.75	.60	□□□□□
3734	37c Greetings From Rhode Island type (3599), self-adhesive................	.75	.60	□□□□□
3735	37c Greetings From South Carolina type (3600), self-adhesive................	.75	.60	□□□□□
3736	37c Greetings From South Dakota type (3601), self-adhesive................	.75	.60	□□□□□
3737	37c Greetings From Tennessee type (3602), self-adhesive................	.75	.60	□□□□□
3738	37c Greetings From Texas type (3603), self-adhesive................	.75	.60	□□□□□
3739	37c Greetings From Utah type (3604), self-adhesive................	.75	.60	□□□□□
3740	37c Greetings From Vermont type (3605), self-adhesive................	.75	.60	□□□□□
3741	37c Greetings From Virginia type (3606), self-adhesive................	.75	.60	□□□□□
3742	37c Greetings From Washington type (3607), self-adhesive................	.75	.60	□□□□□

3754

3755

3757

3756

3758

3766

3770

3772

3771

3773

3774

3776

Scott No.	Description	Unused Value	Used Value	//////
3743	37c Greetings From West Virginia type (3608), self-adhesive..............	.75	.60	☐☐☐☐☐
3744	37c Greetings From Wisconsin type (3609), self-adhesive..............	.75	.60	☐☐☐☐☐
3745	37c Greetings From Wyoming type (3610), self-adhesive..............	.75	.60	☐☐☐☐☐
a.	Pane of 50, #3696-3745	37.50		☐☐☐☐☐

2003 Issues

Scott No.	Description	Unused Value	Used Value	//////
3746	37c Black Heritage Series – Thurgood Marshall (1908-93), Supreme Court Justice, self-adhesive	.75	.25	☐☐☐☐☐
3747	37c Chinese New Year – Year of the Ram, self-adhesive	.80	.25	☐☐☐☐☐
3748	37c Literary Arts – Zora Neale Hurston (1891-1960), Writer, self-adhesive	.85	.25	☐☐☐☐☐
3749	1c American Design Series – Tiffany Lamp (3758), self-adhesive	.25	.25	☐☐☐☐☐
3749A	1c American Design Series – Tiffany Lamp (3758), self-adhesive, with "USPS" microprinting	.25	.25	☐☐☐☐☐
3750	2c American Design Series – Navajo Necklace, self-adhesive, die cut 11	.25	.25	☐☐☐☐☐
3751	2c American Design Series – Navajo Necklace (3750), self-adhesive, serp. die cut 11¼ x 11½	.30	.25	☐☐☐☐☐
3752	2c American Design Series – Navajo Necklace (3750), self-adhesive, serp. die cut 11¼ x 11½, with "USPS" microprinting..............	.25	.25	☐☐☐☐☐
3753	2c American Design Series – Navajo Necklace (3750), dated "2007," serp. die cut 11¼x10¾, self-adhesive, with "USPS" microprinting	.25	.25	☐☐☐☐☐
3754	3c American Design Series – Silver Coffeepot, self-adhesive............	.25	.25	☐☐☐☐☐
3755	4c American Design Series – Chippendale Chair, self-adhesive..............	.25	.25	☐☐☐☐☐
3756	5c American Design Series – Toleware Coffeepot (3612), self-adhesive serp. die cut 11¼ x 11¾	.25	.25	☐☐☐☐☐
3756A	5c American Design Series – Toleware Coffeepot (3612), self-adhesive, serp. die cut 11¼ x 10¾.............	.25	.25	☐☐☐☐☐
3757	10c American Design Series – American Clock, self-adhesive..............	.25	.25	☐☐☐☐☐
a.	Die cutting omitted, pair..............	—		☐☐☐☐☐
3758	1c American Design Series – Tiffany Lamp, coil stamp, dated "2003"	.25	.25	☐☐☐☐☐

3777

3778

3779

3780

3781

3782

3783

3784

3786

3787

3788

3789

3790

3791

3792

Scott No.	Description	Unused Value	Used Value	/ / / / / /
3758A	1c American Design Series – Tiffany Lamp (3758), coil stamp, dated "2008" with "USPS" microprinting........	.25	.25	☐☐☐☐☐
3758B	2c American Design Series - Navajo Necklace (3750), coil stamp......	.25	.25	☐☐☐☐☐
3759	3c American Design Series – Silver Coffeepot (3754), coil stamp...........	.25	.25	☐☐☐☐☐
3761	4c American Design Series – Chippendale Chair (3755), coil stamp...........	.25	.25	☐☐☐☐☐
3762	10c American Design Series – American Clock (3757), coil stamp.............	.25	.25	☐☐☐☐☐
3763	10c American Design Series – American Clock (3757), coil stamp.............	.25	.25	☐☐☐☐☐
3766	$1 American Culture Series – Wisdom, Rockefeller Center, New York City, self-adhesive, dated "2003".........	2.00	.40	☐☐☐☐☐
a.	Dated "2008".................................	2.00	.40	☐☐☐☐☐
3769	10c New York Public Library Lion Type of 2000 (3447), coil stamp, perf. 10 vert................................	.25	.25	☐☐☐☐☐
3770	10c Atlas Statue (3520), self-adhesive, coil stamp, serp. die cut 11 vert.	.25	.25	☐☐☐☐☐
3771	80c Special Olympics – Athlete with Medal, self-adhesive	1.60	.35	☐☐☐☐☐
3772	American Filmmaking: Behind The Scenes, pane of 10, self-adhesive	12.00		☐☐☐☐☐
a.	37c Screenwriting, segment of script from Gone With the Wind	1.20	.50	☐☐☐☐☐
b.	37c Directing, John Cassavetes	1.20	.50	☐☐☐☐☐
c.	37c Costume design, Edith Head........	1.20	.50	☐☐☐☐☐
d.	37c Music, Max Steiner working on score	1.20	.50	☐☐☐☐☐
e.	37c Makeup, Jack Pierce working on Boris Karloff's makeup for Frankenstein	1.20	.50	☐☐☐☐☐
f.	37c Art direction, Perry Ferguson working on sketch for Citizen Kane	1.20	.50	☐☐☐☐☐
g.	37c Cinematography, Paul Hill, assistant cameraman for Nagana..............	1.20	.50	☐☐☐☐☐
h.	37c Film Editing, J. Watson Webb editing The Razor's Edge	1.20	.50	☐☐☐☐☐
i.	37c Special effects, Mark Siegel working on model for E.T. The Extra-Terrestrial	1.20	.50	☐☐☐☐☐
j.	37c Sound, Gary Summers works on control panel	1.20	.50	☐☐☐☐☐
3773	37c Ohio Statehood Bicentennial, self-adhesive	.75	.25	☐☐☐☐☐
3774	37c Pelican Island National Wildlife Refuge, Cent. – Brown Pelican, self-adhesive	.75	.25	☐☐☐☐☐

3793

3802

3803

3804

3805

3806

3807

3808

3809

3810

3811

346

Scott No.	Description	Unused Value	Used Value	/ / / / / /
3775	5c Sea Coast Type of 2002 (3693), coil stamp, perf 9¾ vert., "2003" year date	.25	.25	☐☐☐☐☐
3776	37c Old Glory – Uncle Sam on Bicycle with Liberty Flag, 20th Cent., self-adhesive, booklet stamp......	.75	.50	☐☐☐☐☐
3777	37c Old Glory – 1888 Presidential Campaign Badge, self-adhesive, booklet stamp............................	.75	.50	☐☐☐☐☐
3778	37c Old Glory – 1893 Silk Bookmark, self-adhesive, booklet stamp......	.75	.50	☐☐☐☐☐
3779	37c Old Glory – Modern Hand Fan, self-adhesive, booklet stamp......	.75	.50	☐☐☐☐☐
3780	37c Old Glory – Carving of Woman with Flag and Sword, 19th Cent., self-adhesive, booklet stamp......	.75	.50	☐☐☐☐☐
a.	Horiz. Strip of 5, #3776-3780......	3.75		☐☐☐☐☐
b.	Booklet pane, 2 #3780a	7.50		☐☐☐☐☐
3781	37c Cesar E. Chavez (1927-93), Labor Organizer, self-adhesive.............	.75	.25	☐☐☐☐☐
3782	37c Louisiana Purchase, Bicent., self-adhesive	.95	.40	☐☐☐☐☐
3783	37c First Flight of Wright Brothers, Cent., self-adhesive....................	.90	.40	☐☐☐☐☐
a.	Booklet pane of 9.........................	8.00		☐☐☐☐☐
b.	Booklet pane of 1, booklet stamp	.90		☐☐☐☐☐
3784	37c Purple Heart, self-adhesive serp. die cut 11¼ x 10¾	.75	.25	☐☐☐☐☐
b.	Printed on back of backing paper	—		☐☐☐☐☐
d.	Die cutting omitted, pair	—		☐☐☐☐☐
3784A	37c Purple Heart (3784), self-adhesive, serp. die cut 10¾ x 10¼	.75	.25	☐☐☐☐☐
e.	Die cutting omitted, pair	150.00		☐☐☐☐☐
f.	Die cutting omitted, pane of 20 ...	*1,600.*		☐☐☐☐☐
3785	5c Sea Coast Type of 2002 (3693), self-adhesive, coil stamp, serp. die cut 9½ x 10........................	.25	.25	☐☐☐☐☐
a.	Serp. die cut 9¼ x 10	.25	.25	☐☐☐☐☐
3786	37c Legends of Hollywood – Audrey Hepburn (1929-93), self-adhesive	1.25	.25	☐☐☐☐☐
✓3787	37c Southeastern Lighthouses – Old Cape Henry, Virginia, self-adhesive	1.10	.25	☐☐☐☐☐
✓3788	37c Southeastern Lighthouses – Cape Lookout, North Carolina, self-adhesive	1.10	.25	☐☐☐☐☐

3812

3813

Scarlet Kingsnake

3814

Blue-spotted Salamander

3815

Reticulate Collared Lizard

3816

Ornate Chorus Frog

3817

Ornate Box Turtle

3818

3821

3822

3823

3824

3825

3826

3827

3828

Scott No.	Description	Unused Value	Used Value	/ / / / / /
a.	Bottom of 'USA' even with top of upper half-diamond of lighthouse, pos. 2	4.00	2.50	☐☐☐☐☐
3789	37c Southeastern Lighthouses – Morris Island, South Carolina, self-adhesive	1.10	.25	☐☐☐☐☐
3790	37c Southeastern Lighthouses – Tybee Island, Georgia, self-adhesive	1.10	.25	☐☐☐☐☐
3791	37c Southeastern Lighthouses – Hillsboro Inlet, Florida, self-adhesive	1.10	.25	☐☐☐☐☐
a.	Strip of 5, #3587-3791	5.50		☐☐☐☐☐
b.	Strip of 5, #3767, 3788a, 3789-3791	9.50		☐☐☐☐☐
3792	25c Eagle in gold on gray background, self-adhesive, coil stamp	.50	.25	☐☐☐☐☐
d.	Dated "2005"	.50	.25	☐☐☐☐☐
3793	25c Red eagle on gold background, self-adhesive, coil stamp	.50	.25	☐☐☐☐☐
d.	Dated "2005"	.50	.25	☐☐☐☐☐
3794	25c Eagle in gold on dull blue background, self-adhesive, coil stamp	.50	.25	☐☐☐☐☐
d.	Dated "2005"	.50	.25	☐☐☐☐☐
3795	25c Prussian blue eagle on gold background, self-adhesive, coil stamp	.50	.25	☐☐☐☐☐
d.	Dated "2005"	.50	.25	☐☐☐☐☐
3796	25c Eagle in gold on green background, self-adhesive, coil stamp	.50	.25	☐☐☐☐☐
d.	Dated "2005"	.50	.25	☐☐☐☐☐
3797	25c Gray eagle on gold background, self-adhesive, coil stamp	.50	.25	☐☐☐☐☐
d.	Dated "2005"	.50	.25	☐☐☐☐☐
3798	25c Eagle in gold on Prussian blue background, self-adhesive, coil stamp	.50	.25	☐☐☐☐☐
d.	Dated "2005"	.50	.25	☐☐☐☐☐
3799	25c Dull blue eagle on gold background, self-adhesive, coil stamp	.50	.25	☐☐☐☐☐
d.	Dated "2005"	.50	.25	☐☐☐☐☐
3800	25c Eagle in gold on red background, self-adhesive, coil stamp	.50	.25	☐☐☐☐☐
d.	Dated "2005"	.50	.25	☐☐☐☐☐
3801	25c Green eagle on gold background, self-adhesive, coil stamp	.50	.25	☐☐☐☐☐
b.	Strip of 10 #3792-3801	5.00		☐☐☐☐☐
d.	Dated "2005"	.50	.25	☐☐☐☐☐
e.	Strip of 10, #3792d-3801d	5.00		☐☐☐☐☐
3802	Arctic Tundra, Pane of 10, self-adhesive	8.50		☐☐☐☐☐
a.	37c Gyrfalcon	.85	.50	☐☐☐☐☐

3829

PACIFIC CORAL REEF

3831

3832

3833

3834

3835

3836

3837

HOW TO USE THIS BOOK

The number in the first column is its Scott number or identifying number. Following that is the denomination of the stamp and its color or description. Finally, the values, unused and used, are shown.

Scott No.	Description	Unused Value	Used Value	/ / / / / /
b.	37c Gray wolf, vert.	.85	.50	☐☐☐☐☐
c.	37c Common raven, vert......................	.85	.50	☐☐☐☐☐
d.	37c Musk oxen and caribou...............	.85	.50	☐☐☐☐☐
e.	37c Grizzly bears, caribou	.85	.50	☐☐☐☐☐
f.	37c Caribou, willow ptarmigans.........	.85	.50	☐☐☐☐☐
g.	37c Arctic ground squirrel, vert.	.85	.50	☐☐☐☐☐
h.	37c Willow ptarmigan, bearberry.......	.85	.50	☐☐☐☐☐
i.	37c Arctic grayling	.85	.50	☐☐☐☐☐
j.	37c Singing vole, thin-legged wolf spider, lingonberry, Labrador tea	.85	.50	☐☐☐☐☐
3803	37c Korean War Veterans Memorial, self-adhesive	.75	.25	☐☐☐☐☐
3804	37c Mary Cassatt Paintings – Young Mother, 1888, self-adhesive, booklet stamp............................	.75	.25	☐☐☐☐☐
3805	37c Mary Cassatt Paintings – Children Playing on the Beach, 1884, self-adhesive, booklet stamp......	.75	.25	☐☐☐☐☐
3806	37c Mary Cassatt Paintings – On a Balcony, 1878-79, self-adhesive, booklet stamp............................	.75	.25	☐☐☐☐☐
3807	37c Mary Cassatt Paintings – Child in a Straw Hat, c. 1886, self-adhesive, booklet stamp......	.75	.25	☐☐☐☐☐
a.	Block of 4, #3804-3807	3.00		☐☐☐☐☐
b.	Booklet pane of 20, 5 each #3807a	15.00		☐☐☐☐☐
3808	37c Early Football Heroes – Bronko Nagurski (1908-90), self-adhesive	.75	.25	☐☐☐☐☐
3809	37c Early Football Heroes – Ernie Nevers (1903-96), self-adhesive	.75	.25	☐☐☐☐☐
3810	37c Early Football Heroes – Walter Camp (1859-1925), self-adhesive	.75	.25	☐☐☐☐☐
3811	37c Early Football Heroes – Red Grange (1903-91), self-adhesive	.75	.25	☐☐☐☐☐
a.	Block of 4, #3808-3811	3.00		☐☐☐☐☐
3812	37c Roy Acuff (1903-92), Country Music Artist, self-adhesive	.75	.25	☐☐☐☐☐
3813	37c District of Columbia, self-adhesive	.85	.25	☐☐☐☐☐
3814	37c Reptiles and Amphibians - Scarlet Kingsnake, self-adhesive	.80	.25	☐☐☐☐☐
3815	37c Reptiles and Amphibians – Blue-Spotted Salamander, self-adhesive	.80	.25	☐☐☐☐☐
3816	37c Reptiles and Amphibians – Reticulate Collared Lizard, self-adhesive	.80	.25	☐☐☐☐☐
3817	37c Reptiles and Amphibians - Orange Chorus Frog, self-adhesive	.80	.25	☐☐☐☐☐

3838

3839

3840

3841

3842

3843

3854

3855

3856

352

Scott No.	Description	Unused Value	Used Value	/ / / / / /
3818	37c Reptiles and Amphibians – Ornate Box Turtle, self-adhesive	.80	.25	☐☐☐☐☐
a.	Vert. strip of 5, #3814-3818........	3.75		☐☐☐☐☐
3819	37c George Washington (3468A), self-adhesive, serp. die cut 11....	1.00	.25	☐☐☐☐☐
3820	37c Christmas Type of 2002 (3675), self-adhesive, booklet stamp, 19½ x 28mm design size...........	.75	.25	☐☐☐☐☐
a.	Booklet pane of 20.......................	15.00		☐☐☐☐☐
b.	Die cutting omitted, pair	—		☐☐☐☐☐
3821	37c Reindeer with Pan Pipes, self-adhesive, serp. die cut 11¾ x 11	1.00	.25	☐☐☐☐☐
3822	37c Santa Claus with Drum, self-adhesive, serp. die cut 11¾ x 11....................................	1.00	.25	☐☐☐☐☐
3823	37c Santa Claus with Trumpet, self-adhesive, serp. die cut 11¾ x 11	1.00	.25	☐☐☐☐☐
3824	37c Reindeer with Horn, self-adhesive, serp. die cut 11¾ x 11..............	1.00	.25	☐☐☐☐☐
a.	Block of 4, #3821-3824	4.00		☐☐☐☐☐
b.	Booklet pane of 20, 5 each #3821-3824	20.00		☐☐☐☐☐
3825	37c Reindeer with Pan Pipes, booklet stamp, serpentine die cut 10½ x 10¾................................	1.10	.25	☐☐☐☐☐
3826	37c Santa Claus with Drum, booklet stamp, serpentine die cut 10½ x 10¾................................	1.10	.25	☐☐☐☐☐
3827	37c Santa Claus with Trumpet, booklet stamp, serpentine die cut 10½ x 10¾	1.10	.25	☐☐☐☐☐
3828	37c Reindeer with Horn, booklet stamp, serpentine die cut 10½ x 10¾ .	1.10	.25	☐☐☐☐☐
a.	Block of 4, #3825-3828	4.40		☐☐☐☐☐
b.	Booklet pane of 4, #3825-3828 ..	4.40		☐☐☐☐☐
c.	Booklet pane of 6, #3827-3828 2 each #3825-3826	6.60		☐☐☐☐☐
d.	Booklet pane of 6, #3825-3826, 2 each #3827-3828....................	6.60		☐☐☐☐☐

2003-05 Issues

Scott No.	Description	Unused Value	Used Value	/ / / / / /
3829	37c Snowy Egret, self-adhesive, coil stamp, serp. die cut 8½ vert.	.75	.25	☐☐☐☐☐
b.	Black omitted	—		☐☐☐☐☐
3829A	37c Snowy Egret (3829), self-adhesive, coil stamp, serp. die cut 9½ vert..	.85	.25	☐☐☐☐☐
3830	37c Snowy Egret (3829), self-adhesive, booklet stamp, serp. die cut 11½ x 11......................................	.75	.25	☐☐☐☐☐

3857

3858

3859

3860

3861

3862

3863

3865

3866

Scott No.	Description	Unused Value	Used Value	/ / / / /
a.	Booklet pane of 20......................	15.00		
b.	As "a," die cutting omitted...........	—		
3830D	37c Snowy Egret (3829), self-adhesive, with "USPS" Microprinted on Bird's Breast	5.50	.50	
e.	Booklet pane of 20	*110.00*		
f.	Die cutting omitted, pair	*250.00*		
g.	As "e," die cutting omitted...........	—		
2004 Issues				
3831	37c Pacific Coral Reef – Marine Life, pane of 10, self-adhesive	9.00		
a.	37c Emperor angelfish, blue coral, mound coral	.90	.25	
b.	37c Humphead wrasse, Moorish idol .	.90	.25	
c.	37c Bumphead parrotfish	.90	.25	
d.	37c Black-spotted puffer, threadfin butterflyfish, staghorn coral	.90	.25	
e.	37c Hawksbill turtle, palette surgeonfish	.90	.25	
f.	37c Pink amemonefish, magnificent sea anemone..............................	.90	.25	
g.	37c Snowflake moray eel, spanish dance	.90	.25	
h.	37c Lionfish...	.90	.25	
i.	37c Triton's trumpet............................	.90	.25	
j.	37c Oriental sweetlips, bluestreak cleaner wrasse, mushroom coral ..	.90	.25	
3832	37c Chinese New Year – Year of the Monkey, self-adhesive	.75	.25	
3833	37c Love – Candy Hearts, self-adhesive, booklet stamp............................	.75	.25	
a.	Booklet pane of 20......................	15.00		
3834	37c Black Heritage Series – Paul Robeson (1898-1976), Actor, Singer, Athlete and Activist, self-adhesive	.75	.25	
3835	37c Theodor Seuss Geisel (Dr. Seuss), Children's Book Writer, and Book Characters, self-adhesive..	.85	.25	
a.	Die cutting omitted, pair	*2,750.*		
3836	37c Flowers: White Lilacs and Pink Roses, self-adhesive, booklet stamp......	.75	.25	
a.	Booklet pane of 20......................	15.00		
3837	60c Flowers: Five Varieties of Pink Roses, self-adhesive, booklet stamp......	1.40	.25	
3838	37c U.S. Air Force Academy, 50th Anniv., self-adhesive	.75	.25	
3839	37c Henry Mancini (1924-94), Composer, and Pink Panther, self-adhesive .	.75	.25	
3840	37c American Choreographers, Martha Graham (1893-1991), self-adhesive	.75	.25	

3867

3868

3869

3870

3871

3873

3872

3876

3877

356

Scott No.	Description	Unused Value	Used Value	/ / / / / /
3841	37c American Choreographers, Alvin Ailey (1931-89), and Dancers, self-adhesive	.75	.25	☐☐☐☐☐
3842	37c American Choreographers, Agnes de Mille (1909-93), and Dancers, self-adhesive	.75	.25	☐☐☐☐☐
3843	37c American Choreographers, George Balanchine (1904-83), and Dancers, self-adhesive	.75	.25	☐☐☐☐☐
a.	Horiz. strip of 4, #3840-3843	3.00		☐☐☐☐
b.	Strip of 4, die cutting omitted......	*500.00*		☐☐☐☐
3844	25c Eagle Type of 2003 (3792), coil stamp, perf. 9¾ vert.	.50	.25	☐☐☐☐☐
3845	25c Eagle Type of 2003 (3801), coil stamp, perf. 9¾ vert.	.50	.25	☐☐☐☐☐
3846	25c Eagle Type of 2003 (3800), coil stamp, perf. 9¾ vert.	.50	.25	☐☐☐☐☐
3847	25c Eagle Type of 2003 (3799), coil stamp, perf. 9¾ vert.	.50	.25	☐☐☐☐☐
3848	25c Eagle Type of 2003 (3798), coil stamp, perf. 9¾ vert.	.50	.25	☐☐☐☐☐
3849	25c Eagle Type of 2003 (3797), coil stamp, perf. 9¾ vert.	.50	.25	☐☐☐☐☐
3850	25c Eagle Type of 2003 (3796), coil stamp, perf. 9¾ vert.	.50	.25	☐☐☐☐☐
3851	25c Eagle Type of 2003 (3795), coil stamp, perf. 9¾ vert.	.50	.25	☐☐☐☐☐
3852	25c Eagle Type of 2003 (3794), coil stamp, perf. 9¾ vert.	.50	.25	☐☐☐☐☐
3853	25c Eagle Type of 2003 (3801), coil stamp, perf. 9¾ vert.	.50	.25	☐☐☐☐☐
a.	25c Strip of 10, #3844-3853...............	5.00	—	☐☐☐☐☐
3854	37c Lewis & Clark Expedition, Bicent., Meriwether Lewis (1774-1809) and William Clark (1770-1838), On Hill, self-adhesive	1.10	.25	☐☐☐☐☐
3855	37c Lewis & Clark Expedition, Bicent., Meriwether Lewis, self-adhesive, booklet stamp.............................	.90	.45	☐☐☐☐☐
3856	37c Lewis & Clark Expedition, Bicent., William Clark, self-adhesive, booklet stamp.............................	.90	.45	☐☐☐☐☐
a.	Horiz. or vert. Pair, #3855-3856..	1.80	—	☐☐☐☐☐
b.	Booklet pane, 5 each #3855-3856	9.00	—	☐☐☐☐☐
3857	37c Isamu Naguchi (1904-88), Sculptor, Akari 25N, self-adhesive............	.90	.25	☐☐☐☐☐
3858	37c Isamu Naguchi (1904-88), Sculptor, Margaret la Farge Osborn, self-adhesive......................................	.90	.25	☐☐☐☐☐

C L O U D S C A P E S

3878

3879

3880

3881

3882

3883

3884

3885

3886

3887

3888

3889

3890

Scott No.	Description	Unused Value	Used Value	/ / / / / /
3859	37c Isamu Naguchi (1904-88), Sculptor, Black Sun, self-adhesive............	.90	.25	☐☐☐☐☐
3860	37c Isamu Naguchi (1904-88), Scultpor, Mother and Child, self-adhesive	.90	.25	☐☐☐☐☐
3861	37c Isamu Naguchi (1904-88), Scultpor, Figure (Detail), self-adhesive	.90	.25	☐☐☐☐☐
a.	Horiz. strip of 5, #3857-3861	4.50	—	☐☐☐☐☐
3862	37c National World War II Memorial, self-adhesive	.75	.25	☐☐☐☐☐
3863	37c Summer Olympic Games, Athens, Greece, Stylized Runner, self-adhesive.....................................	.75	.25	☐☐☐☐☐
3864	5c Sea Coast Type of 2002 (3693), coil stamp, perf. 9¾ vert., "2004" year date....................................	.25	.25	☐☐☐☐☐
3865	37c Disney Characters: Goofy, Mickey Mouse, Donald Duck, self-adhesive	1.00	.25	☐☐☐☐☐
3866	37c Disney Characters: Bambi, Thumper, self-adhesive	1.00	.25	☐☐☐☐☐
3867	37c Disney Characters: Mufasa, Simba, self-adhesive	1.00	.25	☐☐☐☐☐
3868	37c Disney Characters: Jiminy Cricket, Pinocchio, self-adhesive	1.00	.25	☐☐☐☐☐
a.	Block or vert. strip of 4, #3865-3868	4.00	—	☐☐☐☐☐
3869	37c U.S.S. Constellation, self-adhesive	.75	.25	☐☐☐☐☐
3870	37c R. Buckminster Fuller (1895-1983), Engineer; Time Magazine Cover Depicting Fuller, by Boris Artzybasheff, self-adhesive.........	.75	.25	☐☐☐☐☐
✓3871	37c Literary Arts – James Baldwin (1924-87), Writer, self-adhesive	.75	.25	☐☐☐☐☐
3872	37c Giant Magnolias, by M.J. Heade, self-adhesive	.70	.25	☐☐☐☐☐
a.	Booklet pane of 20	15.00		☐☐☐☐☐
b.	Die cutting omitted, pair, in #3872a with foldover	—		☐☐☐☐☐
3873	37c Art of the American Indian, pane of 10	25.00		☐☐☐☐☐
a.-j.	Any single	2.50	.25	☐☐☐☐☐
3874	5c Sea Coast Type of 2002 (3693), self-adhesive, coil stamp, serp. die cut 10 vert., large "2003" date...	.25	.25	☐☐☐☐☐
a.	Small "2003" date	.25	.25	☐☐☐☐☐
3875	5c Sea Coast Type of 2002 (3693), self-adhesive, coil stamp, serp. die cut 11½ vert., "2004" date...	.25	.25	☐☐☐☐☐

3895

3896

3897

3898

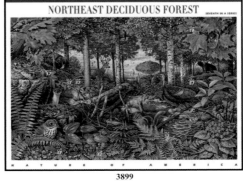

3899

Scott No.	Description	Unused Value	Used Value	/ / / / / /
3876	37c Legends of Hollywood – John Wayne (1907-79), self-adhesive	.85	.25	☐☐☐☐☐
3877	37c Sickle Cell Disease Awareness, self-adhesive	.75	.25	☐☐☐☐☐
3878	Cloudscapes, pane of 15, self-adhesive..............................	15.00		☐☐☐☐☐
a.	37c Cirrus radiatus.............................	1.00	.25	☐☐☐☐☐
b.	37c Cirrostratus fibratus.....................	1.00	.25	☐☐☐☐☐
c.	37c Cirrocumulus undulatus..............	1.00	.25	☐☐☐☐☐
d.	37c Cumulonimbus mammatus	1.00	.25	☐☐☐☐☐
e.	37c Cumolonimbus incus	1.00	.25	☐☐☐☐☐
f.	37c Altocumulus stratiformis.............	1.00	.25	☐☐☐☐☐
g.	37c Altostratus translucidus..............	1.00	.25	☐☐☐☐☐
h.	37c Altocumulus undulatus...............	1.00	.25	☐☐☐☐☐
i.	37c Altocumullus castellanus............	1.00	.25	☐☐☐☐☐
j.	37c Altocumulus lenticularis	1.00	.25	☐☐☐☐☐
k.	37c Stratocumulus undulatus.............	1.00	.25	☐☐☐☐☐
l.	37c Stratus opacus	1.00	.25	☐☐☐☐☐
m.	37c Cumulus humilis	1.00	.25	☐☐☐☐☐
n.	37c Cumulus congestus	1.00	.25	☐☐☐☐☐
o.	37c Cumulonimbus with tornado.......	1.00	.25	☐☐☐☐☐
3879	37c Christmas, Madonna and Child, self-adhesive, booklet stamp	.75	.25	☐☐☐☐☐
a.	Booklet pane of 20	15.00		☐☐☐☐☐
b.	As "a," die cutting omitted...........	—		☐☐☐☐☐
3880	37c Hanukkah, Dreidel, self-adhesive	.75	.25	☐☐☐☐☐
a.	Die cut applied to wrong side of stamp (hyphen hole cuts on face, die cut 10¾ on reverse)	—	—	☐☐☐☐☐
3881	37c Kwanzaa, self-adhesive...............	.75	.25	☐☐☐☐☐
3882	37c Literary Arts – Moss Hart (1904-61), Playwright, self-adhesive..............................	.80	.25	☐☐☐☐☐
3883	37c Christmas, Purple Santa Ornament, self-adhesive..............................	1.00	.25	☐☐☐☐☐
3884	37c Christmas, Green Santa Ornament, self-adhesive..............................	1.00	.25	☐☐☐☐☐
3885	37c Christmas, Blue Santa Ornament, self-adhesive..............................	1.00	.25	☐☐☐☐☐
3886	37c Christmas, Red Santa Ornament, self-adhesive..............................	1.00	.25	☐☐☐☐☐
a.	Block or strip of 4, #3883-3886 ...	4.00		☐☐☐☐☐
b.	Booklet pane of 20, 5 #3886a	20.00		☐☐☐☐☐
3887	37c Christmas, Purple Santa Ornament, self-adhesive, booklet stamp, serp. die cut 10¼ x 10¾ on 2 or 3 sides	1.00	.25	☐☐☐☐☐

3900

3901

3902

3903

ROBERT PENN WARREN

3904

somewhere over the rainbow skies are blue...

YIP HARBURG

3905

BARBARA McCLINTOCK
GENETICIST

3906

JOSIAH WILLARD GIBBS
THERMODYNAMICIST

3907

JOHN von NEUMANN
MATHEMATICIAN

3908

RICHARD FEYNMAN
PHYSICIST

3909

Masterworks of Modern American Architecture

3910

Henry Fonda

3911

362

Scott No.	Description	Unused Value	Used Value	/ / / / / /
3888	37c Christmas, Green Santa Ornament, self-adhesive, booklet stamp, serp. die cut 10¼ x 10¾ on 2 or 3 sides	1.00	.25	☐☐☐☐☐
3889	37c Christmas, Blue Santa Ornament, self-adhesive, booklet stamp, serp. die cut 10¼ x 10¾ on 2 or 3 sides	1.00	.25	☐☐☐☐☐
3890	37c Christmas, Red Santa Ornament, self-adhesive, booklet stamp, serp. die cut 10¼ x 10¾ on 2 or 3 sides	1.00	.25	☐☐☐☐☐
a.	Block of 4, #3887-3890	4.00		☐☐☐☐☐
b.	Booklet pane of 4, #3887-3890....	4.00		☐☐☐☐☐
c.	Booklet pane of 6, #3889-3890, 2 each #3887-3888	6.00		☐☐☐☐☐
d.	Booklet pane of 6, #3887-3888, 2 each #3889-3890	6.00		☐☐☐☐☐
3891	37c Christmas, Green Santa Ornament (3888), self-adhesive, booklet stamp, serp. die cut 8 on 2, 3 or 4 sides.....................................	1.35	.25	☐☐☐☐☐
3892	37c Christmas, Purple Santa Ornament, (3887), self-adhesive, booklet stamp, serp. die cut 8 on 2, 3 or 4 sides.....................................	1.35	.25	☐☐☐☐☐
3893	37c Christmas, Red Santa Ornament (3890), self-adhesive, booklet stamp, serp. die cut 8 on 2, 3 or 4 sides.....................................	1.35	.25	☐☐☐☐☐
3894	37c Christmas, Blue Santa Ornament (3889), self-adhesive, booklet stamp, serp. die cut 8 on 2, 3 or 4 sides.....................................	1.35	.25	☐☐☐☐☐
a.	Block of 4, #3891-3894	5.40		☐☐☐☐☐
b.	Booklet pane of 18, 6 each #3891, 3893, 3 each #3892, 3894	24.50		☐☐☐☐☐
2005 Issues				
3895	Chinese New Year – Types of 1992-2004, double sided pane of 24, 2 each #a-l, dated "2005", self-adhesive, serp. die cut 10¼ .	18.00		☐☐☐☐☐
a.	37c Rat...	.75	.25	☐☐☐☐☐
b.	37c Ox..	.75	.25	☐☐☐☐☐
c.	37c Tiger..	.75	.25	☐☐☐☐☐
d.	37c Rabbit..	.75	.25	☐☐☐☐☐
e.	37c Dragon...	.75	.25	☐☐☐☐☐
f.	37c Snake...	.75	.25	☐☐☐☐☐

Scott No.	Description	Unused Value	Used Value	/ / / / / /
g.	37c Horse	.75	.25	☐☐☐☐☐
h.	37c Ram	.75	.25	☐☐☐☐☐
i.	37c Monkey	.75	.25	☐☐☐☐☐
j.	37c Rooster	.75	.25	☐☐☐☐☐
k.	37c Dog	.75	.25	☐☐☐☐☐
l.	37c Boar	.75	.25	☐☐☐☐☐
m.	As No. 3895, die cutting omitted on "a," "b," and "c" on reverse side	1,250.		☐☐☐☐☐

2005 Issues

Scott No.	Description	Unused Value	Used Value	/ / / / / /
3896	37c Black Heritage Series – Marian Anderson (1897-1903), Singer, self-adhesive	.75	.25	☐☐☐☐☐
3897	37c Ronald Reagan (1911-2004), 40th President, self-adhesive	.75	.25	☐☐☐☐☐
3898	37c Love – Hand and Flower Bouquet, self-adhesive, booklet stamp	.75	.25	☐☐☐☐☐
a.	Booklet pane of 20	15.00		☐☐☐☐☐
3899	Northeast Deciduous Forest – Wildlife, pane of 10, self-adhesive	8.50		☐☐☐☐☐
a.	37c Eastern buckmoth, vert.	.85	.25	☐☐☐☐☐
b.	37c Red-shouldered hawk	.85	.25	☐☐☐☐☐
c.	37c Eastern red bat	.85	.25	☐☐☐☐☐
d.	37c White-tailed deer	.85	.25	☐☐☐☐☐
e.	37c Black bear	.85	.25	☐☐☐☐☐
f.	37c Long-tailed weasel, vert.	.85	.25	☐☐☐☐☐
g.	37c Wild turkey, vert.	.85	.25	☐☐☐☐☐
h.	37c Ovenbird, vert.	.85	.25	☐☐☐☐☐
i.	37c Red eft	.85	.25	☐☐☐☐☐
j.	37c Eastern Chipmunk	.85	.25	☐☐☐☐☐
3900	37c Spring Flowers, Hyacinth, self-adhesive, booklet stamp	.85	.25	☐☐☐☐☐
3901	37c Spring Flowers, Daffodil, self-adhesive, booklet stamp	.85	.25	☐☐☐☐☐
3902	37c Spring Flowers, Tulip, self-adhesive, booklet stamp	.85	.25	☐☐☐☐☐
3903	37c Spring Flowers, Iris, self-adhesive, booklet stamp	.85	.25	
a.	Block of 4, #3900-3903	3.40		☐☐☐☐☐
b.	Booklet pane, 5 each #3900-3903	17.00		☐☐☐☐☐
c.	As "b," die cutting omitted on side with 8 stamps	—		☐☐☐☐☐
3904	37c Literary Arts – Robert Penn Warren (1905-89), Writer, self-adhesive	.75	.25	☐☐☐☐☐
3905	37c Edgar Y. "Yip" Harburg (1896-1981), Lyricist, self-adhesive	.75	.25	☐☐☐☐☐

Scott No.	Description	Unused Value	Used Value	/ / / / / /
3906	37c American Scientists, Barbara McClintock (1902-92), Geneticist, self-adhesive	1.00	.25	☐☐☐☐☐
3907	37c American Scientists, Josiah Willard Gibbs (1839-1903), Thermodynamicist, self-adhesive	1.00	.25	☐☐☐☐☐
3908	37c American Scientists, John von Neumann (1903-57), Mathematician, self-adhesive.....	1.00	.25	☐☐☐☐☐
a.	Vert. pair, die cutting omitted, #3906 and 3908.......................	—		☐☐☐☐☐
3909	37c American Scientists, Richard Feynman (1918-88), Physicist, self-adhesive...............................	1.00	.25	☐☐☐☐☐
a.	Block or horiz. strip of 4, #3906-3909	4.00		☐☐☐☐☐
b.	All colors omitted, tagging omitted, pane of 20....................	—		☐☐☐☐☐
c.	As "a," printing on back of stamps omitted	—		☐☐☐☐☐
d.	Vert. pair, die cutting omitted, #3907 and 3909.......................	—		☐☐☐☐☐
3910	Modern American Architecture, pane of 12, self-adhesive............	11.00		
a.	37c Guggenheim Museum, New York	.90	.25	☐☐☐☐☐
b.	37c Chrysler Building, New York	.90	.25	☐☐☐☐☐
c.	37c Vanna Venturi House, Philadelphia.............................	.90	.25	☐☐☐☐☐
d.	37c TWA Terminal, New York	.90	.25	☐☐☐☐☐
e.	37c Walt Disney Concert Hall, Los Angeles................................	.90	.25	☐☐☐☐☐
f.	37c 860-880 Lake Shore Drive, Chicago	.90	.25	☐☐☐☐☐
g.	37c National Gallery of Art, Washington, DC	.90	.25	☐☐☐☐☐
h.	37c Glass House, New Canaan, CT	.90	.25	☐☐☐☐☐
i.	37c Yale Art and Architecture Building, New Haven, CT..........	.90	.25	☐☐☐☐☐
j.	37c High Museum of Art, Atlanta.......	.90	.25	☐☐☐☐☐
k.	37c Exeter Academy Library, Exeter, NH................................	.90	.25	☐☐☐☐☐
l.	37c Hancock Center, Chicago............	.90	.25	☐☐☐☐☐
m.	As No. 3910, orange yellow omitted	300.00	—	☐☐☐☐☐
3911	37c Legends of Hollywood – Henry Fonda (1905-82), self-adhesive...............................	.90	.25	☐☐☐☐☐

3912

3913

3914

3915

3916

3917

3918

3919

3920

3921

3922

3923

3924

3925

3926

3927

3928

3929

3930

3931

3932

3933

3934

3935

3936

3938

TO FORM A MORE PERFECT UNION

SEEKING EQUAL RIGHTS FOR AFRICAN AMERICANS

"FOR IN A REAL SENSE
AMERICA IS ESSENTIALLY A DREAM...
A DREAM AS YET UNFULFILLED.
IT IS A DREAM OF A LAND WHERE MEN
OF ALL RACES, OF ALL NATIONALITIES
AND OF ALL CREEDS CAN LIVE
TOGETHER AS BROTHERS."

MARTIN LUTHER KING, JR.

3937

3939

3940

3941

3942

Scott No.	Description	Unused Value	Used Value	//////
3912	37c Disney Characters: Pluto, Mickey Mouse, self-adhesive.....	.85	.25	☐☐☐☐☐
3913	37c Disney Characters: Mad Hatter, Alice, self-adhesive	.85	.25	☐☐☐☐☐
3914	37c Disney Characters: Flounder, Ariel, self-adhesive....................	.85	.25	☐☐☐☐☐
3915	37c Disney Characters: Snow White, Dopey, self-adhesive	.85	.25	☐☐☐☐☐
a.	Block or vert. strip of 4 #3812-3815	3.40		☐☐☐☐☐
b.	Die cutting omitted, pane of 20....	—	1,400.	☐☐☐☐☐
c.	Printed on backing paper.............	—		
3916	37c Boeing 247, self-adhesive	.80	.25	☐☐☐☐☐
3917	37c Consolidated PBY Catalina, self-adhesive................................	.80	.25	☐☐☐☐☐
3918	37c Grumman F6F Hellcat, self-adhesive	.80	.25	☐☐☐☐☐
3919	37c Republic P-47 Thunderbolt, self-adhesive	.80	.25	☐☐☐☐☐
3920	37c Engineering and Research Corporation Ercoupe, self-adhesive...............	.80	.25	☐☐☐☐☐
3921	37c Lockheed P-80 Shooting Star, self-adhesive	.80	.25	☐☐☐☐☐
3922	37c Consolidated B-24 Liberator, self-adhesive	.80	.25	☐☐☐☐☐
3923	37c Boeing B-29 Superfortress, self-adhesive	.80	.25	☐☐☐☐☐
3924	37c Beechcraft 35 Bonanza, self-adhesive	.80	.25	☐☐☐☐☐
3925	37c Northrop YB-49 Flying Wing, self-adhesive	.80	.25	☐☐☐☐☐
a.	Block of 10, #3916-3925.............	8.00		☐☐☐☐☐
3926	37c Rio Grande Blankets, self-adhesive, booklet stamp......	.75	.25	☐☐☐☐☐
3927	37c Rio Grande Blankets, self-adhesive, booklet stamp......	.75	.25	☐☐☐☐☐
3928	37c Rio Grande Blankets, self-adhesive, booklet stamp......	.75	.25	☐☐☐☐☐
3929	37c Rio Grande Blankets, self-adhesive, booklet stamp......	.75	.25	☐☐☐☐☐
a.	Block of 4, #3926-3929...............	3.00		☐☐☐☐☐
b.	Booklet pane, 5 each #3900-3903	15.00		☐☐☐☐☐
3930	37c Presidential Libraries Act, 50th Anniv., self-adhesive..........	.80	.25	☐☐☐☐☐
3931	37c Sporty Cars of the 1950s, 1953 Studebaker Starliner, self-adhesive	.90	.25	☐☐☐☐☐
3932	37c Sporty Cars of the 1950s, 1954 Kaiser Darrin, self-adhesive	.90	.25	☐☐☐☐☐

3943

3944

3945

3946

3947

3948

Scott No.		Description	Unused Value	Used Value	/ / / / / /
3933	37c	Sporty Cars of the 1950s, 1953 Chevrolet Corvette, self-adhesive	.90	.25	☐☐☐☐☐
3934	37c	Sporty Cars of the 1950s, 1952 Nash Healey, self-adhesive	.90	.25	☐☐☐☐☐
3935	37c	Sporty Cars of the 1950s, 1955 Ford Thunderbird, self-adhesive .	.90	.25	☐☐☐☐☐
a.	37c	Vert. strip of 5, #3931-3935..........	4.50		☐☐☐☐☐
b.	37c	Booklet pane of 20, #3931-3935 ..	18.00		☐☐☐☐☐
3936	37c	Arthur Ashe (1943-93), Tennis Player, self-adhesive....................	.75	.25	☐☐☐☐☐
3937		To Form A More Perfect Union, pane of 10, self-adhesive	9.00		☐☐☐☐☐
a.	37c	1948 Executive Order 9981 (Training for War, by William H. Johnson)	.90	.25	☐☐☐☐☐
b.	37c	1965 Voting Rights Act (Youths on the Selma March, 1965, photograph by Bruce Davidson)	.90	.25	☐☐☐☐☐
c.	37c	1960 Lunch Counter Sit-ins (National Civil Rights Museum exhibits, by Studio EIS)................................	.90	.25	☐☐☐☐☐
d.	37c	1957 Little Rock Nine (America Cares, by George Hunt)	.90	.25	☐☐☐☐☐
e.	37c	1955 Montgomery Bus Boycott (Walking, by Charles Alston)	.90	.25	☐☐☐☐☐
f.	37c	1961 Freedom Riders (Freedom Riders, by May Stevens).........................	.90	.25	☐☐☐☐☐
g.	37c	1964 Civil Rights Act (Dixie Café, by Jacob Larence)	.90	.25	☐☐☐☐☐
h.	37c	1963 March on Washington (March on Washington, by Alma Thomas)	.90	.25	☐☐☐☐☐
i.	37c	1965 Selma March (Selma March, by Bernice Sims).........................	.90	.25	☐☐☐☐☐
j.	37c	1954 Brown v. Board of Education (The Lamp, by Romare Bearden)	.90	.25	☐☐☐☐☐
3938	37c	Child Health, self-adhesive...........	.75	.25	☐☐☐☐☐
3939	37c	Let's Dance, Merengue, self-adhesive	1.00	.25	☐☐☐☐☐
3940	37c	Let's Dance, Salsa, self-adhesive ..	1.00	.25	☐☐☐☐☐
3941	37c	Let's Dance, Cha Cha Cha, self-adhesive..............................	1.00	.25	☐☐☐☐☐
3942	37c	Let's Dance, Mambo, self-adhesive	1.00	.25	☐☐☐☐☐
a.		Vert. strip of 4	4.00		☐☐☐☐☐
3943	37c	Greta Garbo (1905-90), Actress, self-adhesive..............................	.75	.25	☐☐☐☐☐
3944		Jim Henson and The Muppets, pane of 11, self-adhesive	8.25		☐☐☐☐☐
a.	37c	Kermit the Frog.............................	.75	.25	☐☐☐☐☐
b.	37c	Fozzie Bear....................................	.75	.25	☐☐☐☐☐

3949   3950

3951   3952

3957   3958   3959   3960

3961   3962

3963   3964

Scott No.	Description	Unused Value	Used Value	/ / / / / /
c.	37c Sam the Eagle and flag................	.75	.25	☐☐☐☐☐
d.	37c Miss Piggy....................................	.75	.25	☐☐☐☐☐
e.	37c Statler and Waldorf	.75	.25	☐☐☐☐☐
f.	37c The Swedish Chef and fruit..........	.75	.25	☐☐☐☐☐
g.	37c Animal...	.75	.25	☐☐☐☐☐
h.	37c Dr. Bunsen Honeydew and Beaker	.75	.25	☐☐☐☐☐
i.	37c Rowlf the Dog	.75	.25	☐☐☐☐☐
j.	37c The Great Gonzo and Camilla the Chicken	.75	.25	☐☐☐☐☐
k.	37c Jim Henson....................................	.75	.25	☐☐☐☐☐
3945	37c Constellations, Leo, self-adhesive	.85	.25	☐☐☐☐☐
3946	37c Constellations, Orion, self-adhesive	.85	.25	☐☐☐☐☐
3947	37c Constellations, Lyra, self-adhesive	.85	.25	☐☐☐☐☐
3948	37c Constellations, Pegasus, self-adhesive	.85	.25	☐☐☐☐☐
a.	Block or vert. strip of 4, #3945-3948	3.40		☐☐☐☐☐
b.	As "a," die cutting omitted	—		☐☐☐☐☐
3949	37c Christmas Cookies, Santa Claus, self-adhesive................................	.85	.25	☐☐☐☐☐
3950	37c Christmas Cookies, Snowmen, self-adhesive................................	.85	.25	☐☐☐☐☐
3951	37c Christmas Cookies, Angel, self-adhesive................................	.85	.25	☐☐☐☐☐
3952	37c Christmas Cookies, Elves, self-adhesive................................	.85	.25	☐☐☐☐☐
a.	Block or vert. strip of 4, #3949-3952	3.50		
3953	37c Christmas Cookies, Santa Claus (3949), self-adhesive, booklet stamp, serp. die cut 10¾ x 11 on 2 or 3 sides	1.00	.25	☐☐☐☐☐
3954	37c Christmas Cookies, Snowmen (3950), self-adhesive, booklet stamp, serp. die cut 10¾ x 11 on 2 or 3 sides	1.00	.25	☐☐☐☐☐
3955	37c Christmas Cookies, Angel (3951), self-adhesive, booklet stamp, serp. die cut 10¾ x 11 on 2 or 3 sides	1.00	.25	☐☐☐☐☐
3956	37c Christmas Cookies, Elves (3952), self-adhesive, booklet stamp, serp. die cut 10¾ x 11 on 2 or 3 sides	1.00	.25	☐☐☐☐☐
a.	Block of 4, #3953-3956................	4.00		
b.	Booklet pane of 20, 5 #3956a.......	18.00		☐☐☐☐☐
3957	37c Christmas Cookies, Santa Claus, self-adhesive, booklet stamp, serp. die cut 10½ x 10¾ on 2 or 3 sides............................	1.50	.25	☐☐☐☐☐
3958	37c Christmas Cookies, Snowmen, self-adhesive, booklet stamp, serp. die cut 10½ x 10¾ on 2 or 3 sides	1.50	.25	☐☐☐☐☐

3965

3976

3978

3987

3988

3989

3990

3991

3992

3993

3994

3995

Scott No.	Description	Unused Value	Used Value	/ / / / / /
3959	37c Christmas Cookies, Angel, self-adhesive, booklet stamp, serp. die cut 10½ x 10¾ on 2 or 3 sides	1.50	.25	☐☐☐☐☐
3960	37c Christmas Cookies, Elves, self-adhesive, booklet stamp, serp. die cut 10½ x 10¾ on 2 or 3 sides	1.25	.25	☐☐☐☐☐
a.	Block of 4, #3957-3960...............	5.00		☐☐☐☐☐
b.	Booklet pane of 4, #3957-3960	5.00		☐☐☐☐☐
c.	Booklet pane of 6, #3957-3958, 2 each #3957-3958	7.50		☐☐☐☐☐
d.	Booklet pane of 6, #3957-3958, 2 each #3959-3960......................	7.50		☐☐☐☐☐
3961	37c Distinguished Marines, Lt. Gen. John A. Lejeune (1867-1942), 2nd Infantry Division Insignia, self-adhesive..	1.00	.25	☐☐☐☐☐
3962	37c Distinguished Marines, Lt. Gen. Lewis B. Puller (1898-1971), 1st Marine Division Insignia, self-adhesive..	1.00	.25	☐☐☐☐☐
3963	37c Distinguished Marines, Sgt. John Basilone (1916-45), 5th Marine Division Insignia, self-adhesive..	1.00	.25	☐☐☐☐☐
3964	37c Distinguished Marines, Sgt. Major Daniel J. Daly (1873-1937), 73rd Marine Gun Company, 6th Marine Regiment Insignia, self-adhesive	1.00	.25	☐☐☐☐☐
a.	Block or horiz. strip of 4, #3961-3964	4.00		☐☐☐☐☐
2005-06 Issues				
3965	(39c) Flag and Statue of Liberty, perf. 11¼	.80	.25	☐☐☐☐☐
3966	(39c) Flag and Statue of Liberty (3965), self-adhesive, serp. die cut 11¼ x10¾	.80	.25	☐☐☐☐☐
a.	Booklet pane of 20........................	16.00		☐☐☐☐☐
b.	As "a," die cutting omitted	—		☐☐☐☐☐
3967	(39c) Flag and Statue of Liberty (3965), coil stamp, perf. 9¾ vert.............	.80	.25	☐☐☐☐☐
3968	(39c) Flag and Statue of Liberty (3965), self-adhesive, coil stamp, serp. die cut 8½ vert.	.80	.25	☐☐☐☐☐
3969	(39c) Flag and Statue of Liberty (3965), self-adhesive, coil stamp, serp. die cut 10¼ vert., dated 2006	.90	.25	☐☐☐☐☐
3970	(39c) Flag and Statue of Liberty (3965), self-adhesive, coil stamp, serp. die cut 9½ vert.	1.25	.25	☐☐☐☐☐
3972	(39c) Flag and Statue of Liberty (3965), self-adhesive, booklet stamp, serp. die cut 11¼ x 10¾ on 2 or 3 sides	.80	.25	☐☐☐☐☐
a.	Booklet pane of 20........................	16.00		☐☐☐☐☐

Scott No.	Description	Unused Value	Used Value	/ / / / / /
3973	(39c) Flag and Statue of Liberty (3965), self-adhesive, booklet stamp, serp. die cut 10¼ x 10¾ on 2 or 3 sides	.80	.25	
a.	Booklet pane of 20......................	16.00		
3974	(39c) Flag and Statue of Liberty (3965), self-adhesive, booklet stamp, serp. die cut 11¼ x 10¾ on 2 or 3 sides	.80	.25	
a.	Booklet pane of 4.........................	3.20		
b.	Booklet pane of 6.........................	4.80		
3975	(39c) Flag and Statue of Liberty (3965), self-adhesive, booklet stamp, serp. die cut 8 on 2, 3, or 4 sides	.80	.25	
a.	Booklet pane of 18......................	14.50		
2006 Issues				
3976	(39c)Birds, self-adhesive, booklet stamp, serp. die cut 11 on 2, 3, or 4 sides	1.00	.25	
3978	39c Flag and Statue of Liberty, self-adhesive, serp. die cut 11¼ x 10¾	.85	.25	
a.	Booklet pane of 10......................	8.50		
b.	Booklet pane of 20......................	17.00		
c.	As "b," die cutting omitted on side with 8 stamps	—		
d.	Die cutting omitted, pair	—		
3979	39c Flag and Statue of Liberty (3978), coil stamp, perf. 10 vert.	.80	.25	
3980	39c Flag and Statue of Liberty (3978), self-adhesive, coil stamp, serp. die cut 11 vert., no micro-print...	.80	.25	
3981	39c Flag and Statue of Liberty (3978), self-adhesive, coil stamp, serp. die cut 9½ vert.	.80	.25	
a.	Die cutting omitted, pair	—		
3982	39c Flag and Statue of Liberty (3978), self-adhesive, coil stamp, serp. die cut 10¼ vert.	.80	.25	
a.	Vert. pair, unslit btwn.	—		
3983	39c Flag and Statue of Liberty (3978), self-adhesive, coil stamp, serp. die cut 8½ vert.	.80	.25	
3985	39c Flag and Statue of Liberty (3978), self-adhesive, booklet stamp, serp. die cut 11¼ x 10¾ on 2 or 3 sides, no micro print	.80	.25	
a.	Booklet pane of 20......................	16.00		
b.	Serp. die cut 11.1 on 2 or 3 sides.	.80	.25	
c.	Booklet pane of 4 #3985b.............	3.20		
d.	Booklet pane of 6 #3985b.............	4.80		

Scott No.	Description	Unused Value	Used Value	/ / / / /
3987	39c Children's Book Animals - The Very Hungry Caterpillar, from The Very Hungry Caterpillar, by Eric Carle, self-adhesive..................................	.80	.25	☐☐☐☐☐
3988	39c Children's Book Animals - Wilbur, from Charlotte's Web, by E.B. White, self-adhesive..................................	.80	.25	☐☐☐☐☐
3989	39c Children's Book Animals - Fox in Socks, from Fox in Socks, by Dr. Seuss, self-adhesive	.80	.25	☐☐☐☐☐
3990	39c Children's Book Animals - Maisy, from Maisy's ABC, by Lucy Cousins, self-adhesive..................................	.80	.25	☐☐☐☐☐
3991	39c Children's Book Animals - Wild Thing, from Where the Wild Things Are, by Maurice Sendak, self-adhesive...	.80	.25	☐☐☐☐☐
3992	39c Children's Book Animals - Curious George, from Curious George, by Margaret and H.A. Rey, self-adhesive	.80	.25	☐☐☐☐☐
3993	39c Children's Book Animals - Olivia, from Olivia, by Ian Falconer, self-adhesive	.80	.25	☐☐☐☐☐
3994	39c Children's Book Animals - Frederick, from Frederick, by Leo Lionni, self-adhesive..................................	.80	.25	☐☐☐☐☐
a.	Block of 8, #3987-3994	6.50		☐☐☐☐☐
3995	39c 2005 Winter Olympics, Turin, Italy, self-adhesive......................	.80	.25	☐☐☐☐☐
3996	39c Black Heritage Series - Hattie McDaniel (1895-1952), Actress, self-adhesive................................	3.20		☐☐☐☐☐
✓3997	Chinese New Year - Types of 1992-2004, pane of 12, self-adhesive..	12.00		☐☐☐☐☐
a.	39c Rat	1.00	.25	☐☐☐☐☐
b.	39c Ox	1.00	.25	☐☐☐☐☐
c.	39c Tiger	1.00	.25	☐☐☐☐☐
d.	39c Rabbit	1.00	.25	☐☐☐☐☐
e.	39c Dragon	1.00	.25	☐☐☐☐☐
f.	39c Snake	1.00	.25	☐☐☐☐☐
g.	39c Horse	1.00	.25	☐☐☐☐☐
h.	39c Ram	1.00	.25	☐☐☐☐☐
i.	39c Monkey	1.00	.25	☐☐☐☐☐
j.	39c Rooster	1.00	.25	☐☐☐☐☐
k.	39c Dog	1.00	.25	☐☐☐☐☐
l.	39c Boar	1.00	.25	☐☐☐☐☐
3998	39c Wedding Doves, Dove Facing Left, self-adhesive, booklet stamp.......	.80	.25	☐☐☐☐☐
a.	Booklet pane of 20	16.00		☐☐☐☐☐
b.	As "a," die cutting omitted	—		☐☐☐☐☐

3997

3996 3998 3999

4000 4003 4004

4005 4006 4007

Scott No.		Description	Unused Value	Used Value	/ / / / / /
3999	63c	Wedding Doves, Dove Facing Right, self-adhesive, booklet stamp.......	1.40	.50	☐☐☐☐☐
a.		Booklet pane, 20 each #3998-3999	45.00		☐☐☐☐☐
b.		Horiz. pair, #3998-3999 with vert. gutter btwn.	2.25	1.00	☐☐☐☐☐
4000	24c	Common Buckeye Butterfly	.50	.25	☐☐☐☐☐
4001	24c	Common Buckeye Butterfly (4000), self-adhesive, serp. die cut 11	.55	.25	☐☐☐☐☐
a.		Booklet stamp, serp. die cut 10¾ x 11¼ on 3 sides....................................	.50	.25	☐☐☐☐☐
b.		Booklet pane of 10 #4001a...........	5.00		☐☐☐☐☐
c.		Booklet pane of 4 #4001a............	2.00		☐☐☐☐☐
d.		Booklet pane of 6 #4001a............	3.00		☐☐☐☐☐
4002	24c	Common Buckeye Butterfly (4000), self-adhesive, coil stamp, serp. die cut 8½ horiz.	.50	.25	☐☐☐☐☐
4003	39c	Crops of the Americas - Chili Peppers, self-adhesive, coil stamp, serp. die cut 10¼ horiz.	.85	.25	☐☐☐☐☐
4004	39c	Crops of the Americas - Beans, self-adhesive, coil stamp, serp. die cut 10¼ horiz.	.85	.25	☐☐☐☐☐
4005	39c	Crops of the Americas - Sunflower and Seeds, self-adhesive, coil stamp, serp. die cut 10¼ horiz.	.85	.25	☐☐☐☐☐
4006	39c	Crops of the Americas - Squashes, self-adhesive, coil stamp, serp. die cut 10¼ horiz.	.85	.25	☐☐☐☐☐
4007	39c	Crops of the Americas - Corn, self-adhesive, coil stamp, serp. die cut 10¼ horiz.	.85	.25	☐☐☐☐☐
a.		Strip of 5, #4003-4007	4.25		☐☐☐☐☐
4008	39c	Crops of the Americas - Corn (4007), self-adhesive, booklet stamp, serp. die cut 10¾ x 10¼	.90	.25	☐☐☐☐☐
4009	39c	Crops of the Americas - Squash (4006), self-adhesive, booklet stamp, serp. die cut 10¾ x 10¼	1.00	.25	☐☐☐☐☐
4010	39c	Crops of the Americas - Sunflower and Seeds (4005), self-adhesive, booklet stamp, serp. die cut 10¾ x 10¼ .	1.00	.25	☐☐☐☐☐
4011	39c	Crops of the Americas - Beans (4004), self-adhesive, booklet stamp, serp. die cut 10¾ x 10¼	1.00	.25	☐☐☐☐☐
4012	39c	Crops of the Americas - Chili Peppers (4003), self-adhesive, booklet stamp, serp. die cut 10¾ x 10¼	1.00	.25	☐☐☐☐☐
a.		Horiz. strip of 5, #4008-4012	5.00		☐☐☐☐☐

4018

4019

4020

4021

4022

4023

4024

4025

4026

4027

4028

Scott No.	Description	Unused Value	Used Value	/ / / / /
b.	Booklet pane, 4 each #4008-4012	20.00		☐☐☐☐☐
4013	39c Crops of the Americas - Chili Peppers (4003), self-adhesive, booklet stamp, serp. die cut 10¾ x 11¼	1.00	.25	☐☐☐☐☐
4014	39c Crops of the Americas - Corn (4007), self-adhesive, booklet stamp, serp. die cut 10¾ x 11¼	1.00	.25	☐☐☐☐☐
4015	39c Crops of the Americas - Squash (4006), self-adhesive, booklet stamp, serp. die cut 10¾ x 11¼	1.00	.25	☐☐☐☐☐
4016	39c Crops of the Americas - Sunflower and Seeds (4005), self-adhesive, booklet stamp, serp. die cut 10¾ x 11¼	1.00	.25	☐☐☐☐☐
a.	Booklet pane of 4, #4013-4016	1.00		☐☐☐☐☐
4017	39c Crops of the Americas - Beans (4004), booklet stamp, serp. die cut 10¾ x 11¼	1.00	.25	☐☐☐☐☐
a.	Horiz. strip of 5, #4013-4017	5.00		☐☐☐☐☐
b.	Booklet pane of 4, #4013-4015, 4017	4.00		☐☐☐☐☐
c.	Booklet pane of 6, #4013-4016, 2 #40174	6.00		☐☐☐☐☐
d.	Booklet pane of 6, #4013-4015, 4017, 2 #4016..	6.00		☐☐☐☐☐
4018	$4.05 X-Planes, self-adhesive..............	8.00	5.00	☐☐☐☐☐
a.	Silver foil ("X") omitted..............	—		☐☐☐☐☐
4019	$14.40 X-Planes, self-adhesive	27.50	15.00	☐☐☐☐☐
4020	39c Sugar Ray Robinson (1921-89), Boxer, self-adhesive	.80	.25	☐☐☐☐☐
4021	39c Benjamin Franklin (1706-90), Statesman, self-adhesive.............	1.25	.25	☐☐☐☐☐
4022	39c Benjamin Franklin (1706-90), Scientist, self-adhesive.............	1.25	.25	☐☐☐☐☐
4023	39c Benjamin Franklin (1706-90), Printer, self-adhesive...................	1.25	.25	☐☐☐☐☐
4024	39c Benjamin Franklin (1706-90), Postmaster, self-adhesive	1.25	.25	☐☐☐☐☐
a.	Block or horiz. strip of 4..............	5.00		☐☐☐☐☐
4025	39c Disney Characters: Mickey and Minnie Mouse, self-adhesive......	.80	.25	☐☐☐☐☐
4026	39c Disney Characters: Cinderella and Prince Charming, self-adhesive..	.80	.25	☐☐☐☐☐
4027	39c Disney Characters: Beauty and the Beast, self-adhesive.................	.80	.25	☐☐☐☐☐
4028	39c Disney Characters: Lady and Tramp, self-adhesive................................	.80	.25	☐☐☐☐☐
a.	Block or vert. strip of 4, #4025-4028	3.20		☐☐☐☐☐
4029	39c Birds, self-adhesive, booklet stamp, serp. die cut 11...........................	.95	.25	☐☐☐☐☐

4029

4030

4031

4073

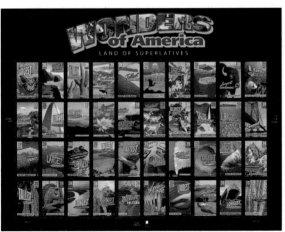

4072a

Scott No.	Description	Unused Value	Used Value	/ / / / / /
a.	Booklet pane of 20.........................	19.00		☐☐☐☐☐
4030	39c Literary Arts, Katherine Anne Porter (1890-1980), Author, self-adhesive	.80	.25	☐☐☐☐☐
4031	39c Amber Alert, Mother and Child, self-adhesive...............................	.80	.25	☐☐☐☐☐
4032	39c Purple Heart Type of 2003 (3784), self-adhesive...............................	.80	.25	☐☐☐☐☐
4033	39c Wonders of America, American alligator, largest reptile, self-adhesive	.80	.45	☐☐☐☐☐
4034	39c Wonders of America, Moloka'I, highest sea cliffs, self-adhesive ..	.80	.45	☐☐☐☐☐
4035	39c Wonders of America, Saguaro, tallest cactus, self-adhesive	.80	.45	☐☐☐☐☐
4036	39c Wonders of America, Bering Glacier, largest glacier, self-adhesive......	.80	.45	☐☐☐☐☐
4037	39c Wonders of America, Great Sand Dunes, tallest dunes, self-adhesive	.80	.45	☐☐☐☐☐
4038	39c Wonders of America, Chesapeake Bay, largest estuary, self-adhesive	.80	.45	☐☐☐☐☐
4039	39c Wonders of America, Cliff Palace, largest cliff dwelling, self-adhesive	.80	.45	☐☐☐☐☐
4040	39c Wonders of America, Crater Lake, deepest lake, self-adhesive..........	.80	.45	☐☐☐☐☐
4041	39c Wonders of America, American bison, largest land mammal, self-adhesive	.80	.45	☐☐☐☐☐
4042	39c Wonders of America, Off the Florida Keys, longest reef, self-adhesive	.80	.45	☐☐☐☐☐
4043	39c Wonders of America, Pacific Crest Trail, longest hiking trail, self-adhesive......................................	.80	.45	☐☐☐☐☐
4044	39c Wonders of America, Gateway Arch, tallest man-made monument, self-adhesive...............................	.80	.45	☐☐☐☐☐
4045	39c Wonders of America, Appalachians, oldest mountains, self-adhesive..	.80	.45	☐☐☐☐☐
4046	39c Wonders of America, American lotus, largest flower, self-adhesive........	.80	.45	☐☐☐☐☐
4047	39c Wonders of America, Lake Superior, largest lake, self-adhesive..........	.80	.45	☐☐☐☐☐
4048	39c Wonders of America, Pronghorn, fastest land animal, self-adhesive	.80	.45	☐☐☐☐☐
4049	39c Wonders of America, Bristlecone pines, oldest trees, self-adhesive	.80	.45	☐☐☐☐☐
4050	39c Wonders of America, Yosemite Falls, tallest waterfall, self-adhesive	.80	.45	☐☐☐☐☐
4051	39c Wonders of America, Great Basin, largest desert, self-adhesive........	.80	.45	☐☐☐☐☐

4074

4075

4076

384

Scott No.	Description	Unused Value	Used Value	/ / / / / /
4052	39c Wonders of America, Verrazano-Narrows Bridge, longest span, self-adhesive..............................	.80	.45	☐☐☐☐☐
4053	39c Wonders of America, Mount Washington, windiest place, self-adhesive..............................	.80	.45	☐☐☐☐☐
4054	39c Wonders of America, Grand Canyon, largest canyon, self-adhesive	.80	.45	☐☐☐☐☐
4055	39c Wonders of America, American bullfrog, largest frog, self-adhesive	.80	.45	☐☐☐☐☐
4056	39c Wonders of America, Oroville Dam, tallest dam, self-adhesive...........	.80	.45	☐☐☐☐☐
4057	39c Wonders of America, Peregrine falcon, fastest bird, self-adhesive...........	.80	.45	☐☐☐☐☐
4058	39c Wonders of America, Mississippi River Delta, largest delta, self-adhesive	.80	.45	☐☐☐☐☐
4059	39c Wonders of America, Steamboat, tallest geyser, self-adhesive	.80	.45	☐☐☐☐☐
4060	39c Wonders of America, Rainbow Bridge, largest natural bridge, self-adhesive	.80	.45	☐☐☐☐☐
4061	39c Wonders of America, White sturgeon, largest freshwater fish, self-adhesive	.80	.45	☐☐☐☐☐
4062	39c Wonders of America, Rocky Mountains, longest mountain chain, self-adhesive	.80	.45	☐☐☐☐☐
4063	39c Wonders of America, Coast redwoods, tallest trees, self-adhesive	.80	.45	☐☐☐☐☐
4064	39c Wonders of America, American beaver, largest rodent, self-adhesive	.80	.45	☐☐☐☐☐
4065	39c Wonders of America, Mississippi-Missouri, longest river system, self-adhesive..............................	.80	.45	☐☐☐☐☐
4066	39c Wonders of America, Mount Wai'ale'ale, rainiest spot, self-adhesive..........	.80	.45	☐☐☐☐☐
4067	39c Wonders of America, Kilauea, most active volcano, self-adhesive	.80	.45	☐☐☐☐☐
4068	39c Wonders of America, Mammoth Cave, longest cave, self-adhesive...........	.80	.45	☐☐☐☐☐
4069	39c Wonders of America, Blue whale, loudest animal, self-adhesive......	.80	.45	☐☐☐☐☐
4070	39c Wonders of America, Death Valley, hottest spot, self-adhesive...........	.80	.45	☐☐☐☐☐
4071	39c Wonders of America, Cornish-Windsor Bridge, longest covered bridge, self-adhesive..............................	.80	.45	☐☐☐☐☐
4072	39c Wonders of America, Quaking aspen, largest plant, self-adhesive..........	.80	.45	☐☐☐☐☐
a.	Pane of 40, #4033-4072................	32.00		☐☐☐☐☐

4077

4080

4081

4082

4083

4084

Scott No.	Description	Unused Value	Used Value	/ / / / / /
4073	39c Exploration of East Coast By Samuel De Champlain, 400th Anniv., Ship and Map, self-adhesive, serp. die cut 10¾	.85	.25	☐☐☐☐☐
4074	39c Exploration of East Coast By Samuel De Champlain, 400th Anniv., Ship and Map, Souvenir Sheet, 2 each #4074a, Canada #2156a	8.50	2.00	☐☐☐☐☐
a.	Sheet single, USA, perf. 11	2.00	.25	☐☐☐☐☐
4075	Washington 2006 World Philatelic Exhibition, Souvenir Sheet, pane of 3	16.00	6.00	☐☐☐☐☐
a.	1.00 Reproduction of 1922 issue, Scott 571	2.00	.50	☐☐☐☐☐
b.	2.00 Reproduction of 1922 issue, Scott 572	4.00	1.00	☐☐☐☐☐
c.	5.00 Reproduction of 1922 issue, Scott 573	10.00	2.50	☐☐☐☐☐
4076	Distinguished American Diplomats, Souvenir Sheet, self-adhesive, pane of 6	6.00		☐☐☐☐☐
a.	39c Robett D. Murphy (1894-1978)	1.00	.25	☐☐☐☐☐
b.	39c Frances E. Willis (1899-1983)	1.00	.25	☐☐☐☐☐
c.	39c Hiram Bingham IV (1903-88)	1.00	.25	☐☐☐☐☐
d.	39c Philip C. Habib (1920-92)	1.00	.25	☐☐☐☐☐
e.	39c Charles E. Bohlen (1904-74)	1.00	.25	☐☐☐☐☐
f.	39c Clifton R. Wharton, Sr. (1899-1990)	1.00	.25	☐☐☐☐☐
4077	39c Legends of Hollywood – Judy Garland (1922-69), self-adhesive	1.00	.25	☐☐☐☐☐
a.	Pair, die cutting omitted	—		☐☐☐☐☐
4078	39c Ronald Reagan Type of 2005 (3897), self-adhesive	.80	.25	☐☐☐☐☐
4079	39c Happy Birthday Type of 2002 (3558), self-adhesive	.80	.25	☐☐☐☐☐
4080	39c Baseball Sluggers, Roy Campanella (1921-93), self-adhesive	.80	.25	☐☐☐☐☐
4081	39c Baseball Sluggers, Hank Greenberg (1911-86), self-adhesive	.80	.25	☐☐☐☐☐
4082	39c Baseball Sluggers, Mel Ott (1909-58), self-adhesive	.80	.25	☐☐☐☐☐
4083	39c Baseball Sluggers, Mickey Mantle (1931-95), self-adhesive	.80	.25	☐☐☐☐☐
a.	Block or vert. strip of 4, #4080-4083	3.20		☐☐☐☐☐
4084	D.C. Comics Superheroes, pane of 20, self-adhesive	16.00		☐☐☐☐☐
a.	39c Superman	.80	.25	☐☐☐☐☐
b.	39c Green Lantern	.80	.25	☐☐☐☐☐
c.	39c Wonder Woman	.80	.25	☐☐☐☐☐
d.	39c Green Arrow	.80	.25	☐☐☐☐☐
e.	39c Batman	.80	.25	☐☐☐☐☐
f.	39c The Flash	.80	.25	☐☐☐☐☐

4085

4086

4087

4088

4089

4090

4091

4092

4093

4094

4095

4096

4097

4098

Scott No.	Description	Unused Value	Used Value	/ / / / / /
g.	39c Plastic Man..................................	.80	.25	
h.	39c Aquaman	.80	.25	
i.	39c Supergirl......................................	.80	.25	
j.	39c Hawkman......................................	.80	.25	
k.	39c Cover of Superman #11	.80	.25	
l.	39c Cover of Green Lantern #4...........	.80	.25	
m.	39c Cover of Wonder Woman #22, Second Series...........................	.80	.25	
n.	39c Cover of Green Arrow #15	.80	.25	
o.	39c Cover of Batman #1	.80	.25	
p.	39c Cover of The Flash #111..............	.80	.25	
q.	39c Cover of Plastic Man #4	.80	.25	
r.	39c Cover of Aquaman #5, of 5	.80	.25	
s.	39c Cover of The Daring New Adventures of Supergirl #1	.80	.25	
t.	39c Cover of The Brave and the Bold Presents Hawkman #36	.80	.25	
u.	As #4084, all inscriptions omitted on reverse	—		
4085	39c Motorcycles - 1940 Indian Four, self-adhesive....................................	1.00	.25	
4086	39c Motorcycles - 1918 Cleveland, self-adhesive..............................	1.00	.25	
4087	39c Motorcycles - Generic "Chopper", c.1970, self-adhesive..................	1.00	.25	
4088	39c Motorcycles - 1965 Harley-Davidson Electra-Glide, self-adhesive........	1.00	.25	
a.	Block or horiz. strip of 4, #4085-4088	4.00		
4089	39c American Treasures Series, Quilts - Housetop Variation, By Mary Lee Bendolph, self-adhesive.............	1.00	.25	
4090	39c American Treasures Series, Quilts - Pig In A Pen Medallion, By Minnie Sue Coleman, self-adhesive.........	1.00	.25	
4091	39c American Treasures Series, Quilts - Nine Patch, By Ruth P. Mosely, self-adhesive................................	1.00	.25	
4092	39c American Treasures Series, Quilts - Housetop Four Block Half Log Cabin Variation, By Lottie Mooney, self-adhesive................................	1.00	.25	
4093	39c American Treasures Series, Quilts - Roman Stripes Variation, By Loretta Pettway, self-adhesive	1.00	.25	
4094	39c American Treasures Series, Quilts - Chinese Coins Variation, By Arlonzia Pettway, self-adhesive..	1.00	.25	

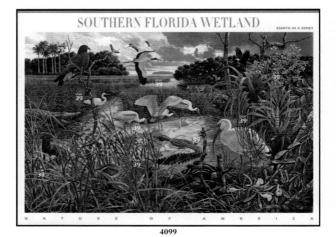

4099

4100

4101

4102

4103

4104

4120

4121

4122

390

Scott No.	Description	Unused Value	Used Value	/ / / / / /
4095	39c American Treasures Series, Quilts - Blocks And Strips, By Annie Mae Young, self-adhesive	1.00	.25	☐☐☐☐☐
4096	39c American Treasures Series, Quilts - Medallion, By Loretta Pettway, self-adhesive	1.00	.25	☐☐☐☐☐
4097	39c American Treasures Series, Quilts - Bars And String-Pieced Columns, By Jessie T. Pettway, self-adhesive	1.00	.25	☐☐☐☐☐
4098	39c American Treasures Series, Quilts - Medallion With Checkerboard Center, by Patty Ann Williams, self-adhesive	1.00	.25	☐☐☐☐☐
a.	Block of 10, #4089-4098	10.00		☐☐☐☐☐
b.	Booklet pane of 20, 2 each #4089-4098	20.00		☐☐☐☐☐
4099	Southern Florida Wetland, Wildlife, pane of 10, self-adhesive	9.00		☐☐☐☐☐
a.	39c Snail Kite	.90	.25	☐☐☐☐☐
b.	39c Wood Storks	.90	.25	☐☐☐☐☐
c.	39c Florida Panther	.90	.25	☐☐☐☐☐
d.	39c Bald Eagle	.90	.25	☐☐☐☐☐
e.	39c American Crocodile	.90	.25	☐☐☐☐☐
f.	39c Roseate Spoonbills	.90	.25	☐☐☐☐☐
g.	39c Everglades Mink	.90	.25	☐☐☐☐☐
h.	39c Cape Sable Seaside Sparrow	.90	.25	☐☐☐☐☐
i.	39c American Alligator	.90	.25	☐☐☐☐☐
j.	39c White Ibis	.90	.25	☐☐☐☐☐
4100	39c Christmas, Madonna and Child with Bird, by Ignacio Chacon, self-adhesive, booklet stamp	.80	.25	☐☐☐☐☐
a.	Booklet pane of 20	16.00		☐☐☐☐☐
4101	39c Christmas - Snowflake, self-adhesive, booklet stamp, serp. die cut 11¼ x 11, base of denomination higher than year date	.90	.25	☐☐☐☐☐
4102	39c Christmas - Snowflake, self-adhesive, booklet stamp, serp. die cut 11¼ x 11, base of denomination higher than year date	.90	.25	☐☐☐☐☐
4103	39c Christmas - Snowflake, self-adhesive, booklet stamp, serp. die cut 11¼ x 11, base of denomination higher than year date	.90	.25	☐☐☐☐☐
4104	39c Christmas - Snowflake, self-adhesive, booklet stamp, serp. die cut 11¼ x 11, base of denomination higher than year date	.90	.25	☐☐☐☐☐
a.	Block or vert. strip of 4, # 4101-4104	3.60		☐☐☐☐☐

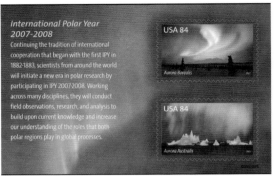

4123

4124   **4125**   **4129**

4136

Scott No.	Description	Unused Value	Used Value	/ / / / / /
4105	39c Christmas - Snowflake (4101), self-adhesive, booklet stamp, serp. die cut 11¼ x 11½ on 2 or 3 sides, base of denomination even with year date	.80	.25	☐☐☐☐☐
4106	39c Christmas - Snowflake (4102), self-adhesive, booklet stamp, serp. die cut 11¼ x 11½ on 2 or 3 sides, base of denomination even with year date	.80	.25	☐☐☐☐☐
4107	39c Christmas - Snowflake (4103), self-adhesive, booklet stamp, serp. die cut 11¼ x 11½ on 2 or 3 sides, base of denomination even with year date	.80	.25	☐☐☐☐☐
4108	39c Christmas - Snowflake (4104), self-adhesive, booklet stamp, serp. die cut 11¼ x 11½ on 2 or 3 sides, base of denomination even with year date	.80	.25	☐☐☐☐☐
a.	Block of 4, # 4105-4108..............	3.20		☐☐☐☐☐
b.	Booklet pane of 20, 5 #4108a.......	16.00		☐☐☐☐☐
4109	39c Christmas - Snowflake (4101), self-adhesive, booklet stamp, serp. die cut 11¼ x 11 on 2 or 3 sides, base of denomination even with year date	1.00	.25	☐☐☐☐☐
4110	39c Christmas - Snowflake (4102), self-adhesive, booklet stamp, serp. die cut 11¼ x 11 on 2 or 3 sides, base of denomination even with year date	1.00	.25	☐☐☐☐☐
4111	39c Christmas - Snowflake (4103), self-adhesive, booklet stamp, serp. die cut 11¼ x 11 on 2 or 3 sides, base of denomination even with year date	1.00	.25	☐☐☐☐☐
4112	39c Christmas - Snowflake (4104), self-adhesive, booklet stamp, serp. die cut 11¼ x 11 on 2 or 3 sides, base of denomination even with year date	1.00	.25	☐☐☐☐☐
a.	Block of 4, # 4109-4112..............	4.00		☐☐☐☐☐
b.	Booklet pane of 4, # 4109-4112...	4.00		☐☐☐☐☐
c.	Booklet pane of 6, # 4111-4112, 2 each # 4109-4110	6.00		☐☐☐☐☐
d.	Booklet pane of 6, # 4109-4110, 2 each # 4111-4112	6.00		☐☐☐☐☐
4113	39c Christmas - Snowflake (4101), self-adhesive, booklet stamp, serp. die cut 8 on 2, 3 or 4 sides	1.20	.25	☐☐☐☐☐
4114	39c Christmas - Snowflake (4102), self-adhesive, booklet stamp, serp. die cut 8 on 2, 3 or 4 sides	1.20	.25	☐☐☐☐☐
4115	39c Christmas - Snowflake (4103), self-adhesive, booklet stamp, serp. die cut 8 on 2, 3 or 4 sides	1.20	.25	☐☐☐☐☐

Scott No.	Description	Unused Value	Used Value	/ / / / / /
4116	39c Christmas - Snowflake (4104), self-adhesive, booklet stamp, serp. die cut 8 on 2, 3 or 4 sides	1.20	.25	☐☐☐☐☐
a.	Block of 4, # 4113-4116...............	4.40		☐☐☐☐☐
b.	Booklet pane of 18, 4 each # 4114, 4116, 5 each # 4113, 4115	22.00		☐☐☐☐☐
4117	39c Eid Type of 2001 (3532), self-adhesive	.80	.25	☐☐☐☐☐
4118	39c Hanukkah Type of 2004 (3880), self-adhesive..............................	.80	.25	☐☐☐☐☐
a.	Die cutting omitted, pane of 20	—		☐☐☐☐☐
4119	39c Kwanzaa Type of 2004 (3881), self-adhesive..............................	.80	.25	☐☐☐☐☐

2007 Issues

Scott No.	Description	Unused Value	Used Value	/ / / / / /
4120	39c Black Heritage Series - Ella Fitzgerald (1917-96), Singer, self-adhesive.	.80	.25	☐☐☐☐☐
4121	39c Oklahoma Statehood, self-adhesive	.80	.25	☐☐☐☐☐
4122	39c Love - Hershey's Kiss, self-adhesive, booklet stamp, serp. die cut 10¾ x 11 on 2, 3 or 4 sides..........................	.80	.25	☐☐☐☐☐
a.	Booklet pane of 20......................	16.00		☐☐☐☐☐
4123	International Polar Year, souvenir sheet, pane of 2, self-adhesive	4.00		☐☐☐☐☐
a.	84c International Polar Year - Aurora Borealis	2.00	.50	☐☐☐☐☐
b.	84c International Polar Year - Aurora Australis	2.00	.50	☐☐☐☐☐
4124	39c Literary Arts - Henry Wadsworth Longfellow (1807-82), Poet, self-adhesive..............................	.80	.25	☐☐☐☐☐
4125	(41c) Forever Stamp - Liberty Bell, self-adhesive, booklet stamp, serp. die cut 11¼ x 10¾ on 2 or 3 sides, large microprinting, bell 16mm wide, dated 2007	.90	.25	☐☐☐☐☐
a.	Booklet pane of 20......................	18.00		☐☐☐☐☐
b.	(42c) Dated 2008	.90	.25	☐☐☐☐☐
c.	Booklet pane of 20 #4125b	18.00		☐☐☐☐☐
d.	As "c," copper ("FOREVER") omitted	—		☐☐☐☐☐
e.	As "c," copper ("FOREVER") omitted on side with 12 stamps, copper splatters on side with 8 stamps	—		☐☐☐☐☐
f.	(44c) Dated 2009	.90	.25	☐☐☐☐☐
g.	Booklet pane of 20 #4125f............	18.00		☐☐☐☐☐
h.	As No. 4125, copper ("FOREVER") omitted, on cover........................	—		☐☐☐☐☐
i.	As No. 4125, die cutting missing (from perforation shift)..............	—		☐☐☐☐☐

Scott No.	Description	Unused Value	Used Value	/ / / / / /
4126	(41c) Forever Stamp - Liberty Bell (4125), self-adhesive, booklet stamp, serp. die cut 11¼ x 10¾ on 2 or 3 sides, small microprinting, bell 16mm wide, dated 2007	.90	.25	
a.	Booklet pane of 20	18.00		
b.	(42c) Dated 2008	.90	.25	
c.	Booklet pane of 20 #4126b	18.00		
d.	(44c) Dated 2009 in copper	.90	.25	
e.	Booklet pane of 20 #4126d	18.00		
f.	As "b," copper ("FOREVER") omitted	—		
4127	(41c) Forever Stamp - Liberty Bell (4125), self-adhesive, booklet stamp, serp. die cut 11¼ x 10¾ on 2 or 3 sides, medium microprinting, bell 15mm wide	.90	.25	
a.	Booklet pane of 20	18.00		
b.	Booklet pane of 4	3.60		
c.	Booklet pane of 6	5.50		
d.	(42c) Dated "2008"	.90	.25	
e.	Booklet pane of 20, #4127d	18.00		
f.	(42c) Dated 2008, date in smaller type	.85	.25	
g.	Booklet pane of 4 #4127f	3.40		
h.	Booklet pane of 6 #4127f	5.10		
i.	(44c) Dated 2009 in copper	.90	.25	
j.	Booklet pane of 20 #4127i	18.00		
k.	As "i," die cutting omitted, pair	—		
l.	As No 4127, copper ("FOREVER") and "USA FIRST-CLASS" missing (from perf. shift)	—		
m.	As "e," die cutting omitted	—		
4128	(41c) Forever Stamp - Liberty Bell (4125), self-adhesive, booklet stamps, serp. die cut 8 on 2, 3 or 4 sides, large microprinting, bell 16mm wide, dated 2007	.85	.25	
a.	Booklet pane of 18	15.50		
b.	(42c) Dated 2009	.85	.25	
c.	Booklet pane of 18 #4128b	15.50		
4129	41c Flag, perf. 11¼	.90	.40	
4130	41c Flag (4129), self-adhesive, serp. die cut 11¼ x 10¾	.90	.25	
4131	41c Flag (4129), coil stamp, perf. 9¾ vert.	.90	.40	
4132	41c Flag (4129), self-adhesive, coil stamp, serp. die cut 9½ Vert., with perpendicular corners	.90	.25	
4133	41c Flag (4129), self-adhesive, coil stamp, serp. die cut 11 vert.	.90	.25	
a.	Die cutting omitted, pair	—		

4137

4138

4143

Scott No.	Description	Unused Value	Used Value	/ / / / / /
4134	41c Flag (4129), self-adhesive, coil stamp, serp. die cut 8½ vert.	.90	.25	☐☐☐☐☐
4135	41c Flag (4129), self-adhesive, coil stamp, serp. die cut 11 vert., with rounded corners	.90	.75	☐☐☐☐☐
4136	41c Settlement of Jamestown, self-adhesive	1.10	.25	☐☐☐☐☐
4137	26c Wildlife - Florida Panther, perf. 11¼ x 11	.60	.25	☐☐☐☐☐
4138	17c Wildlife - Bighorn Sheep, self-adhesive, serp. die cut 11	.35	.25	☐☐☐☐☐
4139	26c Wildlife - Florida Panther (4137), self-adhesive, serp. die cut 11¼ x 11	.55	.25	☐☐☐☐☐
4140	17c Wildlife - Bighorn Sheep (4138), self-adhesive, coil stamp, serpentine die cut 11 vert.	.35	.25	☐☐☐☐☐
4141	26c Wildlife - Florida Panther (4137), self-adhesive, coil stamp, serp. die cut 11 vert.	.55	.25	☐☐☐☐☐
a.	Die cutting omitted, pair	—		☐☐☐☐☐
4142	26c Wildlife - Florida Panther (4137), self-adhesive, booklet stamp, serp. die cut 11¼ x 11 on 3 sides........	.55	.25	☐☐☐☐☐
a.	Booklet pane of 10........................	5.50		☐☐☐☐☐
4143	Premiere of Movie "Star Wars," 30th Anniv., pane of 15, self-adhesive	13.00		☐☐☐☐☐
a.	41c Darth Vader	.85	.25	☐☐☐☐☐
b.	41c Millennium Falcon......................	.85	.25	☐☐☐☐☐
c.	41c Emperor Palpatine........................	.85	.25	☐☐☐☐☐
d.	41c Anakin Skywalker and Obi-Wan Kenobi	.85	.25	☐☐☐☐☐
e.	41c Luke Skywalker............................	.85	.25	☐☐☐☐☐
f.	41c Princess Leia and R2-D2	.85	.25	☐☐☐☐☐
g.	41c C-3PO...	.85	.25	☐☐☐☐☐
h.	41c Queen Padme Amidala	.85	.25	☐☐☐☐☐
i.	41c Obi-Wan Kenobi	.85	.25	☐☐☐☐☐
j.	41c Boba Fett	.85	.25	☐☐☐☐☐
k.	41c Darth Maul	.85	.25	☐☐☐☐☐
l.	41c Chewbacca and Han Solo	.85	.25	☐☐☐☐☐
m.	41c X-wing Starfighter.......................	.85	.25	☐☐☐☐☐
n.	41c Yoda...	.85	.25	☐☐☐☐☐
o.	41c Stormtroopers.............................	.85	.25	☐☐☐☐☐
4144	$4.60 Air Force One, self-adhesive......	9.25	5.00	☐☐☐☐☐
a.	Black (engr.) omitted	275.00		☐☐☐☐☐
4145	$16.25 Marine One, self-adhesive	27.50	16.00	☐☐☐☐☐
4146	41c Pacific Lighthouses - Diamond Head Lighthouse, Hawaii, self-adhesive	1.20	.25	☐☐☐☐☐
4147	41c Pacific Lighthouses - Five Finger Lighthouse, Alaska, self-adhesive	1.20	.25	☐☐☐☐☐

4144

4145

4146

4147

4148

4149

4150

4151

4152

4153

4154

4155

4156

4157

4159

4160

4161

4162

4163

LOUIS COMFORT TIFFANY

4165

USA 41

4166

USA 41

4167

USA 41

4168

USA 41

4169

USA 41

4170

USA 41

4171

USA 41

4172

USA 41

4173

USA 41

4174

USA 41

4175

41 USA

4186

41 USA

4192

41 USA

4193

4196

41 USA

4194

41 USA

4195

James Stewart

USA 41

4197

Scott No.	Description	Unused Value	Used Value	/ / / / / /
4148	41c Pacific Lighthouses - Grays Harbor Lighthouse, Washington, self-adhesive	1.20	.25	☐☐☐☐☐
4149	41c Pacific Lighthouses - Umpqua River Lighthouse, Oregon, self-adhesive	1.20	.25	☐☐☐☐☐
4150	41c Pacific Lighthouses - St. George Reef Lighthouse, California, self-adhesive..............................	1.20	.25	☐☐☐☐☐
a.	Horiz, Strip of 5, #4146-4150	6.00		☐☐☐☐☐
4151	41c Wedding Heart, self-adhesive, booklet stamp.............................	1.00	.25	☐☐☐☐☐
a.	Booklet pane of 20........................	20.00		☐☐☐☐☐
4152	58c Wedding Heart, self-adhesive	1.25	.25	☐☐☐☐☐
4153	41c Pollination - Purple Nightshade, Morrison's Bumblebee, Type I, self-adhesive, booklet stamp	.85	.25	☐☐☐☐☐
a.	Type II, bee at right straight edge.	.85	.25	☐☐☐☐☐
4154	41c Pollination - Hummingbird Trumpet, Calliope Hummingbird, Type I, self-adhesive, booklet stamp	.85	.25	☐☐☐☐☐
a.	Type II, bird at left straight edge ..	.85	.25	☐☐☐☐☐
4155	41c Pollination - Saguaro, Lesser Long-nosed Bat, Type I, self-adhesive, booklet stamp	.85	.25	☐☐☐☐☐
a.	Type II, bat at right straight edge..	.85	.25	☐☐☐☐☐
4156	41c Pollination - Prairie Ironweed, Southern Dogface Butterfly, Type I, self-adhesive, booklet stamp.............................	.85	.25	☐☐☐☐☐
a.	Type II, butterfly at left straight edge	.85	.25	☐☐☐☐☐
b.	Block of 4, #4153-4156...............	3.40		☐☐☐☐☐
c.	Block of 4, #4153a-4156a	3.40		☐☐☐☐☐
d.	Booklet pane of 20, 3 each #4153-4156, 2 each #4153a-4156a	17.00		☐☐☐☐☐
4157	(10c) Patriotic Banner, self-adhesive, coil stamp, serp. die cut 11 vert., photo.	.25	.25	☐☐☐☐☐
4158	(10c) Patriotic Banner (4157), self-adhesive, coil stamp, serp. die cut 11¾ vert., litho.	.25	.25	☐☐☐☐☐
4159	Marvel Comics Superheroes, pane of 20, self-adhesive	17.00		☐☐☐☐☐
a.	41c Spider-Man....................................	.85	.25	☐☐☐☐☐
b.	41c The Hulk.......................................	.85	.25	☐☐☐☐☐
c.	41c Sub-Mariner	.85	.25	☐☐☐☐☐
d.	41c The Thing	.85	.25	☐☐☐☐☐
e.	41c Captain America............................	.85	.25	☐☐☐☐☐
f.	41c Silver Surfer	.85	.25	☐☐☐☐☐
g.	41c Spider-Woman..............................	.85	.25	☐☐☐☐☐
h.	41c Iron Man.......................................	.85	.25	☐☐☐☐☐
i.	41c Elektra	.85	.25	☐☐☐☐☐
j.	41c Wolverine	.85	.25	☐☐☐☐☐

Scott No.	Description	Unused Value	Used Value	/ / / / / /
k.	41c Cover of The Amazing Spider-Man #1	.85	.25	
l.	41c Cover of The Incredible Hulk #1..	.85	.25	
m.	41c Cover of Sub-Mariner #1.............	.85	.25	
n.	41c Cover of The Fantastic Four #3	.85	.25	
o.	41c Cover of Captain America #100...	.85	.25	
p.	41c Cover of The Silver Surfer #1.......	.85	.25	
q.	41c Cover of Marvel Spotlight on The Spider-Woman #32..............	.85	.25	
r.	41c Cover of Iron Man #1	.85	.25	
s.	41c Cover of Daredevil #176 Featuring Elektra........................	.85	.25	
t.	41c Cover of The X-Men #1...............	.85	.25	
4160	41c Vintage Mahogany Speedboats - 1915 Hutchinson, self-adhesive .	.85	.25	
4161	41c Vintage Mahogany Speedboats - 1954 Chris-Craft, self-adhesive..	.85	.25	
4162	41c Vintage Mahogany Speedboats - 1939 Hacker-Craft, self-adhesive	.85	.25	
4163	41c Vintage Mahogany Speedboats - 1931 Gar Wood, self-adhesive....	.85	.25	
a.	Horiz. strip of 4, #4160-4163	3.40		
4164	41c Purple Heart Type of 2003 (3784), self-adhesive.................................	.85	.25	
4165	41c American Treasures Series - Magnolia & Irises, Stained Glass by Louis Comfort Tiffany, self-adhesive, booklet stamp	.85	.25	
a.	Booklet pane of 20........................	17.00		
4166	41c Flowers - Iris, self-adhesive, coil stamp	.85	.25	
4167	41c Flowers - Dahlia, self-adhesive, coil stamp....................................	1.50	.25	
4168	41c Flowers - Magnolia, self-adhesive, coil stamp....................................	1.50	.25	
4169	41c Flowers - Red Gerbera Daisy, self-adhesive, coil stamp.............	1.50	.25	
4170	41c Flowers - Coneflower, self-adhesive, coil stamp....................................	1.50	.25	
4171	41c Flowers - Tulip, self-adhesive, coil stamp....................................	1.50	.25	
4172	41c Flowers - Water Lily, self-adhesive, coil stamp....................................	1.50	.25	
4173	41c Flowers - Poppy, self-adhesive, coil stamp....................................	1.50	.25	
4174	41c Flowers - Chrysanthemum, self-adhesive, coil stamp.............	1.50	.25	
4175	41c Flowers - Orange Gerbera Daisy, self-adhesive, coil stamp.............	1.50	.25	
a.	Strip of 10, #4166-4175...............	15.00		

Scott No.	Description	Unused Value	Used Value	/ / / / / /
4176	41c Flowers - Chrysanthemum (4174), self-adhesive, booklet stamp, serp. die cut 11¼ x 11½ on 2 or 3 sides	.85	.25	☐☐☐☐☐
4177	41c Flowers - Orange Gerbera Daisy (4175), self-adhesive, booklet stamp, serp. die cut 11¼ x 11½ on 2 or 3 sides	.85	.25	☐☐☐☐☐
4178	41c Flowers - Iris (4166), self-adhesive, booklet stamp, serp. die cut 11¼ x 11½ on 2 or 3 sides	.85	.25	☐☐☐☐☐
4179	41c Flowers - Dahlia (4167), self-adhesive, booklet stamp, serp. die cut 11¼ x 11½ on 2 or 3 sides	.85	.25	☐☐☐☐☐
4180	41c Flowers - Magnolia (4168), self-adhesive, booklet stamp, serp. die cut 11¼ x 11½ on 2 or 3 sides............	.85	.25	☐☐☐☐☐
4181	41c Flowers - Red Gerbera Daisy (4169), self-adhesive, booklet stamp, serp. die cut 11¼ x 11½ on 2 or 3 sides	.85	.25	☐☐☐☐☐
4182	41c Flowers - Water Lily (4172), self-adhesive, booklet stamp, serp. die cut 11¼ x 11½ on 2 or 3 sides............	.85	.25	☐☐☐☐☐
4183	41c Flowers - Poppy (4173), self-adhesive, booklet stamp, serp. die cut 11¼ x 11½ on 2 or 3 sides............	.85	.25	☐☐☐☐☐
4184	41c Flowers - Coneflower (4170), self-adhesive, booklet stamp, serp. die cut 11¼ x 11½ on 2 or 3 sides............	.85	.25	☐☐☐☐☐
4185	41c Flowers - Tulip (4171), self-adhesive, booklet stamp, serp. die cut 11¼ x 11½ on 2 or 3 sides	.85	.25	☐☐☐☐☐
a.	Booklet pane of 20, 2 each #4176-4185	17.00		☐☐☐☐☐
b.	As "a," die cutting missing on Nos. 4178 & 4183 on side with 8 stamps (from perforation shift)...............	—		☐☐☐☐☐
4186	41c Flag, self-adhesive, coil stamp, serp. die cut 9½ vert., with "USPS" microprinted on right side of flagpole	.85	.25	☐☐☐☐☐
4187	41c Flag (4186), self-adhesive, coil stamp, serp. die cut 11 vert., with "USPS" microprinted on left side of flagpole	.85	.25	☐☐☐☐☐
4188	41c Flag (4186), self-adhesive, coil stamp, serp. die cut 8½ vert.	.85	.25	☐☐☐☐☐
4189	41c Flag (4186), self-adhesive, coil stamp, serp. die cut 11 vert., with rounded corners	.85	.25	☐☐☐☐☐
4190	41c Flag (4186), self-adhesive, booklet stamp, serp. die cut 11¼ x 10¾ on 2 or 3 sides, with "USPS" mircoprinted on right side of flagpole	.85	.25	☐☐☐☐☐

4198

4199

4200

4201

4203

4204

4205

4206

Scott No.	Description	Unused Value	Used Value	/ / / / / /
a.	Booklet pane of 10........................	8.50		
4191	41c Flag (4186), self-adhesive, booklet stamp, serp. die cut 11¼ x 10¾ on 2 or 3 sides, with "USPS" microprinted on left side of flagpole..............	.85	.25	
a.	Booklet pane of 20........................	17.00		
4192	41c Disney Characters - Mickey Mouse, self-adhesive..............................	.85	.25	
4193	41c Disney Characters - Peter Pan and Tinker Bell, self-adhesive...........	.85	.25	
4194	41c Disney Characters - Dumbo and Timothy Mouse, self-adhesive....	.85	.25	
4195	41c Disney Characters - Aladdin and Genie, self-adhesive..................	.85	.25	
a.	Block of 4, #4192-4195...............	3.40		
4196	41c Celebrate, self-adhesive	.85	.25	
4197	41c Legends of Hollywood – James Stewart (1908-97), self-adhesive	.85	.25	
4198	Alpine Tundra - Wildlife, pane of 10, self-adhesive...............................	8.50		
a.	41c Elk...	.85	.25	
b.	41c Golden eagle.................................	.85	.25	
c.	41c Yellow-bellied marmot..................	.85	.25	
d.	41c American pika	.85	.25	
e.	41c Bighorn sheep	.85	.25	
f.	41c Magdalena alpine butterfly...........	.85	.25	
g.	41c White-tailed ptarmigan..................	.85	.25	
h.	41c Rocky Mountain parnassian butterfly	.85	.25	
i.	41c Melissa arctic butterfly	.85	.25	
j.	41c Brown-capped rosy-finch	.85	.25	
4199	41c Gerald R. Ford (1913-2006), 38th President, self-adhesive	.85	.25	
4200	41c Jury Duty - Twelve Jurors, self-adhesive	.85	.25	
4201	41c Mendez vs. Westminster, 60th Anniv., self-adhesive...............................	.85	.25	
4202	41c Eid Type of 2001 (3532), self-adhesive	.90	.25	
4203	41c Auroras - Aurora Borealis, self-adhesive	1.25	.25	
4204	41c Auroras - Aurora Australis, self-adhesive	1.25	.25	
a.	Horiz. or vert. pair, #4203-4204...	2.50		
4205	41c Yoda, self-adhesive........................	.85	.25	
4206	41c Christmas - Madonna of the Carnation, by Bernardino Luini, self-adhesive, booklet stamp..............................	.85	.25	
a.	Booklet pane of 20........................	17.00		
4207	41c Christmas - Knit Reindeer, self-adhesive, serp. die cut 10¾........................	.85	.25	

4207

4208

4209

4210

4221

4222

4223

4224

4225

4226

4227

4228

4229

4230

4231

Scott No.	Description	Unused Value	Used Value	/ / / / / /
4208	41c Christmas - Knit Christmas Tree, self-adhesive, serp. die cut 10¾ .	.85	.25	☐☐☐☐☐
4209	41c Christmas - Knit Snowman, self-adhesive, serp. die cut 10¾ .	.85	.25	☐☐☐☐☐
4210	41c Christmas - Knit Bear, self-adhesive, serp. die cut 10¾........................	.85	.25	☐☐☐☐☐
b.	Block or vert. strip of 4, #4207-4210	3.40		☐☐☐☐☐
4211	41c Christmas - Knit Reindeer (4207), self-adhesive, booklet stamp, serp. die cut 11¼ x 11 on 2 or 3 sides	.85	.25	☐☐☐☐☐
4212	41c Christmas - Knit Christmas Tree (4208), self-adhesive, booklet stamp, serp. die cut 11¼ x 11 on 2 or 3 sides	.85	.25	☐☐☐☐☐
4213	41c Christmas - Knit Snowman (4209), self-adhesive, booklet stamp, serp. die cut 11¼ x 11 on 2 or 3 sides	.85	.25	☐☐☐☐☐
4214	41c Christmas - Knit Bear (4210), self-adhesive, booklet stamp, serp. die cut 11¼ x 11 on 2 or 3 sides	.85	.25	☐☐☐☐☐
a.	Block of 4, #4211-4214................	3.40		☐☐☐☐☐
b.	Booklet pane of 4, #4211-4214	3.40		☐☐☐☐☐
c.	Booklet pane of 6, #4213-4214, 2 each #4211-4212	5.10		☐☐☐☐☐
d.	Booklet pane of 6, #4211-4212, 2 each #4213-4214	5.10		☐☐☐☐☐
4215	41c Christmas - Knit Reindeer (4207), self-adhesive, booklet stamp, serp. die cut 8 on 2, 3 or 4 sides	.90	.25	☐☐☐☐☐
4216	41c Christmas - Knit Christmas Tree (4208), self-adhesive, booklet stamp, serp. die cut 8 on 2, 3 or 4 sides	.90	.25	☐☐☐☐☐
4217	41c Christmas - Knit Snowman (4209), self-adhesive, booklet stamp, serp. die cut 8 on 2, 3 or 4 sides	.90	.25	☐☐☐☐☐
4218	41c Christmas - Knit Bear (4210), self-adhesive, booklet stamp, serp. die cut 8 on 2, 3 or 4 sides	.90	.25	☐☐☐☐☐
a.	Block of 4, #4215-4218................	3.60		☐☐☐☐☐
b.	Booklet pane of 18, 4 each #4215, 4218, 5 each #4216, 4217	17.00		☐☐☐☐☐
4219	41c Hanukkah Type of 2004 (3880), self-adhesive..............................	.85	.25	☐☐☐☐☐
4220	41c Kwanzaa Type of 2004 (3881), self-adhesive..............................	.85	.25	☐☐☐☐☐

2008 Issues

| 4221 | 41c Chinese New Year - Year of the Rat, lanterns, self-adhesive................ | .85 | .25 | ☐☐☐☐☐ |

4248

4249

4250

4251

4252

4253

4254

4255

4256

4257

4265

4266

4267

Scott No.	Description	Unused Value	Used Value	//////
4222	41c Black Heritage Series - Charles W. Chesnutt (1858-1932), Writer, self-adhesive..............................	.85	.25	☐☐☐☐☐
4223	41c Literary Arts Series - Marjorie Kinnan Rawlings (1896-1953), Writer, self-adhesive..............................	.85	.25	☐☐☐☐☐
4224	41c American Scientists - Gerty Cori (1896-1957), Biochemist, self-adhesive..............................	1.00	.30	☐☐☐☐☐
4225	41c American Scientists - Linus Pauling (1901-94), Structural Chemist, self-adhesive..............................	1.00	.30	☐☐☐☐☐
4226	41c American Scientists - Edwin Hubble (1889-1953), Astronomer, self-adhesive..............................	1.00	.30	☐☐☐☐☐
4227	41c American Scientists - John Bardeen (1908-91), Theoretical Physicist, self-adhesive..............................	1.00	.30	☐☐☐☐☐
a.	Horiz. strip of 4, #4224-4227	4.00		☐☐☐☐☐
4228	42c Flag at Dusk, coil stamp	1.25	.40	☐☐☐☐☐
4229	42c Flag at Night, coil stamp	1.25	.40	☐☐☐☐☐
4230	42c Flag at Dawn, coil stamp	1.25	.40	☐☐☐☐☐
4231	42c Flag at Midday, coil stamp............	1.25	.40	☐☐☐☐☐
a.	Horiz. strip of 4, #4228-4231	5.00	1.60	☐☐☐☐☐
4232	42c Flag at Dusk (4228), self-adhesive, coil stamp, serp. die cut 9½ vert.	1.25	.25	☐☐☐☐☐
4233	42c Flag at Night (4229), self-adhesive, coil stamp, serp. die cut 9½ vert.	1.25	.25	☐☐☐☐☐
4234	42c Flag at Dawn (4230), self-adhesive, coil stamp, serp. die cut 9½ vert.	1.25	.25	☐☐☐☐☐
4235	42c Flag at Midday (4231), self-adhesive, coil stamp, serp. die cut 9½ vert.	1.25	.25	☐☐☐☐☐
a.	Horiz. strip of 4, #4232-4235	5.00		☐☐☐☐☐
4236	42c Flag at Dusk (4228), self-adhesive, coil stamp, serp. die cut 11 vert., with perpendicular corners.........	1.25	.25	☐☐☐☐☐
4237	42c Flag at Night (4229), self-adhesive, coil stamp, serp. die cut 11 vert., with perpendicular corners.........	1.25	.25	☐☐☐☐☐
4238	42c Flag at Dawn (4230), self-adhesive, coil stamp, serp. die cut 11 vert., with perpendicular corners.........	1.25	.25	☐☐☐☐☐
4239	42c Flag at Midday (4231), self-adhesive, coil stamp, serp. die cut 11 vert., with perpendicular corners.........	1.25	.25	☐☐☐☐☐
a.	Horiz. strip of 4, #4236-4239	5.00		☐☐☐☐☐
4240	42c Flag at Dusk (4228), self-adhesive, coil stamp, serp. die cut 8½ vert.	1.25	.25	☐☐☐☐☐

4268

4269

4270

4271

4272

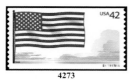

4273

4274

4275

4276

4277

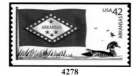

4278

4279

4280

Scott No.	Description	Unused Value	Used Value	/ / / / / /
4241	42c Flag at Night (4229), self-adhesive, coil stamp, serp. die cut 8½ vert.	1.25	.25	☐☐☐☐☐
4242	42c Flag at Dawn (4230), self-adhesive, coil stamp, serp. die cut 8½ vert.	1.25	.25	☐☐☐☐☐
4243	42c Flag at Midday (4231), self-adhesive, coil stamp, serp. die cut 8½ vert.	1.25	.25	☐☐☐☐☐
a.	Horiz. strip of 4, #4240-4243	5.00		☐☐☐☐☐
4244	42c Flag at Dusk (4228), self-adhesive, coil stamp, serp. die cut 11 vert., with rounded corners	1.00	.25	☐☐☐☐☐
4245	42c Flag at Night (4229), self-adhesive, coil stamp, serp. die cut 11 vert., with rounded corners	1.00	.25	☐☐☐☐☐
4246	42c Flag at Dawn (4230), self-adhesive, coil stamp, serp. die cut 11 vert., with rounded corners	1.00	.25	☐☐☐☐☐
4247	42c Flag at Midday (4231), self-adhesive, coil stamp, serp. die cut 11 vert., with rounded corners	1.00	.25	☐☐☐☐☐
a.	Horiz. strip of 4, #4244-4247	5.00		☐☐☐☐☐
4248	42c American Journalists - Martha Gellhorn (1908-98), self-adhesive	1.25	.25	☐☐☐☐☐
4249	42c American Journalists - John Hersey (1914-93), self-adhesive	1.25	.25	☐☐☐☐☐
4250	42c American Journalists - George Polk (1913-48), self-adhesive	1.25	.25	☐☐☐☐☐
4251	42c American Journalists - Ruben Salazar (1928-70), self-adhesive	1.25	.25	☐☐☐☐☐
4252	42c American Journalists - Eric Sevareid (1912-92), self-adhesive	1.25	.25	☐☐☐☐☐
a.	Vert. strip of 5, #4248-4252..........	6.25		☐☐☐☐☐
4253	27c Tropical Fruit - Pomegranate, self-adhesive...............................	.65	.25	☐☐☐☐☐
4254	27c Tropical Fruit - Star Fruit, self-adhesive	.65	.25	☐☐☐☐☐
4255	27c Tropical Fruit - Kiwi, self-adhesive	.65	.25	☐☐☐☐☐
4256	27c Tropical Fruit - Papaya, self-adhesive	.65	.25	☐☐☐☐☐
4257	27c Tropical Fruit - Guava, self-adhesive	.65	.25	☐☐☐☐☐
a.	Horiz. strip of 5, #4253-4257	3.25		☐☐☐☐☐
4258	27c Tropical Fruit - Pomegranate (4253), self-adhesive, coil stamp............	.90	.25	☐☐☐☐☐
4259	27c Tropical Fruit - Star Fruit (4254), self-adhesive, coil stamp............	.90	.25	☐☐☐☐☐
4260	27c Tropical Fruit - Kiwi (4255), self-adhesive, coil stamp............	.90	.25	☐☐☐☐☐
4261	27c Tropical Fruit - Papaya (4256), self-adhesive, coil stamp............	.90	.25	☐☐☐☐☐
4262	27c Tropical Fruit - Guava (4257), self-adhesive, coil stamp............	.90	.25	☐☐☐☐☐

4281

4282

4283

4284

4285

4286

4287

4288

4289

4290

4291

4292

4293

4294

412

Scott No.	Description	Unused Value	Used Value	/ / / / /
a.	Horiz. strip of 5, #4258-4262	4.50		☐☐☐☐☐
b.	As No. 4262, light green ("27 USA", "Kiwi" and year date) omitted ...	—		☐☐☐☐☐
4263	42c Purple Heart Type of 2003 (3784)	.90	.25	☐☐☐☐☐
4264	42c Purple Heart Type of 2003 (3784), self-adhesive.................................	.85	.25	☐☐☐☐☐
4265	42c Frank Sinatra (1915-98), Singer and Actor, self-adhesive	.85	.25	☐☐☐☐☐
4266	42c Minnesota Statehood, 150th Anniv. - Bridge Over Mississippi River, self-adhesive.................................	.85	.25	☐☐☐☐☐
4267	62c Dragonfly, self-adhesive...............	1.25	.25	☐☐☐☐☐
4268	$4.80 American Landmarks - Mount Rushmore, self-adhesive.	9.75	5.00	☐☐☐☐☐
4269	$16.50 American Landmarks - Hoover Dam, self-adhesive.....................	30.00	17.00	☐☐☐☐☐
4270	42c Love - Man carrying heart, self-adhesive, booklet stamp	.85	.25	☐☐☐☐☐
a.	Booklet pane of 20........................	17.00		☐☐☐☐☐
4271	42c Wedding Heart, self-adhesive, booklet stamp.............................	.85	.25	☐☐☐☐☐
a.	Booklet pane of 20........................	17.00		☐☐☐☐☐
4272	59c Wedding Heart, self-adhesive	1.25	.25	☐☐☐☐☐
4273	42c Flags Of Our Nation - American flag and clouds, self-adhesive, coil stamp	.85	.25	☐☐☐☐☐
4274	42c Flags Of Our Nation - Alabama flag and shrimp boat, self-adhesive, coil stamp....................................	.85	.25	☐☐☐☐☐
4275	42c Flags Of Our Nation - Alaska flag and humpback whale, self-adhesive, coil stamp....................................	.85	.25	☐☐☐☐☐
4276	42c Flags Of Our Nation - American Samoa flag and island peaks and trees, self-adhesive, coil stamp.	.85	.25	☐☐☐☐☐
4277	42c Flags Of Our Nation - Arizona flag and saguaro cacti, self-adhesive, coil stamp....................................	.85	.25	☐☐☐☐☐
a.	Strip of 5, #4273-4277	4.25		☐☐☐☐☐
4278	42c Flags Of Our Nation - Arkansas flag and wood duck, self-adhesive, coil stamp....................................	.85	.25	☐☐☐☐☐
4279	42c Flags Of Our Nation - California flag and coast, self-adhesive, coil stamp	.85	.25	☐☐☐☐☐
4280	42c Flags Of Our Nation - Colorado flag and mountain, self-adhesive, coil stamp....................................	.85	.25	☐☐☐☐☐
4281	42c Flags Of Our Nation - Connecticut flag, sailboats and buoy, self-adhesive, coil stamp....................................	.85	.25	☐☐☐☐☐

413

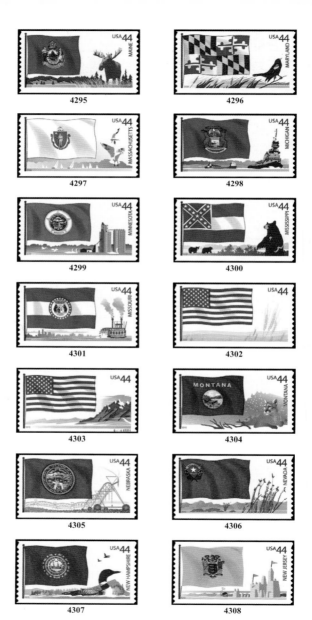

USA44 MAINE

4295

USA44 MARYLAND

4296

USA44 MASSACHUSETTS

4297

USA44 MICHIGAN

4298

USA44 MINNESOTA

4299

USA44 MISSISSIPPI

4300

USA44 MISSOURI

4301

USA44

4302

USA44

4303

USA44 MONTANA

4304

USA44 NEBRASKA

4305

USA44 NEVADA

4306

USA44 NEW HAMPSHIRE

4307

USA44 NEW JERSEY

4308

414

Scott No.	Description	Unused Value	Used Value	/ / / / / /
4282	42c Flags Of Our Nation - Delaware flag and beach, self-adhesive, coil stamp	.85	.25	☐☐☐☐☐
a.	Strip of 5, #4278-4282..................	4.25		☐☐☐☐☐
b.	Plate # set of 10, #4277a + 4282a	8.50		☐☐☐☐☐
4283	42c Flags Of Our Nation - District of Columbia flag and cherry tree, self-adhesive, coil stamp............	.85	.25	☐☐☐☐☐
4284	42c Flags Of Our Nation - Florida flag and anhinga, self-adhesive, coil stamp..................................	.85	.25	☐☐☐☐☐
4285	42c Flags Of Our Nation - Georgia flag, fence and lamppost, self-adhesive, coil stamp..................................	.85	.25	☐☐☐☐☐
4286	42c Flags Of Our Nation - Guam flag, fish and tropicbird, self-adhesive, coil stamp..................................	.85	.25	☐☐☐☐☐
4287	42c Flags Of Our Nation - Hawaii flag and ohia lehua flowers, self-adhesive, coil stamp..................................	.85	.25	☐☐☐☐☐
a.	Strip of 5, #4283-4287..................	4.25		☐☐☐☐☐
4288	42c Flags Of Our Nation - Idaho flag and rainbow trout, self-adhesive, coil stamp..................................	.85	.25	☐☐☐☐☐
4289	42c Flags Of Our Nation - Illinois flag and windmill, self-adhesive, coil stamp..................................	.85	.25	☐☐☐☐☐
4290	42c Flags Of Our Nation - Indiana flag and tractor, self-adhesive, coil stamp	.85	.25	☐☐☐☐☐
4291	42c Flags Of Our Nation - Iowa flag, farm field and cornstalks, self-adhesive, coil stamp............	.85	.25	☐☐☐☐☐
4292	42c Flags Of Our Nation - Kansas flag and farm buildings, self-adhesive, coil stamp..................................	.85	.25	☐☐☐☐☐
a.	Strip of 5, #4288-4292..................	4.25		☐☐☐☐☐
b.	Plate # set of 10, #4287a +4192a .	8.50		☐☐☐☐☐
4293	44c Flags of Our Nation - Kentucky flag, fence and horses, self-adhesive, coil stamp..................................	.90	.25	☐☐☐☐☐
4294	44c Flags of Our Nation - Louisiana flag and brown pelicans, self-adhesive, coil stamp..................................	.90	.25	☐☐☐☐☐
4295	44c Flags of Our Nation - Maine flag and moose, self-adhesive, coil stamp	.90	.25	☐☐☐☐☐
4296	44c Flags of Our Nation - Maryland flag and red-winged blackbird, self-adhesive, coil stamp............	.90	.25	☐☐☐☐☐

4309

4310

4311

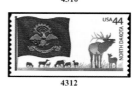

4312

4313

4314

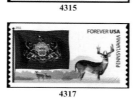

4315

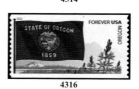

4316

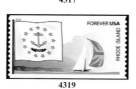

4317

4318

4319

4320

4321

4322

416

Scott No.	Description	Unused Value	Used Value	/ / / / / /
4297	44c Flags of Our Nation - Massachusetts flag, sea birds and sailboats, self-adhesive, coil stamp.....................................	.90	.25	☐☐☐☐☐
a.	Strip of 5, #4293-4297..................	4.50		☐☐☐☐☐
4298	44c Flags of Our Nation - Michigan flag and Great Lakes ships, self-adhesive, coil stamp.....................................	.90	.25	☐☐☐☐☐
4299	44c Flags of Our Nation - Minnesota flag, swans and grain elevator, self-adhesive, coil stamp.....................................	.90	.25	☐☐☐☐☐
4300	44c Flags of Our Nation - Mississippi flag and black bears, self-adhesive, coil stamp.....................................	.90	.25	☐☐☐☐☐
4301	44c Flags of Our Nation - Missouri flag and paddle wheeler, self-adhesive, coil stamp.....................................	.90	.25	☐☐☐☐☐
4302	44c Flags of Our Nation - American flag and wheat, self-adhesive, coil stamp	.90	.25	☐☐☐☐☐
a.	Strip of 5 #4298-4302..................	4.50		☐☐☐☐☐
b.	Plate # set of 10, #4297a + 4302a	9.00		☐☐☐☐☐
4303	44c Flags of Our Nation - American flag and mountains, self-adhesive, coil stamp.....................................	.90	.25	☐☐☐☐☐
4304	44c Flags of Our Nation - Montana flag and mountain lion, self-adhesive, coil stamp.....................................	.90	.25	☐☐☐☐☐
4305	44c Flags of Our Nation - Nebraska flag and central-pivot irrigation system, self-adhesive, coil stamp.............	.90	.25	☐☐☐☐☐
4306	44c Flags of Our Nation - Nevada flag, mountains and ocotillos, self-adhesive, coil stamp.............	.90	.25	☐☐☐☐☐
4307	44c Flags of Our Nation - New Hampshire flag and loon, self-adhesive, coil stamp	.90	.25	☐☐☐☐☐
a.	Strip of 5, #4303-4307..................	4.50		☐☐☐☐☐
4308	44c Flags of Our Nation - New Jersey flag and sand castle, self-adhesive, coil stamp.....................................	.90	.25	☐☐☐☐☐
4309	44c Flags of Our Nation - New Mexico flag, mountains and hot air balloons, self-adhesive, coil stamp.............	.90	.25	☐☐☐☐☐
4310	44c Flags of Our Nation - New York flag, fireboats and city skyline, self-adhesive, coil stamp.....................................	.90	.25	☐☐☐☐☐
4311	44c Flags of Our Nation - North Carolina flag, great blue heron and Cape Hatteras Lighthouse, self-adhesive, coil stamp	.90	.25	☐☐☐☐☐

4333

4334   4336   4337

4338   4339   4340

Scott No.	Description	Unused Value	Used Value	/ / / / /
4312	44c Flags of Our Nation - North Dakota flag and elk, self-adhesive, coil stamp	.90	.25	☐☐☐☐☐
a.	Strip of 5, #4308-4312..................	4.50		☐☐☐☐☐
b.	Plate # set of 10, #4307a + 4312a	9.00		☐☐☐☐☐
4313	(44c)Flags of Our Nation - Northern Marianas flag, beach and palm trees, self-adhesive, coil stamp............	.90	.25	☐☐☐☐☐
4314	(44c) Flags of Our Nation - Ohio flag, butterfly, milkweed flowers and river, self-adhesive, coil stamp............	.90	.25	☐☐☐☐☐
4315	(44c) Flags of Our Nation - Oklahoma flag and oil pumps, self-adhesive, coil stamp....................	.90	.25	☐☐☐☐☐
4316	(44c) Flags of Our Nation - Oregon flag, Mount Hood and camas lilies, self-adhesive, coil stamp............	.90	.25	☐☐☐☐☐
4317	(44c) Flags of Our Nation - Pennsylvania flag and white-tailed deer, self-adhesive, coil stamp............	.90	.25	☐☐☐☐☐
a.	Strip of 5, #4313-4317..................	4.50		☐☐☐☐☐
4318	(44c) Flags of Our Nation - Puerto Rico flag and Puerto Rican tody bird, self-adhesive, coil stamp............	.90	.25	☐☐☐☐☐
4319	(44c) Flags of Our Nation - Rhode Island flag and sailboat, self-adhesive, coil stamp	.90	.25	☐☐☐☐☐
4320	(44c) Flags of Our Nation - South Carolina flag, marsh and gazebo, self-adhesive, coil stamp............	.90	.25	☐☐☐☐☐
4321	(44c) Flags of Our Nation - South Dakota flag and bison, self-adhesive, coil stamp....................	.90	.25	☐☐☐☐☐
4322	(44c) Flags of Our Nation - Tennessee flag and scarlet tanagers, self-adhesive, coil stamp....................	.90	.25	☐☐☐☐☐
a.	Strip of 5, #4318-4322..................	4.50		☐☐☐☐☐
b.	P# set of 10, #4317a + 4322a.......	9.00		☐☐☐☐☐
4333	Charles (1907-78) and Ray (1912-88) Eames, Designers, self-adhesive, pane of 16....................	18.00		☐☐☐☐☐
a.	42c Christmas card depicting Charles and Ray Eames	1.10	.25	☐☐☐☐☐
b.	42c "Crosspatch" fabric design	1.10	.25	☐☐☐☐☐
c.	42c Stacking chairs	1.10	.25	☐☐☐☐☐
d.	42c Case Study House #8, Pacific Palisades, CA	1.10	.25	☐☐☐☐☐
e.	42c Wire-base table.............................	1.10	.25	☐☐☐☐☐
f.	42c Lounge chair and ottoman	1.10	.25	☐☐☐☐☐

4341

4342

4343

4344

4345

4346

4347

4349

4350

Scott No.	Description	Unused Value	Used Value	/ / / / / /
g.	42c Hang-it-all	1.10	.25	☐☐☐☐☐
h.	42c La Chaise..............................	1.10	.25	☐☐☐☐☐
i.	42c Scene from film, "Tops"...........	1.10	.25	☐☐☐☐☐
j.	42c Wire mesh chair	1.10	.25	☐☐☐☐☐
k.	42c Cover of May 1943 edition of California Arts & Architecture magazine..	1.10	.25	☐☐☐☐☐
l.	42c House of Cards.......................	1.10	.25	☐☐☐☐☐
m.	42c Molded plywood sculpture	1.10	.25	☐☐☐☐☐
n.	42c Eames Storage Unit	1.10	.25	☐☐☐☐☐
o.	42c Aluminum group chair................	1.10	.25	☐☐☐☐☐
p.	42c Molded plywood chair	1.10	.25	☐☐☐☐☐
4334	42c Summer Olympic Games, Beijing, China - Gymnast, self-adhesive .	.85	.25	☐☐☐☐☐
4335	42c Celebrate type of 2007 (4196), self-adhesive...................................	.85	.25	☐☐☐☐☐
4336	42c Vintage Black Cinema - Poster for Black and Tan, self-adhesive	.85	.25	☐☐☐☐☐
4337	42c Vintage Black Cinema - Poster for The Sport Of The Gods, self-adhesive...............................	.85	.25	☐☐☐☐☐
4338	42c Vintage Black Cinema - Poster for Prinsesse Tam-Tam, self-adhesive	.85	.25	☐☐☐☐☐
4339	42c Vintage Black Cinema - Poster for Caldonia, self-adhesive...............	.85	.25	☐☐☐☐☐
4340	42c Vintage Black Cinema - Poster for Hallelujah, self-adhesive...........	.85	.25	☐☐☐☐☐
a.	Horiz. strip of 5, #4336-4340	4.25		☐☐☐☐☐
4341	42c Take Me Out To The Ballgame, Centenary, self-adhesive.............	.85	.25	☐☐☐☐☐
4342	42c The Art Of Disney: Imagination - Pongo and Pup, self-adhesive.....	.85	.25	☐☐☐☐☐
4343	42c The Art Of Disney: Imagination - Steamboat Willie, self-adhesive .	.85	.25	☐☐☐☐☐
4344	42c The Art Of Disney: Imagination - Princess Aurora, Flora, Fauna and Merryweather, self-adhesive.......	.85	.25	☐☐☐☐☐
4345	42c The Art Of Disney: Imagination - Mowgli and Baloo, self-adhesive	.85	.25	☐☐☐☐☐
a.	Block of 4, #4342-4345	3.40		☐☐☐☐☐
4346	42c American Treasures Series - Valley of the Yosemite, by Albert Bierstadt, self-adhesive, booklet stamp	.85	.25	☐☐☐☐☐
a.	Booklet pane of 20........................	17.00		☐☐☐☐☐
4347	42c Sunflower, self-adhesive, booklet stamp.............................	.85	.25	☐☐☐☐☐
a.	Booklet pane of 20........................	17.00		☐☐☐☐☐

4352

4353

4354

4355

4356

4357

4358

4359

Scott No.	Description	Unused Value	Used Value	//////
4348	(5c) Sea Coast type of 2002 (3693), coil stamp, perf. 9½ vert............	.25	.25	☐☐☐☐☐
4349	42c Latin Jazz, self-adhesive	.85	.25	☐☐☐☐☐
4350	42c Legends Of Hollywood – Bette Davis (1908-89), self-adhesive	.85	.25	☐☐☐☐☐
4351	42c Eid Type of 2001 (3532), self-adhesive	.85	.25	☐☐☐☐☐
4352	Great Lakes Dunes - Wildlife, pane of 10, self-adhesive	8.50		☐☐☐☐☐
a.	42c Vesper sparrow............................	.85	.25	☐☐☐☐☐
b.	42c Red fox	.85	.25	☐☐☐☐☐
c.	42c Piping plover	.85	.25	☐☐☐☐☐
d.	42c Eastern hognose snake.................	.85	.25	☐☐☐☐☐
e.	42c Common mergansers	.85	.25	☐☐☐☐☐
f.	42c Spotted sandpiper........................	.85	.25	☐☐☐☐☐
g.	42c Tiger beetle.................................	.85	.25	☐☐☐☐☐
h.	42c White-footed mouse.....................	.85	.25	☐☐☐☐☐
i.	42c Piping plover nestlings................	.85	.25	☐☐☐☐☐
j.	42c Red admiral butterfly...................	.85	.25	☐☐☐☐☐
4353	42c Automobiles of the 1950s - 1959 Cadillac Eldorado, self-adhesive	.85	.25	☐☐☐☐☐
4354	42c Automobiles of the 1950s - 1957 Studebaker Golden Hawk, self-adhesive.............................	.85	.25	☐☐☐☐☐
4355	42c Automobiles of the 1950s - 1957 Pontiac Safari, self-adhesive.......	.85	.25	☐☐☐☐☐
4356	42c Automobiles of the 1950s - 1957 Lincoln Premiere, self-adhesive.	.85	.25	☐☐☐☐☐
4357	42c Automobiles Of The 1950s - 1957 Chrysler 300C, self-adhesive	.85	.25	☐☐☐☐☐
a.	Vert. strip of 5, #4353-4357..........	4.25		☐☐☐☐☐
4358	42c Alzheimer's Disease Awareness, self-adhesive...............................	.85	.25	☐☐☐☐☐
4359	42c Christmas - Virgin and Child with the young John the Baptist, by Sandro Botticelli, self-adhesive, booklet stamp............................	.85	.25	☐☐☐☐☐
a.	Booklet pane of 20......................	17.00		☐☐☐☐☐
b.	Die cutting omitted, pair	—		☐☐☐☐☐
4360	42c Christmas - Drummer Nutcracker, self-adhesive, booklet stamp, serp. die cut 10¾ x 11 on 2 or 3 sides	1.00	.25	☐☐☐☐☐
4361	42c Christmas - Santa Claus Nutcracker, self-adhesive, booklet stamp, serp. die cut 10¾ x 11 on 2 or 3 sides	1.00	.25	☐☐☐☐☐
4362	42c Christmas - King Nutcracker, self-adhesive, booklet stamp, serp. die cut 10¾ x 11 on 2 or 3 sides	1.00	.25	☐☐☐☐☐
4363	42c Christmas - Soldier Nutcracker, self-adhesive, booklet stamp, serp. die cut 10¾ x 11 on 2 or 3 sides	1.00	.25	☐☐☐☐☐

4360

4361

4362

4363

4364

4365

4366

4367

4374

4375

4376

4377

4378

4379

Scott No.	Description	Unused Value	Used Value	/ / / / / /
a.	Block of 4, #4360-4363	4.00		☐☐☐☐☐
b.	Booklet pane of 20, 5 each			
	#4360-4363	20.00		☐☐☐☐☐
4364	42c Christmas - Drummer Nutcracker,			
	self-adhesive, booklet stamp, serp.			
	die cut 11¼ x 11 on 2 or 3 sides	1.00	.25	☐☐☐☐☐
4365	42c Christmas - Santa Claus Nutcracker,			
	self-adhesive, booklet stamp, serp.			
	die cut 11¼ x 11 on 2 or 3 sides	1.00	.25	☐☐☐☐☐
4366	42c Christmas - King Nutcracker,			
	self-adhesive, booklet stamp, serp.			
	die cut 11¼ x 11 on 2 or 3 sides	1.00	.25	☐☐☐☐☐
4367	42c Christmas - Soldier Nutcracker,			
	self-adhesive, booklet stamp, serp.			
	die cut 11¼ x 11 on 2 or 3 sides	1.00	.25	☐☐☐☐☐
a.	Block of 4, #4364-4367	4.00		☐☐☐☐☐
b.	Booklet pane of 4, #4364-4367	4.00		☐☐☐☐☐
c.	Booklet pane of 6, #4366-4367,			
	2 each #4364-4365	6.00		☐☐☐☐☐
d.	Booklet pane of 6, #4364-4365,			
	2 each #4366-4367	6.00		☐☐☐☐☐
4368	42c Christmas - Drummer Nutcracker			
	(4364), self-adhesive, booklet stamp,			
	serp. die cut 8 on 2, 3 or 4 sides	1.00	.25	☐☐☐☐☐
4369	42c Christmas - Santa Claus Nutcracker			
	(4365), self-adhesive, booklet stamp,			
	serp. die cut 8 on 2, 3 or 4 sides	1.00	.25	☐☐☐☐☐
4370	42c Christmas - King Nutcracker (4366),			
	self-adhesive, booklet stamp, serp.			
	die cut 8 on 2, 3 or 4 sides	1.00	.25	☐☐☐☐☐
4371	42c Christmas - Soldier Nutcracker (4367),			
	self-adhesive, booklet stamp, serp.			
	die cut 8 on 2, 3 or 4 sides	1.00	.25	☐☐☐☐☐
a.	Block of 4, #4368-4371	4.00		☐☐☐☐☐
b.	Booklet pane of 18, 5 each #4368-4369,			
	4 each #4370-4371	18.00		☐☐☐☐☐
4372	42c Hanukkah type of 2004 (3880),			
	self-adhesive...............................	.85	.25	☐☐☐☐☐
4373	42c Kwanzaa type of 2004 (3881),			
	self-adhesive...............................	.85	.25	☐☐☐☐☐
2009 Issues				
4374	42c Alaska Statehood, self-adhesive ...	.85	.25	☐☐☐☐☐
4375	42c Chinese New Year - Year of the Ox,			
	self-adhesive...............................	.85	.25	☐☐☐☐☐
4376	42c Oregon Statehood, 150th Anniv.,			
	self-adhesive...............................	.85	.25	☐☐☐☐☐
4377	42c Edgar Allan Poe (1809-49), Writer,			
	self-adhesive...............................	.90	.25	☐☐☐☐☐

4380

4381

4382

4383

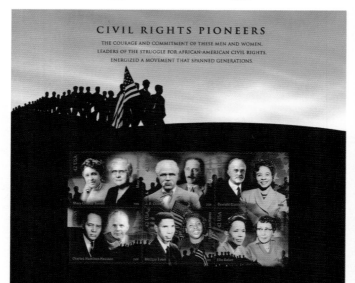
4384

4386

Scott No.	Description	Unused Value	Used Value	//////
4378	$4.95 American Landmarks - Redwood Forest, self-adhesive...	10.00	5.00	☐☐☐☐☐
4379	$17.50 American Landmarks - Old Faithful, self-adhesive..............................	32.50	18.00	☐☐☐☐☐
4380	42c Abraham Lincoln (1809-65), 16th President - Lincoln As Rail-splitter, self-adhesive	1.00	.25	☐☐☐☐☐
4381	42c Abraham Lincoln (1809-65), 16th President - Lincoln As Lawyer, self-adhesive..............................	1.00	.25	☐☐☐☐☐
4382	42c Abraham Lincoln (1809-65), 16th President - Lincoln As Politician, self-adhesive..............................	1.00	.25	☐☐☐☐☐
4383	42c Abraham Lincoln (1809-65), 16th President - Lincoln As President, self-adhesive..............................	1.00	.25	☐☐☐☐☐
a.	Horiz. strip of, #4380-4383	4.00		☐☐☐☐☐
4384	Civil Rights Pioneers, pane of 6, self-adhesive..............................	5.10		☐☐☐☐☐
a.	42c Mary Terrell (1863-1954), writer; Mary White Ovington (1865-1951), journalist.....................................	.85	.25	☐☐☐☐☐
b.	42c J.R. Clifford (1848-1933), attorney; Joel Elias Spingarn (1875-1939), educator.....................................	.85	.25	☐☐☐☐☐
c.	42c Oswald Garrison Villard (1872-1949), co-founder of National Association for the Advancement of Colored People (NAACP); Daisy Gatson Bates (1914-99), mentor of black Little Rock Central High School students..................	.85	.25	☐☐☐☐☐
d.	42c Charles Hamilton Houston (1895-1950), lawyer; Walter White (1893-1955), chief secretary of NAACP..........	.85	.25	☐☐☐☐☐
e.	42c Medgar Evans (1925-63), assassinated Mississippi NAACP field secretary; Fannie Lou Hamer (1917-77), voting rights activist...............................	.85	.25	☐☐☐☐☐
f.	42c Ella Baker (1903-86), activist; Ruby Hurley (1909-80), NAACP southeast regional director..........	.85	.25	☐☐☐☐☐
4385	(10c) Patriotic Banner Type of 2007 (4157), self-adhesive, coil stamp, perf 9¾ vert................................	.25	.25	☐☐☐☐☐
4386	61c Literary Arts - Richard Wright (1908-60), author, self-adhesive	1.25	.25	☐☐☐☐☐
4387	28c Wildlife - Polar Bear, self-adhesive	.60	.25	☐☐☐☐☐
4388	64c Wildlife - Dolphin, self-adhesive..	1.40	.25	☐☐☐☐☐

4387   4388   4389   4391

4397   4398

4399   4400

4401   4402   4403

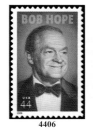

4404   4405   4406   4408

Scott No.	Description	Unused Value	Used Value	/ / / / / /
4389	28c Wildlife - Polar Bear, self-adhesive, coil stamp....................................	.60	.25	☐☐☐☐☐
4390	44c Purple Heart type of 2003 (3784), self-adhesive..............................	.90	.25	☐☐☐☐☐
4391	44c Flag, coil stamp, perf. 9¾ vert......	.90	.75	☐☐☐☐☐
4392	44c Flag, coil stamp (4391), self-adhesive, with pointed corners, serp. die cut 11 vert	1.50	.25	☐☐☐☐☐
a.	Die cutting omitted, pair...............	—		☐☐☐☐☐
4393	44c Flag (4391), coil stamp, self-adhesive, serp. die cut 9½ vert	.90	.25	☐☐☐☐☐
4394	44c Flag (4391), coil stamp, self-adhesive, serp. die cut 8½ vert.....................	.90	.25	☐☐☐☐☐
4395	44c Flag (4391), coil stamp, self-adhesive, with rounded corners, serp. die cut 11 vert	.90	.25	☐☐☐☐☐
4396	44c Flag (4391), booklet stamp, self-adhesive, serp. die cut 11¼ x 10¾ on 3 sides	.90	.25	☐☐☐☐☐
a.	Booklet pane of 10......................	9.00		☐☐☐☐☐
4397	44c Weddings - Wedding Rings, self-adhesive..............................	.90	.25	☐☐☐☐☐
4398	61c Weddings - Wedding Cake, self-adhesive..............................	1.25	.25	☐☐☐☐☐
4399	44c The Simpsons Television Show, 20th Anniv. - Homer Simpson, self-adhesive, booklet stamp	.90	.25	☐☐☐☐☐
4400	44c The Simpsons Television Show, 20th Anniv. - Marge Simpson, self-adhesive, booklet stamp	.90	.25	☐☐☐☐☐
4401	44c The Simpsons Television Show, 20th Anniv. - Bart Simpson, self-adhesive, booklet stamp	.90	.25	☐☐☐☐☐
4402	44c The Simpsons Television Show, 20th Anniv. - Lisa Simpson, self-adhesive, booklet stamp	.90	.25	☐☐☐☐☐
4403	44c The Simpsons Television Show, 20th Anniv. - Maggie Simpson, self-adhesive, booklet stamp	.90	.25	☐☐☐☐☐
a.	Horiz. strip of 5, #4399-4403	4.50		☐☐☐☐☐
b.	Booklet pane of 20, 4 each #4399-4403	18.00		☐☐☐☐☐
4404	44c Love - Kings of Hearts, self-adhesive, booklet stamp..............................	1.00	.25	☐☐☐☐☐
4405	44c Love - Queen of Hearts, self-adhesive, booklet stamp..............................	1.00	.25	☐☐☐☐☐
a.	Horiz. or vert. pair #4404-4405....	2.00		☐☐☐☐☐
b.	Booklet pane of 20, 10 each #4404-4405	20.00		☐☐☐☐☐

4409

4410

4411

4412

4413

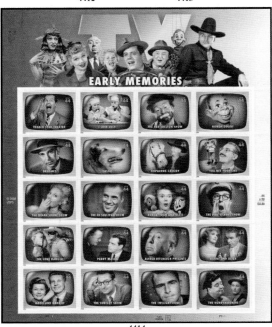

4414

Scott No.	Description	Unused Value	Used Value	/ / / / / /
4406	44c Bob Hope (1903-2003), Actor and Comedian, self-adhesive.............	.90	.25	☐☐☐☐☐
4407	44c Celebrate type of 2007 (4196), self-adhesive.................................	.90	.25	☐☐☐☐☐
a.	Die cutting omitted, pair	275.00		☐☐☐☐☐
4408	44c Black Heritage - Anna Julia Cooper (1858-1964), educator, self-adhesive	.90	.25	☐☐☐☐☐
4409	44c Gulf Coast Lighthouses - Matagorda Island Lighthouse, Texas, self-adhesive	.90	.25	☐☐☐☐☐
4410	44c Gulf Coast Lighthouses - Sabine Pass Lighthouse, Louisiana, self-adhesive	.90	.25	☐☐☐☐☐
4411	44c Gulf Coast Lighthouses - Biloxi Lighthouse, Mississippi, self-adhesive	.90	.25	☐☐☐☐☐
4412	44c Gulf Coast Lighthouses - Sand Island Lighthouse, Alabama, self-adhesive	.90	.25	☐☐☐☐☐
4413	44c Gulf Coast Lighthouses - Fort Jefferson Lighthouse, Florida, self-adhesive	.90	.25	☐☐☐☐☐
a.	Horiz. strip of 5, #4409-4413	4.50		☐☐☐☐☐
4414	Early TV Memories, pane of 20, self-adhesive.................................	20.00		☐☐☐☐☐
a.	44c Milton Berle in Texaco Star Theater.................................	1.00	.25	☐☐☐☐☐
b.	44c Lucille Ball and Vivian Vance In I Love Lucy	1.00	.25	☐☐☐☐☐
c.	44c Red Skelton in The Red Skelton Show	1.00	.25	☐☐☐☐☐
d.	44c Marionette Howdy Doody In Howdy Doody	1.00	.25	☐☐☐☐☐
e.	44c Jack Webb in Dragnet	1.00	.25	☐☐☐☐☐
f.	44c Lassie in Lassie	1.00	.25	☐☐☐☐☐
g.	44c William Boyd and Horse, Topper, in Hopalong Cassidy	1.00	.25	☐☐☐☐☐
h.	44c Groucho Marx in You Bet Your Life	1.00	.25	☐☐☐☐☐
i.	44c Dinah Shore in The Dinah Shore Show	1.00	.25	☐☐☐☐☐
j.	44c Ed Sullivan In The Ed Sullivan Show	1.00	.25	☐☐☐☐☐
k.	44c Fran Allison and Puppets, Kukla and Ollie in Kukla, Fran and Ollie....	1.00	.25	☐☐☐☐☐
l.	44c Phil Silvers In The Phil Silvers Show	1.00	.25	☐☐☐☐☐
m.	44c Clayton Moore and Horse, Silver, In The Lone Ranger...................	1.00	.25	☐☐☐☐☐
n.	44c Raymond Burr and Will Talman in Perry Mason...........................	1.00	.25	☐☐☐☐☐
o.	44c Alfred Hitchcock in Alfred Hitchcock Presents..........	1.00	.25	☐☐☐☐☐
p.	44c George Burns and Gracie Allen In Burns and Allen.....................	1.00	.25	☐☐☐☐☐
q.	44c Ozzie and Harriet Nelson in Ozzie and Harriet	1.00	.25	☐☐☐☐☐

4415

4417

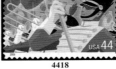
4418

4419

4420

4421

JUSTICES OF THE SUPREME COURT OF THE UNITED STATES

4422

432

Scott No.	Description	Unused Value	Used Value	/ / / / / /
r.	44c Steve Allen In The Tonight Show .	1.00	.25	☐☐☐☐☐
s.	44c Rod Serling in The Twilight Zone	1.00	.25	☐☐☐☐☐
t.	44c Jackie Gleason and Art Carney in The Honeymooners................	1.00	.25	☐☐☐☐☐
4415	44c Hawaii Statehood, 50th Anniv., self-adhesive..............................	1.00	.25	☐☐☐☐☐
4416	44c Eid Type of 2001 (3532), self-adhesive..............................	.90	.25	☐☐☐☐☐
4417	44c Thanksgiving Day Parade - Crowd, Street Sign, Bear Balloon, self-adhesive..............................	.90	.25	☐☐☐☐☐
4418	44c Thanksgiving Day Parade - Drum Major, Musicians, self-adhesive	.90	.25	☐☐☐☐☐
4419	44c Thanksgiving Day Parade - Musicians, Balloon, Horse, self-adhesive.....	.90	.25	☐☐☐☐☐
4420	44c Thanksgiving Day Parade - Cowboy, Turkey Balloon, Crowd, Television Cameraman, self-adhesive............	.90	.25	☐☐☐☐☐
a.	Horiz. strip of 4, #4417-4420	3.60		☐☐☐☐☐
4421	44c Legends of Hollywood – Gary Cooper (1901-61), self-adhesive	1.00	.25	☐☐☐☐☐
4422	Supreme Court Justices, sheet of 4, self-adhesive..............................	3.60		☐☐☐☐☐
a.	44c Felix Frankfurter (1882-1965)......	.90	.25	☐☐☐☐☐
b.	44c William J. Brennan Jr. (1906-97) .	.90	.25	☐☐☐☐☐
c.	44c Louis D. Brandeis (1865-1941)....	.90	.25	☐☐☐☐☐
d.	44c Joseph Story (1779-1845).............	.90	.25	☐☐☐☐☐
4423	Kelp Forest, pane of 10, self-adhesive	9.00		☐☐☐☐☐
a.	44c Brown pelican	.90	.25	☐☐☐☐☐
b.	44c Western gull, southern sea otters, red sea urchin............................	.90	.25	☐☐☐☐☐
c.	44c Harbor seal	.90	.25	☐☐☐☐☐
d.	44c Lion's mane nudibranch...............	.90	.25	☐☐☐☐☐
e.	44c Yellowtail rockfish, white-spotted rose anemone	.90	.25	☐☐☐☐☐
f.	44c Vermilion rockfish	.90	.25	☐☐☐☐☐
g.	44c Copper rockfish............................	.90	.25	☐☐☐☐☐
h.	44c Pacific rock crab, jeweled top snail	.90	.25	☐☐☐☐☐
i.	44c Northern kelp crab	.90	.25	☐☐☐☐☐
j.	44c Treefish, Monterey turban snail, brooding sea anemones	.90	.25	☐☐☐☐☐
4424	44c Christmas - Madonna and Sleeping Child, by Sassoferrato (Giovanni Battista Salvi), self-adhesive, booklet stamp.............................	.90	.25	☐☐☐☐☐
a.	Booklet pane of 20......................	18.00		☐☐☐☐☐
4425	44c Christmas - Reindeer, self-adhesive, booklet stamp, serp. die cut 10¾ x 11 on 2 or 3 sides	.90	.25	☐☐☐☐☐

4423

4424

4425-4428

4429-4432

434

Scott No.	Description	Unused Value	Used Value	/ / / / / /
4426	44c Christmas - Snowman, self-adhesive, booklet stamp, serp. die cut 10¾ x 11 on 2 or 3 sides	.90	.25	☐☐☐☐☐
4427	44c Christmas - Gingerbread Man, self-adhesive, booklet stamp, serp. die cut 10¾ x 11 on 2 or 3 sides	.90	.25	☐☐☐☐☐
4428	44c Christmas - Toy Soldier, self-adhesive, booklet stamp, serp. die cut 10¾ x 11 on 2 or 3 sides............................	.90	.25	☐☐☐☐☐
a.	Block of 4, #4425-4428	3.60		☐☐☐☐☐
b.	Booklet pane of 20, 5 each #4425-4428	18.00		☐☐☐☐☐
c.	As "b," die cutting omitted on side with 12 stamps............................	—		☐☐☐☐☐
d.	As "b," die cutting omitted on side with 8 stamps	—		☐☐☐☐☐
4429	44c Christmas - Reindeer, self-adhesive, booklet stamp, serp. die cut 8 on 2, 3 or 4 sides.............................	1.00	.25	☐☐☐☐☐
4430	44c Christmas - Snowman, self-adhesive, booklet stamp, serp. die cut 8 on 2, 3 or 4 sides........................	1.00	.25	☐☐☐☐☐
4431	44c Christmas - Gingerbread Man, self-adhesive, booklet stamp, serp. die cut 8 on 2, 3 or 4 sides	1.00	.25	☐☐☐☐☐
4432	44c Christmas - Toy Soldier, self-adhesive, booklet stamp, serp. die cut 8 on 2, 3 or 4 sides.............................	1.00	.25	☐☐☐☐☐
a.	Block of 4, #4429-4432	4.00		☐☐☐☐☐
b.	Booklet pane of 18, 5 each #4429, #4431, 4 each #4430, #4432	18.00		☐☐☐☐☐
4433	44c Hanukkah - Menorah, self-adhesive	.90	.25	☐☐☐☐☐
4434	44c Kwanzaa, self-adhesive................	.90	.25	☐☐☐☐☐
2010 Issues				
4435	44c Chinese New Year - Year of the Tiger, self-adhesive..............................	1.10	.25	☐☐☐☐☐
4436	44c 2010 Winter Olympics, Vancouver - Snowboarder, self-adhesive	.90	.25	☐☐☐☐☐
4437	(44c) Forever Liberty Bell Type of 2007 (4125), dated 2009, medium microprinting, Bell 16mm wide, self-adhesive, booklet stamp..............................	.90	.25	☐☐☐☐☐
a.	Booklet pane of 18, #4437............	16.50		☐☐☐☐☐
4438	$4.90 American Landmarks - Mackinac Bridge, self-adhesive	10.00	5.00	☐☐☐☐☐
4439	$18.30 American Landmarks - Bixby Creek Bridge, self-adhesive	35.00	18.00	☐☐☐☐☐

4433

4434

4435

4436

4438

4439

4440-4443

Scott No.	Description	Unused Value	Used Value	/ / / / / /
4440	44c Distinguished Sailors - Admiral William S. Sims (1858-1936), Emblem of USS W.S. Sims, self-adhesive	.90	.25	☐☐☐☐☐
4441	44c Distinguished Sailors - Admiral Arleigh A. Burke (1901-96), Emblem of USS Arleigh Burke, self-adhesive	.90	.25	☐☐☐☐☐
4442	44c Distinguished Sailors - Lieutenant Commander John McCloy (1876-1945), Emblem of USS McCloy, self-adhesive	.90	.25	☐☐☐☐☐
4443	44c Distinguished Sailors - Petty Officer 3rd Class Doris Miller (1919-43), Emblem of USS Miller, self-adhesive	.90	.25	☐☐☐☐☐
a.	Block or horiz. strip of 4, #4440-4443	3.60		☐☐☐☐☐
4444	Abstract Expressionists, pane of 10, self-adhesive..............................	9.00		☐☐☐☐☐
a.	44c The Golden Wall, by Hans Hofmann	.90	.25	
b.	44c Asheville, by Willem de Kooning	.90	.25	
c.	44c Orange and Yellow, by Mark Rothko	.90	.25	
d.	44c Convergence, by Jackson Pollock	.90	.25	
e.	44c The Liver is the Cock's Comb, by Arshile Gorky.........................	.90	.25	☐☐☐☐☐
f.	44c 1948-C, by Clyfford Still	.90	.25	
g.	44c Elegy to the Spanish Republic No. 34, by Robert Motherwell.................	.90	.25	☐☐☐☐☐
h.	44c La Grande Vallee O, by Joan Mitchell	.90	.25	☐☐☐☐☐
i.	44c Romanesque Façade, by Adolph Gottlieb	.90	.25	☐☐☐☐☐
j.	44c Achilles, by Barnett Newman.......	.90	.25	
4445	44c Mauldin and His Characters, Willie and Joe, self-adhesive......	.90	.25	☐☐☐☐☐
4446	44c Cowboys of the Silver Screen - Roy Rogers (1911-98), self-adhesive	1.25	.25	☐☐☐☐☐
4447	44c Cowboys of the Silver Screen - Tom Mix (1880-1940), self-adhesive	1.25	.25	☐☐☐☐☐
4448	44c Cowboys of the Silver Screen - William S. Hart (1864-1946), self-adhesive..............................	1.25	.25	☐☐☐☐☐
4449	44c Cowboys of the Silver Screen - Gene Autry (1907-98), self-adhesive	1.25	.25	☐☐☐☐☐
a.	Block of 4, #4446-4449	5.00		☐☐☐☐☐
4450	44c Love - Pansies In a Basket, self-adhesive..............................	.90	.25	☐☐☐☐☐
4451	44c Animal Rescue - Wire-haired Jack Russell Terrier, self-adhesive	.90	.25	☐☐☐☐☐
4452	44c Animal Rescue - Maltese, self-adhesive	.90	.25	☐☐☐☐☐
4453	44c Animal Rescue - Calico, self-adhesive	.90	.25	
4454	44c Animal Rescue - Yellow Labrador Retriever, self-adhesive..............	.90	.25	☐☐☐☐☐

The function of the artist is to express reality as *felt*. Robert Motherwell

ABSTRACT EXPRESSIONISTS

The abstract expressionists revolutionized art and moved the U.S. to the center of the international art scene during the 1940s and 1950s. Based primarily in New York City, this group of artists with radically different styles created a new visual language based on color, motion, and the expression of universal truths. In the process, they transformed the act of painting into a means of self-discovery, which was both uniquely American and utterly new.

4444

4445

4446-4449

438

4451-4460

4450

4461

4462

4463

4464

4465

4466

4467

4468

4469

4470

4471

4472

4473

4475

4476

4477

Scott No.	Description	Unused Value	Used Value	/ / / / / /
4455	44c Animal Rescue - Golden Retriever, self-adhesive	.90	.25	☐☐☐☐☐
4456	44c Animal Rescue - Gray, White and Tan Cat, self-adhesive	.90	.25	☐☐☐☐☐
4457	44c Animal Rescue - Black, White and Tan Cat, self-adhesive	.90	.25	☐☐☐☐☐
4458	44c Animal Rescue - Australian Shepherd, self-adhesive	.90	.25	☐☐☐☐☐
4459	44c Animal Rescue - Boston Terrier, self-adhesive	.90	.25	☐☐☐☐☐
4460	44c Animal Rescue - Orange Tabby, self-adhesive	.90	.25	☐☐☐☐☐
a.	Block of 10, #4451-4460	9.00		☐☐☐☐☐
4461	44c Legends of Hollywood – Katharine Hepburn (1907-2003), self-adhesive	1.00	.25	☐☐☐☐☐
4462	64c Monarch Butterfly, self-adhesive	1.30	2.00	☐☐☐☐☐
4463	44c Kate Smith (1907-1986), Singer, self-adhesive	.90	.25	☐☐☐☐☐
4464	44c Black Heritage - Oscar Micheaux (1884-1951), Film Director, self-adhesive	.90	.25	☐☐☐☐☐
4465	44c Negro Leagues Baseball - Play at the Plate, self-adhesive	.90	.25	☐☐☐☐☐
4466	44c Negro Leagues Baseball - Andres "Rube" Foster, self-adhesive	.90	.25	☐☐☐☐☐
a.	Horiz. pair, #4465-4466	1.80		☐☐☐☐☐
4467	44c Sunday Funnies - Beetle Bailey, self-adhesive	.90	.25	☐☐☐☐☐
4468	44c Sunday Funnies - Calvin and Hobbes, self-adhesive	.90	.25	☐☐☐☐☐
4469	44c Sunday Funnies - Archie, self-adhesive	.90	.25	☐☐☐☐☐
4470	44c Sunday Funnies - Garfield, self-adhesive	.90	.25	☐☐☐☐☐
4471	44c Sunday Funnies - Dennis the Menace, self-adhesive	.90	.25	☐☐☐☐☐
a.	Horiz. strip of 5, #4467-4471	4.50		☐☐☐☐☐
4472	44c Boy Scouts of America, Centennial, self-adhesive	.90	.25	☐☐☐☐☐
4473	44c American Treasures Series - Boys in a pasture, by Winslow Homer, self-adhesive	.90	.25	☐☐☐☐☐
4474	Hawaiian Rainforest, pane of 10, self-adhesive	9.00		☐☐☐☐☐
a.	44c Hawaii 'amakihi, Hawaii 'elepaio, ohi'a lehua	.90	.25	☐☐☐☐☐
b.	44c Akepa, 'ope'ape'a	.90	.25	☐☐☐☐☐
c.	44c I'iwi, haha	.90	.25	☐☐☐☐☐
d.	44c Oma'o, kanawao, 'ohelo kau la'au	.90	.25	☐☐☐☐☐

4474

4478 4479 4480 4481

4482 4483 4484 4485

4486 4487 4495 4496

Scott No.	Description	Unused Value	Used Value	/ / / / / /
e.	44c Oha...	.90	.25	☐☐☐☐☐
f.	44c Pulelehua butterfly, kolea lau nui, 'ilihia......................	.90	.25	☐☐☐☐☐
g.	44c Koele mountain damselfly, 'akala .	.90	.25	☐☐☐☐☐
h.	44c Apapane, Hawaiian mint	.90	.25	☐☐☐☐☐
i.	44c Jewel orchid	.90	.25	☐☐☐☐☐
j.	44c Happyface spider, 'ala'ala wai nui	.90	.25	☐☐☐☐☐
4475	44c Mother Teresa (1910-97), Humanitarian, self-adhesive	.90	.25	☐☐☐☐☐
4476	44c Literary Arts - Julia de Burgos (1914-53), Poet, self-adhesive	.90	.25	☐☐☐☐☐
4477	44c Christmas - Angel With Lute, by Melozzo da Forli, self-adhesive ..	.90	.25	☐☐☐☐☐
4478	(44c) Christmas - Ponderosa Pine, self-adhesive, booklet stamp, serp. die cut 11 on 2 or 3 sides	.90	.25	☐☐☐☐☐
4479	(44c) Christmas - Eastern Red Cedar, self-adhesive, booklet stamp, serp. die cut 11 on 2 or 3 sides	.90	.25	☐☐☐☐☐
4480	(44c) Christmas - Balsam Fir, self-adhesive, booklet stamp, serp. die cut 11 on 2 or 3 sides	.90	.25	☐☐☐☐☐
4481	(44c) Christmas - Blue Spruce, self-adhesive, booklet stamp, serp. die cut 11 on 2 or 3 sides	.90	.25	☐☐☐☐☐
a.	Block of 4, #4478-4481...............	3.60		☐☐☐☐☐
b.	Booklet pane of 20, 5 each #4478-4481	18.00		☐☐☐☐☐
c.	As "a," die cutting omitted............	—	—	☐☐☐☐☐
d.	As "b," die cutting omitted on side with 12 stamps............................	—		☐☐☐☐☐
e.	As "b," die cutting omitted on side with 8 stamps...............................	—		☐☐☐☐☐
f.	As "b," die cutting omitted on side with 12 stamps, die cutting omitted on bottom 4 stamps on side with 8 stamps	—		☐☐☐☐☐
4482	(44c) Christmas - Ponderosa Pine, self-adhesive, booklet stamp, serp. die cut 11¼ x 10¾ on 2, 3 or 4 sides......	.90	.25	☐☐☐☐☐
4483	(44c) Christmas - Eastern Red Cedar, self-adhesive, booklet stamp, serp. die cut 11¼ x 10¾ on 2, 3 or 4 sides......	.90	.25	☐☐☐☐☐
4484	(44c) Christmas - Balsam Fir, self-adhesive, booklet stamp, serp. die cut 11¼ x 10¾ on 2, 3 or 4 sides......	.90	.25	☐☐☐☐☐
4485	(44c) Christmas - Blue Spruce, self-adhesive, booklet stamp, serp. die cut 11¼ x 10¾ on 2, 3 or 4 sides......	.90	.25	☐☐☐☐☐
a.	Block of 4, #4482-4485...............	3.60		☐☐☐☐☐

4492

4493

4494

4497

4498

4499

4500

4501

4502

4503

4504

4505

4506

4507

4508

4509

444

Scott No.	Description	Unused Value	Used Value	/ / / / / /
b.	Booklet pane of 18, 5 each #4482, 4484, 4 each #4483, 4485	16.50		☐☐☐☐☐
4486	(44c) Statue of Liberty, self-adhesive, coil stamp, serp. die cut 9½ vert.	.90	.25	☐☐☐☐☐
4487	(44c) Flag, self-adhesive, coil stamp, serp. die cut 9½ vert.....................	.90	.25	☐☐☐☐☐
a.	Pair, #4486-4487.............................	1.80		☐☐☐☐☐
4488	(44c) Statue of Liberty (4486), self-adhesive, coil stamp, serp. die cut 11 vert..	.90	.25	☐☐☐☐☐
a.	Vert. pair, horiz. unslit btwn..........	—		☐☐☐☐☐
4489	(44c) Flag (4487), self-adhesive, coil stamp, serp. die cut 11 vert.....................	.90	.25	☐☐☐☐☐
a.	Pair, #4488-4489.............................	1.80		☐☐☐☐☐
4490	(44c) Statue of Liberty (4486), self-adhesive, coil stamp, serp. die cut 8½ vert.	.90	.25	☐☐☐☐☐
4491	(44c) Flag (4487), self-adhesive, coil stamp, serp. die cut 8½ vert...................	.90	.25	☐☐☐☐☐
a.	Pair, #4490-4491.............................	1.80		☐☐☐☐☐
2011 Issues				
4492	(44c) Chinese New Year - Year of the rabbit, self-adhesive	.90	.25	☐☐☐☐☐
4493	(44c) Kansas Statehood, 150th Anniv., self-adhesive	.90	.25	☐☐☐☐☐
4494	(44c) Pres. Ronald Reagan, self-adhesive	.90	.25	☐☐☐☐☐
4495	(5c) Art Deco Bird, self-adhesive, coil stamp....................................	.25	.25	☐☐☐☐☐
4496	44c Quill and Inkwell, self-adhesive, coil stamp....................................	.90	.25	☐☐☐☐☐
4497	(44c) Latin Music Legends - Tito Puente (1923-2000), self-adhesive..........	.90	.25	☐☐☐☐☐
4498	(44c) Latin Music Legends - Carmen Miranda (1909-55), self-adhesive..........	.90	.25	☐☐☐☐☐
4499	(44c) Latin Music Legends - Selena (1971-95), self-adhesive.............	.90	.25	☐☐☐☐☐
4500	(44c) Latin Music Legends - Carlos Gardel (1890-1935), self-adhesive..........	.90	.25	☐☐☐☐☐
4501	(44c) Latin Music Legends - Celia Cruz (1925-2003), self-adhesive..........	.90	.25	☐☐☐☐☐
a.	Horiz. strip of 5, #4497-4501........	4.50		☐☐☐☐☐
4502	(44c) Celebrate, self-adhesive................	.90	.25	☐☐☐☐☐
4503	(44c) Jazz - Musicians, self-adhesive	.90	.25	☐☐☐☐☐
4504	20c George Washington, self-adhesive	.40	.25	☐☐☐☐☐
4505	29c Herbs - Oregano, self-adhesive	.60	.25	☐☐☐☐☐
4506	29c Herbs - Flax, self-adhesive............	.60	.25	☐☐☐☐☐
4507	29c Herbs - Foxglove, self-adhesive	.60	.25	☐☐☐☐☐
4508	29c Herbs - Lavender, self-adhesive	.60	.25	☐☐☐☐☐
4509	29c Herbs - Sage, self-adhesive	.60	.25	☐☐☐☐☐
a.	Horiz. strip of 5, #4505-4509........	3.00		☐☐☐☐☐

4510

4511

4520

4522

4523

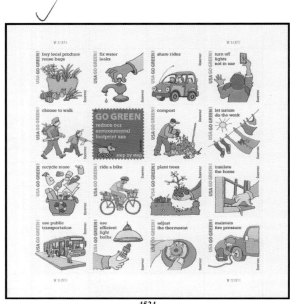

4524

Scott No.	Description	Unused Value	Used Value	/ / / / / /
4510	84c Oveta Culp Hobby (1905-95), self-adhesive	1.75	.35	
4511	$4.95 American Landmarks - New River Gorge Bridge, self-adhesive	10.00	5.00	
4512	20c George Washington (4504), self-adhesive, coil stamp	.40	.25	
4513	29c Herbs - Foxglove (4507), self-adhesive, coil stamp	.60	.25	
4514	29c Herbs - Lavender (4508), self-adhesive, coil stamp	.60	.25	
4515	29c Herbs - Sage (4509), self-adhesive, coil stamp	.60	.25	
4516	29c Herbs - Oregano (4505), self-adhesive, coil stamp	.60	.25	
4517	29c Herbs - Flax (4506), self-adhesive, coil stamp	.60	.25	
a.	Horiz. strip of 5, #4513-4517	3.00		
4518	(44c) Statue of Liberty Type of 2010 (4486), booklet stamp, serp. die cut 11¼ x 10¾ on 2, 3 or 4 sides	.90	.25	
4519	(44c) Flag Type of 2010 (4487), booklet stamp, serp. die cut 11¼ x 10¾ on 2, 3 or 4 sides	.90	.25	
a.	Pair, #4518-4519	1.80		
b.	Booklet pane of 18, 9 each #4518-4519	16.50		
4520	(44c) Wedding Roses, self-adhesive	.90	.25	
a.	Die cutting omitted, pair	—		
4521	64c Wedding Cake Type of 2009 (4398), USA in serifed type, self-adhesive	1.30	.25	
4522	(44c) Civil War Sesquicentennial - Battle of Fort Sumter, self-adhesive	.90	.25	
4523	(44c) Civil War Sesquicentennial - First Battle of Bull Run, self-adhesive	.90	.25	
a.	Pair, #4522-4523	1.80		
	Pane of 12	10.80		
4524	Go Green - Messages, pane of 16, self-adhesive	14.50		
a.	(44c) Buy local produce, reuse bags	.90	.25	
b.	(44c) Fix water leaks	.90	.25	
c.	(44c) Share rides	.90	.25	
d.	(44c) Turn off lights not in use	.90	.25	
e.	(44c) Choose to walk	.90	.25	
f.	(44c) Go Green, reduce our environmental footprint step by step	.90	.25	
g.	(44c) Compost	.90	.25	
h.	(44c) Let nature do the work	.90	.25	
i.	(44c) Recycle more	.90	.25	

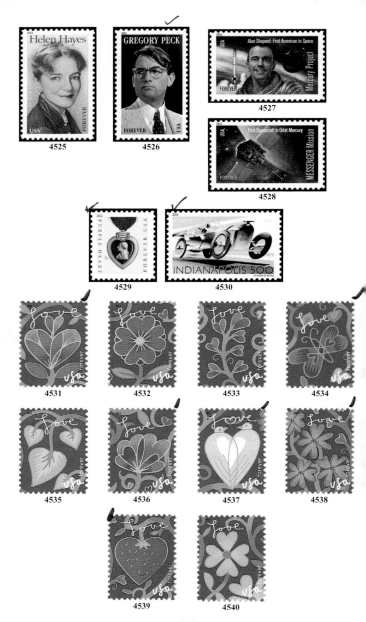

4525

4526

4527

4528

4529

4530

4531

4532

4533

4534

4535

4536

4537

4538

4539

4540

448

Scott No.	Description	Unused Value	Used Value	/ / / / / /
j.	(44c) Ride a bike	.90	.25	☐☐☐☐☐
k.	(44c) Plant Trees	.90	.25	☐☐☐☐☐
l.	(44c) Insulate the home...........................	.90	.25	☐☐☐☐☐
m.	(44c) Use public transportation..............	.90	.25	☐☐☐☐☐
n.	(44c) Use efficient light bulbs	.90	.25	☐☐☐☐☐
o.	(44c) Adjust the thermostat.....................	.90	.25	☐☐☐☐☐
p.	(44c) Maintain tire pressure	.90	.25	☐☐☐☐☐
4525	(44c) Helen Hayes (1900-93), Actress, self-adhesive	.90	.25	☐☐☐☐☐
4526	(44c) Legends of Hollywood – Gregory Peck (1916-2003), self-adhesive..........	.90	.25	☐☐☐☐☐
4527	(44c) Space Firsts - Alan B. Shepard, Jr. (1923-98), First American In Space, self-adhesive	.90	.25	☐☐☐☐☐
4528	(44c) Space Firsts - Messenger, First Spacecraft to Orbit Mercury, self-adhesive ..	.90	.25	☐☐☐☐☐
a.	Horiz. pair, #4527-4528	1.80		☐☐☐☐☐
4529	(44c) Purple Heart and Ribbon, self-adhesive	.90	.25	☐☐☐☐☐
4530	(44c) Indianapolis 500, Cent., self-adhesive	.90	.25	☐☐☐☐☐
4531	(44c) Garden of Love - Pink Flower, self-adhesive	.90	.25	☐☐☐☐☐
4532	(44c) Garden of Love - Red Flower, self-adhesive	.90	.25	☐☐☐☐☐
4533	(44c) Garden of Love - Blue Flowers, self-adhesive	.90	.25	☐☐☐☐☐
4534	(44c) Garden of Love - Butterfly, self-adhesive	.90	.25	☐☐☐☐☐
4535	(44c) Garden of Love - Green Vine Leaves, self-adhesive	.90	.25	☐☐☐☐☐
4536	(44c) Garden of Love - Blue Flower, self-adhesive	.90	.25	☐☐☐☐☐
4537	(44c) Garden of Love - Doves, self-adhesive	.90	.25	☐☐☐☐☐
4538	(44c) Garden of Love - Orange Red Flowers, self-adhesive	.90	.25	☐☐☐☐☐
4539	(44c) Garden of Love - Strawberry, self-adhesive	.90	.25	☐☐☐☐☐
4540	(44c) Garden of Love - Yellow Orange Flowers, self-adhesive	.90	.25	☐☐☐☐☐
a.	Block of 10, #4531-4540..............	9.00		☐☐☐☐☐
4541	(44c) American Scientists - Melvin Calvin (1911-97), Chemist, self-adhesive	.90	.25	☐☐☐☐☐
4542	(44c) American Scientists - Asa Gray (1810-88), Botanist, self-adhesive	.90	.25	☐☐☐☐☐
4543	(44c) American Scientists - Maria Goeppert Mayer (1906-72), Physicist, self-adhesive	.90	.25	☐☐☐☐☐

4541   4542

4543   4544

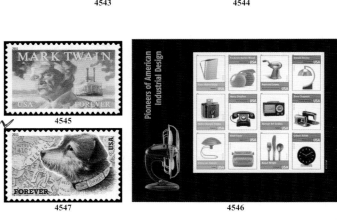

4545

4547

4546

4548   4549

4550   4551

Scott No.	Description	Unused Value	Used Value	/ / / / / /
4544	(44c) American Scientists - Severo Ochoa (1905-93), Biochemist, self-adhesive	.90	.25	☐☐☐☐☐
a.	Horiz. strip of 4, #4541-4544........	3.60		☐☐☐☐☐
b.	Horiz. strip of 4, cie cutting omitted on backing paper (from misaligned die-cutting mat)	—		☐☐☐☐☐
4545	(44c) Literary Arts - Mark Twain (Samuel L. Clemens) (1835-1910), Writer, self-adhesive...................	.90	.25	☐☐☐☐☐
4546	Pioneers of American Industrial Design, pane of 12, self-adhesive.............	11.00		☐☐☐☐☐
a.	(44c) Normandie pitcher, designed by Peter Muller-Munk (1904-67).....	.90	.25	☐☐☐☐☐
b.	(44c) Fiesta dinnerware, designed by Frederick Hurten Rhead (1880-1942)	.90	.25	☐☐☐☐☐
c.	(44c) Streamlined pencil sharpener, designed by Raymond Loewy (1893-1986)	.90	.25	☐☐☐☐☐
d.	(44c) Table lamp, designed by Donald Deskey (1894-1989)...................	.90	.25	☐☐☐☐☐
e.	(44c) Kodak Baby Brownie camera, designed by Walter Dorwin Teague (1883-1960)	.90	.25	☐☐☐☐☐
f.	(44c) Model 302 Bell telephone, designed by Henry Dreyfuss (1904-72).....	.90	.25	☐☐☐☐☐
g.	(44c) Emerson Patriot radio, designed by Norman Bel Geddes (1893-1958)	.90	.25	☐☐☐☐☐
h.	(44c) Streamlined sewing machines, designed by Dave Chapman (1909-78)......	.90	.25	☐☐☐☐☐
i.	(44c) Anywhere lamp, designed by Greta von Nessen (1900-74).......	.90	.25	☐☐☐☐☐
j.	(44c) IBM Selectric typewriter, designed by Eliot Noyes (1910-77).................	.90	.25	☐☐☐☐☐
k.	(44c) Highlight/Pinch flatware, designed by Russel Wright (1904-76).............	.90	.25	☐☐☐☐☐
l.	(44c) Herman Miller electric clock, designed by Gilbert Rohde (1894-1944)...	.90	.25	
✓4547	(44c) Owney, The Postal Dog, self-adhesive	.90	.25	
4548	(44c) U.S. Merchant Marine - Clipper Ship, self-adhesive	.90	.25	☐☐☐☐☐
4549	(44c) U.S. Merchant Marine - Auxiliary Steamship, self-adhesive..............	.90	.25	☐☐☐☐☐
4550	(44c) U.S. Merchant Marine - Liberty Ship, self-adhesive	.90	.25	☐☐☐☐☐
4551	(44c) U.S. Merchant Marine - Container Ship, self-adhesive......................	.90	.25	☐☐☐☐☐
a.	Block or horiz. strip of 4, #4548-4551	3.60		☐☐☐☐☐
4552	(44c) EID - "Eid Mubarak", self-adhesive	.90	.25	☐☐☐☐☐
✓4553	(44c) Characters From Disney - Pixar Films: Lightning McQueen and Mater from Cars, self-adhesive..............	.90	.25	☐☐☐☐☐

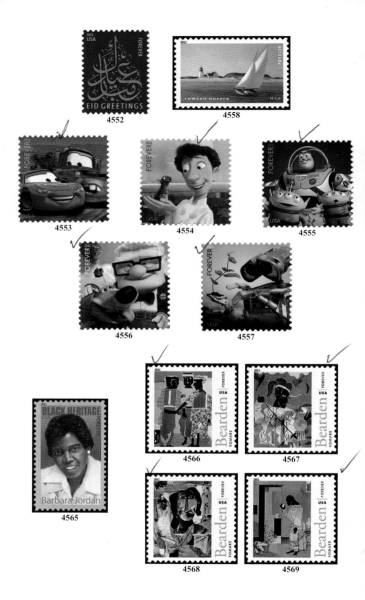

4552

4558

4553

4554

4555

4556

4557

4565

4566

4567

4568

4569

Scott No.	Description	Unused Value	Used Value	/ / / / /
4554 (44c)	Characters From Disney - Pixar Films: Remy the Rat and Linguini from Ratatouille, self-adhesive	.90	.25	☐☐☐☐☐
4555 (44c)	Characters From Disney - Pixar Films: Buzz Lightyear and Aliens from Toy Story, self-adhesive..............	.90	.25	☐☐☐☐☐
4556 (44c)	Characters From Disney - Pixar Films: Carl Fredricksen and Dug the Dog from Up, self-adhesive	.90	.25	☐☐☐☐☐
4557 (44c)	Characters From Disney - Pixar Films: WALL-E from WALL-E, self-adhesive	.90	.25	☐☐☐☐☐
a.	Horiz. strip of 5, #4553-4557........	4.50		☐☐☐☐☐
4558 (44c)	American Treasures Series - The Long Leg, by Edward Hopper (1882-1967), self-adhesive..........	.90	.25	☐☐☐☐☐
4559 (44c)	Statue of Liberty Type of 2010 (4486) - microprinted "4evR", self-adhesive, booklet stamp..............................	.90	.25	☐☐☐☐☐
4560 (44c)	Flag Type of 2010 (4487) - microprinted "4evR", self-adhesive, booklet stamp			☐☐☐☐☐
a.	Pair, #4559-4560...........................	1.80		☐☐☐☐☐
b.	Booklet pane of 20, 10 each #4559-4560.................................	18.00		☐☐☐☐☐
4561 (44c)	Statue of Liberty Type of 2010 (4486) - microprinted "4evr", self-adhesive, booklet stamp..............................	.90	.25	☐☐☐☐☐
4562 (44c)	Flag Type of 2010 (4487) - microprinted "4evr", self-adhesive, booklet stamp	.90	.25	☐☐☐☐☐
a.	Pair, #4561-4562...........................	1.80		☐☐☐☐☐
b.	Booklet pane of 20, 10 each #4561-4562.................................	18.00		☐☐☐☐☐
4563 (44c)	Statue of Liberty Type of 2010 (4486) - microprinted "4EVR", self-adhesive, booklet stamp..............................	.90	.25	☐☐☐☐☐
4564 (44c)	Flag Type of 2010 (4487) - microprinted "4EVR", self-adhesive, booklet stamp..............................	.90	.25	☐☐☐☐☐
a.	Pair, #4563-4564...........................	1.80		☐☐☐☐☐
b.	Booklet pane of 20, 10 each #4563-4564.................................	18.00		☐☐☐☐☐
4565 (44c)	Black Heritage - Barbara Jordan (1936-96), Congresswoman, self-adhesive	.90	.25	☐☐☐☐☐
4566 (44c)	Art of Romare Bearden (1911-88) - Conjunction, self-adhesive	.90	.25	☐☐☐☐☐
4567 (44c)	Art of Romare Bearden (1911-88) - Odysseus, self-adhesive...............	.90	.25	☐☐☐☐☐
4568 (44c)	Art of Romare Bearden (1911-88) - Prevalence of Ritual, self-adhesive	.90	.25	☐☐☐☐☐

4570

4571

4572

4573

4574

4579

4580

4581

4582

4583

4584

4585

4586

4587

4588

4589

4590

Scott No.	Description	Unused Value	Used Value	/ / / / / /
4569	(44c) Art of Romare Bearden (1911-88) - Falling Star, self-adhesive	.90	.25	☐☐☐☐☐
a.	Horiz. strip of 4, #4566-4569........			☐☐☐☐☐
4570	(44c) Christmas - Madonna of the Candelabra, by Raphael, self-adhesive............	.90	.25	☐☐☐☐☐
a.	Booklet pane of 20	18.00		☐☐☐☐☐
4571	(44c) Christmas - Ornaments, self-adhesive, booklet stamp, USPS microprinted on collar of ornament..................	.90	.25	☐☐☐☐☐
4572	(44c) Christmas - Ornaments, self-adhesive, booklet stamp, USPS microprinted on collar of ornament..................	.90	.25	☐☐☐☐☐
4573	(44c) Christmas - Ornaments, self-adhesive, booklet stamp, USPS microprinted on collar of ornament..................	.90	.25	☐☐☐☐☐
4574	(44c) Christmas - Ornaments, self-adhesive, booklet stamp, USPS microprinted on collar of ornament.................	.90	.25	☐☐☐☐☐
a.	Block of 4, #4571-4574.............	3.60		☐☐☐☐☐
b.	Booklet pane of 20, 5 each #4571-4574................................	18.00		☐☐☐☐☐
4575	(44c) Christmas - Ornaments (4571), self-adhesive, booklet stamp, microprinted USPS in places other than collar of ornament	.90	.25	☐☐☐☐☐
4576	(44c) Christmas - Ornaments (4572), self-adhesive, booklet stamp, microprinted USPS in places other than collar of ornament	.90	.25	☐☐☐☐☐
4577	(44c) Christmas - Ornaments (4573), self-adhesive, booklet stamp, microprinted USPS in places other than collar of ornament	.90	.25	☐☐☐☐☐
4578	(44c) Christmas - Ornaments (4574), self-adhesive, booklet stamp, microprinted USPS in places other than collar of ornament	.90	.25	☐☐☐☐☐
a.	Block of 4, #4575-4578................	3.60		☐☐☐☐☐
b.	Booklet pane of 20, 5 each #4575-4578.................................	18.00		☐☐☐☐☐
4579	(44c) Christmas - Ornaments, self-adhesive, booklet stamp, microprinted USPS in places other than collar of ornament, serp. die cut 11¼ x 11 on 2, 3 or 4 sides..............................	.90	.25	☐☐☐☐☐
4580	(44c) Christmas - Ornaments, self-adhesive, booklet stamp, microprinted USPS in places other than collar of ornament, serp. die cut 11¼ x 11 on 2, 3 or 4 sides..............................	.90	.25	☐☐☐☐☐

4591

4592

4593

4594

4595

4596

4597

4598

4599

4600

4601

4603

4604

4605

4606

4607

456

Scott No.	Description	Unused Value	Used Value	/ / / / / /
4581	(44c) Christmas - Ornaments, self-adhesive, booklet stamp, microprinted USPS in places other than collar of ornament, serp. die cut 11¼ x 11 on 2, 3 or 4 sides..............................	.90	.25	☐☐☐☐☐
4582	(44c) Christmas - Ornaments, self-adhesive, booklet stamp, microprinted USPS in places other than collar of ornament, serp. die cut 11¼ x 11 on 2, 3 or 4 sides..............................	.90	.25	☐☐☐☐☐
a.	Block of 4, #4579-4582.................	3.60		☐☐☐☐☐
b.	Booklet pane of 18, 5 each #4579, 4582, 4 each #4580-4581	16.50		☐☐☐☐☐
4583	(44c) Hanukkah, self-adhesive..............	.90	.25	☐☐☐☐☐
4584	(44c) Kwanzaa, self-adhesive	.90	.25	☐☐☐☐☐
2012 Issues				
4585	(25c) Eagle, self-adhesive, coil stamp	.50	.25	☐☐☐☐☐
4586	(25c) Eagle, self-adhesive, coil stamp	.50	.25	☐☐☐☐☐
4587	(25c) Eagle, self-adhesive, coil stamp	.50	.25	☐☐☐☐☐
4588	(25c) Eagle, self-adhesive, coil stamp	.50	.25	☐☐☐☐☐
4589	(25c) Eagle, self-adhesive, coil stamp	.50	.25	☐☐☐☐☐
4590	(25c) Eagle, self-adhesive, coil stamp	.50	.25	☐☐☐☐☐
a.	Strip of 6, #4585-4590	3.00		☐☐☐☐☐
4591	(44c) New Mexico Statehood Centennial, self-adhesive...............................	.90	.25	☐☐☐☐☐
4592	32c Aloha Shirts, Surfers and Palm Trees, self-adhesive...............................	.65	.25	☐☐☐☐☐
4593	32c Aloha Shirts, Surfers, self-adhesive	.65	.25	☐☐☐☐☐
4594	32c Aloha Shirts, Fossil Fish, self-adhesive	.65	.25	☐☐☐☐☐
4595	32c Aloha Shirts, Shells, self-adhesive	.65	.25	☐☐☐☐☐
4596	32c Aloha Shirts, Fish and Starfish, self-adhesive...............................	.65	.25	☐☐☐☐☐
a.	Horiz. strip of 5, #4592-4596........	3.25		☐☐☐☐☐
4597	32c Aloha Shirts, Fish and Starfish, self-adhesive, coil stamp	.65	.25	☐☐☐☐☐
4598	32c Aloha Shirts, Surfers and Palm Trees, self-adhesive, coil stamp	.65	.25	☐☐☐☐☐
4599	32c Aloha Shirts, Surfers, self-adhesive, coil stamp....................................	.65	.25	☐☐☐☐☐
4600	32c Aloha Shirts, Fossil Fish, self-adhesive, coil stamp	.65	.25	☐☐☐☐☐
4601	32c Aloha Shirts, Shells, self-adhesive, coil stamp....................................	.65	.25	☐☐☐☐☐
a.	Strip of 5, #4597-4601	3.25		☐☐☐☐☐
4602	65c Wedding Cake Type of 2009 (4398), self-adhesive...............................	1.30	.25	☐☐☐☐☐

Northern Goshawk USA 85 2012
4608

Peregrine Falcon USA 85 2012
4609

Golden Eagle 85 USA 2012
4610

Osprey USA 85 2012
4611

Northern Harrier USA 85 2012
4612

USA 45
4613

USA 45
4614

USA 45
4615

USA 45
4616

USA 45
4617

BONSAI SIERRA JUNIPER FOREVER 2012
4618

BONSAI BLACK PINE FOREVER 2012
4619

BONSAI BANYAN FOREVER 2012
4620

BONSAI TRIDENT MAPLE FOREVER 2012
4621

BONSAI AZALEA FOREVER 2012
4622

4623

forever Love USA
4626

USA FOREVER ARIZONA 1912-2012
4627

BLACK HERITAGE USA John H. Johnson FOREVER
4624

DANNY THOMAS USA FOREVER 2012
4628

Heart Health USA FOREVER 2012
4625

458

Scott No.	Description	Unused Value	Used Value	/ / / / /
4603	65c Baltimore Checkerspot Butterfly, self-adhesive	1.30	.25	☐☐☐☐☐
4604	65c Dogs at Work - Seeing Eye Dog, self-adhesive	1.30	.25	☐☐☐☐☐
4605	65c Dogs at Work - Therapy Dog, self-adhesive	1.30	.25	☐☐☐☐☐
4606	65c Dogs at Work - Military Dog, self-adhesive	1.30	.25	☐☐☐☐☐
4607	65c Dogs at Work - Rescue Dog, self-adhesive	1.30	.25	☐☐☐☐☐
a.	Block or vert. strip of 4, #4604-4607	5.20		☐☐☐☐☐
4608	85c Birds of Prey - Northern Goshawk,	1.75	.35	☐☐☐☐☐
4609	85c Birds of Prey - Peregrine Falcon, self-adhesive	1.75	.35	☐☐☐☐☐
4610	85c Birds of Prey - Golden Eagle, self-adhesive	1.75	.35	☐☐☐☐☐
4611	85c Birds of Prey - Osprey, self-adhesive	1.75	.35	☐☐☐☐☐
4612	85c Birds of Prey - Northern Harrier, self-adhesive	1.75	.35	☐☐☐☐☐
a.	Horiz. strip of 5, #4608-4612........	8.75		☐☐☐☐☐
4613	45c Weather Vanes - Rooster Without Perch, self-adhesive, coil stamp	.90	.25	☐☐☐☐☐
4614	45c Weather Vanes - Cow, self-adhesive, coil stamp..............................	.90	.25	☐☐☐☐☐
4615	45c Weather Vanes - Eagle, self-adhesive, coil stamp..............................	.90	.25	☐☐☐☐☐
4616	45c Weather Vanes - Rooster With Perch, self-adhesive, coil stamp	.90	.25	☐☐☐☐☐
4617	45c Weather Vanes - Centaur, self-adhesive, coil stamp..............................	.90	.25	☐☐☐☐☐
a.	Strip of 5, #4613-4617	4.50		☐☐☐☐☐
4618	(45c) Bonsai - Sierra Juniper, self-adhesive, booklet stamp..............................	.90	.25	☐☐☐☐☐
4619	(45c) Bonsai - Black Pine, self-adhesive, booklet stamp..............................	.90	.25	☐☐☐☐☐
4620	(45c) Bonsai - Banyan, self-adhesive, booklet stamp..............................	.90	.25	☐☐☐☐☐
4621	(45c) Bonsai - Trident Maple, self-adhesive, booklet stamp..............................	.90	.25	☐☐☐☐☐
4622	(45c) Bonsai - Azalea, self-adhesive, booklet stamp..............................	.90	.25	☐☐☐☐☐
a.	Vert. strip of 5, #4618-4622	4.50		☐☐☐☐☐
4623	(45c) Chinese New Year - Year of the Dragon, self-adhesive	.90	.25	☐☐☐☐☐
4624	(45c) Black Heritage - John H. Johnson (1918-2005), Magazine Publisher, self-adhesive	.90	.25	☐☐☐☐☐
4625	(45c) Heart Health, self-adhesive	.90	.25	☐☐☐☐☐

4629

4630

4631

4632

4641

4642

4643

4644

4649

4650

4651

4652

Scott No.	Description	Unused Value	Used Value	/ / / / /
4626	(45c) Love - Ribbons, self-adhesive	.90	.25	☐☐☐☐☐
4627	(45c) Arizona Statehood Cent., self-adhesive	.90	.25	☐☐☐☐☐
4628	(45c) Danny Thomas (1912-91) - Comedian, self-adhesive	.90	.25	☐☐☐☐☐
4629	(45c) Flag and Equality, self-adhesive, coil stamp, serp. die cut 8½ vert.	.90	.25	☐☐☐☐☐
4630	(45c) Flag and Justice, self-adhesive, coil stamp, serp. die cut 8½ vert.	.90	.25	☐☐☐☐☐
4631	(45c) Flag and Freedom, self-adhesive, coil stamp, serp. die cut 8½ vert.	.90	.25	☐☐☐☐☐
4632	(45c) Flag and Liberty, self-adhesive, coil stamp, serp. die cut 8½ vert.	.90	.25	☐☐☐☐☐
a.	Strip of 4, #4629-4632	3.60		☐☐☐☐☐
4633	(45c) Flag and Equality (4629), self-adhesive, coil stamp, serp. die cut 9½ vert.	.90	.25	☐☐☐☐☐
4634	(45c) Flag and Justice (4630), self-adhesive, coil stamp, serp. die cut 9½ vert..	90	.25	☐☐☐☐☐
4635	(45c) Flag and Freedom (4631), self-adhesive, coil stamp, serp. die cut 9½ vert.	.90	.25	☐☐☐☐☐
4636	(45c) Flag and Liberty (4632), self-adhesive, coil stamp, serp. die cut 9½ vert.	.90	.25	☐☐☐☐☐
a.	Strip of 4, #4633-4636	3.60		☐☐☐☐☐
4637	(45c) Flag and Equality (4629), self-adhesive, coil stamp, serp. die cut 11 vert..	.90	.25	☐☐☐☐☐
4638	(45c) Flag and Justice (4630), self-adhesive, coil stamp, serp. die cut 11 vert..	.90	.25	☐☐☐☐☐
4639	(45c) Flag and Freedom (4631), self-adhesive, coil stamp, serp. die cut 11 vert..	.90	.25	☐☐☐☐☐
4640	(45c) Flag and Liberty (4632), self-adhesive, coil stamp, serp. die cut 11 vert..	.90	.25	☐☐☐☐☐
a.	Strip of 4, #4637-4640	3.60		☐☐☐☐☐
4641	(45c) Flag and Freedom, self-adhesive, booklet stamp, colored dots in stars	.90	.25	☐☐☐☐☐
4642	(45c) Flag and Liberty, self-adhesive, booklet stamp, colored dots in stars	.90	.25	☐☐☐☐☐
4643	(45c) Flag and Equality, self-adhesive, booklet stamp, colored dots in stars	.90	.25	☐☐☐☐☐
4644	(45c) Flag and Justice, self-adhesive, booklet stamp, colored dots in stars	.90	.25	☐☐☐☐☐
a.	Block of 4, #4641-4644................	3.60		☐☐☐☐☐
b.	Booklet Pane of 20, 5 each #4641-4644..............................	18.00		☐☐☐☐☐
4645	(45c) Flag and Freedom (4641), self-adhesive, booklet stamp, dark dots only in stars	.90	.25	☐☐☐☐☐
4646	(45c) Flag and Liberty (4642), self-adhesive, booklet stamp, dark dots only in stars	.90	.25	☐☐☐☐☐
4647	(45c) Flag and Equality (4643), self-adhesive, booklet stamp, dark dots only in stars	.90	.25	☐☐☐☐☐

WILLIAM H. JOHNSON

4653

Brodsky
JOSEPH BRODSKY | USA

4654

Brooks
GWENDOLYN BROOKS | USA

4655

Williams
WILLIAM CARLOS WILLIAMS | USA

4656

Hayden
ROBERT HAYDEN | USA

4657

Plath
SYLVIA PLATH | USA

4658

Bishop
ELIZABETH BISHOP | USA

4659

Stevens
WALLACE STEVENS | USA

4660

Levertov
DENISE LEVERTOV | USA

4661

Cummings
E. E. CUMMINGS | USA

4662

Roethke
THEODORE ROETHKE | USA

4663

New Orleans April 24-May 1, 1862 USA

FOREVER

4664

FOREVER

USA   Antietam September 17, 1862

4665

Scott No.	Description	Unused Value	Used Value	//////
4648	(45c) Flag and Justice (4644), self-adhesive, booklet stamp, dark dots only in stars	.90	.25	☐☐☐☐☐
a.	Block of 4, #4645-4648..............	3.60		☐☐☐☐☐
b.	Booklet Pane of 20, 5 each #4645-4648..............................	18.00		☐☐☐☐☐
4649	$5.15 American Landmarks - Sunshine Skyway Bridge, self-adhesive.....	10.50	5.75	
4650	$18.95 American Landmarks - Carmel Mission, self-adhesive..............................	37.50	19.00	☐☐☐☐☐
4651	(45c) Cherry Blossom Centennial - Cherry Blossoms and Washington Monument, self-adhesive..............................	.90	.25	☐☐☐☐☐
4652	(45c) Cherry Blossom Centennial - Cherry Blossoms and Jefferson Memorial, self-adhesive..............................	.90	.25	☐☐☐☐☐
a.	Horiz. pair, #4651-4652	1.80		☐☐☐☐☐
4653	(45c) American Treasures Series - Flowers, by William H. Johnson (1901-70), self-adhesive..............................	.90	.25	☐☐☐☐☐
4654	(45c) Twentieth Century Poets - Joseph Brodsky (1940-96), self-adhesive.............	.90	.25	☐☐☐☐☐
4655	(45c) Twentieth Century Poets - Gwendolyn Brooks (1917-2000), self-adhesive..........	.90	.25	☐☐☐☐☐
4656	(45c) Twentieth Century Poets - William Carlos Williams (1883-1963), self-adhesive	.90	.25	☐☐☐☐☐
4657	(45c) Twentieth Century Poets - Robert Hayden (1913-80), self-adhesive.............	.90	.25	☐☐☐☐☐
4658	(45c) Twentieth Century Poets - Sylvia Plath (1932-63), self-adhesive.............	.90	.25	☐☐☐☐☐
4659	(45c) Twentieth Century Poets - Elizabeth Bishop (1911-79), self-adhesive.............	.90	.25	☐☐☐☐☐
4660	(45c) Twentieth Century Poets - Wallace Stevens (1879-1955), self-adhesive..........	.90	.25	☐☐☐☐☐
4661	(45c) Twentieth Century Poets - Denise Levertov (1923-97), self-adhesive.............	.90	.25	☐☐☐☐☐
4662	(45c) Twentieth Century Poets - E.E. Cummings (1894-1962), self-adhesive..........	.90	.25	☐☐☐☐☐
4663	(45c) Twentieth Century Poets - Theodore Roethke (1908-63), self-adhesive	.90	.25	☐☐☐☐☐
a.	Block of 10, #4654-4663..............	9.00		☐☐☐☐☐
4664	(45c) Civil War Sesquicentennial - Battle of New Orleans, self-adhesive	.90	.25	☐☐☐☐☐
4665	(45c) Civil War Sesquicentennial - Battle of Antietam, self-adhesive.	90	.25	☐☐☐☐☐
a.	Pair, #4664-4665............................	1.80		☐☐☐☐☐
4666	(45c) Distinguished Americans - Jose Ferrer (1912-92), Actor, self-adhesive...	.90	.25	☐☐☐☐☐
4667	(45c) Louisiana Statehood Bicentennial, self-adhesive	.90	.25	☐☐☐☐☐

4666

4667

4668

4669

4670

4671

4672

4677

4678

4679

4680

4681

464

Scott No.	Description	Unused Value	Used Value	/ / / / / /
4668	(45c) Great Film Directors - John Ford (1894-1973), self-adhesive..........	.90	.25	☐☐☐☐☐
4669	(45c) Great Film Directors - Frank Capra (1897-1991), self-adhesive..........	.90	.25	☐☐☐☐☐
4670	(45c) Great Film Directors - Billy Wilder (1906-2002), self-adhesive..........	.90	.25	☐☐☐☐☐
4671	(45c) Great Film Directors - John Huston (1906-87), self-adhesive..............	.90	.25	☐☐☐☐☐
a.	Block or horiz. strip of 4, #4668-4671	3.60		☐☐☐☐☐
4672	1c Wildlife - Bobcat, self-adhesive, coil stamp.....................................	.25	.25	☐☐☐☐☐
4673	(45c) Flags Type of 2012 (4641), self-adhesive, booklet stamp, colored dots in stars, 19¼ mm from lower left to lower right corners of flag.............................	.90	.25	☐☐☐☐☐
4674	(45c) Flags Type of 2012 (4641), self-adhesive, booklet stamp, colored dots in stars, 19¼ mm from lower left to lower right corners of flag.............................	.90	.25	☐☐☐☐☐
4675	(45c) Flags Type of 2012 (4641), self-adhesive, booklet stamp, colored dots in stars, 19¼ mm from lower left to lower right corners of flag.............................	.90	.25	☐☐☐☐☐
4676	(45c) Flags Type of 2012 (4641), self-adhesive, booklet stamp, colored dots in stars, 19¼mm from lower left to lower right corners of flag.............................	.90	.25	☐☐☐☐☐
a.	Block of 4, #4673-4676................	3.60		☐☐☐☐☐
b.	Booklet pane of 10, 3 each #4673-4674, 2 each #4675-4676	9.00		☐☐☐☐☐
4677	(45c) Characters From Disney - Pixar Films: Flik and Dot from A Bug's Life, self-adhesive	.90	.25	☐☐☐☐☐
4678	(45c) Characters From Disney - Pixar Films: Bob Parr and Dashiell Parr from The Incredibles, self-adhesive	.90	.25	☐☐☐☐☐
4679	(45c) Characters From Disney - Pixar Films: Nemo and Squirt from Finding Nemo, self-adhesive	.90	.25	☐☐☐☐☐
4680	(45c) Characters From Disney - Pixar Films: Jessie, Woody and Bullseye from Toy Story 2, self-adhesive	.90	.25	☐☐☐☐☐
4681	(45c) Characters From Disney - Pixar Films: Boo, Mike Wazowski and James P. "Sulley" Sullivan from Monsters, Inc., self-adhesive	.90	.25	☐☐☐☐☐
a.	Horiz. strip of 5, #4677-4681........	4.50		☐☐☐☐☐

4687

4688

4689

4690

4691

4692

4693

B1

B2

B3

B4

466

Scott No.	Description	Unused Value	Used Value	/ / / / / /
4682	32c Aloha Shirts Type of 2012 (4592), self-adhesive, booklet stamp, serp. die cut on 3 sides	.65	.25	☐☐☐☐☐
4683	32c Aloha Shirts Type of 2012 (4592), self-adhesive, booklet stamp, serp. die cut on 3 sides	.65	.25	☐☐☐☐☐
4684	32c Aloha Shirts Type of 2012 (4592), self-adhesive, booklet stamp, serp. die cut on 3 sides	.65	.25	☐☐☐☐☐
4685	32c Aloha Shirts Type of 2012 (4592), self-adhesive, booklet stamp, serp. die cut on 3 sides	.65	.25	☐☐☐☐☐
4686	32c Aloha Shirts Type of 2012 (4592), self-adhesive, booklet stamp, serp. die cut on 3 sides	.65	.25	☐☐☐☐☐
a.	Vert. strip of 5, #4682-4686	3.25		☐☐☐☐☐
b.	Booklet pane of 10, 2 each #4682-4686	6.50		☐☐☐☐☐
4687	(45c) Bicycling - Child on Bicycle with Training Wheels, self-adhesive	.90	.25	☐☐☐☐☐
4688	(45c) Bicycling - Commuter on Bicycle with Panniers, self-adhesive	.90	.25	☐☐☐☐☐
4689	(45c) Bicycling - Road Racer, self-adhesive	.90	.25	☐☐☐☐☐
4690	(45c) Bicycling - BMX Rider, self-adhesive	.90	.25	☐☐☐☐☐
a.	Horiz. strip of 4 #4687-4690	3.60		☐☐☐☐☐
4691	(45c) Girl Scouts of America, Cent., self-adhesive	.90	.25	☐☐☐☐☐
4692	(45c) Musicians - Edith Piaf (1915-63), Singer, self-adhesive	.90	.25	☐☐☐☐☐
4693	(45c) Musicians - Miles Davis (1926-91), Jazz Trumpet Player, self-adhesive	.90	.25	☐☐☐☐☐
a.	Horiz. pair, #4692-4693	1.80		☐☐☐☐☐

SEMI-POSTAL STAMPS

1998, July 29

B1 (32c+8c) Breast Cancer Research, self-adhesive		.80	.25	☐☐☐☐☐

2002, June 7

B2 (34c+11c) Heroes of 2001, Firemen Atop World Trade Center Rubble, self adhesive		.90	.35	☐☐☐☐☐

2003, Oct. 8

B3 (37c+8c) Stop Family Violence, self-adhesive		.90	.45	☐☐☐☐☐

2011, Sept. 20

B4 (44c+11c) Save Vanishing Species, Amur Tiger Cub, self-adhesive		1.10	.55	☐☐☐☐☐

☐☐☐☐☐
☐☐☐☐☐
☐☐☐☐☐

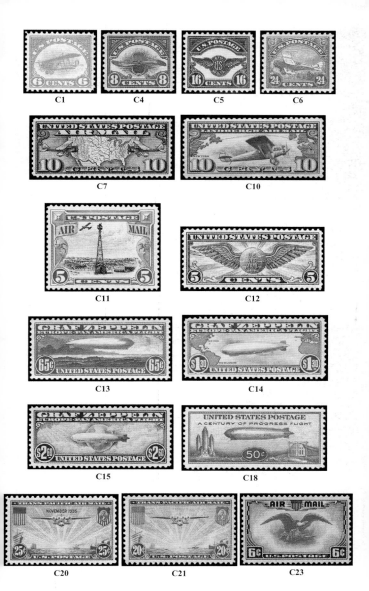

C1 C4 C5 C6

C7 C10

C11 C12

C13 C14

C15 C18

C20 C21 C23

Scott No.	Description	Unused Value	Used Value	/ / / / / /

AIR POST STAMPS

1918

Scott No.	Description	Unused Value	Used Value	
C1	6c Curtiss Jenny, orange	65.00	30.00	☐☐☐☐☐
C2	16c Curtiss Jenny (C1), green	65.00	35.00	☐☐☐☐☐
C3	24c Curtiss Jenny (C1), car rose & blue	75.00	35.00	☐☐☐☐☐
a.	Center inverted	*450,000.*		☐☐☐☐☐

1923

C4	8c Propeller	21.00	14.00	☐☐☐☐☐
C5	16c Air Service Emblem	70.00	30.00	☐☐☐☐☐
C6	24c Biplane	75.00	30.00	☐☐☐☐☐

1926-30

C7	10c Map & Planes, dark blue	2.50	.35	☐☐☐☐☐
C8	15c Map & Planes (C7), olive brown	2.75	2.50	☐☐☐☐☐
C9	20c Map & Planes (C7), yellow green	7.00	2.00	☐☐☐☐☐
C10	10c "Spirit of St. Louis"	7.00	2.50	☐☐☐☐☐
a.	Booklet pane of 3	75.00	*65.00*	☐☐☐☐☐
C11	5c Beacon	5.00	.75	☐☐☐☐☐
a.	Vertical pair, imperf. btwn.	*7,000.*		☐☐☐☐☐
C12	5c Winged Globe, violet, perf. 11	9.50	.50	☐☐☐☐☐
a.	Horiz. pair, imperf. btwn.	*4,500.*		☐☐☐☐☐

1930

C13	65c Zeppelin over Atlantic	180.00	165.00	☐☐☐☐☐
C14	$1.30 Zeppelin between Continents	400.00	375.00	☐☐☐☐☐
C15	$2.60 Zeppelin passing Globe	575.00	600.00	☐☐☐☐☐

1931-32, Perf. 10½ x 11

C16	5c Winged Globe (C12), violet	5.00	.60	☐☐☐☐☐
C17	8c Winged Globe (C12), olive bister	2.25	.40	☐☐☐☐☐

1933

C18	50c Century of Progress	55.00	55.00	☐☐☐☐☐

1934

C19	6c Winged Globe (C12), dull orange	3.50	.25	☐☐☐☐☐

1935

C20	25c Transpacific (dated 1935), blue	1.40	1.00	☐☐☐☐☐

1937

C21	20c Transpacific (no date), green	11.00	1.75	☐☐☐☐☐
C22	50c Transpacific (C21), carmine	11.00	5.00	☐☐☐☐☐

1938

C23	6c Eagle & Shield	.60	.25	☐☐☐☐☐
a.	Vert. pair, imperf. horiz.	325.00		☐☐☐☐☐
b.	Horiz. pair, imperf. vert	*12,500.*		☐☐☐☐☐

C24

C25

C33

C32

C34

C35

C36

C40

C38

C42

C43

C44

C45

C46

C47

471

Scott No.	Description	Unused Value	Used Value	/ / / / /
1939				
C24	30c Winged Globe (inscribed "Transatlantic"), dull blue..............	12.00	1.50	☐☐☐☐☐
1941-44				
C25	6c Airplane, carmine.............................	.25	.25	☐☐☐☐☐
a.	Booklet pane of 3.............................	4.00	1.50	☐☐☐☐☐
b.	Horiz. pair, imperf. btwn.	2,250.		☐☐☐☐☐
C26	8c Airplane (C25), olive green..............	.25	.25	☐☐☐☐☐
a.	All color omitted..............................	—		☐☐☐☐☐
C27	10c Airplane (C25), violet......................	1.25	.25	☐☐☐☐☐
C28	15c Airplane (C25), brown carmine.......	2.25	.35	☐☐☐☐☐
C29	20c Airplane (C25), bright green	2.25	.30	☐☐☐☐☐
C30	30c Airplane (C25), blue........................	2.25	.35	☐☐☐☐☐
C31	50c Airplane (C25), orange	11.00	3.25	☐☐☐☐☐
1946				
C32	5c DC-4 Skymaster (entire plane)........	.25	.25	☐☐☐☐☐
1947, Perf. 10½ x 11				
C33	5c DC-4 Skymaster	.25	.25	☐☐☐☐☐
C34	10c Pan American Union Building..........	.25	.25	☐☐☐☐☐
C35	15c Statue of Liberty	.35	.25	☐☐☐☐☐
a.	Horiz. pair, imperf. btwn.	2,750.		☐☐☐☐☐
C36	25c San Francisco-Oakland Bay Bridge .	.90	.25	☐☐☐☐☐
1948, Coil Stamp, Perf. 10 Horizontally				
C37	5c DC-4 Skymaster (C33)	1.00	.80	☐☐☐☐☐
1948				
C38	5c New York City.................................	.25	.25	☐☐☐☐☐
1949, Perf. 10½ x 11				
C39	6c DC-4 Skymaster (C33)	.25	.25	☐☐☐☐☐
a.	Booklet pane of 6..............................	12.00	5.00	☐☐☐☐☐
1949				
C40	6c Alexandria Bicentennial...................	.25	.25	☐☐☐☐☐
Coil Stamp, Perf. 10 Horizontally				
C41	6c DC-4 Skymaster (C33)	3.00	.25	☐☐☐☐☐
1949				
C42	10c Universal Postal Union	.25	.25	☐☐☐☐☐
C43	15c Universal Postal Union	.30	.25	☐☐☐☐☐
C44	25c Universal Postal Union	.60	.40	☐☐☐☐☐
C45	6c Wright Brothers...............................	.25	.25	☐☐☐☐☐
1952-58				
C46	80c Diamond Head, Hawaii....................	4.75	1.25	☐☐☐☐☐
C47	6c Powered Flight.................................	.25	.25	☐☐☐☐☐

C48

C49

C51

C53

C55

C57

C58

C59

C63-Redrawn

C54

C56

C68

C70

C64

C66

C67

C69

Scott No.	Description	Unused Value	Used Value	//////
C48	4c Eagle, bright blue	.25	.25	
C49	6c Air Force	.25	.25	
C50	5c Eagle (C48), red	.25	.25	

Perf. 10½x11

C51	7c Jet, blue	.25	.25	
a.	Booklet pane of 6	8.00	6.00	

Coil Stamp, Perf. 10 Horizontally

C52	7c Jet (C51), blue	2.00	.25	

1959

C53	7c Alaska Statehood	.25	.25	
C54	7c Balloon Jupiter	.30	.25	
C55	7c Hawaii Statehood	.25	.25	
C56	10c Pan American Games	.25	.25	

1959-66

C57	10c Liberty Bell, black & green	1.00	.70	
C58	15c Statue of Liberty, black & orange	.35	.25	
C59	25c Abraham Lincoln, black & maroon, untagged	.50	.25	
a.	Tagged	.60	.30	

Perf. 10½ x 11

C60	7c Jet (C51), carmine	.25	.25	
a.	Booklet pane of 6	8.50	7.00	
b.	Vert. pair, imperf. btwn. (from booklet pane)	5,500.	—	

Coil Stamp, Perf. 10 Horizontally

C61	7c Jet (C51), carmine	4.00	.25	

1961-67

C62	13c Liberty Bell (C57), black & red, untagged	.40	.25	
a.	Tagged	.75	.50	
C63	15c Statue of Liberty (redrawn), blk & org, untagged	.30	.25	
a.	Tagged	.35	.25	
b.	As "a," horiz. pair, imperf. vert.	15,000.		
c.	As "a," horiz. pair, imperf. btwn. and at left	2,750.		
d.	All color omitted	100.00		

Perf. 10½ x 11

C64	8c Jet & Capitol, untagged	.25	.25	
a.	Tagged	.25	.25	
b.	Booklet pane 5 + label, tagged	6.00	3.00	
c.	As "b," tagged	1.75	.75	

Coil Stamp, Perf. 10 Horizontally

C65	8c Jet & Capitol (C64), untagged	.40	.25	
a.	Tagged	.35	.25	

C72

C77

C78

C79

C71

C76

C84

C74

C75

C80

C85

C86

C87

C89

C88

C90

C97

Scott No.	Description	Unused Value	Used Value	/ / / / / /
1963-67				
C66	15c Montgomery Blair	.55	.50	
C67	6c Eagle, untagged	.25	.25	
a.	Tagged	4.00	3.00	
C68	8c Amelia Earhart	.25	.25	
C69	8c Robert H. Goddard	.35	.25	
C70	8c Alaska Purchase	.25	.25	
C71	20c Columbia Jays by Audubon	.75	.25	
1968, Perf. 11 x 10½				
C72	10c Star Runway	.25	.25	
b.	Booklet pane of 8	2.25	2.00	
c.	Booklet pane of 5 + label	3.75	1.25	
d.	Vert. pair, imperf. btwn., in #C72b with foldover	5,000.	—	
Coil Stamp, Perf. 10 Vertically				
C73	10c Star Runway (C72)	.30	.25	
a.	Imperf., pair	550.00		
1968				
C74	10c 50th Anniversary of Air Mail	.25	.25	
C75	20c "USA" & Jet, red, blue & black	.35	.25	
1969				
C76	10c Moon Landing	.25	.25	
a.	Rose red (litho.) omitted	500.00	—	
1971-73				
C77	9c Delta Wing Plane	.25	.25	
C78	11c Jet, tagged	.25	.25	
a.	Booklet pane of 4 + 2 labels	1.25	1.00	
b.	Untagged (Bureau precanceled)	.85	.85	
C79	13c Winged Envelope, tagged	.25	.25	
a.	Booklet pane of 5 + label	1.50	1.00	
b.	Untagged (Bureau precanceled)	.85	.85	
C80	17c Statue of Liberty	.35	.25	
C81	21c "USA" & Jet (C75), red, blue & black	.40	.25	
b.	Black (engr.) omitted	2,750.		
Coil Stamps, Perf. 10 Vertically				
C82	11c Jet (C78)	.25	.25	
a.	Imperf., pair	250.00		
C83	13c Winged Envelope (C79)	.30	.25	
a.	Imperf., pair	65.00		
1972-74				
C84	11c City of Refuge	.25	.25	
a.	Blue & green (litho.) omitted	750.00		
C85	11c Olympics - Skiing	.25	.25	
C86	11c Progress in Electronics	.30	.25	
a.	Vermilion & olive (litho.) omitted	825.00		
c.	Olive omitted	1,150.		

C91-C92   C93-C94   C95-C96

C99   C98   C100

C108   C113   C114

C115   C116   C117

C118   C119

Scott No.	Description	Unused Value	Used Value	//////
C87	18c Statue of Liberty	.35	.30	
C88	26c Mt. Rushmore.................................	.60	.25	
1976				
C89	25c Plane & Globes	.50	.25	
C90	31c Plane, Globes & Flag......................	.60	.25	
1978				
C91	31c Wright Brothers - Portraits at top.....	.65	.30	
C92	31c Wright Brothers - Plane at top..........	.65	.30	
a.	Vertical pair, #C91-C92	1.30	1.20	
b.	As "a," ultra & black (engr.) omitted	600.00		
c.	As "a," black (engr.) omitted	2,500.		
d.	As "a," black, yel, mag, blue & brown (litho.) omitted	2,250.		
1979				
C93	21c Octave Chanute - Portrait at top	.70	.35	
C94	21c Octave Chanute - Plane at top	.70	.35	
a.	Vertical pair, #C93-C94	1.40	1.20	
b.	As "a," ultra & black (engr.) omitted	4,500.		
C95	25c Wiley Post - Portrait at top...............	.95	.45	
C96	25c Wiley Post - Plane at top..................	.95	.45	
a.	Vertical pair, #C95-C96	1.90	1.50	
C97	31c Olympics - High Jump......................	.70	.30	
1980				
C98	40c Philip Mazzei, perf. 11......................	.80	.25	
b.	Imperf., pair......................................	3,500.		
C98A	40c Philip Mazzei, perf. 10½ x 11¼ ('82) (C98)	8.00	1.50	
c.	Horiz. pair, imperf. vert.	4,250.		
C99	28c Blanche Stuart Scott........................	.60	.25	
a.	Imperf., pair......................................	2,350.		
C100	35c Glenn Curtiss..................................	.65	.25	
a.	Light blue (background) omitted......	2,000.		
1983				
C101	28c Olympics - Women's Gymnastics.....	1.00	.30	
C102	28c Olympics - Hurdles..........................	1.00	.30	
C103	28c Olympics - Women's Basketball.......	1.00	.30	
C104	28c Olympics - Soccer...........................	1.00	.30	
a.	Block of 4, #C101-C104..................	4.25	2.50	
b.	As "a," imperf. vert.	7,500.		
C105	40c Olympics - Shot put, Perf. 11.2 bullseye	.90	.40	
a.	Perf. 11 line	1.00	.45	
C106	40c Olympics - Gymnast, Perf. 11.2 bullseye	.90	.40	
a.	Perf. 11 line	1.00	.45	
C107	40c Olympics - Swimmer, Perf. 11.2 bullseye	.90	.40	

C120

C121

C122-C125

C127

C128

C130

C131

C132

C133

C134

C135

C136

C137

C138

479

Scott No.	Description	Unused Value	Used Value	/////
a.	Perf. 11 line	1.00	.45	
C108	40c Olympics - Weightlifting, perf. 11.2 bullseye	.90	.40	
a.	Perf. 11 line	1.00	.45	
b.	Block of 4, #C105-C108	4.25	3.00	
c.	Block of 4, #C105a-C108a	5.00	4.00	
d.	Block of 4, imperf.	1,000.		
C109	35c Olympics - Women's fencing	.90	.55	
C110	35c Olympics - Cycling	.90	.55	
C111	35c Olympics - Women's volleyball	.90	.55	
C112	35c Olympics - Pole vaulting	.90	.55	
a.	Block of 4, #C109-C112	4.00	3.25	

1985

Scott No.	Description	Unused Value	Used Value	/////
C113	33c Alfred V. Verville	.65	.25	
a.	Imperf., pair	825.00		
C114	39c Lawrence & Elmer Sperry	.80	.25	
a.	Imperf., pair	1,750.		
C115	44c Transpacific Airmail	.85	.25	
a.	Imperf., pair	750.00		
C116	44c Father Junipero Serra	1.00	.35	
a.	Imperf., pair	1,300.		

1988

Scott No.	Description	Unused Value	Used Value	/////
C117	44c Settling of New Sweden	1.00	.25	
C118	45c Samuel P. Langley	.90	.25	
C119	36c Igor Sikorsky	.70	.25	
a.	Red, dk blue & black (engr.) omitted	3,000.		

1989

Scott No.	Description	Unused Value	Used Value	/////
C120	45c French Revolution	.95	.25	
C121	45c Carved Figure	.90	.25	
C122	45c Futuristic Space Craft	1.00	.50	
C123	45c Futuristic Hover Car	1.00	.50	
C124	45c Futuristic Moon Rover	1.00	.50	
C125	45c Space Shuttle	1.00	.50	
a.	Block of 4, #C122-C125	4.00	3.00	
b.	As "a.," light blue (engr.) omitted	575.00		
C126	UPU Congress, sheet of 4, imperf.	5.00	4.00	
a.	45c Futuristic Space Craft (C122)	1.25	.50	
b.	45c Futuristic Hover Car (C123)	1.25	.50	
c.	45c Futuristic Moon Rover (C124)	1.25	.50	
d.	45c Space Shuttle (C125)	1.25	.50	

1990

Scott No.	Description	Unused Value	Used Value	/////
C127	45c Tropical Coast	.90	.25	

1991, Perf. 11

Scott No.	Description	Unused Value	Used Value	/////
C128	50c Harriet Quimby, perf. 11	1.00	.25	
a.	Vert. pair, imperf. horiz.	1,500.		

Scott No.	Description	Unused Value	Used Value	/ / / / / /
b.	Perf. 11.2	1.20	.25	☐☐☐☐☐
C129	40c William T. Piper (C132), hair does not touch top edge..........................	.80	.25	☐☐☐☐☐
C130	50c Antarctic Treaty...............................	1.00	.35	☐☐☐☐☐
C131	50c Bering Land Bridge	1.00	.35	☐☐☐☐☐
1993, Perf. 11.2				
C132	40c Piper, hair touches top edge..............	4.00	.65	☐☐☐☐☐
C133	48c Niagara Falls, self-adhesive	.95	.25	☐☐☐☐☐
C134	40c Rio Grande, self-adhesive................	.80	.60	☐☐☐☐☐
2000-05				
C135	60c Grand Canyon, self-adhesive	1.25	.25	☐☐☐☐☐
a.	Imperf, pair..	*1,850.*		☐☐☐☐☐
C136	70c Nine-Mile Prairie, Nebraska, self-adhesive....................................	1.40	.30	☐☐☐☐☐
C137	80c Mt. McKinley, self-adhesive.............	1.60	.35	☐☐☐☐☐
C138	60c Arcadia National Park, self-adhesive, serpentine die cut 11¼ x 11½, dated "2001"	1.25	.25	☐☐☐☐☐
a.	Dated "2001," serp. die cut 11.5x11.9 ..	1.25	.25	☐☐☐☐☐
b.	Dated "2005," serp. die cut 11.5x11.9 ...	1.25	.25	☐☐☐☐☐
c.	As "b," printed on back of backing paper	—		☐☐☐☐☐
C139	63c Scenic American Landscapes - Bryce Canyon National Park, self-adhesive.....	1.25	.25	☐☐☐☐☐
a.	Die cutting omitted, pair........................	—		☐☐☐☐☐
C140	75c Scenic American Landscapes - Great Smoky Mountains National Park, self-adhesive..	1.50	.35	☐☐☐☐☐
a.	Die cutting omitted, pair........................	—		☐☐☐☐☐
C141	84c Scenic American Landscapes - Yosemite National Park, self-adhesive	1.75	.35	☐☐☐☐☐
2007				
C142	69c Scenic American Landscapes - Okefenokee Swamp, self-adhesive	1.40	.30	☐☐☐☐☐
C143	90c Scenic American Landscapes - Hagatna Bay, self-adhesive..........	1.80	.40	☐☐☐☐☐
2008				
C144	72c Scenic American Landscapes - 13-Mile Woods, self-adhesive	1.50	.30	☐☐☐☐☐
C145	94c Scenic American Landscapes - Trunk Bay, self-adhesive..............	1.90	.45	☐☐☐☐☐
2009				
C146	79c Scenic American Landscapes - Zion National Park, self-adhesive ..	1.60	.35	☐☐☐☐☐
C147	98c Scenic American Landscapes - Grand Teton National Park, self-adhesive .	2.00	.45	☐☐☐☐☐
C148	80c Scenic American Landscapes - Voyageurs Ntl. Park, self-adhesive .	1.60	.25	☐☐☐☐☐

C139

C140

C141

C142

C143

C144

C145

C146

C147

C148

C149

C150

CE1

E1

E3

E4

E6

Scott No.	Description	Unused Value	Used Value	/ / / / /
2012				
C149	85c Scenic American Landscapes - Glacier Ntl. Park, self-adhesive......	1.75	.35	☐☐☐☐☐
C150	$1.05 Scenic American Landscapes - Lancaster County, self-adhesive	2.10	.45	☐☐☐☐☐

AIR POST SPECIAL DELIVERY STAMPS
1934, Perf. 11

CE1	16c Great Seal, dark blue......................	.60	.70	☐☐☐☐☐

1936

CE2	16c Great Seal (CE1), red & blue	.45	.25	☐☐☐☐☐
a.	Horiz. pair, imperf. vert.	*4,000.*		☐☐☐☐☐

SPECIAL DELIVERY STAMPS
1885-93

E1	10c Messenger Running, blue	550.00	80.00	☐☐☐☐☐
E2	10c Messenger Running, "Post Office" Curved (E3), blue	500.00	45.00	☐☐☐☐☐
E3	10c Messenger Running, orange	300.00	55.00	☐☐☐☐☐

1894, Line under "TEN CENTS"

E4	10c Messenger Running, blue	900.00	80.00	☐☐☐☐☐

1895, Watermark 191

E5	10c Messenger Running (E4), blue	210.00	10.00	☐☐☐☐☐
b.	Printed on both sides........................	—		☐☐☐☐☐

1902

E6	10c Bicycle Messenger, ultramarine......	230.00	10.00	☐☐☐☐☐
a.	10c blue	300.00	10.00	☐☐☐☐☐

1908

E7	10c Helmet of Mercury...........................	70.00	50.00	☐☐☐☐☐

1911, Watermark 190, Perf. 12

E8	10c Bicycle Messenger (E6), ultramarine	110.00	10.00	☐☐☐☐☐
b.	10c violet blue...	140.00	14.00	☐☐☐☐☐

1914, Perf. 10

E9	10c Bicycle Messenger (E6), ultramarine	190.00	12.00	☐☐☐☐☐
a.	10c blue	250.00	15.00	☐☐☐☐☐

1916, Perf. 10, Unwatermarked

E10	10c Bicycle Messenger (E6), pale ultra ..	320.00	50.00	☐☐☐☐☐
a.	10c blue	375.00	50.00	☐☐☐☐☐

1917-25, Perf. 11

E11	10c Bicycle Messenger (E6), ultramarine	20.00	.75	☐☐☐☐☐

E7

E12

E14

E20

E22

Scott No.	Description	Unused Value	Used Value	/ / / / / /

b.	10c gray violet............................	30.00	3.00	
c.	10c blue.......................................	85.00	5.00	
d.	Perf. 10 at left	—		
E12	10c Motorcycle Delivery, gray violet	45.00	2.25	
a.	10c deep ultramarine....................	55.00	2.75	
E13	15c Motorcycle Delivery (E12), dp orange	40.00	2.25	
E14	20c Post Office Truck	2.00	1.00	

1927-51, Perf. 11 x 10½

E15	10c Motorcycle Delivery (E12), gray violet	.65	.25	
a.	10c red lilac	.70	.25	
b.	10c gray lilac	.90	.25	
c.	Horiz. pair, imperf. btwn..................	300.00		
E16	15c Motorcycle Delivery (E12), orange.	.60	.25	
E17	13c Motorcycle Delivery (E12), blue	.60	.25	
E18	17c Motorcycle Delivery (E12), yellow.	3.50	2.50	
E19	20c Post Office Truck	1.20	.25	

1954-57

E20	20c Hands & Letter, deep blue	.40	.25	
E21	30c Hands & Letter (E20), lake..............	.50	.25	

1969-71

E22	45c Arrows, carmine & violet blue	1.20	.25	
E23	60c Arrows (E22), violet blue & carmine	1.25	.25	

F1   FA1

Scott No.	Description	Unused Value	Used Value	/ / / / / /

REGISTRATION STAMP
1911
F1   10c Eagle..   80.00   13.00   ☐☐☐☐☐

CERTIFIED MAIL STAMP
1955
FA1   15c Mailman 65   .60   ☐☐☐☐☐

J1

J29

J69

J77

J88

Scott No.	Description	Unused Value	Used Value	/ / / / / /

POSTAGE DUE STAMPS

1879, Perf. 12

J1	1c Numeral, brown	100.00	14.00	
J2	2c Numeral (J1), brown	425.00	25.00	
J3	3c Numeral (J1), brown	105.00	6.00	
J4	5c Numeral (J1), brown	825.00	70.00	
J5	10c Numeral (J1), brown	1,000.00	70.00	
a.	Imperf., pair	3,000.		
J6	30c Numeral (J1), brown	400.00	65.00	
J7	50c Numeral (J1), brown	650.00	90.00	

1879, Special Printing

J8	1c Numeral (J1), deep brown	22,500.		
J9	2c Numeral (J1), deep brown	19,000.		
J10	3c Numeral (J1), deep brown	25,000.		
J11	5c Numeral (J1), deep brown	15,000.		
J12	10c Numeral (J1), deep brown	8,500.		
J13	30c Numeral (J1), deep brown	9,750.		
J14	50c Numeral (J1), deep brown	8,750.		

1884-89

J15	1c Numeral (J1), red brown	75.00	7.00	
J16	2c Numeral (J1), red brown	90.00	6.00	
J17	3c Numeral (J1), red brown	1,150.	350.00	
J18	5c Numeral (J1), red brown	625.00	50.00	
J19	10c Numeral (J1), red brown	625.00	35.00	
J20	30c Numeral (J1), red brown	225.00	70.00	
J21	50c Numeral (J1), red brown	1,900.	250.00	

1891-93

J22	1c Numeral (J1), bright claret	35.00	2.00	
J23	2c Numeral (J1), bright claret	37.50	2.00	

Scott No.	Description	Unused Value	Used Value	//////
J24	3c Numeral (J1), bright claret...............	75.00	16.00	☐☐☐☐☐
J25	5c Numeral (J1), bright claret..........	110.00	16.00	☐☐☐☐☐
J26	10c Numeral (J1), bright claret...........	180.00	30.00	☐☐☐☐☐
J27	30c Numeral (J1), bright claret...............	650.00	225.00	☐☐☐☐☐
J28	50c Numeral (J1), bright claret...............	700.00	225.00	☐☐☐☐☐

1894

J29	1c Numeral, vermilion........................	2,750.	725.00	☐☐☐☐☐
J30	2c Numeral (J29), vermilion..................	850.00	350.00	☐☐☐☐☐
J31	1c Numeral (J29), deep claret...............	80.00	12.00	☐☐☐☐☐
b.	Vert. pair, imperf. horiz...............	—		☐☐☐☐☐
J32	2c Numeral (J29), deep claret...........	70.00	10.00	☐☐☐☐☐
J33	3c Numeral (J29), deep claret...............	220.00	50.00	☐☐☐☐☐
J34	5c Numeral (J29), deep claret...............	350.00	55.00	☐☐☐☐☐
J35	10c Numeral (J29), deep clare..............	400.00	40.00	☐☐☐☐☐
J36	30c Numeral (J29), deep claret...............	600.00	250.00	☐☐☐☐☐
a.	30c carmine	750.00	275.00	☐☐☐☐☐
b.	30c pale rose	500.00	200.00	☐☐☐☐☐
J37	50c Numeral (J29), deep claret...............	2,000.	800.00	☐☐☐☐☐
a.	50c pale rose....................................	1,800.	725.00	☐☐☐☐☐

1895, Watermark 191

J38	1c Numeral (J29), deep claret...........	15.00	1.00	☐☐☐☐☐
J39	2c Numeral (J29), deep claret	15.00	1.00	☐☐☐☐☐
J40	3c Numeral (J29), deep claret...............	110.00	5.00	☐☐☐☐☐
J41	5c Numeral (J29), deep claret...............	120.00	5.00	☐☐☐☐☐
J42	10c Numeral (J29), deep claret...........	120.00	7.50	☐☐☐☐☐
J43	30c Numeral (J29), deep claret...........	700.00	75.00	☐☐☐☐☐
J44	50c Numeral (J29), deep claret...........	450.00	60.00	☐☐☐☐☐

1910-12, Watermark 190

J45	1c Numeral (J29), deep claret...............	45.00	5.00	☐☐☐☐☐
a.	1c rose carmine	40.00	5.00	☐☐☐☐☐
J46	2c Numeral (J29), deep claret...............	45.00	2.00	☐☐☐☐☐
a.	2c rose carmine	40.00	2.00	☐☐☐☐☐
J47	3c Numeral (J29), deep claret...............	675.00	60.00	☐☐☐☐☐
J48	5c Numeral (J29), deep claret	130.00	12.00	☐☐☐☐☐
a.	5c rose carmine................................	130.00	12.00	☐☐☐☐☐
J49	10c Numeral (J29), deep claret...............	140.00	20.00	☐☐☐☐☐
a.	10c rose carmine	140.00	20.00	☐☐☐☐☐
J50	50c Numeral (J29), deep claret...............	1,150.	175.00	☐☐☐☐☐
a.	50c rose carmine	1,200.	190.00	☐☐☐☐☐

1914-15, Perf. 10

J52	1c Numeral (J29), carmine lake............	90.00	15.00	☐☐☐☐☐
a.	1c dull rose	95.00	15.00	☐☐☐☐☐
J53	2c Numeral (J29), carmine lake............	70.00	1.00	☐☐☐☐☐
a.	2c dull rose	75.00	2.00	☐☐☐☐☐
b.	2c vermilion......................................	75.00	2.00	☐☐☐☐☐

Scott No.	Description	Unused Value	Used Value	/ / / / / /
J54	3c Numeral (J29), carmine lake............	1,150.	75.00	
a.	3c dull rose	1,100.	75.00	
J55	5c Numeral (J29), carmine lake............	55.00	6.00	
a.	5c dull rose	50.00	4.00	
J56	10c Numeral (J29), carmine lake..........	85.00	4.00	
a.	10c dull rose	90.00	5.00	
J57	30c Numeral (J29), carmine lake..........	250.00	55.00	
J58	50c Numeral (J29), carmine lake	*12,500.*	1,600.	

1916, Perf. 10, Unwatermarked

J59	1c Numeral (J29), rose...........................	4,500.	750.00	
J60	2c Numeral (J29), rose...........................	300.00	85.00	

1917, Perf. 11

J61	1c Numeral (J29), carmine rose	3.00	.25	
a.	1c rose red	3.00	.25	
b.	1c deep claret	3.00	.25	
J62	2c Numeral (J29), carmine rose	3.00	.25	
a.	2c rose red	3.00	.25	
b.	2c deep claret	3.00	.25	
J63	3c Numeral (J29), carmine rose	15.00	.80	
a.	3c rose red	15.00	.80	
b.	3c deep claret	15.00	.80	
J64	5c Numeral (J29), carmine	12.50	.80	
a.	5c rose red	12.50	.80	
b.	5c deep claret	12.50	.80	
J65	10c Numeral (J29), carmine rose	25.00	1.00	
a.	10c rose red	25.00	1.00	
b.	10c deep claret	25.00	1.00	
J66	30c Numeral (J29), carmine rose	90.00	2.00	
a.	30c deep claret	90.00	2.00	
b.	As "a," perf. 10 at top, precanceled..	—	*21,000.*	
J67	50c Numeral (J29), carmine rose	150.00	1.00	
a.	50c rose red	150.00	1.00	
b.	50c deep claret	150.00	1.00	

1925

J68	½c Numeral (J29), dull red....................	1.00	.25	

1930-31, Perf. 11

J69	½c Numeral, carmine..............................	4.50	1.90	
J70	1c Numeral (J69), carmine	3.00	.35	
J71	2c Numeral (J69), carmine	4.00	.35	
J72	3c Numeral (J69), carmine	21.00	2.75	
J73	5c Numeral (J69), carmine	19.00	5.00	
J74	10c Numeral (J69), carmine	45.00	2.00	
J75	30c Numeral (J69), carmine	150.00	4.00	
J76	50c Numeral (J69), carmine	200.00	2.00	
J77	$1 Numeral, carmine..............................	35.00	.35	
a.	$1 scarlet..	30.00	.35	

Scott No.	Description	Unused Value	Used Value	/ / / / / /
J78	$5 Numeral (J77), carmine	40.00	.35	☐☐☐☐☐
a.	$5 scarlet..	35.00	.35	☐☐☐☐☐

1931-56, Perf. 11x10½, 10½x11

J79	½c Numeral (J69), dull carmine............	.90	.25	☐☐☐☐☐
a.	½c scarlet..	.90	.25	☐☐☐☐☐
J80	1c Numeral (J69), dull carmine............	.25	.25	☐☐☐☐☐
a.	1c scarlet..	.25	.25	☐☐☐☐☐
J81	2c Numeral (J69), dull carmine............	.25	.25	☐☐☐☐☐
a.	2c scarlet..	.25	.25	☐☐☐☐☐
J82	3c Numeral (J69), dull carmine............	.25	.25	☐☐☐☐☐
a.	3c scarlet..	.25	.25	☐☐☐☐☐
J83	5c Numeral (J69), dull carmine............	.40	.25	☐☐☐☐☐
a.	5c scarlet..	.40	.25	☐☐☐☐☐
J84	10c Numeral (J69), dull carmine............	1.10	.25	☐☐☐☐☐
a.	10c scarlet..	1.10	.25	☐☐☐☐☐
J85	30c Numeral (J69), dull carmine............	7.50	.25	☐☐☐☐☐
a.	30c scarlet..	7.50	.25	☐☐☐☐☐
J86	50c Numeral (J69), dull carmine............	9.00	.25	☐☐☐☐☐
a.	50c scarlet..	9.00	.25	☐☐☐☐☐
J87	$1 Numeral (J77), scarlet	30.00	.25	☐☐☐☐☐

1959, Black numerals

J88	½c Numeral, carmine rose	1.50	1.10	☐☐☐☐☐
J89	1c Numeral (J88), carmine rose............	.25	.25	☐☐☐☐☐
a.	"1 CENT" omitted	225.00		☐☐☐☐☐
b.	Pair, one without "1 CENT"	*400.00*		☐☐☐☐☐
J90	2c Numeral (J88), carmine rose............	.25	.25	☐☐☐☐☐
J91	3c Numeral (J88), carmine rose............	.25	.25	☐☐☐☐☐
a.	Pair, one without "3 CENTS"..........	*675.00*		☐☐☐☐☐
J92	4c Numeral (J88), carmine rose............	.25		☐☐☐☐☐
J93	5c Numeral (J88), carmine rose............	.25	.25	☐☐☐☐☐
a.	Pair, one without "5 CENTS"..........	*1,500.*		☐☐☐☐☐
J94	6c Numeral (J88), carmine rose............	.25	.25	☐☐☐☐☐
a.	Pair, one without "6 CENTS"..........	*850.00*		☐☐☐☐☐
J95	7c Numeral (J88), carmine rose............	.25	.25	☐☐☐☐☐
J96	8c Numeral (J88), carmine rose............	.25	.25	☐☐☐☐☐
a.	Pair, one without "8 CENTS"..........	*850.00*		☐☐☐☐☐
J97	10c Numeral (J88), carmine rose............	.25	.25	☐☐☐☐☐
J98	30c Numeral (J88), carmine rose............	.70	.25	☐☐☐☐☐
J99	50c Numeral (J88), carmine rose............	1.10	.25	☐☐☐☐☐
J100	$1 Numeral (J88), carmine rose............	2.00	.25	☐☐☐☐☐
J101	$5 Numeral (J88), carmine rose............	9.00	.25	☐☐☐☐☐

1978

J102	11c Numeral (J88), carmine rose............	.25	.25	☐☐☐☐☐
J103	13c Numeral (J88), carmine rose............	.25	.25	☐☐☐☐☐

1985

J104	17c Numeral (J88), carmine rose............	.40	.35	☐☐☐☐☐

United States Stamps
of 1917-19
Surcharged

Scott No.	Description	Unused Value	Used Value	/ / / / / /

U.S. OFFICES IN CHINA
1919

K1	2c on 1c Washington, green..................	25.00	*70.00*	☐☐☐☐☐
K2	4c on 2c Washington, rose, type I	25.00	*70.00*	☐☐☐☐☐
K3	6c on 3c Washington, violet, type II......	60.00	*140.00*	☐☐☐☐☐
K4	8c on 4c Washington, brown	60.00	*140.00*	☐☐☐☐☐
K5	10c on 5c Washington, blue....................	65.00	*140.00*	☐☐☐☐☐
K6	12c on 6c Washington, red orange	85.00	*210.00*	☐☐☐☐☐
K7	14c on 7c Washington, black..................	87.50	*210.00*	☐☐☐☐☐
K8	16c on 8c Washington, olive bister..........	70.00	*160.00*	☐☐☐☐☐
a.	16c on 8c olive green............................	60.00	*140.00*	☐☐☐☐☐
K9	18c on 9c Franklin, salmon red	65.00	*175.00*	☐☐☐☐☐
K10	20c on 10c Franklin, orange yellow	60.00	*140.00*	☐☐☐☐☐
K11	24c on 12c Franklin, brown carmine.......	80.00	*160.00*	☐☐☐☐☐
a.	24c on 12c claret brown.........................	110.00	*225.00*	☐☐☐☐☐
K12	30c on 15c Franklin, gray	87.50	*230.00*	☐☐☐☐☐
K13	40c on 20c Franklin, deep ultramarine....	130.00	*325.00*	☐☐☐☐☐
K14	60c on 30c Franklin, orange red..............	120.00	*275.00*	☐☐☐☐☐
K15	$1 on 50c Franklin, light violet	575.00	*1,000.*	☐☐☐☐☐
K16	$2 on $1 Franklin, violet brown	450.00	*75.00*	☐☐☐☐☐
a.	Double surcharge	*10,500.*	*10,000.*	☐☐☐☐☐

Nos. 498 and 528B
Surcharged

1922, Surcharged locally

K17	2c on 1c Washington, green..................	110.00	*225.00*	☐☐☐☐☐
K18	4c on 2c Washington, carmine, type VII	100.00	*200.00*	☐☐☐☐☐
a.	"SHANGHAI" omitted....................	*7,500.*		☐☐☐☐☐
b.	"CHINA" only.................................	*15,000.*		☐☐☐☐☐

O1   O68   O47

O121   O127   O138A   O144

Scott No.	Description	Unused Value	Used Value	/ / / / / /

OFFICIAL STAMPS
AGRICULTURE DEPT.
Continental Bank Note Printings, Thin Hard Paper

O1	1c Franklin, yellow	280.00	180.00	
O2	2c Jackson (O1), yellow	240.00	85.00	
O3	3c Washington (O1), yellow	220.00	16.00	
O4	6c Lincoln (O1), yellow	260.00	60.00	
O5	10c Jefferson (O1), yellow	525.00	200.00	
O6	12c Clay (O1), yellow	450.00	260.00	
O7	15c Webster (O1), yellow	425.00	230.00	
O8	24c Scott (O1), yellow	425.00	220.00	
O9	30c Hamilton (O1), yellow	550.00	270.00	

EXECUTIVE DEPT.

O10	1c Franklin (O1), carmine	850.00	475.00	
O11	2c Jackson (O1), carmine	550.00	240.00	
O12	3c Washington (O1), carmine	700.00	210.00	
a.	3c violet rose	700.00	210.00	
O13	6c Lincoln (O1), carmine	900.00	550.00	
O14	10c Jefferson (O1), carmine	1,200.	650.00	

INTERIOR DEPT.

O15	1c Franklin (O1), vermilion	75.00	10.00	
O16	2c Jackson (O1), vermilion	70.00	12.00	
O17	3c Washington (O1), vermilion	80.00	6.00	
O18	6c Lincoln (O1), vermilion	70.00	10.00	
O19	10c Jefferson (O1), vermilion	70.00	20.00	
O20	12c Clay (O1), vermilion	90.00	12.00	

491

Scott No.	Description	Unused Value	Used Value	/ / / / / /
O21	15c Webster (O1), vermilion	200.00	25.00	
O22	24c Scott (O1), vermilion	180.00	20.00	
a.	Double impression	—		
O23	30c Hamilton (O1), vermilion	290.00	20.00	
O24	90c Perry (O1), vermilion	325.00	50.00	

JUSTICE DEPT.

O25	1c Franklin (O1), purple	250.00	100.00	
O26	2c Jackson (O1), purple	310.00	110.00	
O27	3c Washington (O1), purple	320.00	35.00	
O28	6c Lincoln (O1), purple	310.00	45.00	
O29	10c Jefferson (O1), purple	310.00	100.00	
O30	12c Clay (O1), purple	260.00	75.00	
O31	15c Webster (O1), purple	475.00	200.00	
O32	24c Scott (O1), purple	1,250.	425.00	
O33	30c Hamilton (O1), purple	1,300.	350.00	
O34	90c Perry (O1), purple	1,900.	900.00	

NAVY DEPT.

O35	1c Franklin (O1), ultramarine	160.00	50.00	
a.	1c dull blue	160.00	50.00	
O36	2c Jackson (O1), ultramarine	160.00	25.00	
a.	2c dull blue	160.00	25.00	
O37	3c Washington (O1), ultramarine	170.00	15.00	
a.	3c dull blue	170.00	15.00	
O38	6c Lincoln (O1), ultramarine	150.00	25.00	
a.	6c dull blue	150.00	25.00	
O39	7c Stanton (O1), ultramarine	650.00	230.00	
a.	7c dull blue	650.00	230.00	
O40	10c Jefferson (O1), ultramarine	210.00	45.00	
a.	10c dull blue	210.00	45.00	
O41	12c Clay (O1), ultramarine	220.00	45.00	
O42	15c Webster (O1), ultramarine	375.00	75.00	
O43	24c Scott (O1), ultramarine	400.00	85.00	
a.	24c dull blue	375.00	80.00	
O44	30c Hamilton (O1), ultramarine	325.00	50.00	
O45	90c Perry (O1), ultramarine	1,050.	375.00	
a.	Double impression		*20,000.*	

POST OFFICE DEPT.

O47	1c Numeral, black	25.00	12.00	
O48	2c Numeral (O47), black	30.00	10.00	
a.	Double impression	600.00	400.00	
O49	3c Numeral (O47), black	10.00	2.00	
a.	Printed on both sides		*7,500.*	
O50	6c Numeral (O47), black	30.00	8.00	
a.	Diagonal half used as 3c on cover		*5,000.*	
O51	10c Numeral (O47), black	140.00	55.00	
O52	12c Numeral (O47), black	120.00	12.00	

Scott No.	Description	Unused Value	Used Value	/ / / / / /
O53	15c Numeral (O47), black......................	140.00	20.00	
O54	24c Numeral (O47), black......................	200.00	25.00	
O55	30c Numeral (O47), black......................	200.00	25.00	
O56	90c Numeral (O47), black......................	220.00	25.00	

STATE DEPT.

Scott No.	Description	Unused Value	Used Value	/ / / / / /
O57	1c Franklin (O1), bright green.............	260.00	75.00	
O58	2c Jackson (O1), dark green	310.00	100.00	
O59	3c Washington (O1), bright green	220.00	25.00	
O60	6c Lincoln (O1), bright green..............	220.00	30.00	
O61	7c Stanton (O1), dark green.................	290.00	65.00	
O62	10c Jefferson (O1), dark green	230.00	55.00	
O63	12c Clay (O1), dark green.....................	310.00	125.00	
O64	15c Webster (O1), dark green...............	320.00	90.00	
O65	24c Scott (O1), dark green....................	525.00	230.00	
O66	30c Hamilton (O1), dark green..............	500.00	180.00	
O67	90c Perry (O1), dark green	1,050.	325.00	
O68	$2 Seward, green & black	1,750.	1,600.	
O69	$5 Seward (O68), green & black	8,000.	13,000.	
O70	$10 Seward (O68), green & black	5,000.	7,000.	
O71	$20 Seward (O68), green & black	5,250.	5,000.	

TREASURY DEPT.

Scott No.	Description	Unused Value	Used Value	/ / / / / /
O72	1c Franklin (O1), brown......................	120.00	10.00	
O73	2c Jackson (O1), brown	125.00	8.00	
O74	3c Washington (O1), brown.................	110.00	2.00	
a.	Double impression............................		5,000.	
O75	6c Lincoln (O1), brown......................	120.00	4.00	
O76	7c Stanton (O1), brown......................	250.00	35.00	
O77	10c Jefferson (O1), brown....................	240.00	12.00	
O78	12c Clay (O1), brown...........................	300.00	10.00	
O79	15c Webster (O1), brown	300.00	12.00	
O80	24c Scott (O1), brown...........................	675.00	100.00	
O81	30c Hamilton (O1), brown....................	400.00	12.00	
O82	90c Perry (O1), brown	400.00	15.00	

WAR DEPT.

Scott No.	Description	Unused Value	Used Value	/ / / / / /
O83	1c Franklin (O1), rose........................	240.00	15.00	
O84	2c Jackson (O1), rose.........................	240.00	15.00	
O85	3c Washington (O1), rose	240.00	5.00	
O86	6c Lincoln (O1), rose.........................	625.00	10.00	
O87	7c Stanton (O1), rose.........................	160.00	90.00	
O88	10c Jefferson (O1), rose......................	140.00	25.00	
O89	12c Clay (O1), rose..............................	275.00	12.00	
O90	15c Webster (O1), rose	85.00	15.00	
O91	24c Scott (O1), rose..............................	85.00	12.00	
O92	30c Hamilton (O1), rose.......................	130.00	12.00	
O93	90c Perry (O1), rose.............................	225.00	50.00	

Scott No.	Description	Unused Value	Used Value	/ / / / / /

AGRICULTURE DEPT.
1879, American Bank Note Co. Printings, Soft Porous Paper

Scott No.	Description	Unused Value	Used Value	
O94	1c Franklin (O1), yellow, no gum..........	6,000.		☐☐☐☐☐
O95	3c Washington (O1), yellow	550.00	125.00	☐☐☐☐☐

INTERIOR DEPT.

Scott No.	Description	Unused Value	Used Value	
O96	1c Franklin (O1), vermilion...................	300.00	275.00	☐☐☐☐☐
O97	2c Jackson (O1), vermilion....................	10.00	3.00	☐☐☐☐☐
O98	3c Washington (O1), vermilion	10.00	3.00	☐☐☐☐☐
O99	6c Lincoln (O1), vermilion....................	10.00	12.50	☐☐☐☐☐
O100	10c Jefferson (O1), vermilion................	110.00	75.00	☐☐☐☐☐
O101	12c Clay (O1), vermilion......................	230.00	115.00	☐☐☐☐☐
O102	15c Webster (O1), vermilion	400.00	260.00	☐☐☐☐☐
O103	24c Scott (O1), vermilion	4,500.	—	☐☐☐☐☐

JUSTICE DEPT.

Scott No.	Description	Unused Value	Used Value	
O106	3c Washington (O1), bluish purple	190.00	100.00	☐☐☐☐☐
O107	6c Lincoln (O1), bluish purple	475.00	275.00	☐☐☐☐☐

POST OFFICE DEPT.

Scott No.	Description	Unused Value	Used Value	
O108	3c Numeral (O47), black	30.00	10.00	☐☐☐☐☐

TREASURY DEPT.

Scott No.	Description	Unused Value	Used Value	
O109	3c Washington (O1), brown..................	80.00	10.00	☐☐☐☐☐
O110	6c Lincoln (O1), brown	200.00	50.00	☐☐☐☐☐
O111	10c Jefferson (O1), brown	260.00	80.00	☐☐☐☐☐
O112	30c Hamilton (O1), brown....................	2,400.	425.00	☐☐☐☐☐
O113	90c Perry (O1), brown	5,500.	750.00	☐☐☐☐☐

WAR DEPT.

Scott No.	Description	Unused Value	Used Value	
O114	1c Franklin (O1), rose red....................	6.00	4.00	☐☐☐☐☐
O115	2c Jackson (O1), rose red	12.00	4.00	☐☐☐☐☐
O116	3c Washington (O1), rose red	12.00	2.00	☐☐☐☐☐
a.	Imperf., pair...............................	5,000.		☐☐☐☐☐
b.	Double impression	6,500.		☐☐☐☐☐
O117	6c Lincoln (O1), rose red.....................	11.00	3.00	☐☐☐☐☐
O118	10c Jefferson (O1), rose red	65.00	50.00	☐☐☐☐☐
O119	12c Clay (O1), rose red........................	60.00	14.00	☐☐☐☐☐
O120	30c Hamilton (O1), rose red.................	225.00	100.00	☐☐☐☐☐

1875, SPECIAL PRINTINGS, Ovptd. "SPECIMEN" (Type D)
Thin hard white paper
AGRICULTURE DEPT., Carmine Overprint

Scott No.	Description	Unused Value		
O1S	1c Franklin (O1), yellow	32.50		☐☐☐☐☐
a.	"Sepcimen" error..........................	2,500.		☐☐☐☐☐
b.	Horiz. Ribbed paper......................	37.50		☐☐☐☐☐
c.	Small dotted "i" in "Specimen".......	400.00		☐☐☐☐☐
O2S	2c Jackson (O1), yellow......................	55.00		☐☐☐☐☐
a.	"Sepcimen" error...........................	3,000.		☐☐☐☐☐

Scott No.	Description	Unused Value	Used Value	/ / / / / /
O3S	3c Washington (O1), yellow	400.00		
a.	"Sepcimen" error	*12,500.*		
O4S	6c Lincoln (O1), yellow	400.00		
a.	"Sepcimen" error	*20,000.*		
O5S	10c Jefferson (O1), yellow	400.00		
a.	"Sepcimen" error	*17,500.*		
O6S	12c Clay (O1), yellow	400.00		
a.	"Sepcimen" error	*12,500.*		
O7S	15c Webster (O1), yellow	400.00		
a.	"Sepcimen" error	*12,500.*		
O8S	24c Scott (O1), yellow	400.00		
a.	"Sepcimen" error	*12,500.*		
O9S	30c Hamilton (O1), yellow	400.00		
a.	"Sepcimen" error	*13,500.*		

EXECUTIVE DEPT., Blue Overprint

Scott No.	Description	Unused Value	Used Value	/ / / / / /
O10S	1c Franklin (O1), carmine	32.50		
a.	Horiz. Ribbed paper	35.00		
b.	Small dotted "i" in "Specimen"	500.00		
O11S	2c Jackson (O1), carmine	55.00		
O12S	3c Washington (O1), carmine	67.50		
O13S	6c Lincoln (O1), carmine	67.50		
O14S	10c Jefferson (O1), carmine	67.50		

INTERIOR DEPT., Blue Overprint

Scott No.	Description	Unused Value	Used Value	/ / / / / /
O15S	1c Franklin (O1), vermilion	60.00		
O16S	2c Jackson (O1), vermilion	140.00		
a.	"Sepcimen" error	*12,500.*		
O17S	3c Washington (O1), vermilion	*2,500.*		
O18S	6c Lincoln (O1), vermilion	*2,500.*		
O19S	10c Jefferson (O1), vermilion	*2,500.*		
O20S	12c Clay (O1), vermilion	*2,500.*		
O21S	15c Webster (O1), vermilion	*2,500.*		
O22S	24c Scott (O1), vermilion	*2,500.*		
O23S	30c Hamilton (O1), vermilion	*2,500.*		
O24S	90c Perry (O1), vermilion	*2,500.*		

JUSTICE DEPT., Blue Overprint

Scott No.	Description	Unused Value	Used Value	/ / / / / /
O25S	1c Franklin (O1), purple	32.50		
a.	"Sepcimen" error	*1,900.*		
b.	Horiz. Ribbed paper	35.00		
c.	Small dotted "i" in "Specimen"	500.00		
O26S	2c Jackson (O1), purple	55.00		
a.	"Sepcimen" error	*2,500.*		
O27S	3c Washington (O1), purple	1,250.		
a.	"Sepcimen" error	*11,000.*		
O28S	6c Lincoln (O1), purple	1,250.		
O29S	10c Jefferson (O1), purple	1,250.		
O30S	12c Clay (O1), purple	1,250.		

Scott No.	Description	Unused Value	Used Value	/ / / / / /
a.	"Sepcimen" error	*17,500.*		
O31S	15c Webster (O1), purple......................	1,250.		
a.	"Sepcimen" error	*17,500.*		
O32S	24c Scott (O1), purple	1,250.		
a.	"Sepcimen" error	*20,000.*		
O33S	30c Hamilton (O1), purple	1,250.		
a.	"Sepcimen" error	*15,000.*		
O34S	90c Perry (O1), purple...........................	1,250.		

NAVY DEPT., Carmine Overprint

Scott No.	Description	Unused Value	Used Value	/ / / / / /
O35S	1c Franklin (O1), ultramarine...............	35.00		
a.	"Sepcimen" error	*2,500.*		
O36S	2c Jackson (O1), ultramarine.................	75.00		
a.	"Sepcimen" error	*3,250.*		
O37S	3c Washington (O1), ultramarine	1,400.		
O38S	6c Lincoln (O1), ultramarine.................	1,400.		
O39S	7c Stanton (O1), ultramarine.................	550.00		
a.	"Sepcimen" error	*10,000.*		
O40S	10c Jefferson (O1), ultramarine..............	1,400.		
a.	"Sepcimen" error	*17,500.*		
O41S	12c Clay (O1), ultramarine.....................	1,400.		
a.	"Sepcimen" error	*17,500.*		
O42S	15c Webster (O1), ultramarine	1,400.		
a.	"Sepcimen" error	*15,000.*		
O43S	24c Scott (O1), ultramarine...................	1,400.		
a.	"Sepcimen" error	*15,000.*		
O44S	30c Hamilton (O1), ultramarine	1,400.		
a.	"Sepcimen" error	*17,500.*		
O45S	90c Perry (O1), ultramarine...................	1,400.		

POST OFFICE DEPT., Carmine Overprint

Scott No.	Description	Unused Value	Used Value	/ / / / / /
O47S	1c Numeral (O47), black	45.00		
a.	"Sepcimen" error	*1,900.*		
b.	Inverted overprint..............................	*2,500.*		
O48S	2c Numeral (O47), black	325.00		
a.	"Sepcimen" error	*3,250.*		
O49S	3c Numeral (O47), black	1,600.		
a.	"Sepcimen" error	—		
O50S	6c Numeral (O47), black	1,600.		
O51S	10c Numeral (O47), black......................	1,100.		
a.	"Sepcimen" error..............................	*15,000.*		
O52S	12c Numeral (O47), black......................	1,600.		
O53S	15c Numeral (O47), black......................	1,600.		
a.	"Sepcimen" error..............................	*20,000.*		
O54S	24c Numeral (O47), black......................	1,600.		
a.	"Sepcimen" error..............................	*20,000.*		
O55S	30c Numeral (O47), black......................	1,600.		
O56S	90c Numeral (O47), black......................	1,600.		
a.	"Sepcimen" error..............................	*20,000.*		

Scott No.	Description	Unused Value	Used Value	/ / / / / /

STATE DEPT., Carmine Overprint

Scott No.	Description	Unused Value	Used Value
O57S	1c Franklin (O1), bluish green..............	32.50	
a.	"Sepcimen" error..............................	*1,900.*	
b.	Horiz. Ribbed paper	35.00	
c.	Small dotted "i" in "Specimen".......	550.00	
d.	Double overprint.............................	3,800.	
O58S	2c Jackson (O1), dark green	90.00	
a.	"Sepcimen" error..............................	2,500.	
O59S	3c Washington (O1), bright green	140.00	
a.	"Sepcimen" error..............................	*6,000.*	
O60S	6c Lincoln (O1), bright green..............	350.00	
a.	"Sepcimen" error..............................	*11,000.*	
O61S	7c Stanton (O1), dark green.................	140.00	
a.	"Sepcimen" error..............................	*8,250.*	
O62S	10c Jefferson (O1), dark green	550.00	
a.	"Sepcimen" error..............................	*17,500.*	
O63S	12c Clay (O1), dark green....................	550.00	
a.	"Sepcimen" error..............................	*17,500.*	
O64S	15c Webster (O1), dark green................	600.00	
O65S	24c Scott (O1), dark green...................	660.00	
a.	"Sepcimen" error..............................	*17,500.*	
O66S	30c Hamilton (O1), dark green..............	600.00	
a.	"Sepcimen" error..............................	*17,500.*	
O67S	90c Perry (O1), dark green	600.00	
a.	"Sepcimen" error..............................	*15,000.*	
O68S	$2 Seward (O68), green & black	25,000.	
O69S	$5 Seward (O68), green & black	30,000.	
O70S	$10 Seward (O68), green & black	60,000.	
O71S	$20 Seward (O68), green & black	100,000.	

TREASURY DEPT., Blue Overprint

Scott No.	Description	Unused Value	Used Value
O72S	1c Franklin (O1), brown......................	80.00	
O73S	2c Jackson (O1), brown	450.00	
O74S	3c Washington (O1), brown.................	1,600.	
O75S	6c Lincoln (O1), brown.......................	1,600.	
O76S	7c Stanton (O1), brown.......................	950.00	
O77S	10c Jefferson (O1), brown...................	1,600.	
O78S	12c Clay (O1), brown..........................	1,600.	
O79S	15c Webster (O1), brown.....................	1,600.	
O80S	24c Scott (O1), brown.........................	1,600.	
O81S	30c Hamilton (O1), brown...................	1,600.	
O82S	90c Perry (O1), brown	1,650.	

WAR DEPT., Blue Overprint

Scott No.	Description	Unused Value	Used Value
O83S	1c Franklin (O1), deep rose	35.00	
a.	"Sepcimen" error	*1,600.*	
O84S	2c Jackson (O1), deep rose..................	125.00	
a.	"Sepcimen" error	*2,000.*	
O85S	3c Washington (O1), deep rose	1,300.	

Scott No.	Description	Unused Value	Used Value	/ / / / / /
a.	"Sepcimen" error	*11,000.*		
O86S	6c Lincoln (O1), deep rose	1,300.		
a.	"Sepcimen" error	*27,500.*		
O87S	7c Stanton (O1), deep rose	425.00		
a.	"Sepcimen" error	10,000.		
O88S	10c Jefferson (O1), deep rose	1,400.		
a.	"Sepcimen" error	*13,500.*		
O89S	12c Clay (O1), deep rose	1,400.		
a.	"Sepcimen" error	*13,500.*		
O90S	15c Webster (O1), deep rose	1,400.		
a.	"Sepcimen" error	*13,500.*		
O91S	24c Scott (O1), deep rose	1,400.		
a.	"Sepcimen" error	*13,500.*		
O92S	30c Hamilton (O1), deep rose	1,400.		
a.	"Sepcimen" error	*13,500.*		
O93S	90c Perry (O1), deep rose	1,400.		
a.	"Sepcimen" error	*13,500.*		

Soft, porous paper
EXECUTIVE DEPT., Blue Overprint

O10xS	1c Franklin (O1), violet rose	95.00		

NAVY DEPT., Carmine Overprint

O35xS	1c Franklin (O1), gray blue	100.00		
a.	Double overprint	1,200.		

STATE DEPT., Carmine Overprint

O57xS	1c Franklin (O1), yellow green	180.00		

OFFICIAL POSTAL SAVINGS MAIL
1911, Watermark 191

O121	2c Text, black	17.50	2.00	
O122	50c Text (O121), dark green	160.00	60.00	
O123	$1 Text (O121), ultramarine	200.00	15.00	

Watermark 190

O124	1c Text (O121), dark violet	10.00	2.00	
O125	2c Text (O121), black	55.00	7.00	
O126	10c Text (O121), carmine	20.00	2.00	

1983-85

O127	1c Great Seal	.25	.25	
O128	4c Great Seal (O127)	.25	.25	
O129	13c Great Seal (O127)	.50	*15.00*	
O129A	14c Great Seal (O127)	.45	.50	
O130	17c Great Seal (O127)	.60	.40	
O132	$1 Great Seal (O127)	2.25	1.00	
O133	$5 Great Seal (O127)	9.50	9.00	

Coil Stamps, Perf 10 Vertically

O135	20c Great Seal (O127)	1.75	2.00	
a.	Imperf., pair	*2,000.*		
O136	22c Great Seal (O127)	1.00	*2.00*	

Scott No.	Description	Unused Value	Used Value	/ / / / / /

1985

O138 (14c) Great Seal (O127), inscribed "Postal Card Rate D" ...... 7.50 *15.00* ☐☐☐☐☐

1985-88, Coil Stamps, Perf. 10 Vertically

O138A 15c Great Seal, frame line completely around design .... .50 .50 ☐☐☐☐☐

O138B 20c Great Seal (O138A) .... .50 .30 ☐☐☐☐☐

O139 (22c) Great Seal (O127), inscribed "Domestic Letter Rate D" .... 5.25 *10.00* ☐☐☐☐☐

O140 (25c) Great Seal (O138A), inscribed "Domestic Letter Rate E" .... .75 2.00 ☐☐☐☐☐

O141 25c Great Seal (O138A) .... .65 .50 ☐☐☐☐☐

a. Imperf., pair .... *1,250.* — ☐☐☐☐☐

1989

O143 1c Great Seal (O138A) .... .25 .25 ☐☐☐☐☐

1991, Coil Stamps, Perf. 10 Vertically

O144 (29c) Great Seal .... .80 .50 ☐☐☐☐☐

O145 29c Great Seal (O138A) .... .70 .30 ☐☐☐☐☐

1991-93

O146 4c Great Seal (O138A) .... .25 .30 ☐☐☐☐☐

O146A 10c Great Seal (O138A) .... .30 .30 ☐☐☐☐☐

O147 19c Great Seal (O138A) .... .40 .50 ☐☐☐☐☐

O148 23c Great Seal (O138A) .... .50 .30 ☐☐☐☐☐

O151 $1 Great Seal (O138A) .... 5.00 .75 ☐☐☐☐☐

Coil Stamps, Perf. 10 Vertically

O152 (32c) Great Seal (O144), inscribed "G" ..... .65 .50 ☐☐☐☐☐

O153 32c Great Seal (O138A), with micro text 1.50 .50 ☐☐☐☐☐

1995

O154 1c Great Seal (O138A), with micro text .25 *.50* ☐☐☐☐☐

O155 20c Great Seal (O138A), with micro text .55 *.50* ☐☐☐☐☐

O156 23c Great Seal (O138A), with micro text .60 .50 ☐☐☐☐☐

1999, Oct. 8 Perf. 9¾ Vertically Coil Stamp

O157 33c Great Seal (O138A), with micro text 2.25 — ☐☐☐☐☐

2001-2006

O158 34c Great Seal (O138A), coil stamp .... 2.25 .50 ☐☐☐☐☐

O159 37c Great Seal (O138A), coil stamp .... .75 .50 ☐☐☐☐☐

O160 39c Great Seal (O138A), coil stamp .... .80 .50 ☐☐☐☐☐

O161 $1 Great Seal (O138A), background is crosshatched lines .... 3.00 .90 ☐☐☐☐☐

2007

O162 41c Great Seal (O138A), coil stamp ...... 1.00 .50 ☐☐☐☐☐

2009, Feb. 24, Serpentine Die Cut 11½ x 10¾

O163 1c Great Seal (O138A), self-adhesive...... .25 .25 ☐☐☐☐☐

PR1

PR2

PR3

PR9

PR16

PR24

PR25

PR26

PR27

PR28

PR29

PR30

PR31

PR32

PR102

PR106

PR108

PR109

PR110

PR111

PR112

PR113

HOW TO USE THIS BOOK

In cases where two or more Scott numbers share a common design, the illustration shows the first Scott number that bears that design. Subsequent Scott numbers showing the same design will have the first Scott number in parentheses following the description to guide the user to the correct design.

Scott No.	Description	Unused Value	Used Value	/ / / / /
NEWSPAPER STAMPS				
1865, Thin Hard Paper, No Gum				
PR1	5c Washington, dark blue	750.00	*2,000.*	
a.	5c light blue	1,000.00	—	
PR2	10c Franklin, blue green	300.00	*1,800.*	
a.	10c green	300.00	*1,800.*	
b.	Pelure paper	350.00	*1,800.*	
PR3	25c Lincoln, orange red	400.00	*2,500.*	
a.	25c carmine red	350.00	*2,500.*	
b.	Pelure paper	400.00		
White Border, Yellowish Paper				
PR4	5c Washington (PR1), light blue	500.00	2,400.	
a.	5c dark blue	500.00	—	
b.	Pelure paper	550.00	—	
1875, Reprints, Hard White Paper, No Gum				
PR5	5c Washington (PR1), dull blue	225.00		
a.	Printed on both sides	*5,750.*		
PR6	10c Franklin (PR2), dark bluish green	250.00		
a.	Printed on both sides	*4,250.*		
PR7	25c Lincoln (PR3), dark carmine	300.00		
1881, Reprint, Soft Porous Paper, White Border				
PR8	5c Washington (PR1), dark blue	750.00		
1875, Thin Hard Paper				
PR9	2c Statue of Freedom, black	300.00	40.00	
PR10	3c Statue of Freedom (PR9), black	300.00	45.00	
PR11	4c Statue of Freedom (PR9), black	300.00	40.00	
PR12	6c Statue of Freedom (PR9), black	300.00	45.00	
PR13	8c Statue of Freedom (PR9), black	350.00	65.00	
PR14	9c Statue of Freedom (PR9), black	500.00	125.00	
PR15	10c Statue of Freedom (PR9), black	550.00	140.00	
PR16	12c "Justice" (PR16), rose	800.00	100.00	
PR17	24c "Justice" (PR16), rose	850.00	125.00	
PR18	36c "Justice" (PR16), rose	850.00	150.00	
PR19	48c "Justice" (PR16), rose	1,250.	400.00	
PR20	60c "Justice" (PR16), rose	1,250.	115.00	
PR21	72c "Justice" (PR16), rose	1,500.	375.00	
PR22	84c "Justice" (PR16), rose	1,850.	375.00	
PR23	96c "Justice" (PR16), rose	1,350.	250.00	
PR24	$1.92 Ceres, dark brown	1,650.	250.00	
PR25	$3 "Victory," vermilion	1,800.	450.00	
PR26	$6 Clio, ultramarine	3,600.	550.00	
PR27	$9 Minerva, yellow orange	4,000.	*1,000.*	
PR28	$12 Vesta, blue green	4,500.	*1,100.*	
PR29	$24 "Peace," dark gray violet	4,750.	*1,200.*	

Scott No.	Description	Unused Value	Used Value	/ / / / / /
PR30	$36 "Commerce," brown rose	5,000.	*1,400.*	
PR31	$48 Hebe, red rose	6,250.	*1,600.*	
PR32	$60 Indian Maiden, violet	6,500.	*1,750.*	

1875, Special Printing, Hard White Paper, No Gum

Scott No.	Description	Unused Value	Used Value	/ / / / / /
PR33	2c Statue of Freedom (PR9), gray black	650.00		
a.	Horiz. ribbed paper	450.00		
PR34	3c Statue of Freedom (PR9), gray black	650.00		
a.	Horiz. ribbed paper	500.00		
PR35	4c Statue of Freedom (PR9), gray black	700.00		
a.	Horiz. ribbed paper	1,000.		
PR36	6c Statue of Freedom (PR9), gray black	900.00		
PR37	8c Statue of Freedom (PR9), gray black	975.00		
PR38	9c Statue of Freedom (PR9), gray black	1,050.		
PR39	10c Statue of Freedom (PR9), gray black	1,400.		
a.	Horiz. ribbed paper	—		
PR40	12c "Justice" (PR16), pale rose	1,500.		
PR41	24c "Justice" (PR16), pale rose	2,100.		
PR42	36c "Justice" (PR16), pale rose	2,800.		
PR43	48c "Justice" (PR16), pale rose	4,000.		
PR44	60c "Justice" (PR16), pale rose	4,000.		
PR45	72c "Justice" (PR16), pale rose	4,500.		
PR46	84c "Justice" (PR16), pale rose	*5,000.*		
PR47	96c "Justice" (PR16), pale rose	*8,500.*		
PR48	$1.92 Ceres (PR24), dark brown	*22,500.*		
PR49	$3 "Victory" (PR25), vermilion	*45,000.*		
PR50	$6 Clio (PR26), ultramarine	*80,000.*		
PR51	$9 Minerva (PR27), yellow orange	*250,000.*		
PR52	$12 Vesta (PR28), blue green	*125,000.*		
PR53	$24 "Peace" (PR29), dark gray violet	—		
PR54	$36 "Commerce" (PR30), brown rose	*250,000.*		
PR55	$48 Hebe (PR31), red brown	—		
PR56	$60 Indian Maiden (PR32), violet	—		

1879, Soft Porous Paper

Scott No.	Description	Unused Value	Used Value	/ / / / / /
PR57	2c Statue of Freedom (PR9), black	75.00	15.00	
PR58	3c Statue of Freedom (PR9), black	85.00	20.00	
PR59	4c Statue of Freedom (PR9), black	95.00	27.50	
PR60	6c Statue of Freedom (PR9), black	125.00	35.00	
PR61	8c Statue of Freedom (PR9), black	135.00	35.00	
PR62	10c Statue of Freedom (PR9), black	135.00	35.00	
PR63	12c "Justice" (PR16), red	500.00	125.00	
PR64	24c "Justice" (PR16), red	500.00	125.00	
PR65	36c "Justice" (PR16), red	1,000.	325.00	
PR66	48c "Justice" (PR16), red	1,000.	300.00	
PR67	60c "Justice" (PR16), red	1,000.	275.00	
a.	Imperf., pair	*4,000.*		
PR68	72c "Justice" (PR16), red	1,250.	425.00	

Scott No.	Description	Unused Value	Used Value	/ / / / / /
PR69	84c "Justice" (PR16), red	1,250.	350.00	
PR70	96c "Justice" (PR16), red	1,200.	275.00	
PR71	$1.92 Ceres (PR24), pale brown	550.00	175.00	
PR72	$3 "Victory" (PR25), red vermilion	625.00	200.00	
PR73	$6 Clio (PR26), blue	1,050.	300.00	
PR74	$9 Minerva (PR27), orange	800.00	225.00	
PR75	$12 Vesta (PR28), yellow green	850.00	250.00	
PR76	$24 "Peace" (PR29), dark violet	800.00	300.00	
PR77	$36 "Commerce" (PR30), Indian red	850.00	350.00	
PR78	$48 Hebe (PR31), yellow brown	900.00	450.00	
PR79	$60 Indian Maiden (PR32), purple	850.00	400.00	

1883, Special Printing

PR80	2c Statue of Freedom (PR9), intense black	1,600.		

1885

PR81	1c Statue of Freedom (PR9), black	95.00	12.50	
PR82	12c "Justice" (PR16), carmine	200.00	30.00	
PR83	24c "Justice" (PR16), carmine	200.00	32.50	
PR84	36c "Justice" (PR16), carmine	300.00	57.50	
PR85	48c "Justice" (PR16), carmine	425.00	75.00	
PR86	60c "Justice" (PR16), carmine	550.00	100.00	
PR87	72c "Justice" (PR16), carmine	550.00	110.00	
PR88	84c "Justice" (PR16), carmine	520.00	250.00	
PR89	96c "Justice" (PR16), carmine	750.00	190.00	

1894

PR90	1c Statue of Freedom (PR9), intense black	425.00	4,500.	
PR91	2c Statue of Freedom (PR9), intense black	500.00		
PR92	4c Statue of Freedom (PR9), intense black	525.00	13,500.	
PR93	6c Statue of Freedom (PR9), intense black	4,500.		
PR94	10c Statue of Freedom (PR9), intense black	1,200.		
PR95	12c "Justice" (PR16), pink	2,600.	4,500.	
PR96	24c "Justice" (PR16), pink	3,750.	4,750.	
PR97	36c "Justice" (PR16), pink	50,000.		
PR98	60c "Justice" (PR16), pink	55,000.	16,000.	
PR99	96c "Justice" (PR16), pink	52,500.		
PR100	$3 "Victory" (PR25), scarlet	60,000.		
PR101	$6 Clio (PR26), pale blue	60,000.	—	

1895

PR102	1c Statue of Freedom, black	230.00	125.00	
PR103	2c Statue of Freedom (PR102), black	230.00	125.00	

Scott No.	Description	Unused Value	Used Value	/ / / / / /
PR104	5c Statue of Freedom (PR102), black ...	300.00	*175.00*	
PR105	10c Statue of Freedom (PR102), black ...	550.00	*400.00*	
PR106	25c "Justice," carmine.............................	750.00	*500.00*	
PR107	50c "Justice" (PR106), carmine	*2,750.*	*600.00*	
PR108	$2 "Victory"	1,500.	*1,100.*	
PR109	$5 Clio, ultramarine	2,100.	*1,750.*	
PR110	$10 Vesta	2,500.	*2,000.*	
PR111	$20 "Peace"	3,250.	*2,500.*	
PR112	$50 "Commerce".....................................	2,900.	*750.00*	
PR113	$100 Indian Maiden	3,500.	*7,000.*	

1895-97, Watermark 191

Scott No.	Description	Unused Value	Used Value	/ / / / / /
PR114	1c Statue of Freedom (PR102), black ...	8.00	*25.00*	
PR115	2c Statue of Freedom (PR102), black ...	8.00	*25.00*	
PR116	5c Statue of Freedom (PR102), black ...	13.00	*40.00*	
PR117	10c Statue of Freedom (PR102), black ...	13.00	*25.00*	
PR118	25c "Justice" (PR106), carmine	20.00	*65.00*	
PR119	50c "Justice" (PR106), carmine	25.00	*75.00*	
PR120	$2 "Victory" (PR108)	30.00	*110.00*	
PR121	$5 Clio (PR109), dark blue...................	40.00	*160.00*	
a.	$5 light blue..	200.00	*500.00*	
PR122	$10 Vesta (PR110).................................	42.50	*160.00*	
PR123	$20 "Peace" (PR111)	45.00	*180.00*	
PR124	$50 "Commerce" (PR112).......................	75.00	*225.00*	
PR125	$100 Indian Maiden (PR113).................	65.00	*240.00*	

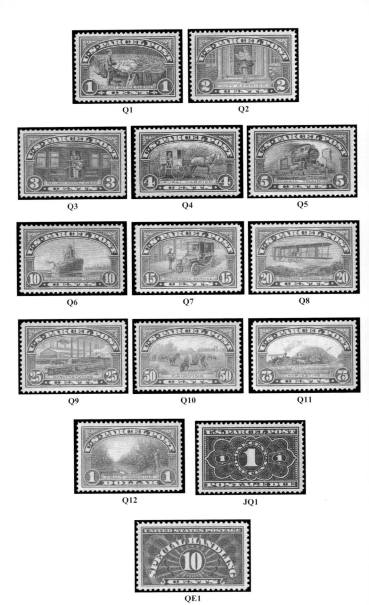

Q1 Q2

Q3 Q4 Q5

Q6 Q7 Q8

Q9 Q10 Q11

Q12 JQ1

QE1

506

Scott No.	Description	Unused Value	Used Value	/ / / / / /

PARCEL POST STAMPS
1913

Scott No.	Description	Unused Value	Used Value	
Q1	1c Post Office Clerk	4.75	1.75	☐☐☐☐☐
Q2	2c City Carrier	5.50	1.40	☐☐☐☐☐
Q3	3c Railway Postal Clerk	10.00	6.50	☐☐☐☐☐
Q4	4c Rural Carrier	30.00	3.50	☐☐☐☐☐
Q5	5c Mail Train	25.00	2.50	☐☐☐☐☐
Q6	10c Steamship & Mail Tender	42.50	3.50	☐☐☐☐☐
Q7	15c Automobile Service	62.50	15.00	☐☐☐☐☐
Q8	20c Airplane Carrying Mail	120.00	30.00	☐☐☐☐☐
Q9	25c Manufacturing	62.50	8.50	☐☐☐☐☐
Q10	50c Dairying	250.00	50.00	☐☐☐☐☐
Q11	75c Harvesting	85.00	40.00	☐☐☐☐☐
Q12	$1 Fruit Growing	300.00	45.00	☐☐☐☐☐

PARCEL POST POSTAGE DUE STAMPS
1912

Scott No.	Description	Unused Value	Used Value	
JQ1	1c Numeral, dark green	9.00	4.50	☐☐☐☐☐
JQ2	2c Numeral (JQ1), dark green	70.00	17.50	☐☐☐☐☐
JQ3	5c Numeral (JQ1), dark green	11.00	5.50	☐☐☐☐☐
JQ4	10c Numeral (JQ1), dark green	140.00	45.00	☐☐☐☐☐
JQ5	25c Numeral (JQ1), dark green	80.00	5.00	☐☐☐☐☐

SPECIAL HANDLING STAMPS
1925-28

Scott No.	Description	Unused Value	Used Value	
QE1	10c Numeral, yellow green	2.00	1.00	☐☐☐☐☐
QE2	15c Numeral (QE1), yellow green	2.25	.90	☐☐☐☐☐
QE3	20c Numeral (QE1), yellow green	3.75	1.50	☐☐☐☐☐
QE4	25c Numeral (QE1), deep green	20.00	3.75	☐☐☐☐☐
a.	25c yellow green	16.50	15.00	☐☐☐☐☐

CVP1

CVP3

CVP31

CVP32

CVP34

CVP35

CVP42

CVP43

CVP54

HOW TO USE THIS BOOK

In cases where two or more Scott numbers share a common design, the illustration shows the first Scott number that bears that design. Subsequent Scott numbers showing the same design will have the first Scott number in parentheses following the description to guide the user to the correct design.

COMPUTER VENDED POSTAGE
1989, Aug. 23, Washington, D.C., Machine 82

Scott No.	Description	Unused Value	Used Value	/ / / / / /
CVP1	25c USA, 1st Class.................................	6.00	—	
a.	1st day dated, serial #12501-15500	4.50	—	
b.	1st day dated, serial #00001-12500	4.50	—	
c.	1st day dated, serial over #27500....	—	—	
CVP2	$1 USA (CVP1), 3rd Class	—	—	
a.	1st day dated, serial #24501-27500	—	—	
b.	1st day dated, serial over #27500....	—	—	
CVP3	$1.69 Bar code, Parcel Post......................	—	—	
a.	1st day dated, serial #21501-24500	—	—	
b.	1st day dated, serial over #27500....	—	—	
CVP4	$2.40 USA (CVP1), Priority Mail	—	—	
a.	1st day dated, serial #18501-21500	—	—	
b.	Priority Mail ($2.74), with bar code	*100.00*	—	
c.	1st day dated, serial over #27500....	—	—	
CVP5	$8.75 USA (CVP1), Express Mail	—	—	
a.	1st day dated, serial #15501-18500	—	—	
b.	1st day dated, serial over #27500....	—	—	
	Nos. 1a-5a.....................................	82.50	—	

Washington, D.C., Machine 83

CVP6	25c USA (CVP1), 1st Class	6.00	—	
a.	1st day dated, serial #12501-15500 .	4.50	—	
b.	1st day dated, serial #00001-12500 .	4.50	—	
c.	1st day dated, serial over #27500.....	—	—	
CVP7	$1 USA (CVP1), 3rd Class...................	—	—	
a.	1st day dated, serial #24501-27500	—	—	
b.	1st day dated, serial over #27500...	—	—	
CVP8	$1.69 Bar Code (CVP3), Parcel Post.......	—	—	
a.	1st day dated, serial #21501-24500	—	—	
b.	1st day dated, serial over #27500...	—	—	
CVP9	$2.40 USA (CVP1), Priority Mail	—	—	
a.	1st day dated, serial #18501-21500	—	—	
b.	1st day dated, serial over #27500...	—	—	
c.	Priority Mail ($2.74), with bar code	*100.00*	—	
CVP10	$8.75 USA (CVP1), Express Mail	—	—	
a.	1st day dated, serial #15501-18500	—	—	
b.	1st day dated, serial over #27500...	—	—	
	Nos. 6a-10a.....................................	57.50	—	

1989, Sept. 1, Kensington, MD, Machine 82

CVP11	25c USA (CVP1), 1st Class.................	6.00	—	
a.	1st day dated, serial #12501-15500	4.50	—	
b.	1st day dated, serial #00001-12500	4.50	—	
c.	1st day dated, serial over #27500...	—	—	
CVP12	$1 USA (CVP1), 3rd Class.................	—	—	
a.	1st day dated, serial #24501-27500	—	—	
b.	1st day dated, serial over #27500...	—	—	
CVP13	$1.69 Bar Code (CVP3), Parcel Post......	—	—	

Scott No.	Description	Unused Value	Used Value	/ / / / / /
a.	1st day dated, serial #21501-24500	—	—	
b.	1st day dated, serial over #27500 ...	—	—	
CVP14 $2.40	USA (CVP1), Priority Mail...........	—	—	
a.	1st day dated, serial #18501-21500	—	—	
b.	1st day dated, serial over #27500 ...	—	—	
c.	Priority Mail ($2.74), with bar code	*100.00*		
CVP15 $8.75	USA (CVP1), Express Mail	—	—	
a.	1st day dated, serial #15501-18500	—	—	
b.	1st day dated, serial over #27500 ...	—	—	
	Nos. 11a-15a.................................	57.50	—	
	Nos. 1b-11b	9.00	—	

Kensington, MD, Machine 83

Scott No.	Description	Unused Value	Used Value	/ / / / / /
CVP16 25c	USA (CVP1), 1st Class.................	6.00	—	
a.	1st day dated, serial #12501-15500	4.50	—	
b.	1st day dated, serial #00001-12500	4.50	—	
c.	1st day dated, serial over #27500 ...	—	—	
CVP17 $1	USA (CVP1), 3rd Class	—	—	
a.	1st day dated, serial #24501-27500	—	—	
b.	1st day dated, serial over #27500 ..	—	—	
CVP18 $1.69	Bar Code (CVP3), Parcel Post......	—	—	
a.	1st day dated, serial #21501-24500	—	—	
b.	1st day dated, serial over #27500 ..	—	—	
CVP19 $2.40	USA (CVP1), Priority Mail..........	—	—	
a.	1st day dated, serial #18501-21500	—	—	
b.	1st day dated, serial over #27500 ..	—	—	
c.	Priority Mail ($2.74), with bar code	100.00		
CVP20 $8.75	USA (CVP1), Express Mail	—	—	
a.	1st day dated, serial #15501-18500...............	—	—	
b.	1st day dated, serial over #27500 .	—	—	
	Nos. 16a-20a.................................	57.50	—	
	Nos. 6b, 16b.................................	9.00	—	

1989, Nov., Washington, D.C., Machine 11

Scott No.	Description	Unused Value	Used Value	/ / / / /
CVP21 25c	USA (CVP1), 1st Class.................	*150.00*		
a.	1st Class, with bar code	—		
CVP22 $1	USA (CVP1), 3rd Class	*500.00*		
CVP23 $1.69	Bar Code (CVP3), Parcel Post......	*500.00*		
CVP24 $2.40	USA (CVP1), Priority Mail..........	*500.00*		
a.	Priority Mail ($2.74), with bar code	—		
CVP25 $8.75	USA (CVP1), Express Mail	*500.00*		

Washington, D.C., Machine 12

Scott No.	Description	Unused Value	Used Value	/ / / / /
CVP26 25c	USA (CVP1), 1st Class.................	*150.00*		
CVP27 $1	USA (CVP1), 3rd Class	—		
CVP28 $1.69	Bar Code (CVP3), Parcel Post......	—		
CVP29 $2.40	USA (CVP1), Priority Mail..........	—		
a.	Priority Mail ($2.74), with bar code	—		
CVP30 $8.75	USA (CVP1), Express Mail	—		

Scott No.	Description	Unused Value	Used Value	/ / / / / /

1992, Coil Stamp

CVP31 29c	Shield, red & blue, Type I	.75	.25	☐☐☐☐☐
b.	Type II...	.90	.40	☐☐☐☐☐

Type I has small serifed numerals preceded by an asterisk 1½ mm across. Type II has large sans-serif numerals preceded by an asterisk 2 mm across.

1994, Coil Stamp

CVP32 29c	Shield, red & blue.........................	.70	.35	☐☐☐☐☐

1996, Coil Stamp

CVP33 32c	Shield (32), bright red & blue dated "1996"..............................	.60	.25	☐☐☐☐☐
CVP34 33c	NCR Automated Postal machine .	22.50	—	☐☐☐☐☐
CVP35 33c	IBM Postal machine.....................	—	—	☐☐☐☐☐
a.	With Priority Mail inscription......	—	—	☐☐☐☐☐

1999

CVP34 33c	NCR Automated Postal Machine	50.00	—	☐☐☐☐☐
a.	With Priority Mail inscription.....	—	—	☐☐☐☐☐
b.	With Express Mail inscription	—	—	☐☐☐☐☐

1999, May 7

CVP35 33c	IBM Postal Machine, Microprinting Above Red Orange Line, numbers only at LL, square corners	220.00	—	
	Round corners	20.00	—	☐☐☐☐☐
a.	"Priority Mail" at LL, square corners...................................	150.00	—	☐☐☐☐☐
	Round corners	—	—	
b.	"Priority Mail AS" at LL, square corners	150.00	—	
	Round corners	—	—	☐☐☐☐☐
CVP36 33c	IBM Postal Machine (CVP35), No Microprinting Above Red Orange Line, numbers only at LL, square corners.................	220.00	—	
	Round corners	10.00	—	☐☐☐☐☐
a.	"Priority Mail" at LL, square corners...................................	125.00	—	
	Round corners	—	—	☐☐☐☐☐
b.	"Priority Mail AS" at LL, square corners	125.00	—	
	Round corners	—	—	☐☐☐☐☐
CVP37 33c	IBM Postal Machine (CVP35), numbers only at LL...................	3.75	—	☐☐☐☐☐
a.	"Priority Mail" at LL	5.00	—	☐☐☐☐☐
b.	"Priority Mail AS" at LL............	5.00	—	☐☐☐☐☐

2001

CVP39 34c	Simplypostage.com, Eagle and stars	—	—	☐☐☐☐☐
CVP40 34c	Simplypostage.com, Eagle and stars, with machine number...............	—	—	☐☐☐☐☐

511

CVP55

CVP56

CVP57

CVP66A

CVP69

CVP75

CVP78

CVP79

CVP82

CVP84

CVP85

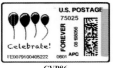

CVP86

CVP87

Scott No.	Description	Unused Value	Used Value	/ / / / /
CVP41 34c	Simplypostage.com, Flag............	—	—	☐☐☐☐☐
CVP42 34c	Simplypostage.com, Flag, with machine number......................	—	20.00	☐☐☐☐☐
2002, June - 2003				
CVP43 21c	Neopostage.com..........................	—	—	☐☐☐☐☐
a.	Booklet pane of 10.....................	—		☐☐☐☐☐
CVP44 23c	Neopostage.com (CVP43)	—	—	☐☐☐☐☐
a.	Booklet pane of 10.....................	—		☐☐☐☐☐
CVP45 34c	black, blue & orange, (CVP43)...	—	—	☐☐☐☐☐
a.	Booklet pane of 10.....................	—		☐☐☐☐☐
CVP46 37c	Neopostage.com (CVP43)	—	—	☐☐☐☐☐
a.	Booklet pane of 10.....................	—		☐☐☐☐☐
CVP47 50c	Neopostage.com (CVP43)	—	—	☐☐☐☐☐
a.	Booklet pane of 10.....................	—		☐☐☐☐☐
CVP48 60c	Neopostage.com (CVP43)	—	—	☐☐☐☐☐
a.	Booklet pane of 10.....................	—		☐☐☐☐☐
CVP49 70c	Neopostage.com (CVP43)	—	—	☐☐☐☐☐
a.	Booklet pane of 10.....................	—		☐☐☐☐☐
CVP50 80c	Neopostage.com (CVP43)	—	—	☐☐☐☐☐
a.	Booklet pane of 10.....................	—		☐☐☐☐☐
CVP51 $3.50	black, blue & orange	—	—	☐☐☐☐☐
a.	Booklet pane of 1	—		☐☐☐☐☐
b.	Booklet pane of 2.......................	—		☐☐☐☐☐
c.	Booklet pane of 5.......................	—		☐☐☐☐☐
d.	Booklet pane of 10.....................	—		☐☐☐☐☐
CVP52 $3.85	Neopostage.com (CVP43)	—	—	☐☐☐☐☐
a.	Booklet pane of 1	—		☐☐☐☐☐
b.	Booklet pane of 2.......................	—		☐☐☐☐☐
c.	Booklet pane of 5.......................	—		☐☐☐☐☐
d.	Booklet pane of 10.....................	—		☐☐☐☐☐
CVP53 $13.65	Neopostage.com (CVP43)..........	—	—	☐☐☐☐☐
a.	Booklet pane of 1	—		☐☐☐☐☐
b.	Booklet pane of 2.......................	—		☐☐☐☐☐
c.	Booklet pane of 5.......................	—		☐☐☐☐☐
d.	Booklet pane of 10.....................	—		☐☐☐☐☐
2004, Apr. 14				
CVP54 37c	IBM Pitney Bowes	5.75	—	☐☐☐☐☐
a.	With First Class Mail inscription	2.50	—	☐☐☐☐☐
b.	With Priority Mail inscription.....	2.50	—	☐☐☐☐☐
c.	With Parcel Post inscription........	2.50	—	☐☐☐☐☐
d.	With International inscription	2.50	—	☐☐☐☐☐
CVP55 37c	IBM Pitney Bowes, US Postage..	2.50	—	☐☐☐☐☐
a.	With First Class Mail inscription	—	—	☐☐☐☐☐
b.	With Priority Mail inscription.....	—	—	☐☐☐☐☐
c.	With Parcel Post inscription........	—	—	☐☐☐☐☐
d.	With International inscription	—	—	☐☐☐☐☐

Scott No.	Description	Unused Value	Used Value	/ / / / /
2004, Nov. 19 -2009				
CVP56 37c	IBM Pitney Bowes	2.50	.25	
CVP57 37c	IBM Pitney Bowes	1.00	.25	
CVP58 60c	IBM Pitney Bowes, with "IM" and Numbers (CVP57).............	3.00	.50	☐☐☐☐☐
CVP59 80c	IBM Pitney Bowes, with "IM" and Numbers (CVP57).............	3.75	.50	☐☐☐☐☐
CVP60 $3.85	IBM Pitney Bowes, with "PM" and Numbers (CVP57).............	15.00	.50	☐☐☐☐☐
CVP61 $13.65	IBM Pitney Bowes, with "EM" and Numbers (CVP57).............	42.50	1.00	☐☐☐☐☐
CVP62 $1	IBM Pitney Bowes, with "IB" and Numbers (CVP57).............	4.00	.25	☐☐☐☐☐
2006				
CVP63 48c	IBM Pitney Bowes, with "IM" and Numbers (CVP57).............	1.25	.40	☐☐☐☐☐
CVP64 63c	IBM Pitney Bowes, with "IM" and Numbers (CVP57).............	1.50	.50	☐☐☐☐☐
CVP65 84c	IBM Pitney Bowes, with "IM" and Numbers(CVP57).............	2.00	.50	☐☐☐☐☐
CVP66 $4.05	IBM Pitney Bowes, with "PM" and Numbers (CVP57)	9.50	1.00	☐☐☐☐☐
CVP66A $8.10	IBM Pitney Bowes, with "PM" and Numbers (CVP57)	35.00	1.00	☐☐☐☐☐
CVP67 $14.40	IBM Pitney Bowes, with "EM" and Numbers (CVP57).............	30.00	1.00	☐☐☐☐☐
2006-2008				
CVP69 39c	IBM Pitney Bowes........................	2.25	.25	☐☐☐☐☐
2006-07				
CVP70 39c	IBM Pitney Bowes, with "IB" and Numbers (CVP57).............	1.00	.50	☐☐☐☐☐
CVP71 41c	IBM Pitney Bowes, with "IB" and Numbers (CVP57).............	1.00	.50	☐☐☐☐☐
CVP72 69c	IBM Pitney Bowes, with "IB" and Numbers (CVP57).............	1.40	.70	☐☐☐☐☐
CVP73 61c	IBM Pitney Bowes, with "IM" and Numbers (CVP57).............	1.25	.50	☐☐☐☐☐
CVP74 90c	IBM Pitney Bowes, with "IM" and Numbers (CVP57).............	1.90	.95	☐☐☐☐☐
2006, Dec. - 2011				
CVP75 41c	IBM Pitney Bowes, black & pink, with "First Class Mail" inscription	—		☐☐☐☐☐
a.	With "Mailed From Zip Code..." inscription	.25	—	☐☐☐☐☐
b.	With "Postcard" inscription	.55	—	☐☐☐☐☐
c.	With "First Class Mail Intl" inscription	1.25	—	☐☐☐☐☐
d.	With "Parcel Post" inscription	7.50	—	☐☐☐☐☐

Scott No.	Description	Unused Value	Used Value	/ / / / /
e.	With "Priority" inscription..........	9.25	—	
f.	With "Express Mail" inscription.	33.00	—	
g.	Encryption at right, numeric code and date sold on bottom line	—	—	
h.	Encryption at right, Postcard on bottom line	—	—	
i.	Encryption at right, First Class Mail on bottom line	—	—	
j.	Encryption at right, First Class Mail Intl on bottom line	—	—	
k.	Encryption at right, Priority Envelope on bottom line	—	—	
l.	Encryption at right, Priority Mail on bottom line	—	—	
m.	Encryption at right, Priority Tube on bottom line	—	—	
n.	Encryption at right, Priority Box on bottom line	—	—	
o.	Encryption at right, Priority - Irregular Shape on bottom line	—	—	
p.	Encryption at right, Parcel Post on bottom line	—	—	
q.	Encryption at right, Express Mail on bottom line	—	—	

2008

CVP76 94c	IBM Pitney Bowes, with IM and numbers (CVP57)..............	2.00	.60	
CVP77 $1.20	IBM Pitney Bowes, with IM and numbers (CVP57)..............	2.40	1.25	
CVP78 42c	IBM Pitney Bowes, black & pink, with rounded corners................	—	—	
CVP79 42c	IBM Pitney Bowes, black & pink, with perpendicular corners	—	—	

2009

CVP80 98c	IBM Pitney Bowes, with IM and numbers (CVP57).	2.00	.60	
CVP81 $1.24	IBM Pitney Bowes, with IM and numbers (CVP57).	2.50	1.25	

2009, June 5

CVP82 44c	IBM Pitney Bowes, Statue of Liberty, with rounded corners................	7.50	—	
CVP83 44c	IBM Pitney Bowes, Statue of Liberty, with perpendicular corners	7.50	—	
a.	Pane of 6, 1c to $16.66...............	—		
b.	Pane of 7, 1c to $14.28...............	—		
c.	Pane of 8, 1c to $12.50...............	—		

Scott No.	Description	Unused Value	Used Value	/ / / / / /
d.	Pane of 9, 1c to $11.11...............	—		
e.	Pane of 10, 1c to $10..................	—		

2011, Oct. 18

CVP84 44c	IBM Pitney Bowes - Flag............	—	—	
a.	Date sold and Postcard on bottom line	—	—	
b.	Date sold and First-Class on bottom line..	—	—	

2012, Apr. 12

CVP85 45c	APC, die cut with rounded corners	—	—	
a.	Die cut with perpendcular corners, Fold Here at center, 105x33mm	—	—	
CPV86 (45c)	APC Variable Vignette Stamp, die cut with rounded corners.....	—	—	
a.	Die cut with perpendcular corners, Fold Here at center, 105x33mm	—	—	
CPV87 45c	APC, die cut with perpendicular corners......................................	—	—	

POSTAL CARDS

1990, July 5, Postal Buddy Machine

| CVUX1 | 15c Eagle.................................... | 6.00 | *10.00* | |

1991, Feb. 3, Postal Buddy Machine

| CVUX2 | 19c Eagle (CVUX1).................... | 3.00 | *8.00* | |

1992, Nov. 13, Postal Buddy Machine

| CVUX3 | 19c Star .... | 6.00 | *15.00* | |

Scott No.	Description	Unused Value	Used Value	/ / / / / /

1CVP1

1CVP2

1CVP10

1CVP16

1CVP22

1CVP32

1CVP37

1CVP38

1CVP39

1CVP43

1CVP44

1CVP51

518

1CVP55

1CVP59

1CVP60

1CVP61

1CVP62

1CVP63

1CVP64

1CVP65

1CVP66

1CVP67

1CVP68

1CVP69

1CVP70

1CVP71

1CVP72

1CVP73

1CVP74

1CVP78

1CVP82

1CVP86

1CVP90

1CVP94

1CVP98

1CVP102

1CVP106

1CVP107

1CVP108

1CVP112

1CVP116

1CVP120

1CVP124

1CVP127

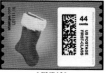

1CVP130

1CVP133

1CVP136

Scott No.	Description	Unused Value	Used Value	/ / / / / /
PERSONAL COMPUTER POSTAGE				
2000, Simply Postage				
1CVP1 33c	Simplypostage.com......................	—	—	☐☐☐☐☐
2002, Stamps.com				
1CVP2 37c	Flag and star...............................	4.00	3.00	☐☐☐☐☐
a.	"First Class" below "US Postage".	2.75	2.00	☐☐☐☐☐
b.	"Priority" below "US Postage"	8.25	2.50	☐☐☐☐☐
c.	"Express" below "US Postage".....	25.00	5.00	☐☐☐☐☐
d.	"Media Mail" below "US Postage"	7.75	2.50	☐☐☐☐☐
e.	"Parcel Post" below "US Postage"	7.75	2.50	☐☐☐☐☐
f.	"Bound Printed Matter" below			
	"US Postage"..............................	7.75	2.50	☐☐☐☐☐
g.	"BPM" below "US Postage"	7.75	2.50	☐☐☐☐☐
1CVP2A 37c	Flag and star...............................	7.00	3.00	☐☐☐☐☐
a.	"First Class" below zip code	2.75	2.00	☐☐☐☐☐
b.	"Priority" below zip code..............	8.25	2.50	☐☐☐☐☐
c.	"Express" below zip code	25.00	5.00	☐☐☐☐☐
d.	"Media Mail" below zip code	7.75	2.50	☐☐☐☐☐
e.	"Parcel Post" below zip code	7.75	2.50	☐☐☐☐☐
1CVP3 37c	Heart..	4.00	4.00	☐☐☐☐☐
a.	"First Class" below "US Postage".	2.75	2.00	☐☐☐☐☐
b.	"Priority" below "US Postage"	8.25	2.50	☐☐☐☐☐
c.	"Express" below "US Postage".....	25.00	5.00	☐☐☐☐☐
d.	"Media Mail" below "US Postage"	7.75	2.50	☐☐☐☐☐
e.	"Parcel Post" below "US Postage"	7.75	2.50	☐☐☐☐☐
f.	"Bound Printed Matter" below			
	"US Postage"..............................	7.75	2.50	☐☐☐☐☐
g.	""BPM"" below "US Postage"......	7.75	2.50	☐☐☐☐☐
2003, June, Stamps.com				
1CVP4 37c	Statue of Liberty and Flag.............	3.50	2.00	☐☐☐☐☐
a.	"First Class" below "US Postage".	3.25	2.00	☐☐☐☐☐
b.	"Priority" below "US Postage"	8.00	1.00	☐☐☐☐☐
c.	"Express" below "US Postage".....	25.00	3.00	☐☐☐☐☐
d.	"Media Mail" below "US Postage"	7.50	1.00	☐☐☐☐☐
e.	"Parcel Post" below "US Postage"	7.50	1.00	☐☐☐☐☐
f.	"Bound Printed Matter" below			
	"US Postage"..............................	7.50	1.00	☐☐☐☐☐
g.	""BPM"" below "US Postage"......	7.50	1.00	☐☐☐☐☐
1CVP5 37c	Liberty Bell and Flag	3.50	2.00	☐☐☐☐☐
a.	"First Class" below "US Postage".	3.25	2.00	☐☐☐☐☐
b.	"Priority" below "US Postage"	8.00	1.00	☐☐☐☐☐
c.	"Express" below "US Postage".....	25.00	3.00	☐☐☐☐☐
d.	"Media Mail" below "US Postage"	7.50	1.00	☐☐☐☐☐
e.	"Parcel Post" below "US Postage"	7.50	1.00	☐☐☐☐☐
f.	"Bound Printed Matter" below			
	"US Postage"..............................	7.50	1.00	☐☐☐☐☐
g.	""BPM"" below "US Postage"......	7.50	1.00	☐☐☐☐☐

Scott No.	Description	Unused Value	Used Value	/ / / / / /
1CVP6 37c	Eagle and Flag..............................	3.50	2.00	
a.	"First Class" below "US Postage".	3.25	2.00	
b.	"Priority" below "US Postage"	8.00	1.00	
c.	"Express" below "US Postage".....	25.00	3.00	
d.	"Media Mail" below "US Postage"	7.50	1.00	
e.	"Parcel Post" below "US Postage"	7.50	1.00	
f.	"Bound Printed Matter" below			
	"US Postage"...............................	7.50	1.00	
g.	"BPM" below "US Postage"	7.50	1.00	
1CVP7 37c	George Washington and Flag	3.50	2.00	
a.	"First Class" below "US Postage".	3.25	.25	
b.	"Priority" below "US Postage"	8.00	1.00	
c.	"Express" below "US Postage".....	25.00	3.00	
d.	"Media Mail" below "US Postage"	7.50	1.00	
e.	"Parcel Post" below "US Postage"	7.50	1.00	
f.	"Bound Printed Matter" below			
	"US Postage"...............................	7.50	1.00	
g.	"BPM" below "US Postage"	7.50	1.00	
1CVP8 37c	Capitol Building and Flag	3.50	2.00	
a.	"First Class" below "US Postage".	3.25	.25	
b.	"Priority" below "US Postage"	8.00	1.00	
c.	"Express" below "US Postage".....	25.00	3.00	
d.	"Media Mail" below "US Postage"	7.50	1.00	
e.	"Parcel Post" below "US Postage"	7.50	1.00	
f.	"Bound Printed Matter" below			
	"US Postage"...............................	7.50	1.00	
g.	"BPM" below "US Postage"	7.50	1.00	
h.	Strip of 5, #1CVP4-1CVP8...........	17.50		
1CVP9 37c	Flag and Star type of 2002 (1CVP2) Redrawn with Stamps.com in upper case letters	3.00	1.50	
a.	"First Class" below "US Postage".	2.00	.25	
b.	"Priority" below "US Postage"	8.00	1.00	
c.	"Express" below "US Postage".....	25.00	3.00	
d.	"Media Mail" below "US Postage"	7.50	1.00	
e.	"Parcel Post" below "US Postage"	7.50	1.00	
f.	"Bound Printed Matter" below			
	"US Postage"...............................	7.50	1.00	
g.	"BPM" below "US Postage"	7.50	1.00	

2003, Dec., Stamps.com

1CVP10 37c	Snowman......................................	3.00	1.50	
a.	"First Class" below "US Postage".	2.00	1.00	
b.	"Priority" below "US Postage"	8.00	1.00	
c.	"Express" below "US Postage".....	25.00	3.00	
d.	"Media Mail" below "US Postage"	7.50	1.00	
e.	"Parcel Post" below "US Postage"	7.50	1.00	

Scott No.	Description	Unused Value	Used Value	/ / / / / /
f.	"Bound Printed Matter" below "US Postage"	7.50	1.00	
g.	"BPM" below "US Postage"	7.50	1.00	
1CVP11 37c	Snowflakes	3.00	1.50	
a.	"First Class" below "US Postage".	2.00	1.00	
b.	"Priority" below "US Postage"	8.00	1.00	
c.	"Express" below "US Postage"	25.00	3.00	
d.	"Media Mail" below "US Postage"	7.50	1.00	
e.	"Parcel Post" below "US Postage"	7.50	1.00	
f.	"Bound Printed Matter" below "US Postage"	7.50	1.00	
g.	"BPM" below "US Postage"	7.50	1.00	
1CVP12 37c	Holly	3.00	1.50	
a.	"First Class" below "US Postage".	2.00	1.00	
b.	"Priority" below "US Postage"	8.00	1.00	
c.	"Express" below "US Postage"	25.00	3.00	
d.	"Media Mail" below "US Postage"	7.50	1.00	
e.	"Parcel Post" below "US Postage"	7.50	1.00	
f.	"Bound Printed Matter" below "US Postage"	7.50	1.00	
g.	"BPM" below "US Postage"	7.50	1.00	
1CVP13 37c	Dove	3.00	1.50	
a.	"First Class" below "US Postage".	2.00	1.00	
b.	"Priority" below "US Postage"	8.00	1.00	
c.	"Express" below "US Postage"	25.00	3.00	
d.	"Media Mail" below "US Postage"	7.50	1.00	
e.	"Parcel Post" below "US Postage"	7.50	1.00	
f.	"Bound Printed Matter" below "US Postage"	7.50	1.00	
g.	"BPM" below "US Postage"	7.50	1.00	
1CVP14 37c	Gingerbread Man and Candy	3.00	1.50	
a.	"First Class" below "US Postage".	2.00	1.00	
b.	"Priority" below "US Postage"	8.00	1.00	
c.	"Express" below "US Postage"	25.00	3.00	
d.	"Media Mail" below "US Postage"	7.50	1.00	
e.	"Parcel Post" below "US Postage"	7.50	1.00	
f.	"Bound Printed Matter" below "US Postage"	7.50	1.00	
g.	"BPM" below "US Postage"	7.50	1.00	
h.	Strip of 5, #1CVP10-1CVP14	12.50		

2004, Mar., Stamps.com

Scott No.	Description	Unused Value	Used Value	/ / / / / /
1CVP15 37c	Mailbox	25.00	15.00	
a.	"First Class" below "US Postage".	25.00	15.00	
b.	"Priority" below "US Postage"	—	—	
c.	"Express" below "US Postage"	—	—	
d.	"Media Mail" below "US Postage"	—	—	
e.	"Parcel Post" below "US Postage"	—	—	

Scott No.	Description	Unused Value	Used Value	/ / / / / /
f.	"Bound Printed Matter" below			
	"US Postage"..............................	—	—	☐☐☐☐☐
g.	"BPM" below "US Postage"	—	—	☐☐☐☐☐
2004, Apr., Stamps.com				
1CVP16 37c	George Washington	2.00	1.00	☐☐☐☐☐
a.	"First Class" below "US Postage".	1.10	.75	☐☐☐☐☐
b.	"Priority" below "US Postage"	5.00	2.50	☐☐☐☐☐
c.	"Express" below "US Postage".....	20.00	5.00	☐☐☐☐☐
d.	"Media Mail" below "US Postage"	5.00	2.50	☐☐☐☐☐
e.	"Parcel Post" below "US Postage"	5.00	2.50	☐☐☐☐☐
f.	"Bound Printed Matter" below			
	"US Postage"..............................	5.00	2.50	☐☐☐☐☐
g.	"BPM" below "US Postage"	5.00	2.50	☐☐☐☐☐
1CVP17 37c	Thomas Jefferson	2.00	1.00	☐☐☐☐☐
a.	"First Class" below "US Postage".	1.10	.75	☐☐☐☐☐
b.	"Priority" below "US Postage"	5.00	2.50	☐☐☐☐☐
c.	"Express" below "US Postage".....	20.00	5.00	☐☐☐☐☐
d.	"Media Mail" below "US Postage"	5.00	2.50	☐☐☐☐☐
e.	"Parcel Post" below "US Postage"	5.00	2.50	☐☐☐☐☐
f.	"Bound Printed Matter" below			
	"US Postage"..............................	5.00	2.50	☐☐☐☐☐
g.	"BPM" below "US Postage"	5.00	2.50	☐☐☐☐☐
1CVP18 37c	Abraham Lincoln	2.00	1.00	☐☐☐☐☐
a.	"First Class" below "US Postage".	1.10	.75	☐☐☐☐☐
b.	"Priority" below "US Postage"	5.00	2.50	☐☐☐☐☐
c.	"Express" below "US Postage".....	20.00	5.00	☐☐☐☐☐
d.	"Media Mail" below "US Postage"	5.00	2.50	☐☐☐☐☐
e.	"Parcel Post" below "US Postage"	5.00	2.50	☐☐☐☐☐
f.	"Bound Printed Matter" below			
	"US Postage"..............................	5.00	2.50	☐☐☐☐☐
g.	"BPM" below "US Postage"	5.50	2.50	☐☐☐☐☐
1CVP19 37c	Theodore Roosevelt......................	2.00	1.00	☐☐☐☐☐
a.	"First Class" below "US Postage".	1.10	.75	☐☐☐☐☐
b.	"Priority" below "US Postage"	5.00	2.50	☐☐☐☐☐
c.	"Express" below "US Postage".....	20.00	5.00	☐☐☐☐☐
d.	"Media Mail" below "US Postage"	5.00	2.50	☐☐☐☐☐
e.	"Parcel Post" below "US Postage"	5.00	2.50	☐☐☐☐☐
f.	"Bound Printed Matter" below			
	"US Postage"..............................	5.00	2.50	☐☐☐☐☐
g.	"BPM" below "US Postage"	5.00	2.50	☐☐☐☐☐
1CVP20 37c	John F. Kennedy	2.00	1.00	☐☐☐☐☐
a.	"First Class" below "US Postage".	1.10	.75	☐☐☐☐☐
b.	"Priority" below "US Postage"	5.00	2.50	☐☐☐☐☐
c.	"Express" below "US Postage".....	20.00	5.00	☐☐☐☐☐
d.	"Media Mail" below "US Postage"	5.00	2.50	☐☐☐☐☐
e.	"Parcel Post" below "US Postage"	5.00	2.50	☐☐☐☐☐
f.	"Bound Printed Matter" below			
	"US Postage"..............................	5.00	2.50	☐☐☐☐☐

Scott No.	Description	Unused Value	Used Value	/ / / / /
g.	"BPM" below "US Postage"	5.00	2.50	
h.	Strip of 5, #1CVP16-1CVP20.......	10.00		
1CVP21 37c	Flag and Star Type of 2002 (1CVP1) Redrawn with Orange Stars and Text at Left, "Stamps.com" in upper case letters......................	2.00	1.00	
a.	"First Class" below "US Postage".	1.35	.75	
b.	"Priority" below "US Postage"	6.00	2.50	
c.	"Express" below "US Postage".....	22.50	5.00	
d.	"Media Mail" below "US Postage"	6.00	2.50	
e.	"Parcel Post" below "US Postage"	6.00	2.50	
f.	"Bound Printed Matter" below "US Postage"..............................	6.00	2.50	
g.	"BPM" below "US Postage"	6.00	2.50	
1CVP22 37c	Bicycling	3.00	2.00	
a.	"First Class" below "US Postage".	2.50	1.50	
b.	"Priority" below "US Postage"	8.00	1.00	
c.	"Express" below "US Postage".....	25.00	3.00	
d.	"Media Mail" below "US Postage"	7.50	1.00	
e.	"Parcel Post" below "US Postage"	7.50	1.00	
f.	"Bound Printed Matter" below "US Postage"..............................	7.50	1.00	
g.	"BPM" below "US Postage"	7.50	1.00	
1CVP23 37c	Running	3.00	2.00	
a.	"First Class" below "US Postage".	2.50	1.50	
b.	"Priority" below "US Postage"	8.00	1.00	
c.	"Express" below "US Postage".....	25.00	3.00	
d.	"Media Mail" below "US Postage"	7.50	1.00	
e.	"Parcel Post" below "US Postage"	7.50	1.00	
f.	"Bound Printed Matter" below "US Postage"..............................	7.50	1.00	
g.	"BPM" below "US Postage"	7.50	1.00	
1CVP24 37c	Swimming	3.00	2.00	
a.	"First Class" below "US Postage".	2.50	1.50	
b.	"Priority" below "US Postage"	8.00	1.00	
c.	"Express" below "US Postage".....	25.00	3.00	
d.	"Media Mail" below "US Postage"	7.50	1.00	
e.	"Parcel Post" below "US Postage"	7.50	1.00	
f.	"Bound Printed Matter" below "US Postage"..............................	7.50	1.00	
g.	"BPM" below "US Postage"	7.50	1.00	
1CVP25 37c	Boxing..	3.00	2.00	
a.	"First Class" below "US Postage".	2.50	1.50	
b.	"Priority" below "US Postage"	8.00	1.00	
c.	"Express" below "US Postage".....	25.00	3.00	
d.	"Media Mail" below "US Postage"	7.50	1.00	
e.	"Parcel Post" below "US Postage"	7.50	1.00	

Scott No.	Description	Unused Value	Used Value
f.	"Bound Printed Matter" below "US Postage"	7.50	1.00
g.	"BPM" below "US Postage"	7.50	1.00
1CVP26 37c	Equestrian	3.00	2.00
a.	"First Class" below "US Postage"	2.50	1.50
b.	"Priority" below "US Postage"	8.00	1.00
c.	"Express" below "US Postage"	25.00	3.00
d.	"Media Mail" below "US Postage"	7.50	1.00
e.	"Parcel Post" below "US Postage"	7.50	1.00
f.	"Bound Printed Matter" below "US Postage"	7.50	1.00
g.	"BPM" below "US Postage"	7.50	1.00
1CVP27 37c	Basketball	3.00	2.00
a.	"First Class" below "US Postage"	2.50	1.50
b.	"Priority" below "US Postage"	8.00	1.00
c.	"Express" below "US Postage"	25.00	3.00
d.	"Media Mail" below "US Postage"	7.50	1.00
e.	"Parcel Post" below "US Postage"	7.50	1.00
f.	"Bound Printed Matter" below "US Postage"	7.50	1.00
g.	"BPM" below "US Postage"	7.50	1.00
1CVP28 37c	Judo	3.00	2.00
a.	"First Class" below "US Postage"	2.50	1.50
b.	"Priority" below "US Postage"	8.00	1.00
c.	"Express" below "US Postage"	25.00	3.00
d.	"Media Mail" below "US Postage"	7.50	1.00
e.	"Parcel Post" below "US Postage"	7.50	1.00
f.	"Bound Printed Matter" below "US Postage"	7.50	1.00
g.	"BPM" below "US Postage"	7.50	1.00
1CVP29 37c	Soccer	3.00	2.00
a.	"First Class" below "US Postage"	2.50	1.50
b.	"Priority" below "US Postage"	8.00	1.00
c.	"Express" below "US Postage"	25.00	3.00
d.	"Media Mail" below "US Postage"	7.50	1.00
e.	"Parcel Post" below "US Postage"	7.50	1.00
f.	"Bound Printed Matter" below "US Postage"	7.50	1.00
g.	"BPM" below "US Postage"	7.50	1.00
1CVP30 37c	Gymnastics	3.00	2.00
a.	"First Class" below "US Postage"	2.50	1.50
b.	"Priority" below "US Postage"	8.00	1.00
c.	"Express" below "US Postage"	25.00	3.00
d.	"Media Mail" below "US Postage"	7.50	1.00
e.	"Parcel Post" below "US Postage"	7.50	1.00
f.	"Bound Printed Matter" below "US Postage"	7.50	1.00
g.	"BPM" below "US Postage"	7.50	1.00

Scott No.	Description	Unused Value	Used Value	/ / / / / /
1CVP31 37c	Tennis	3.00	2.00	
a.	"First Class" below "US Postage".	2.50	1.50	
b.	"Priority" below "US Postage"	8.00	1.00	
c.	"Express" below "US Postage".....	25.00	3.00	
d.	"Media Mail" below "US Postage"	7.50	1.00	
e.	"Parcel Post" below "US Postage"	7.50	1.00	
f.	"Bound Printed Matter" below			
	"US Postage"..............................	7.50	1.00	
g.	"BPM" below "US Postage"	7.50	1.00	
h.	Block of 10, #1CVP22-1CVP31 ...	15.00		

2004, July, Stamps.com

Scott No.	Description	Unused Value	Used Value	/ / / / / /
1CVP32 37c	Leaning Tower of Pisa	3.00	2.00	
a.	"First Class" below "US Postage".	2.30	1.50	
b.	"Priority" below "US Postage"	8.00	1.00	
c.	"Express" below "US Postage".....	25.00	3.00	
d.	"Media Mail" below "US Postage"	7.50	1.00	
e.	"Parcel Post" below "US Postage"	7.50	1.00	
f.	"Bound Printed Matter" below			
	"US Postage"..............................	7.50	1.00	
g.	"BPM" below "US Postage"	7.50	1.00	
1CVP33 37c	Sphinx and Pyramids....................	3.00	2.00	
a.	"First Class" below "US Postage".	2.30	1.50	
b.	"Priority" below "US Postage"	8.00	1.00	
c.	"Express" below "US Postage".....	25.00	3.00	
d.	"Media Mail" below "US Postage"	7.50	1.00	
e.	"Parcel Post" below "US Postage"	7.50	1.00	
f.	"Bound Printed Matter" below			
	"US Postage"..............................	7.50	1.00	
g.	"BPM" below "US Postage"	7.50	1.00	
1CVP34 37c	Sydney Opera House.....................	3.00	2.00	
a.	"First Class" below "US Postage".	2.30	1.50	
b.	"Priority" below "US Postage"	8.00	1.00	
c.	"Express" below "US Postage".....	25.00	3.00	
d.	"Media Mail" below "US Postage"	7.50	1.00	
e.	"Parcel Post" below "US Postage"	7.50	1.00	
f.	"Bound Printed Matter" below			
	"US Postage"..............................	7.50	1.00	
g.	"BPM" below "US Postage"	7.50	1.00	
1CVP35 37c	Mayan Pyramid	3.00	2.00	
a.	"First Class" below "US Postage".	2.30	1.50	
b.	"Priority" below "US Postage"	8.00	1.00	
c.	"Express" below "US Postage".....	25.00	3.00	
d.	"Media Mail" below "US Postage"	7.50	1.00	
e.	"Parcel Post" below "US Postage"	7.50	1.00	
f.	"Bound Printed Matter" below			
	"US Postage"..............................	7.50	1.00	
g.	"BPM" below "US Postage"	7.50	1.00	
1CVP36 37c	Asian Temple................................	3.00	2.00	

Scott No.	Description	Unused Value	Used Value	/ / / / / /
a.	"First Class" below "US Postage".	2.30	1.50	
b.	"Priority" below "US Postage"	8.00	1.00	
c.	"Express" below "US Postage".....	25.00	3.00	
d.	"Media Mail" below "US Postage"	7.50	1.00	
e.	"Parcel Post" below "US Postage"	7.50	1.00	
f.	"Bound Printed Matter" below "US Postage"..............................	7.50	1.00	
g.	"BPM" below "US Postage"	7.50	1.00	
h.	Strip of 5, #1CVP32-1CVP36.......	15.00		
2005, Mar., Stamps.com				
1CVP37 37c	Computer and Letters....................	25.00	15.00	
a.	"First Class" below "US Postage".	25.00	15.00	
b.	"Priority" below "US Postage"	—	—	
c.	"Express" below "US Postage".....	—	—	
d.	"Media Mail" below "US Postage"	—	—	
e.	"Parcel Post" below "US Postage"	—	—	
f.	"Bound Printed Matter" below "US Postage"..............................	—	—	
g.	"BPM" below "US Postage"	—	—	
2005, Aug., Stamps.com				
1CVP38 37c	Logo...	1.00	.30	
a.	"Priority" below "US Postage"	8.00	1.00	
b.	"Express" below "US Postage"......	25.00	3.00	
c.	"Media Mail" below "US Postage"	7.50	1.00	
d.	"Parcel Post" below "US Postage".	7.50	1.00	
e.	"BPM" below "US Postage"	7.50	1.00	
f.	"Aerogramme" below "US Postage"	1.40	1.00	
g.	"Intl Air Letter" below "US Postage"	1.25	1.00	
h.	"Intl Eco Letter" (Economy Letter Mail) below "US Postage"....................	5.50	1.00	
i.	"GXG" (Global Express Guaranteed) below "US Postage"....................	50.00	6.00	
j.	"EMS" (Global Express Mail) below "US Postage"..............................	32.50	4.00	
k.	"GPM" (Global Priority Mail) below "US Postage"..............................	8.00	1.00	
l.	"Intl Air Parcel" (Air Parcel Post) below "US Postage"....................	26.00	3.00	
m.	"Intl Eco Parcel" (Economy Parcel Post) below "US Postage"............	32.50	4.00	
n.	"M-Bag (Air)" below "US Postage"	35.00	5.00	
o.	"M-Bag (Economy)" below "US Postage"..............................	18.00	3.00	
p.	"Mat for Blind" below "US Postage"	1.25	—	
2005, Nov., Stamps.com				
1CVP39 37c	Snowman.......................................	1.60	.25	
a.	"Priority" below "US Postage"	8.00	1.00	
b.	"Express" below "US Postage"......	25.00	3.00	

Scott No.	Description	Unused Value	Used Value	/ / / / /
c.	"Media Mail" below "US Postage"	7.50	1.00	
d.	"Parcel Post" below "US Postage".	7.50	1.00	
e.	"BPM" below "US Postage"	7.50	1.00	
f.	"Aerogramme" below "US Postage"	1.40	1.00	
g.	"Intl Air Letter" below "US Postage"	1.25	1.00	
h.	"Intl Eco Letter" (Economy Letter Mail) below "US Postage"	5.50	1.00	
i.	"GXG" (Global Express Guaranteed) below "US Postage"	50.00	6.00	
j.	"EMS" (Global Express Mail) below "US Postage"	32.50	4.00	
k.	"GPM" (Global Priority Mail) below "US Postage"	8.00	1.00	
l.	"Intl Air Parcel" (Air Parcel Post) below "US Postage"	26.00	3.00	
m.	"Intl Eco Parcel" (Economy Parcel Post) below "US Postage"	32.50	4.00	
n.	"M-Bag (Air)" below "US Postage"	35.00	5.00	
o.	"M-Bag (Economy)" below "US Postage"	18.00	3.00	
p.	"Mat for Blind" below "US Postage"	.25	—	
1CVP40 37c	Candy Cane	1.60	.25	
a.	"Priority" below "US Postage"	8.00	1.00	
b.	"Express" below "US Postage"	25.00	3.00	
c.	"Media Mail" below "US Postage"	7.50	1.00	
d.	"Parcel Post" below "US Postage".	7.50	1.00	
e.	"BPM" below "US Postage"	7.50	1.00	
f.	"Aerogramme" below "US Postage"	1.40	1.00	
g.	"Intl Air Letter" below "US Postage"	1.25	1.00	
h.	"Intl Eco Letter" (Economy Letter Mail) below "US Postage"	5.50	1.00	
i.	"GXG" (Global Express Guaranteed) below "US Postage"	50.00	6.00	
j.	"EMS" (Global Express Mail) below "US Postage"	32.50	4.00	
k.	"GPM" (Global Priority Mail) below "US Postage"	8.00	1.00	
l.	"Intl Air Parcel" (Air Parcel Post) below "US Postage"	26.00	3.00	
m.	"Intl Eco Parcel" (Economy Parcel Post) below "US Postage"	32.50	4.00	
n.	"M-Bag (Air)" below "US Postage"	35.00	5.00	
o.	"M-Bag (Economy)" below "US Postage"	18.00	3.00	
p.	"Mat for Blind" below "US Postage"	.25	—	
1CVP41 37c	Dove	1.60	.25	
a.	"Priority" below "US Postage"	8.00	1.00	

Scott No.	Description	Unused Value	Used Value	/ / / / / /
b.	"Express" below "US Postage"	25.00	3.00	☐☐☐☐☐
c.	"Media Mail" below "US Postage"	7.50	1.00	☐☐☐☐☐
d.	"Parcel Post" below "US Postage".	7.50	1.00	☐☐☐☐☐
e.	"BPM" below "US Postage"	7.50	1.00	☐☐☐☐☐
f.	"Aerogramme" below "US Postage"	1.40	1.00	☐☐☐☐☐
g.	"Intl Air Letter" below "US Postage"	1.25	1.00	☐☐☐☐☐
h.	"Letter Mail (Economy)" below "US Postage"	5.50	1.00	☐☐☐☐☐
i.	"Global Express Guaranteed" below "US Postage"	50.00	6.00	☐☐☐☐☐
j.	"Global Express Mail" below "US Postage"	32.50	4.00	☐☐☐☐☐
k.	"Global Priority Mail" below "US Postage"	8.00	1.00	☐☐☐☐☐
l.	"Pacel Post (Air)" below "US Postage"	26.00	3.00	☐☐☐☐☐
m.	"Parcel Post (Economy)" below "US Postage"	32.50	4.00	☐☐☐☐☐
n.	"M-Bag (Air)" below "US Postage"	35.00	5.00	☐☐☐☐☐
o.	"M-Bag (Economy)" below "US Postage"	18.00	3.00	☐☐☐☐☐
p.	"Mat for Blind" below "US Postage"	.25	—	☐☐☐☐☐
1CVP42 37c	Stylized Christmas Tree and Window	1.60	.25	☐☐☐☐☐
a.	"Priority" below "US Postage"	8.00	1.00	☐☐☐☐☐
b.	"Express" below "US Postage"	25.00	3.00	☐☐☐☐☐
c.	"Media Mail" below "US Postage"	7.50	1.00	☐☐☐☐☐
d.	"Parcel Post" below "US Postage".	7.50	1.00	☐☐☐☐☐
e.	"BPM" below "US Postage"	7.50	1.00	☐☐☐☐☐
f.	"Aerogramme" below "US Postage"	1.40	1.00	☐☐☐☐☐
g.	"Intl Air Letter" below "US Postage"	1.25	1.00	☐☐☐☐☐
h.	"Letter Mail (Economy)" below "US Postage"	5.50	1.00	☐☐☐☐☐
i.	"Global Express Guaranteed" below "US Postage"	50.00	6.00	☐☐☐☐☐
j.	"Global Express Mail" below "US Postage"	32.50	4.00	☐☐☐☐☐
k.	"Global Priority Mail" below "US Postage"	8.00	1.00	☐☐☐☐☐
l.	"Parcel Post (Air)" below "US Postage"	26.00	3.00	☐☐☐☐☐
m.	"Parcel Post (Economy)" below "US Postage"	32.50	4.00	☐☐☐☐☐
n.	"M-Bag (Air)" below "US Postage"	35.00	5.00	☐☐☐☐☐
o.	"M-Bag (Economy)" below "US Postage"	18.00	3.00	☐☐☐☐☐
p.	"Mat for Blind" below "US Postage"	.25	—	☐☐☐☐☐
q.	Vert. Strip, 2 each #CVP39-1CVP42	6.00		☐☐☐☐☐

Scott No.		Description	Unused Value	Used Value	/ / / / / /

2005-6, Endicia.com

1CVP43	24c	"Postcard" under "US Postage"	10.00	4.00	☐☐☐☐☐
a.	39c	"First Class" under "US Postage" ..	2.00	.50	☐☐☐☐☐
b.	63c	"Intl. Mail" under "US Postage"....	3.25	2.50	☐☐☐☐☐
c.	4.05	"Priority Mail." under "US Postage"	12.00	2.50	☐☐☐☐☐
1CVP44	24c	"Postcard" under "US Postage," coil stamp, perf. 10½ x 10¼ on 2 sides	11.00	4.00	☐☐☐☐☐
a.	39c	"First Class" under "US Postage," coil stamp, perf. 10½ x 10¼ on 2 sides	2.25	.50	☐☐☐☐☐
b.	63c	"Intl. Mail." under "US Postage," coil stamp, perf. 10½ x 10¼ on 2 sides	3.50	2.50	☐☐☐☐☐
c.	$4.05	"Priority Mail" under "US Postage," coil stamp, perf. 10½ x 10¼ on 2 sides	12.50	2.50	☐☐☐☐☐

2006, Mar., Stamps.com

1CVP51	39c	Flag and Mount Rushmore............	.80	.25	☐☐☐☐☐
1CVP52	39c	Flag and Eagle	.80	.25	☐☐☐☐☐
1CVP53	39c	Flag and Statue of Liberty.............	.80	.25	☐☐☐☐☐
1CVP54	39c	Flag and Liberty Bell	.80	.25	☐☐☐☐☐
a.		Vert. Strip of 8, 2 each #1CVP51-1CVP54	8.00		☐☐☐☐☐

2006, Stamps.com

1CVP55	39c	Leaning Tower of Pisa	.80	.25	☐☐☐☐☐
1CVP56	39c	Taj Mahal	.80	.25	☐☐☐☐☐
1CVP57	39c	Eiffel Tower....................................	.80	.25	☐☐☐☐☐
1CVP58	39c	Parthenon	.80	.25	☐☐☐☐☐
a.		Vert. Strip, 2 each #1CVP55-1CVP58	8.00		☐☐☐☐☐

2006 Pitney Bowes Stamp Expressions

1CVP59	39c	Any label picture (or without)........	1.35	.80	☐☐☐☐☐

2006, Stamps.com, Personalized Images

1CVP60	39c	Any label picture	1.50	.95	☐☐☐☐☐
a.		Numerals in denomination 2½mm high, thicker text	1.50	.95	☐☐☐☐☐
1CVP61	39c	Any label picture	1.50	.95	☐☐☐☐☐
a.		Numerals in denomination 2½mm high, thicker text	1.50	.95	☐☐☐☐☐
1CVP62	39c	Autumn Leaves...............................	1.25	.25	☐☐☐☐☐
1CVP63	39c	Pumpkins	1.25	.25	☐☐☐☐☐
1CVP64	39c	Basket of Apples, Sheaf of Wheat, Falling Leaves and Pumpkins	1.25	.25	☐☐☐☐☐
1CVP65	39c	Leaves and Carved Pumpkin...........	1.25	.25	☐☐☐☐☐
a.		Vert. Strip, 2 each #1CVP62-1CVP65	10.00		☐☐☐☐☐
1CVP66	39c	Season's Greetings	1.25	.25	☐☐☐☐☐
1CVP67	39c	Christmas Trees	1.25	.25	☐☐☐☐☐
1CVP68	39c	Snowman..	1.25	.25	☐☐☐☐☐

Scott No.	Description	Unused Value	Used Value	/ / / / / /
1CVP69	39c Dove	1.25	.25	
a.	Vert. Strip, 2 each #1CVP66-1CVP69	10.00		

2008, Stamps.com

Scott No.	Description	Unused Value	Used Value	/ / / / / /
1CVP70	42c Flag	1.25	.25	
1CVP71	42c Statue of Liberty and Flag	1.25	.25	
1CVP72	42c Bald Eagle and Flag	1.25	.25	
1CVP73	42c Flag Painted On Building	1.25	.25	
1CVP74	42c Autumn, Oak Leaves	1.25	.25	
1CVP75	42c Autumn, Pumpkin Patch	1.25	.25	
1CVP76	42c Autumn, Autumn Reflection	1.25	.25	
1CVP77	42c Autumn, Pumpkins and Gourds	1.25	.25	
1CVP78	42c Flowers, Sunflowers	1.25	.25	
1CVP79	42c Flowers, Daisies	1.25	.25	
1CVP80	42c Flowers, Sunflower Sky	1.25	.25	
1CVP81	42c Flowers, Treasure Flowers	1.25	.25	
1CVP82	42c Endangered Animals, Bengal Tiger	1.25	.25	
1CVP83	42c Endangered Animals, Hawksbill Turtle	1.25	.25	
1CVP84	42c Endangered Animals, Panda	1.25	.25	
1CVP85	42c Endangered Animals, African Rhino	1.25	.25	
1CVP86	42c Parks, Grand Canyon	1.25	.25	
1CVP87	42c Parks, Yosemite	1.25	.25	
1CVP88	42c Parks, Niagara Falls	1.25	.25	
1CVP89	42c Parks, Arches	1.25	.25	
1CVP90	42c City Skylines, New York City	1.25	.25	
1CVP91	42c City Skylines, St. Louis	1.25	.25	
1CVP92	42c City Skylines, Chicago	1.25	.25	
1CVP93	42c City Skylines, San Francisco	1.25	.25	
1CVP94	42c Presidential Memorials, Washington Monument	1.25	.25	
1CVP95	42c Presidential Memorials, Lincoln Memorial	1.25	.25	
1CVP96	42c Presidential Memorials, Jefferson Memorial	1.25	.25	
1CVP97	42c Presidential Memorials, Mount Rushmore	1.25	.25	
1CVP98	42c Christmas, Ornament	1.25	.25	
1CVP99	42c Christmas, Gingerbread Men	1.25	.25	
1CVP100	42c Christmas, Snowflake	1.25	.25	
1CVP101	42c Christmas, Christmas Tree	1.25	.25	

2009, Stamps.com

Scott No.	Description	Unused Value	Used Value	/ / / / / /
1CVP102	42c Love, Rose	1.25	.25	
1CVP103	42c Love, Small Hearts	1.25	.25	
1CVP104	42c Love, Large Heart	1.25	.25	
1CVP105	42c Love, Hearts on Curtain	1.25	.25	
1CVP106	44c Wavy Lines	1.25	.25	

2009, Endicia.com

Scott No.	Description	Unused Value	Used Value	/ / / / / /
1CVP107	44c Globe	1.25	.25	

Scott No.	Description	Unused Value	Used Value	/ / / / / /

2009, Stamps.com

1CVP108	44c Thank You For Your Business, On Billboard	1.25	.25	☐☐☐☐☐
1CVP109	44c Thank You For Your Business, And Building	1.25	.25	☐☐☐☐☐
1CVP110	44c Thank You For Your Business, On Red Background	1.25	.25	☐☐☐☐☐
1CVP111	44c Thank You For Your Business, And Two People Shaking Hands	1.25	.25	☐☐☐☐☐
1CVP112	44c We're Moving, Stack of Three Boxes, Green Background	1.25	.25	☐☐☐☐☐
1CVP113	44c We're Moving, Eleven Boxes, Orange Background	1.25	.25	☐☐☐☐☐
1CVP114	44c We're Moving, Four Boxes, Green Background	1.25	.25	☐☐☐☐☐
1CVP115	44c We're Moving, Four Boxes, Red Background	1.25	.25	☐☐☐☐☐
1CVP116	44c Special Invitation, And Pen Nib	1.25	.25	☐☐☐☐☐
1CVP117	44c Special Invitation, And Circled 15 On Calendar	1.25	.25	☐☐☐☐☐
1CVP118	44c Special Invitation, On Card On Envelope	1.25	.25	☐☐☐☐☐
1CVP119	44c Special Invitation, On Wax Seal	1.25	.25	☐☐☐☐☐
1CVP120	44c US Flag, On Flagpole	1.25	.25	☐☐☐☐☐
1CVP121	44c US Flag, Behind Statue of Liberty	1.25	.25	☐☐☐☐☐
1CVP122	44c US Flag, Behind Bald Eagle	1.25	.25	☐☐☐☐☐
1CVP123	44c US Flag, On United States Map	1.25	.25	☐☐☐☐☐

2010, Stamps.com

1CVP124	44c Patriotic Symbols, Statue of Liberty	1.25	.25	☐☐☐☐☐
1CVP125	44c Patriotic Symbols, Flag	1.25	.25	☐☐☐☐☐
1CVP126	44c Patriotic Symbols, Bald Eagle	1.25	.25	☐☐☐☐☐
1CVP127	44c Jewish Symbols, Menorah	1.25	.25	☐☐☐☐☐
1CVP128	44c Jewish Symbols, Dreidel	1.25	.25	☐☐☐☐☐
1CVP129	44c Jewish Symbols, Star of David	1.25	.25	☐☐☐☐☐
1CVP130	44c Christmas, Christmas Stocking	1.25	.25	☐☐☐☐☐
1CVP131	44c Christmas, Christmas Tree	1.25	.25	☐☐☐☐☐
1CVP132	44c Christmas, Santa Claus	1.25	.25	☐☐☐☐☐

2011, Stamps.com

1CVP133	44c Valentine's Day, Hearts	1.25	.25	☐☐☐☐☐
1CVP134	44c Valentine's Day, Rose	1.25	.25	☐☐☐☐☐
1CVP135	44c Valentine's Day, Candy Hearts	1.25	.25	☐☐☐☐☐
1CVP136	44c Christian Symbols, Cross	1.25	.25	☐☐☐☐☐
1CVP137	44c Christian Symbols, Fish	1.25	.25	☐☐☐☐☐
1CVP138	44c Christian Symbols, Rosary Beads	1.25	.25	☐☐☐☐☐

☐☐☐☐☐

NON-PERSONALIZABLE POSTAGE

3CVP1   3CVP2

These stamps, approved by the USPS, were non-personalizable stamps that could be purchased directly from private manufacturers, which shipped them to the customer. Other non-personalizable stamps have been created by a variety of companies, all sold at excessive amounts over face value as "collectibles." Such items are not listed here. Most items created that sold for excessive amounts over face value have vignettes that are licensed images, usually depicting sport team emblems or other sports-related themes, or celebrities.

Personalized postage stamps, first available in 2004, created by a variety of different companies, and heretofore listed with Scott numbers having a "2CVP" prefix, are no longer listed. Personalized stamps, though valid for postage, are not sold at any U.S. Postal Service post office. They are available only by on-line ordering through the company's website. Stamps are only available from the companies in full panes of 20. Each pane is sold at a significant premium above the stated face value to cover the costs of personalization, shipping and handling.

In recent years, there has been a steadily increasing number of private companies, either directly licensed by the USPS or created as spinoff companies of these licensees, creating distinctly different personalized stamps. None of the companies has issued fewer than seven stamps for each rate change, with one issuing as many as 42 different stamps. Because mailing rates set by the USPS are expected to change yearly, the collective output of distinctly different, rate-based stamps from these various companies likely will increase. There are no restrictions in place to prevent more firms from bringing personalized stamps to the marketplace, or to keep stamp producers from offering even more customer options. Some personalized stamps do not differ in any appreciable manner from some of the non-personalizable stamps sold as collectibles and not listed here.

Stamps.com
2007, May, Die Cut

3CVP1	2c	Black & gray..........................	.25	.25
a.		Inscribed "US Postag"........	—	—

Die Cut Perf. 5¼ at Right

3CVP2	2c	"Your Photo Here" Ad at Left	.25	.25
a.		Tagged................................	1.40	1.40

2008

3CVP3	1c	Type of 2007 (3CVP1)..........	.25	.25

LO1

LO2

1LB1

1LB6

1LB8

3LB1

3LB2

4LB2

4LB3

4LB5

4LB8

4LB11

4LB13

4LB14

4LB15

4LB16

4LB18

4LB19

9LB1

10LB1

10LB2

CARRIER'S STAMPS
OFFICIAL ISSUES
1851

Scott No.		Description	Unused Value	Used Value	/ / / / / /
LO1	(1c)	Franklin, dull blue on *rose*	*6,500.*	7,500.	☐☐☐☐☐
LO2	1c	Eagle, blue, imperf	50.00	*80.00*	☐☐☐☐☐

1875 REPRINTS, No gum

LO3	(1c)	Franklin (LO1), blue on *rose*, imperf.	50.00		☐☐☐☐☐
LO4	(1c)	Franklin (LO1), blue, perf. 12	*16,000.*		☐☐☐☐☐
LO5	1c	Eagle (LO2), blue, imperf	25.00		☐☐☐☐☐
LO6	1c	Eagle (LO2), blue, perf. 12	175.00		☐☐☐☐☐

SEMI-OFFICIAL ISSUES
1850-55, Imperf.

1LB1	1c	Post Office Despatch, red on *bluish*	180.00	160.00	☐☐☐☐☐
1LB2	1c	Post Office Despatch, blue on *bluish*	200.00	150.00	☐☐☐☐☐
a.		Bluish laid paper	—	—	☐☐☐☐☐
1LB3	1c	Post Office Despatch, blue	160.00	100.00	☐☐☐☐☐
a.		Laid paper	200.00	150.00	☐☐☐☐☐
b.		Block of 14 containing three tete-beche pairs	*4,000.*		☐☐☐☐☐
1LB4	1c	Post Office Despatch, green	—	1.000.	☐☐☐☐☐
1LB5	1c	Post Office Despatch, red	2,250.	1,750.	☐☐☐☐☐

1856

1LB6	1c	Carriers Dispatch, blue	130.00	90.00	☐☐☐☐☐
1LB7	1c	Carriers Dispatch (1LB6), red	130.00	90.00	☐☐☐☐☐

1857

1LB8	1c	Horse & Rider, black	65.00	50.00	☐☐☐☐☐
a.		SENT	100.00	75.00	☐☐☐☐☐
b.		Short rays	100.00	75.00	☐☐☐☐☐
1LB9	1c	Horse & Rider (1LB8), red	100.00	90.00	☐☐☐☐☐
a.		SENT	140.00	110.00	☐☐☐☐☐
b.		Short rays	140.00	110.00	☐☐☐☐☐
c.		As "b," double impression		800.00	☐☐☐☐☐

1849-50

3LB1	1c	"Penny Post.," blue	375.00	180.00	☐☐☐☐☐
a.		Wrong ornament at left		400.00	☐☐☐☐☐

1851

3LB2	1c	"Penny Post. Paid," blue (shades) on *slate*	190.00	100.00	☐☐☐☐☐

1849

4LB1	2c	Honour's City Express, black on *brown rose*	*10,000.*		☐☐☐☐☐

5LB1   5LB2   6LB1

6LB2   6LB7

6LB9   7LB1   7LB8

7LB11   7LB14   7LB18

8LB1   8LB2   8LB3

HOW TO USE THIS BOOK

The number in the first column is its Scott number or identifying number. Following that is the denomination of the stamp and its color or description. Finally, the values, unused and used, are shown.

Scott No.		Description	Unused Value	Used Value	/ / / / /
4LB2	2c	Honour's City Express (4LB1), black on *yellow*, cut to shape	—		☐☐☐☐☐
4LB2A	2c	Honour's City Express (4LB1), black on *bluish gray*, on cover, cut to shape		—	☐☐☐☐☐

1854

4LB3	2c	City Post, black		1,500.	☐☐☐☐☐

1849-50

4LB5	2c	Honour's City Post, black on *bluish*, pelure paper....................	750.00	500.00	☐☐☐☐☐
a.		"Ceuts"...	5,750.		☐☐☐☐☐
4LB7	2c	Honour's City Post (4LB5), black on *yellow*	750.00	1,000.	☐☐☐☐☐
a.		"Ccnts"...		14,500.	☐☐☐☐☐

1851-58

4LB8	2c	Paid, Honour's City Post, black on *bluish*	350.00	175.00	☐☐☐☐☐
a.		Period after Paid..............................	500.00	250.00	☐☐☐☐☐
b.		Cens..	700.00	900.00	☐☐☐☐☐
c.		Conours and Bents............................		—	☐☐☐☐☐
4LB9	2c	Paid, Honour's City Post (4LB8), black on *bluish*, pelure paper..........	850.00	950.00	☐☐☐☐☐
4LB10	2c	Paid, Honour's City Post, black on *pink*, pelure paper, on cover............		7,000.	☐☐☐☐☐
4LB11	(2c)	Honour's Penny Post Paid, black on *bluish*	—	375.00	☐☐☐☐☐
4LB12	(2c)	Honour's Penny Post Paid (4LB11), black on *bluish*, pelure paper..........	—	—	☐☐☐☐☐
4LB13	(2c)	Honour's City Post Paid, black on *bluish*	750.00	400.00	☐☐☐☐☐
a.		Comma after PAID............................	1,100.		☐☐☐☐☐
b.		No period after Post	1,400.		☐☐☐☐☐

1851(?)-58(?)

4LB14	2c	Kingsman's City Post Paid, black on *bluish*	1,400.	900.00	☐☐☐☐☐
a.		"Kingman's" erased..........................		5,000.	☐☐☐☐☐
4LB15	2c	Paid, Kingsman's City Post, black on *bluish*	800.00	800.00	☐☐☐☐☐
a.		"Kingman's" erased on cover with 3c #11, tied by pen cancel (unique)		4,500.	☐☐☐☐☐

1858

4LB16	2c	Martin's City Post, black on *bluish*...	8,000.		☐☐☐☐☐

1860

4LB17	2c	Beckman's City Post (4LB18), black		—	☐☐☐☐☐

1859

4LB18	2c	Circle Frame, Steinmeyer's, black on *bluish*	21,000.		☐☐☐☐☐

Scott No.		Description	Unused Value	Used Value	/ / / / /
4LB19	2c	Steinmeyer's, Rods & Circles Frame, black on *bluish*	4,500.	—	☐☐☐☐☐
4LB20	2c	Steinmeyer's, Rods & Circles (4LB19), black on *pink*	200.00	—	☐☐☐☐☐
4LB21	2c	Steinmeyer's, Rods & Circles (4LB19), black on *yellow*	200.00		☐☐☐☐☐
1854					
9LB1	2c	Williams' City Post, brown	—	4,000.	☐☐☐☐☐
1854					
10LB1		Bishop's, nondenominated, blue	5,000.	4,000.	☐☐☐☐☐
10LB2	2c	Bishop's, black on *bluish*	4,000.	6,000.	☐☐☐☐☐
1857					
5LB1	(2c)	Wharton's, bluish green	125.00		☐☐☐☐☐
1858					
5LB2	(2c)	Brown & McGill's, blue	250.00	750.00	☐☐☐☐☐
5LB3	(2c)	Brown & McGill's (5LB2), black	4,500.	15,000.	☐☐☐☐☐
1842					
6LB1	3c	City Despatch Post, black on *grayish*		2,000.	☐☐☐☐☐
1842-45					
6LB2	3c	United States City Despatch Post black on *rosy buff*	5,000.		☐☐☐☐☐
6LB3	3c	United States City Despatch Post (6LB2) black on *light blue*	1,500.	750.00	☐☐☐☐☐
6LB4	3c	United States City Despatch Post (6LB2) black on *green*	11,500.		☐☐☐☐☐
6LB5	3c	United States City Despatch Post (6LB2) black on *blue green (shades)*	200.00	175.00	
a.		Double impression		1,500.	☐☐☐☐☐
b.	3c	black on *blue*	650.00	300.00	☐☐☐☐☐
c.		As "b.," double impression		850.00	☐☐☐☐☐
d.	3c	black on *green*	1,000.	750.00	☐☐☐☐☐
e.		As "d.," double impression	—		☐☐☐☐☐
6LB6	3c	black on *pink*		14,500.	☐☐☐☐☐
1846					
6LB7		No. 6LB5 surcharged "2" in red		14,000.	☐☐☐☐☐
1849					
6LB9	1c	U.S. Mail, black on *rose*	100.00	100.00	☐☐☐☐☐
1849-50					
6LB10	1c	U.S. Mail (6LB9), black on *yellow*	100.00	100.00	☐☐☐☐☐
6LB11	1c	U.S. Mail (6LB9), black on *buff*	100.00	100.00	☐☐☐☐☐
a.		Pair, one stamp sideways	2,850.		☐☐☐☐☐

Scott No.	Description	Unused Value	Used Value	/ / / / /
1849-50				
7LB1	1c U.S.P.O., black on *rose* (with letters L.P.)	450.00		☐☐☐☐☐
7LB2	1c U.S.P.O. (7LB1), black on *rose* (with letter S)	*3,000.*		☐☐☐☐☐
7LB3	1c U.S.P.O. (7LB1), black on *rose* (with letter H)	275.00		☐☐☐☐☐
7LB4	1c U.S.P.O. (7LB1), black on *rose* (with letters L.S.)	400.00	*500.00*	☐☐☐☐☐
7LB5	1c U.S.P.O. (7LB1), black on *rose* (with letters J.J.)		*7,500.*	☐☐☐☐☐
7LB6	1c U.S.P.O. , no letters, black on *rose*	300.00	250.00	☐☐☐☐☐
7LB7	1c U.S.P.O. (7LB6), black on *blue*, glazed	*1,000.*		☐☐☐☐☐
7LB8	1c U.S.P.O. (7LB6), black on *vermilion*, glazed	*700.00*		☐☐☐☐☐
7LB9	1c U.S.P.O. (7LB6), black on *yellow*, glazed	*2,750.*	*2,250.*	☐☐☐☐☐
1850-52				
7LB11	1c U.S.P.O., fancy frame, gold on *black*, glazed	175.00	110.00	☐☐☐☐☐
7LB12	1c U.S.P.O. (7LB11), fancy frame, blue	400.00	275.00	☐☐☐☐☐
7LB13	1c U.S.P.O. (7LB11), fancy frame, black	750.00	*550.00*	☐☐☐☐☐
7LB14	1c Eagle above oval, blue on *buff*	3,250.		☐☐☐☐☐
1855(?)				
7LB16	1c Eagle above oval (7LB14), black		*5,000.*	☐☐☐☐☐
1856(?)				
7LB18	1c Oval, black	*1,250.*	*2,000.*	☐☐☐☐☐
1849				
8LB1	2c U.S. Penny Post, Numeral, black, type 1	*7,000.*	*3,000.*	☐☐☐☐☐
8LB2	2c U.S. Penny Post, Numeral, black, type 2	*6,000.*	—	☐☐☐☐☐
1857				
8LB3	2c U.S. Penny Post, Star, blue		*22,500.*	☐☐☐☐☐
				☐☐☐☐☐
				☐☐☐☐☐
				☐☐☐☐☐
				☐☐☐☐☐
				☐☐☐☐☐
				☐☐☐☐☐
				☐☐☐☐☐
				☐☐☐☐☐

RW1

RW6

RW16

RW26

RW27

RW36

RW45

RW58

RW64

RW65

RW67

RW68

542

RW69

RW70

RW71

RW72

RW73

RW74

RW75

RW76

RW77

RW78

RW79

HUNTING PERMIT STAMPS

Scott No.		Description	Unused Value	Used Value	//////
1934					
RW1	$1	*Mallards Alighting*	800.00	150.00	☐☐☐☐☐
a.		Imperf., pair.....................................	—		☐☐☐☐☐
b.		Vert. pair, imperf. horiz....................	—		☐☐☐☐☐
1935					
RW2	$1	*Canvasback Ducks Taking to Flight* .	800.00	160.00	☐☐☐☐☐
1936					
RW3	$1	*Canada Geese in Flight*....................	375.00	90.00	☐☐☐☐☐
1937					
RW4	$1	*Scaup Ducks Taking to Flight*...........	425.00	70.00	☐☐☐☐☐
1938					
RW5	$1	*Pintail Drake and Duck Alighting*	475.00	70.00	☐☐☐☐☐
1939					
RW6	$1	*Green-Winged Teal*	275.00	45.00	☐☐☐☐☐
1940					
RW7	$1	*Black Mallards*	275.00	45.00	☐☐☐☐☐
1941					
RW8	$1	*Family of Ruddy Ducks*.....................	275.00	45.00	☐☐☐☐☐
1942					
RW9	$1	*Baldpates*...	275.00	45.00	☐☐☐☐☐
1943					
RW10	$1	*Wood Ducks*	140.00	35.00	☐☐☐☐☐
1944					
RW11	$1	*White-fronted Geese*..........................	135.00	50.00	☐☐☐☐☐
1945					
RW12	$1	*Shoveller Ducks in Flight*	110.00	25.00	☐☐☐☐☐
1946					
RW13	$1	*Redhead Ducks*, red brown..............	55.00	16.00	☐☐☐☐☐
a.	$1	bright rose pink	*35,000.*		☐☐☐☐☐
1947					
RW14	$1	*Snow Geese*	60.00	16.00	☐☐☐☐☐
1948					
RW15	$1	*Bufflehead Ducks in Flight*...............	60.00	16.00	☐☐☐☐☐
1949					
RW16	$2	*Greeneye Ducks*.................................	75.00	15.00	☐☐☐☐☐
1950					
RW17	$2	*Trumpeter Swans in Flight*	95.00	12.00	☐☐☐☐☐
1951					
RW18	$2	*Gadwall Ducks*	95.00	12.00	☐☐☐☐☐
1952					
RW19	$2	*Harlequin Ducks*	95.00	12.00	☐☐☐☐☐
1953					
RW20	$2	*Blue-winged Teal*..............................	95.00	12.00	☐☐☐☐☐

Scott No.	Description	Unused Value	Used Value	/ / / / /
1954				
RW21	$2 *Ring-necked Ducks*............................	95.00	11.00	☐☐☐☐☐
1955				
RW22	$2 *Blue Geese*..	95.00	11.00	☐☐☐☐☐
a.	Back inscription inverted.................	5,500.	4,500.	☐☐☐☐☐
1956				
RW23	$2 *American Merganser*	95.00	11.00	☐☐☐☐☐
1957				
RW24	$2 *American Eider*	95.00	11.00	☐☐☐☐☐
a.	Back inscription inverted.................	5,000.		☐☐☐☐☐
1958				
RW25	$2 *Canada Geese*	95.00	11.00	☐☐☐☐☐
a.	Back inscription inverted.................	—		☐☐☐☐☐
1959				
RW26	$3 *Labrador Retriever carrying Mallard Drake*............................	125.00	15.00	☐☐☐☐☐
a.	Back inscription inverted.................	27,500.	—	☐☐☐☐☐
1960				
RW27	$3 *Redhead Ducks*.................................	95.00	12.00	☐☐☐☐☐
1961				
RW28	$3 *Mallard Hen and Ducklings*	110.00	12.00	☐☐☐☐☐
1962				
RW29	$3 *Pintail Drakes Landing*....................	125.00	12.00	☐☐☐☐☐
a.	Back inscription omitted..................	—		☐☐☐☐☐
1963				
RW30	$3 *Pair of Brant Landing*	115.00	12.00	☐☐☐☐☐
1964				
RW31	$3 *Hawaiian Nene Geese*.......................	120.00	12.00	☐☐☐☐☐
1965				
RW32	$3 *Three Canvasback Drakes*	110.00	12.00	☐☐☐☐☐
1966				
RW33	$3 *Whistling Swans*	110.00	12.00	☐☐☐☐☐
1967				
RW34	$3 *Old Squaw Ducks*.............................	125.00	12.00	☐☐☐☐☐
1968				
RW35	$3 *Hooded Mergansers*..........................	75.00	11.00	☐☐☐☐☐
1969				
RW36	$3 *White-winged Scoters*.......................	75.00	8.00	☐☐☐☐☐
1970				
RW37	$3 *Ross's Geese*	75.00	8.00	☐☐☐☐☐

Scott No.		Description	Unused Value	Used Value	/ / / / /
1971					
RW38	$3	*Three Cinnamon Teal*	45.00	8.00	☐☐☐☐☐
1972					
RW39	$5	*Emperor Geese*	27.50	7.00	☐☐☐☐☐
1973					
RW40	$5	*Stellers Eiders*	20.00	7.00	☐☐☐☐☐
1974					
RW41	$5	*Wood Ducks*	20.00	6.00	☐☐☐☐☐
a.		Back inscription missing, but printed vertically on face of stamp and selvage, from foldover	*4,750.*		☐☐☐☐☐
1975					
RW42	$5	*Canvasback Decoy and three flying Canvasbacks*	17.50	6.00	☐☐☐☐☐
1976					
RW43	$5	*Family of Canada Geese*	17.50	6.00	☐☐☐☐☐
1977					
RW44	$5	*Pair of Ross's Geese*	17.50	6.00	☐☐☐☐☐
1978					
RW45	$5	*Hooded Merganser Drake*	15.00	6.00	☐☐☐☐☐
1979					
RW46	$7.50	*Green-winged teal*	18.00	7.00	☐☐☐☐☐
1980					
RW47	$7.50	*Mallards*	18.00	7.00	☐☐☐☐☐
1981					
RW48	$7.50	*Ruddy Ducks*	18.00	7.00	☐☐☐☐☐
1982					
RW49	$7.50	*Canvasbacks*	18.00	7.00	☐☐☐☐☐
a.		Orange and violet omitted	*10,000.*		☐☐☐☐☐
1983					
RW50	$7.50	*Pintails*	18.00	7.00	☐☐☐☐☐
1984					
RW51	$7.50	*Widgeon*	18.00	7.00	☐☐☐☐☐
1985					
RW52	$7.50	*Cinnamon Teal*	18.00	8.00	☐☐☐☐☐
a.		Light blue (litho.) omitted	*20,000*		☐☐☐☐☐
1986					
RW53	$7.50	*Fulvous Whistling Duck*	18.50	7.00	☐☐☐☐☐
a.		Black omitted	*2,000.*		☐☐☐☐☐
1987					
RW54	$10	*Redheads*	18.00	9.50	☐☐☐☐☐
1988					
RW55	$10	*Snow Goose*	18.00	10.00	☐☐☐☐☐

Scott No.	Description	Unused Value	Used Value	/ / / / / /
1989				
RW56	$12.50 *Lesser Scaups*	20.00	10.00	☐☐☐☐☐
1990				
RW57	$12.50 *Black Bellied Whistling Duck*	20.00	10.00	☐☐☐☐☐
a.	Back inscription omitted	300.00		
b.	Black inscription printed on the stamp paper rather than the gum		3,500.	☐☐☐☐☐
1991				
RW58	$15 *King Eiders*	35.00	12.00	☐☐☐☐☐
a.	Black (engr.) omitted	20,000.		
1992				
RW59	$15 *Spectacled Eider*	35.00	12.00	☐☐☐☐☐
1993				
RW60	$15 *Canvasbacks*	30.00	12.00	☐☐☐☐☐
a.	Black (engr.) omitted	2,250.		
1994				
RW61	$15 *Red-breasted Mergansers*	30.00	12.00	☐☐☐☐☐
1995				
RW62	$15 *Mallards*	35.00	12.00	☐☐☐☐☐
1996				
RW63	$15 *Surf Scoters*	35.00	12.00	☐☐☐☐☐
1997				
RW64	$15 *Canada Goose*	32.50	12.00	☐☐☐☐☐
1998				
RW65	$15 *Barrow's Goldeneye*	50.00	22.50	☐☐☐☐☐
RW65A	$15 *Barrow's Goldeneye* self-adhesive (RW65)	35.00	15.00	☐☐☐☐☐
1999				
RW66	$15 *Greater Scaup*	45.00	20.00	☐☐☐☐☐
RW66A	$15 *Greater Scaup,* self-adhesive (RW66)	25.00	12.00	☐☐☐☐☐
2000				
RW67	$15 *Mottled Duck*	35.00	15.00	☐☐☐☐☐
RW67A	$15 *Mottled Duck*, self-adhesive (RW67)	25.50	14.00	☐☐☐☐☐
2001				
RW68	$15 *Northern Pintail*	32.50	16.00	☐☐☐☐☐
RW68A	$15 *Northern Pintail*, self-adhesive (RW68)	25.00	10.00	☐☐☐☐☐
2002				
RW69	$15 *Black Scoters*	32.50	16.00	☐☐☐☐☐
RW69A	$15 *Black Scoters*, self-adhesive (RW69)	25.00	10.00	☐☐☐☐☐
2003				
RW70	$15 *Snow Geese*	27.50	16.00	☐☐☐☐☐
b.	Imperf, pair	7,000.		
c.	Back inscription omitted	4,500.		
RW70A	$15 *Snow Geese* self-adhesive (RW70)	25.00	10.00	☐☐☐☐☐

Scott No.	Description	Unused Value	Used Value	/ / / / / /
2004				
RW71	$15 *Redheads*	27.50	11.00	☐☐☐☐☐
RW71A	$15 *Redheads,* self-adhesive (RW71)	25.00	10.00	☐☐☐☐☐
2005				
RW72	$15 *Hooded Mergansers,* type I			
	(no outer framelines)	22.50	11.00	☐☐☐☐☐
b.	Souvenir sheet of 1	2,000.		☐☐☐☐☐
c.	Type II (black frameline at top,			
	right and bottom).........................	22.50	11.00	☐☐☐☐☐
RW72A	$15 *Hooded Mergansers,* self-adhesive			
	(RW72)	22.50	11.00	☐☐☐☐☐
2006				
RW73	$15 *Ross's Goose*	22.50	11.00	☐☐☐☐☐
b.	Souvenir sheet of 1	150.00		☐☐☐☐☐
c.	As "b," without artist's signature (error)	*3,000.*		☐☐☐☐☐
RW73A	$15 *Ross's Goose,* self-adhesive (RW73)	22.50	11.00	☐☐☐☐☐
2007				
RW74	$15 *Ring-necked Ducks*............................	22.50	11.00	☐☐☐☐☐
b.	Souvenir sheet of 1	140.00		☐☐☐☐☐
c.	As "b," without artist's signature (error)	*2,750.*		☐☐☐☐☐
RW74A	$15 *Ring-necked Ducks,* self-adhesive			
	(RW74)	22.50	11.00	☐☐☐☐☐
2008				
RW75	$15 *Northern Pintails*.............................	22.50	11.00	☐☐☐☐☐
b.	Souvenir sheet of 1	75.00		☐☐☐☐☐
c.	As "b," without artist's signature			
	(error)	650.00		☐☐☐☐☐
RW75A	$15 *Northern Pintails,* self-adhesive			
	(RW75)..	22.50	11.00	☐☐☐☐☐
RW76	$15 *Long-tailed Duck and Decoy*...........	22.50	11.00	☐☐☐☐☐
b.	Souvenir sheet of 1	60.00		☐☐☐☐☐
c.	As "b," without artist's signature			
	(error)	400.00		☐☐☐☐☐
RW76A	$15 *Long-tailed Duck and Decoy,*			
	self-adhesive (RW76).....................	22.50	11.00	☐☐☐☐☐
2010				
RW77	$15 *American Wigeon*.............................	22.50	11.00	☐☐☐☐☐
b.	Souvenir sheet of 1	60.00		☐☐☐☐☐
c.	As "b," without artist's signature			
	(error)..	200.00		☐☐☐☐☐
RW77A	$15 *American Wigeon,* self-adhesive			
	(RW77)...	22.50	11.00	☐☐☐☐☐
2011				
RW78	$15 *White-fronted Geese*........................	22.50	11.00	☐☐☐☐☐
b.	Souvenir sheet of 1	65.00		☐☐☐☐☐
c.	"As "b," without artist's signature			
	(error)	—		☐☐☐☐☐